本书出版得到《大中华文库》出版经费资助

大中华文库

LIBRARY
OF CHINESE CLASSICS

大中华文库

汉英对照

LIBRARY OF CHINESE CLASSICS

Chinese-English

关汉卿杂剧选

SELECTED PLAYS OF GUAN HANQING

（元）关汉卿　著

吴晓铃　单耀海
李国炎　刘　坚　编校

杨宪益　戴乃迭　译

Written by Guan Hanqing

Edited by Wu Xiaoling, Shan Yaohai, Li Guoyan *and* Liu jian

Translated by Yang Xianyi *and* Gladys Yang

外文出版社

Foreign Languages Press

First Edition 2004
Third Printing 2020

ISBN 978-7-119-03395-2

Published by
Foreign Languages Press
24 Baiwanzhuang Road, Beijing 100037, China
http: // www.flp.com.cn

Printed in the People's Republic of China

总　　序

杨牧之

《大中华文库》终于出版了。我们为之高兴，为之鼓舞，但也倍感压力。

当此之际，我们愿将郁积在我们心底的话，向读者倾诉。

一

中华民族有着悠久的历史和灿烂的文化，系统、准确地将中华民族的文化经典翻译成外文，编辑出版，介绍给全世界，是几代中国人的愿望。早在几十年前，西方一位学者翻译《红楼梦》，将书名译成《一个红楼上的梦》，将林黛玉译为“黑色的玉”。我们一方面对外国学者将中国的名著介绍到世界上去表示由衷的感谢，一方面为祖国的名著还不被完全认识，甚而受到曲解，而感到深深的遗憾。还有西方学者翻译《金瓶梅》，专门摘选其中自然主义描述最为突出的篇章加以译介。一时间，西方学者好像发现了奇迹，掀起了《金瓶梅》热，说中国是“性开放的源头”，公开地在报刊上鼓吹中国要“发扬开放之传统”。还有许多资深、友善的汉学家译介中国古代的哲学著作，在把中华民族文化介绍给全世界的工作方面作出了重大贡献，但或囿于理解有误，或缘于对中国文字认识的局限，质量上乘的并不多，常常是隔靴搔痒，说不到点子上。大哲学家黑格尔曾经说过：中国有最完备的国史。但他认为中国古代没有真正意义上的哲学，还处在哲学史前状态。这么了不起的哲学家竟然作出这样大失水准的评论，何其不幸。正如任何哲学家都要受时间、地点、条件的制约一样，黑格尔也离不开这一规律。当时他也只能从上述水平的汉学家译过去的文字去分析、理解，所以，黑格尔先生对中国古代社会的认识水平是什么状态，也就不难想象了。

中国离不开世界，世界也缺少不了中国。中国文化摄取外域的新成分，丰富了自己，又以自己的新成就输送给别人，贡献于世界。从公元5世纪开始到公元15世纪，大约有一千年，中国走在世界的前列。在这一千多年的时间里，她的光辉照耀全世界。人类要前进，怎么能不全面认识中国，怎么能不认真研究中国的历史呢？

二

中华民族是伟大的，曾经辉煌过，蓝天、白云、阳光灿烂，和平而兴旺；也有过黑暗的、想起来就让人战栗的日子，但中华民族从来是充满理想，不断追求，不断学习，渴望和平与友谊的。

中国古代伟大的思想家孔子曾经说过：“三人行，必有我师焉。择其善者而从之，其不善者而改之。”孔子的话就是要人们向别人学习。这段话正是概括了整个中华民族与人交往的原则。人与人之间交往如此，在与周边的国家交往中也是如此。

秦始皇第一个统一了中国，可惜在位只有十几年，来不及做更多的事情。汉朝继秦而继续强大，便开始走出去，了解自己周边的世界。公元前139年，汉武帝派张骞出使西域。他带着一万头牛羊，总值一万万钱的金帛货物，作为礼物，开始西行，最远到过“安息”（即波斯）。公元73年，班超又率36人出使西域。36个人按今天的话说，也只有一个排的人数，显然是为了拜访未曾见过面的邻居，是去交朋友。到了西域，班超派遣甘英作为使者继续西行，往更远处的大秦国（即罗马）去访问，“乃抵条支而历安息，临西海以望大秦”(《后汉书·西域传》)。“条支”在“安息”以西，即今天的伊拉克、叙利亚一带，“西海”应是今天的地中海。也就是说甘英已经到达地中海边上，与罗马帝国隔海相望，“临大海欲渡”，却被人劝阻而未成行，这在历史上留下了遗恨。可以想见班超、甘英沟通友谊的无比勇气和强烈愿望。接下来是唐代的玄奘，历经千难万险，到“西天”印度取经，带回了南亚国家的古老文化。归国后，他把带回的佛教经典组织人翻译，到后来很多经典印度失传了，但中国却保存完好，以至于今天，没有玄奘的《大唐西域记》，印度人很难完整地编写印度古代史。明代郑和“七下西洋”，把中华文化传到东南亚一带。鸦片战争以后，一代又一代先进的中国人，为了振兴中华，又前赴后继，向西方国家学习先进的科学思想和文明成果。这中间有我们的领导人朱德、周恩来、邓小平；有许许多多大科学家、文学家、艺术家，如郭沫若、李四光、钱学森、冼星海、徐悲鸿等。他们的追求、奋斗，他们的博大胸怀、兼收并蓄的精神，为人类社会增添了光彩。

中国文化的形成和发展过程，就是一个以众为师、以各国人民为师，不断学习和创造的过程。中华民族曾经向周边国家和民族学习过许多东西，假如没有这些学习，中华民族绝不可能创造出昔日的辉煌。回顾历史，我们怎么能够不对伟大的古埃及文明、古希腊文明、古印度文明满怀深深的感激？怎么能够不对伟大的欧洲文明、非洲文明、美洲文明、澳洲文明，以及中国周围的亚洲文明充满温情与敬意？

中华民族为人类社会曾作出过独特的贡献。在15世纪以前，中国的科学技术一直处于世界遥遥领先的地位。英国科学家李约瑟说："中国在公元3世纪到13世纪之间，保持着一个西方所望尘莫及的科学知识水平。"美国耶鲁大学教授、《大国的兴衰》的作者保罗·肯尼迪坦言："在近代以前时期的所有文明中，没有一个国家的文明比中国更发达，更先进。"

世界各国的有识之士千里迢迢来中国观光、学习。在这个过程中，中国唐朝的长安城渐渐发展成为国际大都市。西方的波斯、东罗马，东亚的高丽、新罗、百济，南亚的南天竺、北天竺，频繁前来。外国的王侯、留学生及在长安供职的外国官员、商贾、乐工和舞士，总有几十个国家，几万人之多。日本派出"遣唐使"更是一批接一批。传为美谈的日本人阿倍仲麻吕（晁衡）在长安留学的故事，很能说明外国人与中国的交往。晁衡学成仕于唐朝，前后历时五十余年。晁衡与中国的知识分子结下了深厚的友情。他归国时，传说在海中遇难身亡。大诗人李白作诗哭悼："日本晁卿辞帝都，征帆一片远蓬壶。明月不归沉碧海，白云愁色满苍梧。"晁衡遇险是误传，但由此可见中外学者之间在中国长安交往的情谊。

后来，不断有外国人到中国来探寻秘密，所见所闻，常常让他们目瞪口呆。《希腊纪事》（希腊人波桑尼阿著）记载公元2世纪时，希腊人在中国的见闻。书中写道："赛里斯人用小米和青芦喂一种类似蜘蛛的昆虫，喂到第五年，虫肚子胀裂开，便从里面取出丝来。"从这段对中国古代养蚕技术的描述，可见当时欧洲人与中国人的差距。公元9世纪中叶，阿拉伯人来到中国。一位阿拉伯作家在他所著的《中国印度闻见录》中记载了曾旅居中国的阿拉伯商人的见闻：

——一天，一个外商去拜见驻守广州的中国官吏。会见时，外商总盯着官吏的胸部，官吏很奇怪，便问："你好像总盯着我的胸，这是怎么回事？"那位外商回答说："透过你穿的丝绸衣服，我隐约看到你胸口上长着一个黑痣，这是什么丝绸，我感到十分惊奇。"官吏听后，失声大笑，伸出胳膊，说："请你数数吧，看我穿了几件衣服？"那商人数过，竟然穿了五件之多，黑痣正是透过这五层丝绸衣服显现出来的。外商惊得目瞪口呆，官吏说："我穿的丝绸还不算是最好的，总督穿的要更精美。"

——书中关于茶（他们叫干草叶子）的记载，可见阿拉伯国家当时还没有喝茶的习惯。书中记述："中国国王本人的收入主要靠盐税和泡开水喝的一种干草税。在各个城市里，这种干草叶售价都很高，中国人称这种草叶叫'茶'，这种干草叶比苜蓿的叶子还多，也略比它香，稍有苦味，用开水冲喝，治百病。"

——他们对中国的医疗条件十分羡慕，书中记载道："中国人医疗条件很好，穷人可以从国库中得到药费。"还说："城市里，很多地方立一石碑，高10肘，上面刻有各种疾病和药物，写明某种病用某种药医治。"

——关于当时中国的京城，书中作了生动的描述：中国的京城很大，人口众多，一条宽阔的长街把全城分为两半，大街右边的东区，住着皇帝、宰相、禁军及皇家的总管、奴婢。在这个区域，沿街开凿了小河，流水潺潺；路旁，葱茏的树木整然有序，一幢幢宅邸鳞次栉比。大街左边的西区，住着庶民和商人。这里有货栈和商店，每当清晨，人们可以看到，皇室的总管、宫廷的仆役，或骑马或步行，到这里来采购。

此后的史籍对西人来华的记载，渐渐多了起来。13世纪意大利旅行家马可·波罗，尽管有人对他是否真的到过中国持怀疑态度，但他留下一部记述元代事件的《马可·波罗游记》却是确凿无疑的。这部游记中的一些关于当时中国的描述使得西方人认为是“天方夜谭”。总之，从中西文化交流史来说，这以前的时期还是一个想象和臆测的时代，相互之间充满了好奇与幻想。

从16世纪末开始，由于航海技术的发展，东西方航路的开通，随着一批批传教士来华，中国与西方开始了直接的交流。沟通中西的使命在意大利传教士利玛窦那里有了充分的体现。利玛窦于1582年来华，1610年病逝于北京，在华二十余年。除了传教以外，做了两件具有历史象征意义的事，一是1594年前后在韶州用拉丁文翻译《四书》，并作了注释；二是与明代学者徐光启合作，用中文翻译了《几何原本》。

西方传教士对《四书》等中国经典的粗略翻译，以及杜赫德的《中华帝国志》等书对中国的介绍，在西方读者的眼前展现了一个异域文明，在当时及稍后一段时期引起了一场“中国热”，许多西方大思想家的眼光都曾注目于中国文化。有的推崇中华文明，如莱布尼兹、伏尔泰、魁奈等，有的对中华文明持批评态度，如孟德斯鸠、黑格尔等。莱布尼兹认识到中国文化的某些思想与他的观念相近，如周易的卦象与他发明的二进制相契合，对中国文化给予了热情的礼赞；黑格尔则从他整个哲学体系的推演出发，认为中国没有真正意义上的哲学，还处在哲学史前的状态。但是，不论是推崇还是批评，是吸纳还是排斥，中西文化的交流产生了巨大的影响。随着先进的中国科学技术的西传，特别是中国的造纸、火药、印刷术和指南针四大发明的问世，大大改变了世界的面貌。马克思说："中国的火药把骑士阶层炸得粉碎，指南针打开了世界市场并建立了殖民地，而印刷术则变成了新教的工具，变成对精神发展创造必要前提的最强大的杠杆。"英国的哲学家培根说：中国的四大发明"改变了全世界的面貌和一切事物的状态"。

三

大千世界，潮起潮落。云散云聚，万象更新。中国古代产生了无数伟大的科学家：祖冲之、李时珍、孙思邈、张衡、沈括、毕昇……产生了无数科技成果：《齐民要术》、《九章算术》、《伤寒杂病论》、《本草纲目》……以及保存至今的世界奇迹：浑天仪、地动仪、都江堰、敦煌石窟、大运河、万里长城……但从15世纪下半叶起，风水似乎从东方转到了西方，落后的欧洲只经过400年便成为世界瞩目的文明中心。英国的牛顿、波兰的哥白尼、德国的伦琴、法国的居里、德国的爱因斯坦、意大利的伽利略、俄国的门捷列夫、美国的费米和爱迪生……光芒四射，令人敬仰。

中华民族开始思考了。潮起潮落究竟是什么原因？中国人发明的火药，传到欧洲，转眼之间反成为欧洲列强轰击中国大门的炮弹，又是因为什么？

鸦片战争终于催醒了中国人沉睡的迷梦，最先"睁眼看世界"的一代精英林则徐、魏源迈出了威武雄壮的一步。曾国藩、李鸿章搞起了洋务运动。中国的知识分子喊出"民主与科学”的口号。中国是落后了，中国的志士仁人在苦苦探索。但落后中饱含着变革的动力，探索中孕育着崛起的希望。“向科学进军”，中华民族终于又迎来了科学的春天。

今天，世界毕竟来到了21世纪的门槛。分散隔绝的世界，逐渐变成联系为一体的世界。现在，全球一体化趋势日益明显，人类历史也就在愈来愈大的程度上成为全世界的历史。当今，任何一种文化的发展都离不开对其他优秀文化的汲取，都以其他优秀文化的发展为前提。在近现代，西方文化汲取中国文化，不仅是中国文化的传播，更是西方文化自身的创新和发展；正如中国文化对西方文化的汲取一样，既是西方文化在中国的传播，同时也是中国文化在近代的转型和发展。地球上所有的人类文化，都是我们共同的宝贵遗产。既然我们生活的各个大陆，在地球史上曾经是连成一气的“泛大陆”，或者说是一个完整的“地球村”，那么，我们同样可以在这个以知识和学习为特征的网络时代，走上相互学习、共同发展的大路，建设和开拓我们人类崭新的“地球村”。

西学仍在东渐，中学也将西传。各国人民的优秀文化正日益迅速地为中国文化所汲取，而无论西方和东方，也都需要从中国文化中汲取养分。正是基于这一认识，我们组织出版汉英对照版《大中华文库》，全面系统地翻译介绍中国传统文化典籍。我们试图通过《大中华文库》，向全世界展示，中华民族五千年的追求、五千年的梦想，正在新的历史时期重放光芒。中国人民就像火后的凤凰，万众一心，迎接新世纪文明的太阳。

1999年8月　北京

FOREWORD TO THE *LIBRARY OF CHINESE CLASSICS*

Yang Muzhi

The publication of the *Library of Chinese Classics* is a matter of great satisfaction to all of us who have been involved in the production of this monumental work. At the same time, we feel a weighty sense of responsibility, and take this opportunity to explain to our readers the motivation for undertaking this cross-century task.

1

The Chinese nation has a long history and a glorious culture, and it has been the aspiration of several generations of Chinese scholars to translate, edit and publish the whole corpus of the Chinese literary classics so that the nation's greatest cultural achievements can be introduced to people all over the world. There have been many translations of the Chinese classics done by foreign scholars. A few dozen years ago, a Western scholar translated the title of *A Dream of Red Mansions* into "A Dream of Red Chambers" and Lin Daiyu, the heroine in the novel, into "Black Jade." But while their endeavours have been laudable, the results of their labours have been less than satisfactory. Lack of knowledge of Chinese culture and an inadequate grasp of the Chinese written language have led the translators into many errors. As a consequence, not only are Chinese classical writings widely misunderstood in the rest of the world, in some cases their content has actually been distorted. At one time, there was a "*Jin Ping Mei* craze" among Western scholars, who thought that they had uncovered a miraculous phenomenon, and published theories claiming that China was the "fountainhead of eroticism," and that a Chinese "tradition of permissiveness" was about to be laid bare. This distorted view came about due to the translators of the *Jin Ping Mei (The Golden Lotus)* putting one-sided stress on the raw elements in that novel, to the neglect of its overall literary value. Meanwhile, there have been many distinguished and well-intentioned Sinologists who have attempted to make the culture of the Chinese nation more widely known by translating works of ancient Chinese philosophy. However, the quality of such work, in many cases, is unsatisfactory, often missing the point entirely. The great philosopher Hegel considered that ancient China had no philosophy in the real sense of the word, being stuck in philosophical "prehistory." For such an eminent authority to make such a colossal error of judgment is truly regrettable. But, of course, Hegel was just as subject to the constraints of time, space and other objective conditions as anyone else, and since he had to rely for his knowledge of Chinese philosophy on inadequate translations it is not difficult to imagine why he went so far off the mark.

China cannot be separated from the rest of the world; and the rest of the world cannot ignore China. Throughout its history, Chinese civilization has enriched itself by absorbing new elements from the outside world, and in turn has contributed to the progress of world civilization as a whole by transmitting to other peoples its own cultural achievements. From the 5th to the 15th centuries, China marched in the front ranks of world civilization. If mankind wishes to advance, how can it afford to ignore China? How can it afford not to make a thoroughgoing study of its history?

2

Despite the ups and downs in their fortunes, the Chinese people have always been idealistic, and have never ceased to forge ahead and learn from others, eager to strengthen ties of peace and friendship.

The great ancient Chinese philosopher Confucius once said, "Wherever three persons come together, one of them will surely be able to teach me something. I will pick out his good points and emulate them; his bad points I will reform." Confucius meant by this that we should always be ready to learn from others. This maxim encapsulates the principle the Chinese people have always followed in their dealings with other peoples, not only on an individual basis but also at the level of state-to-state relations.

After generations of internecine strife, China was unified by Emperor

Qin Shi Huang (the First Emperor of the Qin Dynasty) in 221 BC The Han Dynasty, which succeeded that of the short-lived Qin, waxed powerful, and for the first time brought China into contact with the outside world. In 139 BC, Emperor Wu dispatched Zhang Qian to the western regions, i.e. Central Asia. Zhang, who traveled as far as what is now Iran, took with him as presents for the rulers he visited on the way 10,000 head of sheep and cattle, as well as gold and silks worth a fabulous amount. In 73 AD, Ban Chao headed a 36-man legation to the western regions. These were missions of friendship to visit neighbours the Chinese people had never met before and to learn from them. Ban Chao sent Gan Ying to explore further toward the west. According to the "Western Regions Section" in the *History of Later Han*, Gan Ying traveled across the territories of present-day Iraq and Syria, and reached the Mediterranean Sea, an expedition which brought him within the confines of the Roman Empire. Later, during the Tang Dynasty, the monk Xuan Zang made a journey fraught with danger to reach India and seek the knowledge of that land. Upon his return, he organized a team of scholars to translate the Buddhist scriptures, which he had brought back with him. As a result, many of these scriptural classics which were later lost in India have been preserved in China. In fact, it would have been difficult for the people of India to reconstruct their own ancient history if it had not been for Xuan Zang's *A Record of a Journey to the West in the Time of the Great Tang Dynasty*. In the Ming Dynasty, Zheng He transmitted Chinese culture to Southeast Asia during his seven voyages. Following the Opium Wars in the mid-19th century, progressive Chinese, generation after generation, went to study the advanced scientific thought and cultural achievements of the Western countries. Their aim was to revive the fortunes of their own country. Among them were people who were later to become leaders of China, including Zhu De, Zhou Enlai and Deng Xiaoping. In addition, there were people who were to become leading scientists, literary figures and artists, such as Guo Moruo, Li Siguang, Qian Xuesen, Xian Xinghai and Xu Beihong. Their spirit of ambition, their struggles and their breadth of vision were an inspiration not only to the Chinese people but to people all over the world.

Indeed, it is true that if the Chinese people had not learned many things from the surrounding countries they would never have been able to produce the splendid achievements of former days. When we look back upon history, how can we not feel profoundly grateful for the legacies of the civilizations of ancient Egypt, Greece and India? How can we not feel fondness and respect for the cultures of Europe, Africa, America and Oceania?

The Chinese nation, in turn, has made unique contributions to the community of mankind. Prior to the 15th century, China led the world in science and technology. The British scientist Joseph Needham once said, "From the third century AD to the 13th century AD China was far ahead of the West in the level of its scientific knowledge." Paul Kennedy, of Yale University in the U.S., author of *The Rise and Fall of the Great Powers*, said, "Of all the civilizations of the pre-modern period, none was as well-developed or as progressive as that of China."

Foreigners who came to China were often astonished at what they saw and heard. The Greek geographer Pausanias in the second century AD gave the first account in the West of the technique of silk production in China: "The Chinese feed a spider-like insect with millet and reeds. After five years the insect's stomach splits open, and silk is extracted therefrom." From this extract, we can see that the Europeans at that time did not know the art of silk manufacture. In the middle of the 9th century AD, an Arabian writer includes the following anecdote in his *Account of China and India*:

"One day, an Arabian merchant called upon the military governor of Guangzhou. Throughout the meeting, the visitor could not keep his eyes off the governor's chest. Noticing this, the latter asked the Arab merchant what he was staring at. The merchant replied, 'Through the silk robe you are wearing, I can faintly see a black mole on your chest. Your robe must be made out of very fine silk indeed!' The governor burst out laughing, and holding out his sleeve invited the merchant to count how many garments he was wearing. The merchant did so, and discovered that the governor was actually wearing five silk robes, one on top of the other, and they were made of such fine material that a tiny mole could be seen through them all! Moreover, the governor explained that the robes he was wearing were not made of the finest silk at all; silk of the highest grade was reserved for the garments worn by the provincial governor."

The references to tea in this book (the author calls it "dried grass") reveal that the custom of drinking tea was unknown in the Arab countries at that time: "The king of China's revenue comes mainly from taxes on salt and the dry leaves of a kind of grass which is drunk after boiled water is poured on it. This dried grass is sold at a high price in every city in the country. The Chinese call it 'cha.' The bush is like alfalfa, except that it bears more leaves, which are also more fragrant than alfalfa. It has a slightly bitter taste, and when it is infused in boiling water it is said to have medicinal properties."

Foreign visitors showed especial admiration for Chinese medicine. One wrote, "China has very good medical conditions. Poor people are given money to buy medicines by the government."

In this period, when Chinese culture was in full bloom, scholars flocked from all over the world to China for sightseeing and for study. Chang'an, the capital of the Tang Dynasty was host to visitors from as far away as the Byzantine Empire, not to mention the neighboring countries of Asia. Chang'an, at that time the world's greatest metropolis, was packed with thousands of foreign dignitaries, students, diplomats, merchants, artisans and entertainers. Japan especially sent contingent after contingent of envoys to the Tang court. Worthy of note are the accounts of life in Chang'an written by Abeno Nakamaro, a Japanese scholar who studied in China and had close friendships with ministers of the Tang court and many Chinese scholars in a period of over 50 years. The description throws light on the exchanges between Chinese and foreigners in this period. When Abeno was supposedly lost at sea on his way back home, the leading poet of the time, Li Bai, wrote a eulogy for him.

The following centuries saw a steady increase in the accounts of China written by Western visitors. The Italian Marco Polo described conditions in China during the Yuan Dynasty in his *Travels*. However, until advances in the science of navigation led to the opening of east-west shipping routes at the beginning of the 16th century Sino-Western cultural exchanges were coloured by fantasy and conjecture. Concrete progress was made when a contingent of religious missionaries, men well versed in Western science and technology, made their way to China, ushering in an era of direct contacts between China and the West. The experience of this era was embodied in the career of the Italian Jesuit Matteo Ricci. Arriving in China in 1582, Ricci died in Beijing in 1610. Apart from his missionary work, Ricci accomplished two historically symbolic tasks — one was the translation into Latin of the "Four Books," together with annotations, in 1594; the other was the translation into Chinese of Euclid's *Elements*.

The rough translations of the "Four Books" and other Chinese classical works by Western missionaries, and the publication of Père du Halde's *Description Geographique, Historique, Chronologique, Politique, et Physique de l'Empire de la Chine* revealed an exotic culture to Western readers, and sparked a "China fever," during which the eyes of many Western intellectuals were fixed on China. Some of these intellectuals, including Leibniz, held China in high esteem; others, such as Hegel, nursed a critical attitude toward Chinese culture. Leibniz considered that some aspects of Chinese thought were close to his own views, such as the philosophy of the *Book of Changes* and his own binary system. Hegel, on the other hand, as mentioned above, considered that China had developed no proper philosophy of its own. Nevertheless, no matter whether the reaction was one of admiration, criticism, acceptance or rejection, Sino-Western exchanges were of great significance. The transmission of advanced Chinese science and technology to the West, especially the Chinese inventions of paper-making, gunpowder, printing and the compass, greatly changed the face of the whole world. Karl Marx said, "Chinese gunpowder blew the feudal class of knights to smithereens; the compass opened up world markets and built colonies; and printing became an implement of Protestantism and the most powerful lever and necessary precondition for intellectual development and creation." The English philosopher Roger Bacon said that China's four great inventions had "changed the face of the whole world and the state of affairs of everything."

3

Ancient China gave birth to a large number of eminent scientists, such as Zu Chongzhi, Li Shizhen, Sun Simiao, Zhang Heng, Shen Kuo and Bi Sheng. They produced numerous treatises on scientific subjects, including *The Manual of Important Arts for the People's Welfare, Nine Chapters on the Art of Mathematics, Treatise on Febrile Disease Caused by Cold* and *Compendium of Materia Medica*. Their accomplishments included ones whose influence has been felt right down to modern times, such as the armillary sphere, seismograph, Dujiangyan water conservancy project, Dunhuang Grottoes, Grand Canal and Great Wall. But from the latter part of the 15th century, and for the next 400 years, Europe gradually became the cultural centre upon which the world's eyes were fixed. The world's most outstanding scientists then were England's Isaac Newton, Poland's Copernicus, France's Marie Curie, Germany's Rontgen and Einstein, Italy's Galileo, Russia's Mendelev and America's Edison.

The Chinese people then began to think: What is the cause of the rise and fall of nations? Moreover, how did it happen that gunpowder, invented in China and transmitted to the West, in no time at all made Europe powerful enough to batter down the gates of China herself?

It took the Opium War to wake China from its reverie. The first generation to make the bold step of "turning our eyes once again to the rest of the world" was represented by Lin Zexu and Wei Yuan. Zeng Guofan and Li Hongzhang started the Westernization Movement, and later intellectuals raised the slogan of "Democracy and Science." Noble-minded patriots, realizing that China had fallen behind in the race for modernization, set out on a painful quest. But in backwardness lay the motivation for change, and the quest produced the embryo of a towering hope, and the Chinese people finally gathered under a banner proclaiming a "March Toward Science."

On the threshold of the 21st century, the world is moving in the direction of becoming an integrated entity. This trend is becoming clearer by the day. In fact, the history of the various peoples of the world is also becoming the history of mankind as a whole. Today, it is impossible for any nation's culture to develop without absorbing the excellent aspects of the cultures of other peoples. When Western culture absorbs aspects of Chinese culture, this is not just because it has come into contact with Chinese culture, but also because of the active creativity and development of Western culture itself; and vice versa. The various cultures of the world's peoples are a precious heritage which we all share. Mankind no longer lives on different continents, but on one big continent, or in a "global village." And so, in this era characterized by an all-encompassing network of knowledge and information we should learn from each other and march in step along the highway of development to construct a brand-new "global village."

Western learning is still being transmitted to the East, and vice versa. China is accelerating its pace of absorption of the best parts of the cultures of other countries, and there is no doubt that both the West and the East need the nourishment of Chinese culture. Based on this recognition, we have edited and published the *Library of Chinese Classics* in a Chinese-English format as an introduction to the corpus of traditional Chinese culture in a comprehensive and systematic translation. Through this collection, our aim is to reveal to the world the aspirations and dreams of the Chinese people over the past 5,000 years and the splendour of the new historical era in China. Like a phoenix rising from the ashes, the Chinese people in unison are welcoming the cultural sunrise of the new century.

August 1999 Beijing

前　　言

关汉卿不仅属于中国，也属于世界。当 1958 年中国人民纪念关汉卿戏剧活动 700 年之际，经世界和平理事会提名，关汉卿被列为世界文化名人。这是从人类文化发展史的高度对关汉卿作出的评价。关汉卿是当之无愧的。

一

关汉卿是靠戏剧活动谋生的市民剧作家，门第卑微，职位不振，再加上戏剧文体和艺术形式向来不被封建士大夫重视，所以关于他的生平事迹留下的记载很少。我们只知道汉卿是他的字，名不详，号已斋叟。具体生卒年代不详。因为他写有散曲小令【双调·大德歌】10 首，学术界一般把他的卒年定于元成宗大德（1297—1307）初年。至于生年，学者们的不同意见不下十来种。可大体归纳为：金代遗民说，公元 1234 年金朝灭亡时关汉卿已二十多岁；生于金末说，金亡时其年尚幼；生于元代初年说。据已知文献，元代就有人说关汉卿是由金入元的人，到明代以后此说更成为主流，综合诸种说法，学术界推断其生卒年大约为 1225 年左右至 1302 年左右，是比较可信的。

关汉卿的籍贯也有三说：大都（今北京市）人、解州（今属山西省运城专区）人、祁州伍仁村（在今河北省安国县）人。大都说的记载最早，为元人钟嗣成《录鬼簿》；解州说见于清姚之骃《元明事类钞》卷二三引元末朱佑《元史补遗》；祁州说见于清乾隆二十三年（1758 年）修《祁州志》卷八《纪事》。钟嗣成为元人，大都说最为可信。

关汉卿曾在太医院任职（见《录鬼簿》），为人风流倜傥，博学能文，具有多种文艺才能；与当时的杂剧作家和演员有密切交往，他本人也能粉墨登场（见明臧晋叔《元曲选·序二》）。这种种条件使关汉卿熟悉舞台规律，成为一个内行戏剧家。蒙古贵族是以武力征服中原建立元朝的，游牧民族的生活习惯使他们不重视文化，轻视儒生，把隋唐以来读书人传统的入仕阶梯——科举也废止了，读书人纵使想报效国家，也报国无门，于是以有用之才专心致志地靠写作杂剧谋生。从另一面说，元蒙统治者不重视文化教育，对文人创作的约束禁忌便松弛，这又为作家发挥才智自由创作提供了良好的环境。统治者又喜爱歌舞娱乐，就更为杂剧的繁荣创造了氛围。可以说，个人才华和时代环境造就了关汉卿，使他成为当时的剧坛领袖、作家权威、写杂剧的泰斗（《录鬼簿》所附贾仲明【凌波仙】吊关汉卿曲），成为中国写实戏剧的奠基人。

据文献记载，关汉卿一共创作杂剧 67 部，保存到今天的有 18 部（其中个别作品是否关作尚存争议）。在中国的封建社会，言志载道的诗文成为士大夫正统文学，而戏曲小说则被视为小道末技，受人鄙视。那时候又没有著作权意识，创作杂剧不署名，写完便由剧团演出，也任凭剧团改动，散佚作品非常多。如果加上这些散佚作品，关汉卿的作品数量是相当惊人的。

二

中国是诗的王国，在中国文学传统里重抒情不重叙事，而戏曲是抒情与叙事相融合成的第三种文学。中国戏曲成熟晚于古希腊罗马的戏剧和印度梵剧，但中国戏曲却有着鲜明特色和全新面貌。尤其是元代的杂剧，是写实的，面向社会和人生，与百姓的生活和心理、乃至审美情趣息息相关，其生活气息之浓郁、现实性之强烈，都非常独特。而这种戏剧方向的开拓者和奠基者正是关汉卿，所以王国维在《宋元戏曲史》中说:“关汉卿一空倚傍，自铸伟词，而其言曲尽人情，字字本色，故当为元人第一。”可以说，元代戏曲的繁荣离不开关汉卿的卓越贡献，元明清三代戏曲成就压倒诗文，成为中国文学史上辉煌的篇章，与关汉卿的贡献也是分不开的。

从题材来说，关汉卿写过历史剧、婚姻恋爱剧、公案剧和其他社会生活剧，但他没有写过隐居避世的隐逸剧和仙佛之类的宗教剧，这是他直面人生而不回避现实的表现。他又往往把各种生活内容交织在一起构成戏剧情节，从而使戏剧的生活内容深厚。他诅咒金元统治集团之间的战争给人民带来的灾难是“龙斗鱼伤”(《拜月亭》);他挞伐杨衙内杀夫夺妻(《望江亭》)、葛彪残害人命(《蝴蝶梦》)、鲁斋郎强夺人妻(《鲁斋郎》)、周舍骗婚殴妻(《救风尘》)等特权人物践踏人性的兽行；他揭露社会黑暗腐败，官府成为恶人做恶的工具和保护伞，官员判断是非曲直是以权势的大小和金钱的多少为依据的。既无权又无钱的百姓，就只好“有口难言”（《窦娥冤》）了。关汉卿的深刻之处还在于，他指出了这些黑暗势力的靠山是昏庸的皇帝：杨衙内用以斩取白士中首级的势剑金牌是皇帝赐给的，鲁斋郎“大的忒稀诧”的官职是皇帝授予的，周舍仰仗的是他做郑州同知的父亲，打死人不偿命“只当房檐上揭片瓦相似”的葛彪是皇亲，屈杀窦娥的贪官昏官却受重用升了官……昏君贪官构成社会野蛮的统治网，“衙门从古向南开，就中无个不冤哉”（《窦娥冤》），官府成了百姓受苦受难的根源。即使像《陈母教子》这样道德说教明显的戏，其要求官员清正廉洁不受民财，也是针对贪官遍地的现实而发，体现着对社会的干预精神。

关汉卿同情不幸的妇女。在中国封建社会，妇女所受的苦难和压迫比男人更深。关汉卿塑造了各式各样地位不同、性格各异的女性形象：宁舍亲子也要保前妻之子的慈母王婆婆（《蝴蝶梦》），充满幻想又天真幼稚的妓女宋引章、有胆有识的侠妓赵盼儿（《救风尘》），善良又坚强的窦娥（《窦娥冤》），临危不惧从容对敌的谭记儿（《望江亭》），天真美丽渴望摆脱奴婢地位的燕燕（《诈妮子》），争取婚姻自主的王瑞兰（《拜月亭》）……，既有大家闺秀，也有小家碧玉，既有良家妇女，也有风尘娼妓，关汉卿把满腔同情给予她们，希望她们有好的生活。

关剧的着眼点在人，在人应当怎样生活，这是他比前辈作家的进步。在关汉卿的笔下，人性得到承认，人的正常欲望受到肯定。王瑞兰不顾家长威逼阻挠，坚持等待被父亲强行拆散的夫婿；奴婢燕燕为了争取做自由人，像飞蛾扑火一样舍身追求光明；妓女也有权要求从良，做“儿女成双”的“自由人”（《谢天香》），过“对面，并肩”的夫妻生活（《金线池》）的愿望应当得到满足。寡妇再嫁受到鼓励，谭记儿再婚后的生活是幸福的。窦娥用生命向不合理的社会进行抗议，为社会底层的人们呼号生存的权利。关汉卿还以大反世俗的勇气藐视室息妇女人性的贞节观念，认为宋引章错嫁周舍可以原谅，不应当妨碍她与安秀实的爱情；李四张珪并不因为妻子失身于鲁斋郎而心怀芥蒂；甚至妓女也有资格许配状元郎（《谢天香》）。关汉卿没有精心刻画她们美丽的容貌，却着意突出她们的智慧和果敢，勇于面对磨难、战胜磨难，赋予她们几分令人敬畏的辣味和野性。她们已不再是男人的附属物，在中国文学史上第一次体现了女性意识的觉醒。

关汉卿笔下的正面人物身上大都闪耀着理想的光辉——抗争精神。不论是叱咤风云的英雄还是柔弱善良的女性，都在反抗，也都在胜利，有一股使人振奋和鼓舞的激情在跳动。《单刀会》写胜利的英雄，《双赴梦》写败而不馁志在报仇的英雄；谭记儿靠自己的智慧保卫了美满姻缘，赵盼儿抓住对手的弱点解救风尘姊妹宋引章，王婆婆支持儿子们手刃仇人葛彪为亡夫雪恨，窦娥感天动地的抗争精神不仅惩罚了恶人也惩罚了不公平的世道。剧中人靠斗争捍卫人的尊严，也靠斗争掌握自己的命运。而不论多么凶恶的坏人总逃不脱严厉的惩罚。这些恶人都以丑角扮演，作家不仅给他们以有力的鞭挞，也给予无情的讽刺和揶揄，使读者和观众既憎恶他们又鄙视嘲笑他们。关汉卿告诉人们：只有斗争才有出路。作家的社会责任感，对苦难同胞的博爱胸怀，使关汉卿不仅仅是借戏剧鸣一己的不平，他要感染和引导在人生道路上艰难跋涉的人们鼓起直面人生的勇气，靠执着不渝的努力为自己争取美好的前途。

毫无疑问，关汉卿是自立自强精神的呼唤者，是反抗压迫和黑暗的斗士。但同时关汉卿又是浪子，是风流才人。在《玉镜台》里，对温峤以“不本分”的手段骗娶刘倩英，成就老夫少妻婚姻，极有兴致地津津玩味；在散曲【南吕一枝花·不伏老】里又宣称自己是“一世里眠花宿柳”的青楼常客，而且“则除是阎王亲自唤，神鬼自来勾，三魂归地府，七魄丧冥幽，天哪，那其间才不向烟花路儿上走！”除死不休。这虽然不能说是关汉卿生活的真实写照，也可以看出他的浪子情怀和情趣。关汉卿充满了矛盾，《窦娥冤》里既怀疑天地鬼神又要“感天动地”，既反对官府又离不开官府；在剧中也调和，也用幻想安慰无奈的人们。关汉卿是人世间人，作品是带有人间烟火味的作品。

三

关汉卿在艺术上的最大贡献在于，他把中国叙事文学从敷演故事阶段，推进到描写人物阶段。以前的叙事文学是通过人物串联故事，通过故事表现社会政治、伦理道德、经验教训，人物是故事的载体；关汉卿是把故事作为揭示人物心灵的途径，因而剧中人物具有活的血肉和灵魂。

他写出了人物性格的发展变化。以前的中国文学，人物性格几乎始终不变，故事的进展只是使固有性格获得更多的展示机会。关汉卿却写出了人物性格随着自身遭遇和生活环境的变化而发展的轨迹。这以《窦娥冤》里窦娥形象塑造得最为成功。窦娥是由听天由命、逆来顺受逐渐走向反抗的：从恪守封建道德到怀疑天地鬼神，从与世无争到“争到头竞到底”；从反抗张驴儿父子到反抗楚州太守，进而“将那滥官污吏都杀坏”，反抗整个黑暗官场和邪恶势力；从维护自身清白而反抗，到为救婆婆，进而“与一人分忧，万民除害”，精神境界逐渐升华。写出人物性格的发展变化，是对人物性格固定化模式的突破。

他突破了人物性格单一化的模式，写出了人物性格的复杂性。《鲁斋郎》里的张珪是郑州衙门里的六案都孔目。孔目是衙门中的小吏，具体办事人员，无品级无职权，但在元代社会里却有特殊地位，权力也增大了，所以元代有人分十等“一官二吏……”（《谢叠山集》卷一《送方伯载归三山序》、《心史》卷下《大义略叙》）的说法，地位之尊仅次于官。这样的身份使张珪有欺人为恶的一面：“冒支国俸，滥取人钱”，逼得人典卖宅物为自己增加财产。但他又良心未泯，李四害病他相救，为使李四夫妻团圆他又舍俗出家。他欺人也被欺，在鲁斋郎面前他是弱者，鲁斋郎看上他的妻子他会忍辱送上门去。是强人也是弱者，好与坏集于一身，既可恨又可怜。人物的多重性格引起人们复杂的阅读感受。

关汉卿的剧作一般说来矛盾冲突激烈，有相当多的剧目其冲突甚至是性命攸关，这些冲突往往带有很强的社会性，是社会矛盾的反映。一方面是强大的邪恶势力，一方面主人公有执着不渝的追求和坚韧不屈的性格。性格与环境的搏击推动着剧情的发展，通过冲突展示丰厚的社会内容，表现作家民胞物与的情怀。窦娥从为自身到为君为民；王瑞兰由自己夫妻分离而祈祷“愿天下心厮爱的夫妇永无分离”（《拜月亭》）；谢天香由自己从良联想到妓女“越聪明越不得出笼时”（《谢天香》）的普遍现象；《金线池》中的杜蕊娘对卖淫制度产生了怀疑：“我想这一百二十行，门门都是求衣饭，偏俺这一门却是谁人制下的？好低微也呵！”赵盼儿总结出丈夫与嫖客的区别："做子弟的他影儿里会虚脾，那做丈夫的忒老实。"《蝴蝶梦》里的王婆婆提出了“使不着国戚皇亲，玉叶金枝，便是他龙孙帝子，打杀人也吃官司”的朴素法制思想；《单刀会》、《双赴梦》、《哭存孝》等历史剧，其主旨不在描写事件发生朝的历史，也不在反映元代的生活景象，而是要表达凛然无畏的民族精神、死不瞑目的复仇意志和对带有规律性的历史现象发表感慨。

关汉卿创作过“列之于世界大悲剧中亦无愧色”（王国维《宋元戏曲史》）的著名悲剧（《窦娥冤》等），也写出了精彩的喜剧（《救风尘》等）和大气磅礴的正剧（《单刀会》等），可称戏剧全才。从风格学上说，他又是本色派的代表作家。所谓本色就是指按照生活的本来面貌进行描写，情节不枝不蔓，冲突集中紧凑，做到“境无旁溢”，语言符合人物性格和特定情境，不追求辞藻华丽，具有朴素自然的特点。像《窦娥冤》第二折的【斗虾蟆】、第三折的【快活三】【鲍老儿】,《单刀会》第四折的【新水令】【驻马听】等，都是这方面的代表曲文，一向脍炙人口。

在中国，关汉卿被称为“元曲四大家”（关汉卿、郑光祖、白朴、马致远）之首（见元周德清《中原音韵·序》)，具有崇高的地位；在七百多年前的世界上，关汉卿也是无与伦比的，他要比文艺复兴时期英国莎士比亚的戏剧活动早350年左右的时间，而剧作关氏却要比莎翁多出30部。

四

编校关汉卿的作品集是进入二十世纪之后的事，比如吴晓铃等编校《关汉卿戏曲集》(中国戏剧出版社 1958 年版，简称“吴校本”)、王学奇等校注《关汉卿全集校注》(河北教育出版社 1988 年版)、王季思主编《全元戏曲》第一卷（人民文学出版社 1990 年版）等。在古代，关汉卿的作品散见于各种戏曲选本之中,如《元刊杂剧三十种》(简称“元刊本”)、王骥德编《古杂剧》、赵琦美钞校《脉望馆钞校本古今杂剧》(简称“脉望馆本”)、陈与郊编徐龙峰刻《新续古名家杂剧》(简称“陈与郊本”)、息机子编《古今杂剧选》(简称“息机子本”)、臧晋叔编《元曲选》、孟称舜编《古今名剧合选》(分《酹江集》、《柳枝集》)等，以上除《元刊杂剧三十种》为元刊本外，都是明刊本。

本书共选关汉卿戏剧作品 8 部，文字依据 1958 年吴校本移录，并由编辑重新校对、重新标点。

《窦娥冤》，全名《感天动地窦娥冤》，是关汉卿的代表作。题材的最早来源是西汉刘向《说苑》卷五《贵德》所记东海孝妇故事，晋干宝《搜神记》卷十一对这一故事加以发展，说汉代东海郡(治所在今山东省郯城县北)青年寡妇周青非常孝顺，婆婆为不拖累周青上吊而死。小姑告周青杀人，周青被判斩刑：“青将死，车载十丈竹竿，以悬五幡。立誓于众曰：‘青若有罪，愿杀，血当顺下；青若枉死，血当逆流。’既行刑已，其血青黄，缘幡竹而上标，又缘幡竹而下云。”其后郡中枯旱，三年不雨。这便是《窦娥冤》第三折三桩誓愿的来源。周青冤死只是判断失误造成的个案，不具备社会意义。关汉卿借用了其中的传说，反映的是当时贪官遍地冤狱层出的社会现实。窦娥恪守封建道德却没有生存空间，社会造就了窦娥却又毁灭了窦娥，这个社会的存在是不合理的；发自最能忍耐的弱者的抗议，就更有震撼人心的力量。

流传版本有脉望馆本、《元曲选》本、《酹江集》本。

《救风尘》，全名《赵盼儿风月救风尘》，是关汉卿喜剧的代表作。全剧赞美了妓女赵盼儿的智慧、胆量和勇救风尘姊妹宋引章的侠义精神。以风月手段救人，情节新颖别致。

流传版本有脉望馆本、《元曲选》本。

《单刀会》，全名《关大王独赴单刀会》，是关汉卿的正剧力作。题材来源于陈寿《三国志·吴书》卷五四《鲁肃传》及裴松之注等。关汉卿对史实加以改变。史称鲁肃关羽“单刀俱会”、裴注为鲁肃往见关羽，剧中改为关羽往见鲁肃，单刀赴会；会晤结果，史载为割湘水为界双方罢兵、裴注为鲁肃指责关羽贪而弃义而羽无以答，剧中改为关羽大义凛然，述说蜀汉占有荆州的合理性，而东吴并非正统不该占有荆州，凯旋而归。突出关羽的不屈、无畏精神，是为了表现蜀汉政权的正统、正义和正气。艺术上很有特色。前两折主角关羽并不出场，通过各种人物之口对关羽进行渲染，为戏剧冲突进行铺垫，第三折关羽才出场；第四折，赴会途中唱出【新水令】【驻马听】二曲，抒发历史兴亡之感，是历代传诵的名句。矛盾冲突此时才正面展开。剑拔弩张的故事而用抒情曲辞演进,是“武戏文唱”的典型手法。

流传版本有元刊本、脉望馆本、《元曲选》本。

《玉镜台》，全名《温太真玉镜台》。题材来源于南朝宋刘义庆《世说新语·假谲》：温峤一个远房姑母托他给女儿找婆家。温峤正好死了夫人，暗暗打算自娶表妹，就问姑母：“佳婿难得，但如峤比云何？”姑母同意。过几天他对姑母说：“已觅得婚处，门第粗可，婿身名宦，尽不减峤。”并将自己的玉镜台做聘礼。新婚之日新娘掀开盖头，抚掌笑道："我固疑是老奴，果如所卜！”剧中增加了温峤借教表妹弹琴写字之机挑逗表妹及表妹拒不认夫、皇帝调解的情节。追求谐趣是本剧的特点。

流传版本有脉望馆本、《古杂剧》本、《元曲选》本、《柳枝集》本。

《哭存孝》，全名《邓夫人苦痛哭存孝》。题材来源于欧阳修《新五代史》卷三六《义儿传》及宋无名氏《五代史评话·唐史》，这些记载都说李存孝是因为反叛李克用才被杀的，剧中改为李克用听信谗言而杀李存孝。揭示了封建社会君臣之间兔死狗烹、鸟尽弓藏的实质。

流传版本有脉望馆本。

《鲁斋郎》，全名《包待制智斩鲁斋郎》。包拯虽然《宋史》有传，但本剧却与史毫无关系，只是借包公之名揭露元代权豪势要欺压百姓的事实。本剧善于把人物放在特殊情境（如“夫主婚妻招婿”）加以考验，以揭示其内心世界；改“鲁斋郎”为“鱼齐即”智斩的情节，体现了浓厚的民间文学色彩。

流传版本有脉望馆本、《元曲选》本。

《望江亭》，全名《望江亭中秋切鲙旦》，是关汉卿的名作之一。表现女子智慧胜于男子，谭记儿不仅保卫了幸福姻缘，也保护了丈夫。谭记儿妆成渔妇巧斗杨衙内的情节，是别开生面的好戏。

流传版本有《古杂剧》本、息机子本、《元曲选》本。

《蝴蝶梦》，全名《包待制三勘蝴蝶梦》。西汉刘向《列女传》卷五《齐义继母》有后母舍亲子以保前妻之子事；宋苏易简《文房四谱》卷一有蝇集笔端事。关汉卿采用这两件事进行敷演，刻画出一个慈祥仁义又坚韧的崇高母亲形象。

流传版本有脉望馆本、陈与郊本、《元曲选》本。

关汉卿在中国戏曲史上具有崇高的地位，他的作品也较早就被译为英、法、德、俄等文字在国外流传。日本宫原民平曾译《感天动地窦娥冤》为日文，并收入《古典剧大系》第16卷，于1926年由东京近代社编辑出版；1966年俄国斯别阿聂夫（Спеаиев H.A.）译《感天动地窦娥冤》为俄文……诸如此类，非常之多。值得一提的是，曾翻译中国古代文学巨著《红楼梦》的中国著名文学翻译家杨宪益、戴乃迭夫妇，把8部关剧译成英文，北京外文出版社于1958年出版了这本《关汉卿杂剧选》。

首都师范大学
中文系教授　张燕瑾

2003年8月于北京

INTRODUCTION

Guan Hanqing belongs not only to China, but also to the world. When the Chinese people commemorated the 7th centennial of his career in 1958, Guan Hanqing was listed as an eminent person in world culture upon the recommendation of the World Peace Council.

I

Guan Hanqing came from a humble family, and the calling of playwright was regarded as a lowly one in his time. Therefore, there are few records of his life. Hanqing was his style name, but his given name is unknown. He nicknamed himself "Yizhaisou". Both his exact date of birth and date of death are unknown, but he is thought to have lived between 1225 and 1302.

There are also three locations put forward as his birthplace: Dadu (today's Beijing), Xiezhou (in today's Yuncheng Prefecture, Shanxi Province), and Wuren Village in Qizhou (in today's Anguo County, Hebei Province). Of the three, he was most likely to be born in Dadu.

According to the *Ghost Recording Book*, Guan Hanqing once took a post in the Imperial Hospital. He was said to be a flamboyant, gifted and learned scholar with artistic talent. He had close contacts with other playwrights and performers, and he himself also appeared on the stage (see "Preface Two" of *Selected Operas of the Yuan Dynasty* by Zang Jinshu, a Ming Dynasty writer). All these conditions made Guan Hanqing familiar with the stage performances and helped him become an expert dramatist. After the Mongols conquered the Central Plains, they established the new Yuan Dynasty. Preferring the old lifestyle of the nomads, they did not attach importance to culture, looked down upon scholars, and abolished the imperial civil examination system, the traditional ladder to success for scholars. However, the new rulers did not have much prohibition on literary writings. What's more, the new aristocracy was fond of entertainment, so there was a lot of scope for scholars to be creative in the field of drama, opera, etc.

It is recorded that Guan Hanqing wrote 67 operas, of which 18 are extant (there are still disputes about the authorship of one or two of them). In Chinese feudal society, poems and essays that conveyed ideals and philosophical principles were the orthodox literary forms of the literati and the operas and novels were looked down upon as unorthodox and trivial. In those times, there was no such thing as copyright, and the opera scripts did not carry the authors' names. The operas were subject to changes at will when they were performed on stage.

II

In the tradition of the Chinese literature, writers preferred to express their emotions rather than record events, but operas were a third kind of literature that blended the expression of emotions and the recording of events. The Chinese operas matured later than the ancient Greek, Roman and Indian operas, but the Chinese operas have their own distinctive characteristics. Yuan operas, in particular, deal with reality, society and life. They are closely related to the life, psychology and esthetic interests of the common people. It was Guan Hanqing who set the pace and style for such operas. Wang Guowei, a famous Qing Dynasty critic, wrote in his *History of Operas of Song and Yuan Dynasties*: "Guan Hanqing, without any reference, created his great works, and every word in his plays conveys the true feelings of the heroes. He should be rated as number one among the scholars of the Yuan Dynasty". It can thus be said that the thriving of operas in the Yuan Dynasty was inseparable from Guan Hanqing's outstanding contributions.

So far as subject matter is concerned, Guan dealt with history, love and marriage, court trials and social life. He never touches upon religion or the activities of monks or holy men. This shows how he faced life and reality squarely instead of avoiding them. He often wove different aspects of life together to construct the plots of his operas, filling them with rich human experiences. He condemns the disaster brought to the people by the war between the ruling cliques of the Jin Dynasty and the Yuan Dynasty as a "fight between dragons which hurt the fish" ("The Moon-Worshipping Pavilion"). He attacked Lord Yang for killing a man and taking his wife by force ("The Riverside Pavilion"), Ge Biao for committing a murder ("The Butterfly Dream"), Lu Zhailang for taking other's wife by force ("The Wife-Snatcher"), and Zhou She for his fraudulent marriage and beating his wife ("Rescued by A Coquette") and other privileged persons for their crimes. He exposed the darkness and corruption of society by describing government offices as the tools and protective cover for evil persons. Government officials decided right and wrong based on power and money. The common people, without power or money, could only "shut their mouths" ("Snow in Midsummer"). The incisiveness of Guan's remarks lay in the fact that he pointed out that the backing for these dark forces was the fatuous emperor: The sword of authority and golden tally Lord Yang used to cut off Bai Shizhong's head was bestowed by the emperor; Lu Zhailang's official post was bestowed by the emperor; all Zhou She could count on was his father, the Associate Administrator of Zhengzhou; Ge Biao got away with murder because he belonged to the imperial family. Guan attacks the widespread corruption among officials of his time in "Mother Chen Teaches Her Son."

Guan Hanqing showed great sympathy for women, who were in a disadvantageous position in feudal society. He portrayed a wide variety of females: The kind stepmother Wang in "The Butterfly Dream," the naïve and childish prostitute Song Yinzhang and the bold and intelligent chivalrous prostitute Zhao Pan'er in "Rescued by A Coquette," the kind-hearted and unyielding Dou E in "Snow in Midsummer," Tan Ji'er who braves danger in the face of her enemy in "Riverside Pavilion," innocent and pretty Yanyan who longs for freedom from being a servant in "The Tricky Girl," and Wang Ruilan who strives to marry a man of her own choice in "The Moon-worshipping Pavilion," They include daughters of illustrious families, pretty girls from humble families, women of good families, and entertainers.

His focus of attention was on how humans should live. This was an improvement on the work of his predecessors. Under his pen, human nature was recognized and people's normal desires were affirmed. Despite her parents' coercion and hindrance, Wang Ruilan insists on waiting for her husband who has been separated from her by her father. Servant Yanyan is like a moth darting into a flame to sacrifice her life in order to be a free woman. Prostitutes also have the right to live a decent life and get married as "free women" ("Xie Tianxiang"), and their desire to have honest conjugal relations ("The Golden Thread Pond") is justified. Widows are encouraged to remarry. Tan Ji'er's second marriage is a happy one. Dou E goes to her death protesting the injustices done to women of the lower classes. Song Yinzhang's mistaken marriage to Zhou She should not hinder the love between her and An Xiushi. Li Si and Zhang Gui have no ill feelings about their wives losing their chastity to Lu Zhailang, and even a prostitute can marry a Number One Scholar in the imperial examination ("Xie Tianxiang"). Guan does not write much about their beautiful looks, but gives prominence to descriptions of their wisdom, courage and resoluteness. They are no longer appendages of men, and manifest the awakening of female consciousness for the first time in the history of Chinese literature.

The positive figures under Guan's pen mostly shine with the brilliance of ideals - the spirit of resistance. Whether all-conquering heroes or weak-willed and kind women, they all put up resistance and become victorious. They pulsate with a passion of inspiration and encouragement. "Lord Guan Goes to the Feast" portrays an ever-victorious hero, and "Both Have Dreams" portrays a hero determined to get revenge despite earlier failure. Tan Ji'er relies on her wisdom to defend her happy marriage, Zhao Pan'er takes advantage of the opponent's weaknesses to rescue prostitute Song Yinzhang. Old lady Wang helps her sons to kill their enemy Ge Biao to avenge her husband's murder, and Dou E's spirit of resistance brings about the punishment of evil-doers. Guan Hanqing's message is that struggling against a cruel fate is the only way out.

Guan Hanqing was a fighter, but he was also a free-mannered gifted scholar. In "The Jade Minor-Stand," Guan takes great interest in Wen Qiao's using deceptive means to marry Liu Qianying and make an old-man-and-young-woman marriage. In "Refusing to Give in to Age" of his *A Flower in Nanlü*, Guan Hanqing proclaims that he is "a frequent visitor to brothels." saying that he would not stop visiting brothels until he died. Guan Hanqing was full of contradictions. In "Snow in Midsummer," he displays doubts about the gods and other supernatural forces on the one hand, but wants to move Heaven and Earth on the other. He opposes the authorities but cannot live without them. He tries to console the powerless with illusions.

III

Guan's biggest contribution to art is that he pushed Chinese narrative literature forward from the stage of telling stories to the stage of portraying characters. Previously, the characters were simply the carriers of the stories. Guan Hanqing used his stories as ways to expose the souls of his characters. Therefore, the characters in his operas have flesh and blood, and souls.

Guan's characters change and develop. In previous Chinese literature, there was almost no change in the characters; the development of a story merely provided more opportunities for the display of their inherent characteristics. In "Snow in Midsummer," Dou E first resigns herself to her fate and accepts adversity meekly, but then gradually resists - from meekly accepting feudal moral principles to having doubts about Heaven and the gods, from standing aloof from worldly strife to "fighting to the end," from resisting Donkey Zhang and his father to resisting the Governor of Chuzhou, and then further to "killing all evil and corrupt officials" and resisting the whole dark officialdom and all evil forces, from defending her innocence to resistance and further to "eliminating evils to aid the common people" in order to rescue her mother-in-law. Her mental outlook is gradually sublimated.

Guan also departed from the pattern of one single character to introducing a variety of characters. In "The Wife-Snatcher," Zhang Gui is a clerk in the Zhengzhou yamen, a lowly position but one which gives him power, and he uses this power for corrupt ends. However, he still has a conscience. When Li Si falls ill, he helps him. He even leaves home to become a monk in order to bring about the reunion of Li Si and his wife. He bullies others, but he is also bullied. He is weak when he surrenders his wife to Lu Zhailang, but he is strong on other occasions. He does both good and evil. He is both hateful and pitiful.

Guan's operas are full of sharp contradictions and conflicts. These conflicts often have a strong social nature, and reflect the social contradictions of his time, propelling the development of the plots. Dou E's development from defending herself to defending the common people, Wang Ruilan's development from her separation from her husband to praying for "no separation for all affectionate couples in the world" ("The Moon-worshipping Pavilion"), and Xie Tianxiang's connection of her own reform and marriage to a decent man with the fate of other prostitutes "the more intelligent they are, the less chance there is for them to get out of the cage" ("Xie Tianxiang"). Zhao Pan'er summarizes the difference between husbands and the brothel visitors: "The lovers are false, while the husbands at least are honest."

Besides the tragedies, Guan Hanqing wrote excellent comedies ("Rescued by A Coquette" and others) and majestic serious operas, such as "Lord Guan Goes to the Feast." So far as his style of writing is concerned, he is a representative writer of the "natural color" school. Natural color refers to simple, natural and terse description based on the original aspects of life, with a well-knit and well-developed plot and a language conforming to the characters and the given circumstances and scenes. Passages in Act II, Act III in the "Snow in Midsummer" and in Act IV of "Lord Guan Goes to the Feast" are representative of this, and have enjoyed great popularity for centuries.

Guan Hanqing was called the leader of the "four great writers of Yuan operas" (The others were Zheng Guangzu, Bai Pu and Ma Zhiyuan) (see preface to Zhou Deqing's *Poems and Other Literary Writings of the Central Plains*). He was also unparalleled in the world more than 700 years ago. He lived about 350 years earlier than Shakespeare, and produced 30 more works than the English dramatist.

IV

Editing and revising Guan Hanqing's works started in the 20th century. Notable in this respect are *Collection of Guan Hanqing's Operas* edited and revised by Wu Xiaoling (1958 edition, published by the China Theatrical Publishing House, called "Wu's revised edition" for short), *Revised Collected Works of Guan Hanqing with Annotations* revised and annotated by Wang Xueqi and others (1988 edition published by the Hebei Educational Publishing House), and Volume I of *Complete Collection of Yuan Operas* compiled by Wang Jisi (1990 edition, published by the People's Literature Publishing House). Previously, Guan Hanqing's works were scattered in different selections of operas, such as the *Block-Printed Edition of 30 Zaju (operas) of the Yuan Dynasty* (called the "block-printed edition of the Yuan Dynasty"), Wang Jide's *Ancient Zaju, the Maiwang Library Edition of Classical and Modern Operas* copied and revised by Zhao Qimei (called the "Maiwang Library edition" for short), *New Sequel to the Ancient Masters' Operas* edited by Chen Yujiao and carved by Xu Longfeng (called "Chen Yujiao edition" for short), *Selection of Classical and Modern Operas* edited by Xi Jizi (called "Xi Jizi edition" for short), *Selected Operas of the*

Yuan Dynasty edited by Zang Jinshu, *Combined Selection of Classical and Modern Operas* edited by Meng Chengshun (divided into Leijiang collection, Liuzhi collection, etc.) Except for the block-printed edition of the Yuan Dynasty, they were all block-printed in the Ming Dynasty.

This book includes eight of Guan's plays, with scripts transcribed from Wu's revised edition and with new punctuation.

"Snow in Midsummer," (The full title is "The Injustice Done to Dou E Moves Heaven," is Guan's representative work. The story originated in the tale of a filial woman recorded in Volume V of Liu Xiang's *Collection of Stories from the Western Han Dynasty* and developed in Volume XI of Gan Bao's *Records of Spirits* of the Jin Dynasty (265-420). It tells how Zhou Qing, a young widow in Donghai County (located north of Tancheng County in modem Shandong Province) is falsely accused of murdering her mother-in-law, and sentenced to death. On the gallows, she calls out to the crowd: "If I am innocent, my blood will flow upward to Heaven." This is exactly what happens. As a punishment meted out by Heaven, the county suffers severe drought for three consecutive years. By borrowing this legend, Guan Hanqing attacked the corrupt officials and unjust verdicts that were common in his day. Such a society created Dou E, and it also destroyed her.

Editions of this opera can be found in the Maiwang Library edition, *Selected Operas of the Yuan Dynasty* and Leijiang collection.

"Rescued by a Coquette" is Guan's representative comedy. The opera highly praises Zhao Pan'er's wisdom, courage and chivalrous spirit in rescuing her friend Song Yinzhang from a brothel.

Editions of this play can be found in the Maiwang Library edition and *Selected Operas of the Yuan Dynasty*.

"Lord Guan Goes to the Feast," is a powerful serious drama. The story originates in Volume 54, "Biography of Lu Su," in the Kingdom of Wu Volume of Chen Shou's *History of the Three Kingdoms* and Pei Songzhi's annotations. Guan Hanqing changed some historical facts in his opera version. For instance, according to Pei Songzhi's annotation, it was Lu Su who went to see Guan Yu, but in the opera Guan Yu goes to see Lu Su. The opera gives prominence to Guan Yu's unyielding and fearless spirit in order to illustrate the justice and integrity of the Kingdom of Shu. It is noteworthy that Guan Yu does not appear in the first two acts, but we learn much about him from remarks made by other characters to set off the dramatic conflict. In Act IV, Guan Yu sings two songs on his way to the feast to convey his feelings about historical rises and falls. The tension is developed in this act.

Editions of this play can be found in the block-printed edition of the Yuan Dynasty, Maiwang Library edition and *Selected Operas of the Yuan Dynasty*.

"The Jade Mirror-Stand," its full title being "Wen Taizhen's Jade Mirror-Stand," derives its plot from "Falsehood and Trickery" in Liu Yiqing's *New Collection of Anecdotes of Famous Personages* written in the Song Dynasty (420-479) of the Southern Dynasties. The play relies for its comic effect on mistaken identity. In the opera, the emperor helps to arrange the marriage of the protagonists.

Editions of this play can be found in the Maiwang Library edition, *Ancient Zaju, Selected Operas of the Yuan Dynasty* and the Liuzhi collection.

"Death of the Winged-Tiger General," the full title being "Wife Deng Weeps over the Death of the Winged-Tiger General," derives its subject matter from Ouyang Xiu's *New History of the Five Dynasties*, Volume 36, "Biography of the Adopted Son," written during the Northern Song Dynasty, and "The History of Later Tang" in *Anecdotes of the History of the Five Dynasties* by an unknown author of the Song Dynasty (960 - 1279). The accounts given in these records say that the Winged-Tiger General, Li Cunxiao, was killed because he turned against Li Keyong, but in the opera, Li Keyong believes in a false accusation against Li Cunxiao and has him killed. It laid bare the nature of feudal system that trusted aides come to no good end once they have outlived their usefulness.

An edition of this play can be found in the Maiwang Library edition.

"The Wife-Snatcher," or "Bao Zheng Executes Lu Zhailang by Cunning," uses Bao Zheng to expose how those in power bullied the masses. Bao Zheng is a figure who appears in the *History of the Song Dynasty*, but the opera is not based on history. Guan Hanqing uses a variety of twists in the plot of this opera to reveal the characters' psychology.

Editions of this play can be found in the Maiwang Library edition and the *Selected Operas of the Yuan Dynasty*.

In "The Riverside Pavilion" (the full title being "Slicing Fish on the Mid-Autumn Festival in the Riverside Pavilion"), tells how a woman outwits a man. Tan Ji'er not only preserves her happy marriage, but also protects her husband from the wrath of Lord Yang. The scene in which Tan Ji'er disguises herself as a fisherwoman to have a battle of wits with Lord Yang is a novel and exciting one.

Editions of this play can be found in *Ancient Zaju*, Xi Jizi edition, and *Selected Operas of the Yuan Dynasty*.

"The Butterfly Dream," or "Bao Zheng Inquires About the Butterfly Dream Three Times," is based on a story contained in *The Biographies of Chaste Women* by Liu Xiang of the Han Dynasty, Volume V "The Righteous Step-Mother of the State of Qi," which tells how a woman protects her step-son at the sacrifice of her own son. Guan Hanqing also drew on Volume I of *Stories of the Four Treasures of the Study* by Su Yijian of the Song Dynasty for the incident of flies assembling on a writing brush.

Editions of this play can be found in Maiwang Library edition, Chen Yujiao edition and *Selected Operas of the Yuan Dynasty*.

Guan Hanqing's major works have been translated into English, French, German and Russian. A Japanese version of "Snow in Midsummer" was included in Volume 16 of the *Anthology of Classical Operas* published in Tokyo in 1926. N. A. Speanev translated "Snow in Midsummer" into Russian in 1966. It is worth mentioning that Yang Xianyi, a noted Chinese literature translator, and his wife Gladys Yang, who jointly translated the classic *A Dream of Red Mansions*, have translated eight of Guan's plays into English, which was published by the Foreign Languages Press in 1958 under the title *Selected Plays of Guan Hanqing*.

ZhangYanjin
Professor
Chinese Language Department
Capital Normal University

August 2003, Beijing

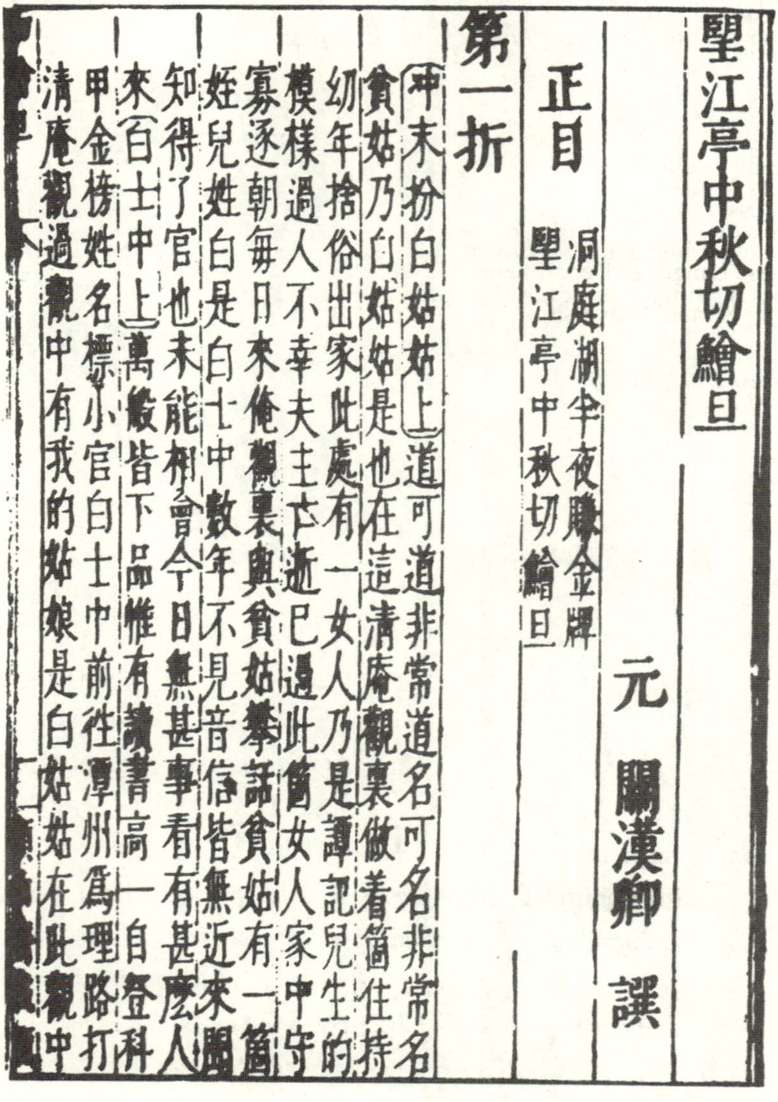
望江亭中秋切鱠旦

元 關漢卿 譔

正目 洞庭湖半夜賺金牌

望江亭中秋切鱠旦

第一折

（冲末扮白姑姑上）道可道非常道名可名非常名貧姑乃白姑姑是也在這清庵觀裏做着箇住持幼年捨俗出家此處有一女人乃是譚記兒生的模樣過人不幸夫主亡逝已過此箇女人家中守寡逐朝每日來俺觀裏與貧姑攀話貧姑有一箇姪兒姓白是白士中數年不見音信皆無近來聞知得了官也未能相會今日無甚事看有甚麼人來（白士中上）萬般皆下品惟有讀書高一自登科甲金榜姓名標小官白士中前往潭州為理路打清庵觀過觀中有我的姑娘是白姑姑在此觀中

《望江亭中秋切鲙旦》　明顾曲斋刊《古杂剧》本书影

The Riverside Pavilion. Facsimile of a page from the Ming Dynasty Guquzhai edition of *Ancient Zaju.*

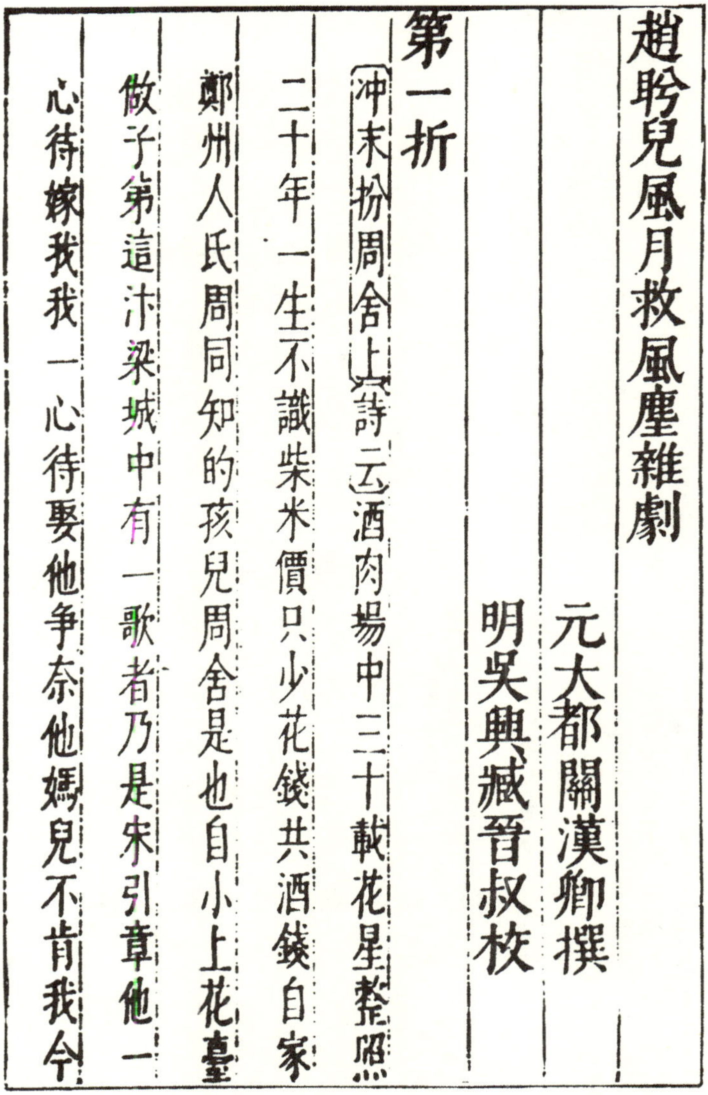
趙盼兒風月救風塵雜劇

元大都關漢卿撰

明吳興臧晉叔校

第一折

（冲末扮周舍上）（詩云）酒肉場中三十載花星整照二十年一生不識柴米價只少花錢共酒錢自家鄭州人氏周同知的孩兒周舍是也自小上花臺做子弟這汴梁城中有一歌者乃是宋引章他一心待嫁我我一心待要他爭奈他媽兒不肯我今

《赵盼儿风月救风尘》　明雕虫馆刊《元曲选》本书影

Rescued by a Coquette. Facsimile of a page from the Ming Dynasty Diaochong Library edition of *Selected Operas of the Yuan Dynasty*.

目　　录

CONTENTS

感天动地窦娥冤

Snow in Midsummer

第一折

（冲末扮卜儿上）花有重开日，人无再少年。老身蔡婆婆是也。楚州人氏。嫡亲的三口儿家属。不幸夫主亡逝已过，止有一个孩儿，年长八岁也。俺娘儿两个过其日月，家中颇有些钱财。这山阳郡有个窦秀才，从去年问我借了五两银子，如今本利该银拾两。我数次索取这银两，他兑付不起。窦秀才有个女儿，我有心看上与我做个媳妇，就准了拾两银子。他说今日好日辰，送来与我。老身今日且不索钱去，专在家中等候。这早晚窦先生敢待来也。（窦天章引俫儿上）腹中晓尽世间事，命里不如天下人。小生姓窦，名天章。祖居长安京兆人也。幼习儒业，颇看诗书。小生未曾进取功名。不幸浑家亡化已过，撇下这个女孩儿，小字端云。从三岁上亡了他母亲，如今孩儿七岁也。小生一贫如洗，今在这楚州山阳郡住坐。此间有个蔡婆

ACT I

(*Enter Mistress Cai.*)

MRS. CAI:

A flower may blossom again,
But youth never returns.

I am Mistress Cai of Chuzhou. There were three of us in my family; but unluckily my husband died, leaving me just one son who is eight years old. We live together, mother and son, and are quite well off. A scholar named Dou of Shanyang Prefecture borrowed five taels of silver from me last year. Now the interest and capital come to ten taels, and I've asked several times for the money; but Mr. Dou cannot pay it. He has a daughter, and I've good mind to make her my daughter-in-law; then he won't have to pay back the ten taels. Mr. Dou chose today as a lucky day, and is bringing the girl to me; so I won't ask him to pay me back, but wait for him at home. He should be here soon.

(*Enter Dou Tianzhang, leading his daughter Duanyun.*)

DOU:

I am master of all the learning in the world,
But my fate is worse than that of other men.

My name is Dou Tianzhang, and the home of my ancestors is Chang'an. I have studied the classics since I was a child and read a good deal; but I haven't yet taken the examinations. Unfortunately my wife has died, leaving me this only daughter, Duanyun. She lost her mother when she was three, and now she is seven. Living from hand to mouth, I moved to Shanyang Prefecture in Chuzhou and took lodgings here. There is a widow

婆，子母二人过日。这婆婆有些钱物，小生因无盘缠，曾借了这婆婆五两银子，到合本利对该银拾两。他数次问小生索取，我着什么还他？谁想蔡婆婆常常着人来说，要小生女儿做他儿媳妇。况如今春榜动，选场开，小生待上朝取应去，争奈欠少盘缠。小生出于无奈，如今将孩儿窦端云送与蔡婆婆做儿媳妇。那里是做媳妇，分明是卖与他一般。就准了他那先取借的银子，分外但借些少东西，够小生应举盘缠，足可够了也。端云孩儿也，是你父亲出于无奈。说话中间，可早来到也。婆婆在家么？（卜）秀才，请家里坐，老身等候多时也。（做相见科）（窦）小生今日一径的将女孩儿送来与婆婆。怎敢说做媳妇，只与婆婆早晚使用咱。小生目下进取功名去，望婆婆看觑则个。（卜）秀才，你本利少我拾两银子，兀的是借钱的文书，还你；再借与你二两银子做盘缠，秀才，休嫌轻少。（窦）多谢了婆婆。先少许多银子，今又与小生盘缠银子，此恩异日必当重报。婆婆，女孩儿早晚呆痴，看小生面看取孩儿咱。（卜）秀才，你只管放心。我做亲女儿一般看承。（窦跪下，云）婆婆，端云孩儿该打呵，看小生面则骂。当骂呵，则处分几句。孩儿，你也不比在我跟前，我是你亲父，将就的你。你若在这里，早晚若顽可，你只讨那打骂哩。儿呵，我这一去了呵，几时再得相见也！（悲科）弹剑自伤悲，文章习仲

in this town named Cai, who lives alone with her son and is fairly well off, and as I had no money for travelling I borrowed five taels from her. Now, with the interest, I owe her ten taels; but though she has asked several times for the money, I haven't been able to pay her. And recently she has sent to say she would like my daughter to marry her son. Since the spring examinations will soon be starting, I should be going to the capital; but I have no money for the road. So I am forced to take Duanyun to Widow Cai as her future daughter-in-law. I'm not marrying my daughter but selling her! For this means the widow will cancel my debt and give me some cash for my journey. This is all I can hope for. Ah! child, your father does this against his will! While talking to myself I've reached her door. Mistress Cai! Are you at home?

(*Enter Mistress Cai.*)

MRS. CAI: So it's Mr. Dou! Come in, please. I've been waiting for you.

(*They greet each other.*)

DOU: I've brought you my daughter, ma'am, not to be your daughter-in-law — that would be asking too much — but to serve you day and night. I must be going to take the examination. I hope you will look after her.

MRS. CAI: Well, you owed me ten taels including interest. Here is your promissory note back and another two taels for your journey. I hope you don't think it too little.

DOU: Thank you, ma'am! Instead of asking for what I owe you, you have given me money for the road. Some day I shall repay your kindness in full. My daughter is a foolish child. Please take care of her, ma'am, for my sake.

MRS. CAI: Don't worry, Mr. Dou. I shall look after your daughter as if she were my own.

DOU (*Kneeling to her*): If the child deserves a beating, ma'am, for my sake just scold her! And if she dserves a scolding, for my sake speak gently to her! As for you, Duan-yun, this isn't like at home, where your father used to put up with your whims. If you're naughty here, you'll be beaten and cursed. When shall I see you again, child? (*He sighs.*)

I drum sadly on my sheath;

尼。不幸妻先丧，父子两分离。（下）（卜）窦秀才留下他这女孩儿与我做媳妇儿，他上朝应举去了。老身无甚事，前后执料去也。（下）

（赛卢医上）行医有斟酌，下药依本草；死的医不活，活的医死了。自家赛卢医。在这荆州开着生药局。在城有个蔡婆婆，我问他借了拾两银子，本利该银二十两。数次来讨这银子，我又无的还他。若不来，便罢；若来呵，我别有个主意。我在这药铺中坐的，看有什么人来。（卜上）老身蔡婆婆。自十三年前窦天章秀才留下端云孩儿与我做媳妇儿，改了他小名，唤做窦娥。自成亲之后，不想我孩儿死了，又早三年光景也。窦娥孩儿守寡。我和媳妇说知："我去城里赛卢医家索钱去也。"早来到他门首，赛卢医在家么？（卢）婆婆，家里来。（卜）我这两个银子长远了，你还了我罢。（卢）婆婆，我家里无银子，你跟我庄上取银子还你。（卜）我跟你去。（做行科）（卢）出的城来，东也无人，西也无人，这里不下手等什么？我随身带着绳子。兀那婆婆，谁唤你哩？（卜）在那里？（做勒卜儿科）（孛老

I have studied the Confucian classics;
My unhappy wife died young,
And now I am parted from my only daughter. (*Exit.*)

MRS. CAI: Now Mr. Dou has left me his daughter, and gone to the capital for the examination. I must see to the house.

(*Exeunt.*)

(*Enter Doctor Lu.*)

DOCTOR:

I diagnose all diseases with care,
And prescribe as the Herbal dictates;
But I cannot bring dead men back to life,
And the live ones I treat often die.

I am Doctor Lu. I own a drug shop here. I've borrowed ten taels of silver from Mistress Cai of this town, and with interest now owe her twenty taels. She keeps coming for the money; but I haven't got it. If she doesn't come back, so much the better. If she does, I have a plan. I'll sit in my shop now, and wait to see who turns up.

(*Enter Mistress Cai.*)

MRS. CAI: I am Mistress Cai. Thirteen years ago Mr. Dou Tianzhang left his daughter Duanyun with me to marry my son, and I changed her name to Dou E. But after their marriage my son died, so now she's a widow. That was nearly three years ago, and she'll soon be out of mourning. I've told her that I'm going to town to collect debt from Doctor Lu. Now I've reached his house. Is Doctor Lu in?

DOCTOR: Yes, ma'am, come in.

MRS. CAI: You've kept my money for a long time, doctor. You must pay me back.

DOCTOR: I've no money at home, ma'am. If you'll come with me to the village, I'll get money for you.

MRS. CAI: Very well. I'll go with you.

(*They start walking.*)

DOCTOR: Now we are outside the city. Here's a good spot, with no one about. Why not do it here? I've got the rope ready. Who's that calling

同副净赶上科）（赛卢医慌走下）（孛老救卜科）（副净云）父亲，是个婆婆。争些勒杀了。（孛老）兀那婆婆，你是那里人氏，姓甚名谁？因甚着这个人将你勒死？（卜）老身姓蔡，在城人氏，婆妇二人过日。有个赛卢医少我二十两银子，赚我到郊外勒死我。若不是老的和哥哥呵，那得老身性命来。（副净）老子，你听的他说么？他家还有个媳妇哩！你要这婆子，我要他媳妇儿。你和他说去。（孛老）兀那婆婆，你无丈夫，我无浑家，你肯与我做个婆婆，意下如何？（卜）是何言语！我当多与些钱钞相谢。（副净）你不肯？我也勒死你！（卜）哥哥，等我慢慢地寻思。（副净）你寻思。你随我老子，我便要你媳妇儿。（卜背云）我不依他，他又勒杀我。（云）你爷儿两个跟我家中去来。（副净）咱去来。（同下）

（正旦扮窦娥上）妾身姓窦，小字端云。祖居楚州人氏。我三岁上亡了母亲，七岁上离了父亲。俺父亲将我嫁与蔡婆婆为儿媳妇，改名窦娥。至十七岁与夫成亲，不幸夫亡化，可早三年光景。我今二十岁也。这在城有个赛卢医，他少俺银子，本利兑该二十两，数

you, ma'am?

MRS. CAI: Where?

(*The Doctor strangles the widow with the rope. Enter Old Zhang and his son Donkey. As they rush forward the Doctor takes to his heels. Old Zhang revives Mistress Cai.*)

DONKEY: It's an old woman, dad, nearly strangled to death.

ZHANG: Hey, you! Who are you? What's your name? Why did that fellow try to strangle you?

MRS. CAI: My name is Cai and I live in town with my widowed daughter-in-law. Doctor Lu owes me twenty taels so he lured me here and tried to strangle me. If not for you and this young man, it would have been all up with me!

DONKEY: Did you hear that, dad? She has a daughter-in-law at home! Suppose you take her as your wife and I take the daugher-in-law? Propose it to her, dad!

ZHANG: Hey, widow! You've no husband and I've no wife. How about the two of us getting married?

MRS. CAI: What an idea! I shall give you a handsome sum of money to thank you.

DONKEY: So you refuse! I'd better strangle you after all.

MRS. CAI: Wait! Let me think a moment, brother!

DONKEY: What do you need to think for? You take my dad, and I'll take your daughter-in-law.

MRS. CAI (*aside*): If I don't agree he'll strangle me! (*To them.*) Very well. Come home with me, both of you.

DONKEY: Let's go.

(*Exeunt.*)

(*Enter Dou E.*)

DOU E: I am Duanyun, and my home was in Chuzhou. When I was three I lost my mother; and when I was seven I had to leave my father, for he sent me to Mistress Cai as her son's child-bride, and she changed my name to Dou E. At seventeen I married; but unluckily my husband died three years ago. Now I am twenty. There is a Doctor Lu in town who

次索取不还。今日俺婆婆亲自索取去了。窦娥也，几时是俺命通时节也呵。（唱）

【仙吕点绛唇】满腹闲愁，数年坐受，常相守，无了无休，朝暮依然有。

【混江龙】黄昏白昼，忘餐废寝两般忧：夜来梦里，今日心头。地久天长难过遣，旧愁新恨几时休？则这业眼苦，愁眉皱，情怀冗冗，心绪悠悠。

似这等，几时是了也呵！

【油葫芦】莫不是八字儿该载着一世忧？谁似我无尽休！便做道人心难似水长流。我从三岁母亲身亡后，七岁与父分离久，嫁的个同住人他可又拔着短筹。撇的俺婆妇每都把空房守。端的有谁问，有谁偢？

【天下乐】莫不是前世里烧香不到头？这前程事一笔勾。劝今世早将来世修：我将这婆侍养，再将这服孝守，我言词须应口。

婆婆索钱去了，怎生这早晚不见回来？（孛老、卜儿、副净同上）（卜云）你爷儿两个且在门首，等我先进去。（净）奶奶，你先进去，就说女婿在门首罢。（卜见旦科）（旦云）奶奶，回来了？你吃饭么？（卜哭科，云）孩儿也，你教怎生说波。（旦唱）

owes my mother-in-law twenty taels including interest; and though she has asked him several times for the money, he hasn't paid her back. She's gone today to try to collect the debt. Ah, when shall I escape from my misery?

My heart is full of grief,
I have suffered for so many years!
Morning or evening it is all the same:
From dawn to dusk I can neither eat nor sleep,
Racked by sad dreams at night, sad thoughts by day,
Unending sorrow which I cannot banish,
Unceasing reasons for fresh misery.
Wretchedness makes me weep, grief makes me frown;

Will this never come to an end?

Is it my fate to be wretched all my life?
Who else knows grief like mine?
For my sorrow, like flowing water, never ceases.
At three I lost my mother, at seven was torn from my father;
Then the life of the husband I married was cut short;
So my mother-in-law and I are left as widows,
With no one to care for us or see to our needs.
Did I burn too little incense in my last life
That my marriage was unlucky?
We should all do good betimes;
So I mourn for my husband and serve my mother-in-law,
Obedient to all her bidding.

My mother-in-law has been gone a long time to collect that debt. What can be keeping her?

(*Enter Mistress Cai with Old Zhang and Donkey.*)

MRS. CAI: Wait here at the door while I go in.

DONKEY: All right, mother. Go in and tell her her husband is at the door.

(*Mistress Cai sees Dou E.*)

DOU E: So you're back, mother. Have you had a meal?

MRS. CAI (*crying*): Ah, Poor child! How am I going to break this to you?

【一半儿】我见他泪漫漫不住点儿流，情脉脉常怀郁闷忧。我这里连忙迎接慌问候，他那里要说缘由。（卜）着我怎生说！（旦）则见他一半儿徘徊一半儿羞。

婆婆，为什么烦恼啼哭那？（卜）我问赛卢医讨银子去，他赚我到郊外勒死我。亏了这张老并他儿子张驴爷儿两个救了我性命。我就招张老做丈夫，因这等烦恼。（旦）婆婆，不中。你再寻思咱，家里又不欠少钱财使用，况你又年纪高大，怎生又招丈夫哪？（卜）孩儿也，是我出于无奈也。（旦）婆婆，你听我说波。（唱）

【后庭花】遇时辰我替你忧，拜家堂我替你愁。梳着个霜雪般白鬏髻，怎戴那销金锦盖头？怪不的可正是“女大不中留”，你如今六旬左右，咱人到中年也万事休。旧恩爱一笔勾，新夫妻两意投，枉着别人笑破口，着别人笑破口。

【青哥儿】你比那搧坟的生受，又不是笄条年幼。刬的你巧画蛾眉成配偶，想当初你夫主遗留。替你耽忧，四时羹粥，又结绸缪。指望你鳏寡孤独，无捱

DOU E:

I see her in floods of tears,
Hiding some grief in her heart;
Greeting her quickly, I beg her to tell me the reason.

MRS. CAI: How can I say this?

DOU E:

She's shilly-shallying and looks ashamed.

What has upset you, mother? Why are you crying?

MRS. CAI: When I asked Doctor Lu for the silver, he lured me outside the town, then tried to strangle me; but an old man called Zhang and his son Donkey saved my life. Now Old Zhang is going to marry me: that's why I'm upset.

DOU E: That would never do, mother! Please think again! We're not short of money. Besides, you are growing old — how can you take another husband?

MRS. CAI: Child, I couldn't do anything else!

DOU E: Mother, listen to me!

What will become of you
If you choose a day and solemnize a wedding?
Now your hair is as white as snow,
How can you wear the bright silk veil of a bride?
No wonder they say it is hard to keep women at home,
If at sixty, when all thought of love should be over,
You've forgotten your former husband,
And taken a fancy to another man!
This will make others split their sides with laughter!
Yes, split their sides with laughter!
Like the widow who fanned her husband's tomb,
You're no tender bamboo shoot, no tender shoot.
How can you paint your eyebrows and remarry?
Your husband left you his property,
Made provision for the future,
For daily food and a good livelihood,

无靠，母子每到白头。公公，你为他干生受！

（卜）孩儿也，事到今日，你也招了女婿罢。今日就都过了门者。（旦）婆婆，你要招，你自招！我并然不要女婿。（卜）实选定今日，敢都过门来也。（净）我们今日招过门去也。帽儿帽儿光光，今日做个新郎；帽儿帽儿窄窄，今日做个娇客。好女婿，好女婿！不枉了，不枉了！（旦）兀那厮，靠后！（唱）

【赚煞】我想这妇人每休信那男儿口，看你那天长地久！招的个村老子，领着个不律头。旧恩情一笔都勾，你可也自穷究。俺公公撞府冲州，阘闒的铜斗儿家缘百事有。兀的是俺公公置就，教张驴儿情受；这的是“前人田土后人收”。（下）

（孛老同卜云）老儿，咱家中吃酒去来。（下）（净）窦娥不肯，则这般罢了不成？好共歹与我做个老婆，和俺老子吃酒去来。（下）

So that you and your son could remain beholden to no one,
And live to a ripe old age.
Did he go to such trouble for nothing?

MRS. CAI: Since it has come to this, I think you'd better take a husband too, and today can be the wedding day.

DOU E: You take a husband if you must. I won't!

MRS. CAI: The date is fixed, and they are already here.

DONKEY: Now we shall marry into their family. Our hats are brushed as good as new, and have narrow brims like bridegrooms'! Good! Fine!

DOU E: Stand back, you fellows!

Women should not believe all men say;
Such a marriage could not last.
Where did she find this old yokel,
And this other ruffian here?
Have you no feeling left for the dead?
You must think this over again.
Your husband worked in different cities and counties
To amass a well-earned fortune, and lack nothing.
How can you let his estate go to Donkey Zhang?
He tilled the land, but others are reaping the harvest. (*Exit.*)

ZHANG (*to Mrs. Cai*): Let us go and drink, ma'am.

(*Exeunt.*)

DONKEY: Dou E refuses to have me, but I shan't let her get away: she will have to be my wife. Now I'll drink with my old man! (*Exit.*)

第二折

（赛卢医上）小子赛卢医的便是。自从赚蔡婆婆到郊外，欲待勒死，撞见两个人救了。今日开这药铺，看有什么人来。（净上）小人张驴儿的便是。有窦娥不肯随顺我。如今那婆子害病，我讨服毒药，与他吃了，药死那婆子。那妮子好歹随顺了我。这里是药铺。太医哥哥，我来讨些药儿。（卢）你讨什么药？（净）我讨服毒药。（卢）谁敢合毒药与你，这厮好大胆也！（净）你不与我这药？你真个不与是怎么？（卢）我不与你，你怎地我？（净做拖卢，云）好呀，好呀！你在城外将那婆子要勒死。好的是你来？你只说我不认的你哩？我拖你见官府去。（卢慌云）大哥，你放我。有药，有药！（做与药科）（净）既然有了药，我往家中去也。（下）（卢云）原来讨药的这人，就是救那婆婆的。我今日与了他这服毒药去了，只怕连累我。今开不成药铺，且往涿州卖药去也。（下）

ACT II

(*Enter Doctor Lu.*)

DOCTOR: I am Doctor Lu. I lured Mistress Cai outside the town and was just going to strangle her when two men rescued her. Today I am opening shop. I wonder who will turn up.

(*Enter Donkey.*)

DONKEY: I am Donkey Zhang. Dou E still refuses to marry me. Now the old woman is ill, I'm going to poison her; for once the old one is dead, the young one will have to be my wife. Ah, here is a drug shop. Doctor! I want a drug!

DOCTOR: What drug do you want?

DONKEY: I want some poison.

DOCTOR: Who dares sell you poison? How can you ask such a thing?

DONKEY: You won't let me have it then?

DOCTOR: I won't. What are you going to do about it?

DONKEY (*seizing him*): Fine! Fine! Aren't you the man who tried to murder Mistress Cai? Do you think I don't recognize you? I'll take you to court.

DOCTOR (*in panic*): Let me go, brother! I've got it! I've got it! (*Gives him the poison.*)

DONKEY: Now that I've got the poison, I'm going home. (*Exit.*)

DOCTOR: So that man who came to buy poison was one of the men who rescued the widow. Since I've given him poison, he may get me into further trouble later. I'd better close my shop and go to Zhuozhou to sell drugs.(*Exit.*)

(*Enter Mistress Cai, supported by Old Zhang and Donkey.*)

（李老同净扶卜儿上）老汉自从来到蔡婆婆家做接脚，谁想婆婆一向染病。多是自己不幸！婆婆，你若想什么吃呵，你便说波。（卜）我思量些羊肚儿汤吃。（孛老）张驴儿，你唤窦娥做些羊肚儿汤与婆婆吃。（净）窦娥，婆婆想羊肚儿汤吃，快安排将来。（旦上）妾身窦娥是也。有俺婆婆不快，想羊肚汤吃。我亲自安排了，与婆婆吃去。我想这妇人心好难保也呵。（唱）

【南吕一枝花】他则待一生鸳帐里眠，那里肯半夜空房里睡；他本是张郎妇，又做了李郎妻。有一等妇女每相随，并不说家克计，则打听些闲是非；说一会那丈夫打凤的机关，使了些不着调虚嚣的见识。

【梁州】哪一个似卓氏般当垆涤器？哪一个似孟光般举案齐眉？近时有等婆娘每，道着难晓，做出难知。旧恩忘却，新爱偏宜。坟头上土脉犹湿，架儿上又换新衣。哪里有走边廷哭倒长城？哪里有浣纱处甘投大水？哪里有上青山便化顽石？可悲，可耻！

ZHANG: I came to Mistress Cai's house hoping to be her second hushand. Who would have thought that the widow would fall ill? I am really too unlucky. If there's anything you fancy to eat, ma'am, just let me know.

MRS.CAI: I'd like some mutton tripe soup.

ZHANG: Son, go and tell Dou E to make some mutton tripe soup for her mother-in-law.

DONKEY: Dou E! Your mother-in-law wants some mutton tripe soup. Look sharp about it!

(*Enter Dou E.*)

DOU E: I am Dou E. My mother-in-law is unwell and wants some mutton tripe soup, so I've made her some. When you think of it, some women are too fickle!

She wants to lie with a husband all her life,
Unwilling to sleep alone;
First she married one, and now she has picked another.
Some women never speak of household matters,
But pick up all the gossip,
Describe their husbands' adventures,
And are always up to some low tricks themselves.
Is there one like Lady Zhuo,[1] *who stooped to serve in a tavern?*
Or like Meng Guang,[2] *who showed such respect to her husband?*
The women today are different:
You can neither tell their character from their speech,
Nor judge them by their actions.
They're all of them faithless, all run after new lovers;
And before their husbands' graves are dry
They set aside their mourning for new clothes.
Where is the woman whose tears for her husband
Caused the Great Wall to crumble?[3]
Where is she who left her washing
And drowned herself in the stream?[4]
Where is she who changed into stone
Through longing for her husband?[5]

妇人家只恁无人意：多淫奔，少志气。亏杀了前人在那里，便休说百步相随。

（旦）羊肚儿汤做成，不免送去。（净）等我拿去。（做接科，云）这里面少盐醋，你取去。（旦虚下）（净放药科）（旦上，云）这不是盐醋！（净）倾下些。（旦唱）

【隔尾】你说道“少盐欠醋无滋味，加料添椒才脆美”。但愿娘亲早痊济，饮羹汤一杯，胜甘露灌体。您三口儿团圆到大来喜。

（孛老）孩儿，汤有了不曾？（净）有了，你拿过去。（孛老将汤，云）婆婆，你吃些汤儿。（卜）有累你，你先吃口儿，我吃。（孛老）你吃。（卜）老儿，你先吃。（孛老吃科）（旦唱）

【贺新郎】一个道你爷先吃，一个道你娘吃。这言语我听也难听，我可是气也不气！新婚的姻眷偏欢喜，不想那旧日夫妻道理，常好是百从千随。这婆娘心如风刮絮，哪里肯身化做望夫石。旧恩情倒不

How shameful that women today are so unfaithful,
So few of them are chaste, so many wanton!
All, all are gone, those virtuous women of old;
For wives will not cleave to their husbands!

Now the soup is ready. I had better take it in.

DONKEY: Let me take it to her. (*He takes the bowl.*) This hasn't much flavour. Bring some salt and vinegar.

(*Dou E goes out. Donkey puts poison in the soup. Dou E comes back.*)

DOU E: Here are the salt and vinegar.

DONKEY: Put some in.

DOU E:

You say that it lacks salt and vinegar,
Adding these will improve the flavour.
I hope my mother will be better soon,
And the soup will serve as a cordial.
Then the three of you can live happily together.

ZHANG: Son, is the soup ready?

DONKEY: Here it is. Take it.

ZHANG (*taking the soup*): Have some soup, ma'am.

MRS. CAI: I am sorry to give you so much trouble. You have some first.

ZHANG: Won't you try it?

MRS. CAI: No, I want *you* to drink it first.

(*Old Zhang drinks the soup.*)

DOU E:

One says: "Won't you try it?"
The other says: "You have it!"
What a shameful way to talk!
How can I help being angry?
The new couple is in transports;
Forgetting her first husband,
She listens to this new man's lightest word.
Now her heart is like a willow seed in the breeze,
Not steadfast as a rock.

比新佳配，他则待百年为婚眷，哪里肯千里送寒衣。

（孛老）我吃下这汤去，自觉昏昏沉沉的。（卜）老儿，你吃下这汤去，怎生不好了也？（卜叫云）老儿也，你放精细着，你扎挣着些儿。（做啼哭）（旦唱）

【斗虾蟆】枉着你烦恼没理会，人生死是轮回。感着这般病疾，趁着这般时气，值着风寒暑湿，或是饥饱劳役，各人病症自知。人命关天关地，别人怎生替的？寿数非干今世。相守三朝五日，常好一家一计。又无羊酒段匹，又无花红财礼。把手为活过日，撒手如同休弃。不怕傍人笑耻，不是窦娥忤逆。劝不的即即世世、哭哭啼啼、烦天恼地。呸！不似你舍不的你那从小里指脚儿夫妻。（孛老死科）（卜云）怎生是好？死了也。（旦）我其实不关心，无半点恓惶泪。休心如醉，意似痴，魂飞，手慌脚乱，哭哭啼啼。

（净）好也啰！把我老子药死了！更待干罢！（卜）孩儿，你

Old love is nothing to new love:
She wants to live with this new man for ever,
Without a thought for the other man far away.

ZHANG: Why has this soup made me dizzy? (*He falls to the ground.*)

MRS. CAI: Why should you feel unwell after that soup? (*Panic-stricken.*) Take a grip on yourself, old man! Don't give up so easily! (*Wails.*)

DOU E:

It's no use grieving for him;
All mortal men must die when their time is up.
Some fall ill, some meet with accidents;
Some catch a chill, some are struck down by heat;
Some die of hunger, surfeit or over-work;
But every death has its cause,
Human life is ruled by fate,
And no man can control it,
For our span of life is predestined.
He has been here a few days only;
He is not of your family,
And he never sent you wedding gifts:
Sheep, wine, silk or money.
For a time you stayed together,
But now he is dead and gone!
I am not an unfilial daughter,
But I fear what the neighbours may say;
So stop your moaning and wailing:
He is not the man you married as a girl.

(*Old Zhang dies.*)

MRS. CAI: What shall we do? He's dead!

DOU E:

He's no relation — I have no tears for him.
There's no need to be so overcome with grief,
Or to cry so bitterly and lose your head!

DONKEY: Fine! You've poisoned my father! What are you going to do

随顺了他罢。(旦)婆婆，怎生说这般言语？(唱)

【隔尾】这厮般调着老母待等成合了你，自药死亲爷，今日唬吓谁？(卜)与他做了浑家罢。(旦)我一马难将两鞍鞴！想男儿在日，俺夫妻道理。你教我改嫁别人，我其实下不的。

(净)窦娥,怎生药杀了俺老子？你要官休？要私休？(旦)怎生是官休？怎生是私休？(净)你要官休呵，我拖你到官司，你招认药死俺老子的罪犯。你要私休呵，你与我做了老婆，我便饶了你。(旦)我心上无事，情愿和你见官去。(净拖旦下)

about it?

MRS. CAI: Child, you had better marry him now.

DOU E: How can you say such a thing, mother?

This fellow forced my mother-in-law to keep him;
Now he's poisoned his father,
But whom does he think he can frighten?

MRS. CAI: You'd better marry him, child.

DOU E:

A horse can't have two saddles;
I was your son's wife when he was alive,
Yet now you are urging me to marry again.
This is unthinkable!

DONKEY: Dou E, you murdered my old man. Do you want to settle this in private or settle it in public?

DOU E: What do you mean?

DONKEY: If you want it settled in public, I'll drag you to the court, and you'll have to confess to the murder of my father! If you want it settled in private, agree to be my wife. Then I'll let you off.

DOU E: I am innocent. I'll go with you to the prefect.

(*Donkey drags Dou E and Mistress Cai out.*)

第三折

（丑扮官人引祗候上）我做官人甚殷勤，告状来的要金银。若是上司来刷卷，在家推病不出门。下官楚州州官是也。今日升厅坐衙。张千，喝撺厢！（张千喝科）（净拖旦上，云）告状，告状！（张千云）过来。（做见科）（旦净同跪科）（丑亦跪科，云）请起。（张千）相公，他是告状的，怎生跪着他？（丑）你不知道，但来告状的，就是我衣食父母。（张千答应科）（丑云）那个是原告？那个是被害？从实说来。（净）小人是原告张驴儿的便是。告媳妇儿合毒药药死俺老子。望大人与孩儿做主。（丑）是那个下毒药？（旦）不干我事。（卜）也不是我。

ACT III

(*Enter the Prefect with an Attendant.*)

PREFECT:

I am a hard-working official;
I make money out of my lawsuits;
But when my superiors come to investigate,
I pretend to be ill and stay at home in bed.

I am prefect of Chuzhou. This morning I am holding court. Attendant, summon the court!

(*The Attendant gives a shout.*)

(*Enter Donkey, dragging in Dou E and Mistress Cai.*)

DONKEY: I want to lodge a charge.

ATTENDANT: Come over here.

(*Donkey and Dou E kneel to the Prefect, who kneels to them.*)

PREFECT (*kneeling*): Please rise.

ATTENDANT: Your Honour, this is a citizen who's come to ask for justice. Why should you kneel to him?

PREFECT: Why? Because such citizens are food and clothes to me!

(*The Attendant assents.*)

PREFECT: Which of you is the plaintiff, which the defendant? Out with the truth now!

DONKEY: I am the plaintiff. I accuse this young woman, Dou E, of poisoning my father with soup. Let justice be done, Your Honour!

PREFECT: Who poisoned the soup?

DOU E: Not I!

MRS. CAI: Not I!

（净）也不是我。（丑）都不是你，敢是我来？（旦唱）

【牧羊关】大人！你明如镜，清似水，照妾身肝胆虚实。那羹本五味俱全，除了此百事不知。他推去尝滋味，吃下去便昏迷。不是妾讼庭上胡支对，相公也！却教我平白地说甚的？

（丑）人是贱虫，不打不招承。张千，与我打着！（张千打旦科，三次科，喷水科）（旦唱）

【骂玉郎】这无情棍棒教我捱不的。婆婆也！须是你自做下，怨他谁？劝普天下前婚后嫁婆娘每，都看取我这般傍州例。

【感皇恩】呀！是谁人唱叫扬疾？不由我哭哭啼啼。我恰还魂，才苏醒，又昏迷。捱千般打拷，见鲜血淋漓。一杖下，一道血，一层皮！

【采茶歌】打的我魄散魂飞，命掩泉石。则我这腹中冤枉有谁知？我不曾药死公公当罪责，告你个相公明镜察虚实。

（丑）你招也不招？（旦）委的不是我下毒药。（丑）既然不

DONKEY: Not I!

PREFECT: If none of you did it, I wonder if I could have done it?

DOU E:

Your Honour is as discerning as a mirror,
And can see my innermost thoughts.
There was nothing wrong with the soup,
I know nothing about the poison;
He made a pretence of tasting it,
Then his father drank it and fell down dead.
It is not that I want to deny my guilt in court;
But I cannot confess to a crime I have not committed!

PREFECT: Low characters are like that: they'll only confess when put to torture. Attendant! Bring the bastinado to beat her.

(*The Attendant beats Dou E. Three times she faints and he has to sprinkle her with water to bring her round.*)

DOU E:

This terrible beating is more than I can bear.
You brought this on yourself, mother. Why complain?
May all women in the world who marry again
Be warned by me!
Why are they shouting so fiercely?
I groan with pain;
I come to myself, then faint away again.
A thousand strokes: I am streaming with blood!
At each blow from the bastinado
My blood spurts out and my skin is torn from my flesh;
My spirit takes flight in fear,
Approaching the nether regions.
Who knows the bitterness in my heart?
It was not I who poisoned the old man;
I beg Your Honour to find out the truth!

PREFECT: Will you confess now?

DOU E: I swear it was not I who put in the poison.

是你，与我打那婆子。（旦）住，住，住。休打我婆婆。我招了罢，是我药死公公。（丑）将枷来枷上，下在死囚牢里去，到来日押赴市曹典刑。（卜）窦娥孩儿，兀的不痛杀我也！都是我送了你命！（旦唱）

【尾声】我做了个衔冤负屈没头鬼，不走了你个好色荒淫漏面贼。想青天不可欺，想人心不可欺，冤枉事天地知。争到头，竞到底，到如今说甚的。冤我便药杀公公，与了招罪。婆婆，我怕把你来便打的，打的来恁的。若是我不死，如何救得你？（下）

（净）明日杀窦娥，我且随衙听候。（下）（卜云）明日市曹中杀窦娥。儿也，兀的不痛杀我也！（下）（丑云）到明日典刑窦娥，今日无事。将马来，后宅去吃酒。（下）

（外扮监斩官上）下官监斩官是也。今日处决犯人，把住巷口，休放往来人走。（丑发鼓三通，打锣三下科）（刽子磨刀科）（刽子磨旗科）（定头通锣鼓科）（正旦带枷上）（刽子云）行动些！把住巷口。（旦唱）

【正宫端正好】没来由犯王法，葫芦提遭刑宪。叫

PREFECT: In that case, beat the old woman.

DOU E (*hastily*): Stop, stop! Don't beat my mother-in-law! Rather than that, I'll say I poisoned the old man.

PREFECT: Fasten her in the cangue and throw her into the gaol for the condemned. Tomorrow she shall be taken to the market-place to be executed.

MRS. CAI (*weeping*): Dou E, my child! It's because of me you are losing your life. Oh, this will be the death of me!

DOU E:

When I am a headless ghost, unjustly killed,
Do you think I will spare that scoundrel?
Men cannot be deceived for ever,
And Heaven will see this injustice.
I struggled as hard as I could, but now I am helpless;
I was forced to confess that I poisoned the old man;
How could I let you be beaten, mother?
How could I save you except by dying myself?

(*She is led off.*)

DONKEY: If she's to be killed tomorrow, I'll hang around. (*Exit*)

MRS. CAI: Poor child! Tomorrow she will be killed in the market-place. This will be the death of me! (*Exit.*)

PREFECT: Tomorrow Dou E will be executed. Today's work is done. Bring me my horse; I am going home to drink.

(*Exeunt.*)

(*Enter the Officer in charge.*)

OFFICER: I am the officer in charge of executions. Today we are putting a criminal to death. We must stand guard at the end of the road, to see that no one comes through.

(*Enter the Attendants. They beat the drum and the gong three times; then the executioner enters, sharpens his sword and waves a flag. Dou E is led on in a cangue. The gong and drum are beaten.*)

EXECUTIONER: Get a move on! Let no one pass this way.

DOU E:

Though no fault of mine I am called a criminal,

声屈动地惊天！我将天地合埋怨：天也！你不与人为方便。

【滚绣球】有日月朝暮显，有山河今古监。天也！却不把清浊分辨，可知道错看了盗跖颜渊。有德的受贫穷更命短，造恶的享富贵又寿延。天也！做得个怕硬欺软！不想天地也顺水推船。地也！你不分好歹难为地。天也！我今日负屈衔冤哀告天，空教我独语独言。

（刽子）窦娥，行动些！误了时辰也。（旦唱）

【倘秀才】则被这枷扭的我左侧右偏，人拥的我前合后偃。窦娥向哥哥行有句言。（刽子）你有什么话说？（旦）前街里去中有怨，后街里去死无冤。非是我自专。

（刽子）你当刑，如今来赴法场，有甚亲眷？（旦唱）

【叨叨令】你道我当刑赴法场何亲眷？（刽子）你前街去是怎生？后街去是如何？（旦）前街里去告您看些颜面，我往后街里去呵不把哥哥怨。前街里去只恐怕俺婆

And condemned to be beheaded —
I cry out to Heaven and Earth of this injustice!
I reproach both Earth and Heaven
For they would not save me.
The sun and moon give light by day and by night,
Mountains and rivers watch over the world of men;
Yet Heaven cannot tell the innocent from the guilty;
And confuses the wicked with the good!
The good are poor, and die before their time;
The wicked are rich, and live to a great old age.
The gods are afraid of the mighty and bully the weak;
They let evil take its course.
Ah, Earth! you will not distinguish good from bad,
And, Heaven! you let me suffer this injustice!
Tears pour down my cheeks in vain!

EXECUTIONER: Get a move on! We are late.

DOU E:

The cangue round my neck makes me stagger this way and that,
And I'm jostled backward and forward by the crowd.
Will you do me a favour, brother?

EXECUTIONER: What do you want?

DOU E:

If you take me the front way, I shall bear you a grudge;
If you take me the back way, I shall die content.
Please do not think me wilful!

EXECUTIONER: Now that you're going to the execution ground, are there any relatives you want to see?

DOU E: I am going to die. What relatives do I need?

EXECUTIONER: Why did you ask me just now to take you the back way?

DOU E:

Please don't go by the front street, brother,
But take me by the back street.
The other way my mother-in-law might see me.

婆见。（刽子）你的性命也顾不的，怕他怎的？（旦）他见我披枷带锁赴法场餐刀去呵！枉将他气杀也么哥，枉将他气杀也么哥。告哥哥临危好与人行方便。

（卜上，云）天呵，兀的不是我媳妇儿？我儿也，不痛杀我也！（刽子）婆子，靠后！（旦）叫俺婆婆来，嘱付他几句话咱。（刽子）那婆子，近前来，你媳妇要嘱付你话里。（卜见，云）孩儿，痛杀我也！（旦）婆婆，都只为你身子不快，思量羊肚儿汤吃。我安排了，又道少盐醋。被张驴儿赚的我取盐醋去，他将毒药放在汤里。可着我拿过去与你吃，谁想你让与他老子吃。实指望药死你，要霸占我为妻，不想把他老子药死了。因报前仇，把我拖去官司。我怕连累婆婆，我屈招了，今日赴法场典刑。婆婆，瀽不了的浆水饭，瀽半碗儿与我吃。烧不了的纸钱，与窦娥烧一陌儿。则是看你死的孩儿面上。（唱）

【快活三】看窦娥葫芦提当罪愆，着窦娥身首不完全，想窦娥从前已往干家缘，婆婆！看窦娥少爷无娘面。

【鲍老儿】看窦娥伏侍婆婆这几年，看时节将碗凉浆奠。（卜）孩儿放心，兀的不痛杀也！（旦）你去那受刑法尸骸上列些纸钱，看你那化去孩儿面。啼啼哭

EXECUTIONER: You can't escape death, so why worry if she sees you?

DOU E: If my mother-in-law were to see me in chains being led to the execution ground —

She would burst with indignation!
She would burst with indignation!
Please grant me this comfort, brother, before I die!

(*Enter Mistress Cai.*)

MRS. CAI: Ah, Heaven! Isn't that my daughter-in-law? This will be the death of me!

EXECUTIONER: Stand back, old woman!

DOU E: Let her come closer so that I can say a few words to her.

EXECUTIONER: Hey, old woman! Come here. Your daughter-in-law wants to speak to you.

MRS. CAI: Poor child! This will be the death of me!

DOU E: Mother, when you were unwell and asked for mutton tripe soup, I prepared some for you. Donkey Zhang made me fetch more salt and vinegar so that he could poison the soup, and then told me to give it to you. He didn't know his old man would drink it. Donkey Zhang poisoned the soup to kill you, so that he could force me to be his wife. He never thought his father would die instead. To take revenge, he dragged me to court. Because I didn't want you to suffer, I had to confess to murder, and now I am going to be killed. In future, mother, if you have gruel to spare, give me half a bowl; and if you have paper money to spare, burn some for me, for the sake of your dead son!

Take pity on one who is dying an unjust death;
Take pity on one whose head will be struck from her body;
Take pity on one who has worked with you in your home;
Take pity on one who has neither mother nor father;
Take pity on one who has served you all these years;
And at festivals offer my spirit a bowl of cold gruel.

MRS. CAI (*weeping*): Don't worry. Ah, this will be the death of me!

DON E:

Burn some paper coins to my headless corpse,

哭，烦烦恼恼，怨气冲天。我不分说，不明不暗负屈衔冤。

（刽子）兀那婆子靠后，时辰到了也。（旦跪下科）（刽子开枷科）（旦）窦娥告监斩官，要一领净席。我有三件事，肯依窦娥，便死无怨。要丈二白练挂在旗枪上，若刀过处头落，一腔热血休落在地下，都飞在白练上者。若委实冤枉，如今是三伏天道，下尺瑞雪，遮了窦娥尸首。着这楚州亢旱三年。（刽子）打嘴，那得此话！（刽子磨旗科）（旦唱）

【尾声】当日个哑妇含药反受殃，耕牛为主遭鞭。（刽子）天色阴了。呀！下雪了。（刽子搧雪天发愿科）（磨旗刽子遮住科）（旦）霜降始知说邹衍，雪飞方表窦娥冤。

（行刃刽子开刀割头）（副净擡尸）（刽子云）好妙手也！咱吃酒去来。（众和下。抬尸下）

For the sake of your dead son.
We wail and complain to Heaven:
There is no justice! Dou E is wrongly slain!

EXECUTIONER: Now then, old woman, stand back! The time has come.

(*Dou E kneels, and the Executioner removes the cangue from her neck.*)

DOU E: I want to say three things, officer. If you will let me, I shall die content. I want a clean mat and a white silk streamer twelve feet long to hang on the flag-pole. When the sword strikes off my head, not a drop of my warm blood will stain the ground. It will all fly up instead to the white silk streamer. This is the hottest time of summer, sir. If injustice has indeed been done, three feet of snow will cover my dead body. Then this district will suffer from drought for three whole years.

EXECUTIONER: Be quiet! What a thing to say!

(*The Executioner waves his flag.*)

DOU E:

A dumb woman was blamed for poisoning herself,
A buffalo is whipped while it toils for its master.

EXECUTIONER: Why is it suddenly so overcast? It is snowing! (*He prays to Heaven.*)

DOU E:

Once Zou Yan caused frost to appear:[6]
Now snow will show the injustice done to me!

(*The Executioner beheads her, and the Attendant sees to her body.*)

EXECUTIONER: A fine stroke! Now let us go and have a drink.

(*The Attendants assent, and carry the body off.*)

第四折

（外上）老夫窦天章是也。自离了我那端云孩儿，可早十三年光景。老夫自到京师，一举及第，官拜参知政事。老夫廉能清正，节操坚刚，谢圣恩可怜，加老夫两淮提刑肃政廉访使之职。随处审囚刷卷，敕赐势剑金牌，体察滥官污吏，老夫先斩后奏。老夫一喜一悲：喜呵，老夫身居台省，职掌刑名；悲呵，有端云孩儿，七岁上与了蔡婆婆为儿媳妇。老夫自得官之后，使人往楚州山阳郡问蔡婆婆家。他邻里街坊道："自当年蔡婆婆不知搬在那里去了，至今音信皆无。"老夫为端云孩儿，啼哭的眼也昏花，忧愁的须发斑白。今日来到这淮南扬州也，不知这楚州为何三年不下雨？老夫今在这扬州府后厅安歇。张千，说与那扬州大小官吏：今日免参，明日早见。（张千）一应大小属官并吏典，今日免参，明日早见。（天章）张千，说与那六房吏典，但有合刷照文卷，都将来。老夫灯下看几宗。（张千送文卷科）（天章）张千，你与我掌上灯。你辛苦了，去歇息罢。我唤你便来，不唤你休来。（张

ACT IV

(*Enter Dou Tianzhang.*)

DOU: I am Dou Tianzhang. It is thirteen years since I left my child Duanyun. I went to the capital, passed the examination and was made a counsellor. And because I am able, just and upright, the emperor appointed me Inspector of the Huai River Area. I have travelled from place to place investigating cases, and I have the sword of authority and golden tally so that I can punish corrupt officials without first reporting to the throne. My heart is torn between grief and happiness. I am glad because I am a high official responsible for seeing that justice is done. I am sad, though, because when Duanyun was seven I gave her to Mistress Cai; and after I became an official and sent for news of the widow to Chuzhou, the neighbours said she had moved away — to what place they did not know — and there has been no word since. I have wept for my child till my eyes are dim and my hair is white. Now I have come south of the Huai River, and am wondering why this district has had no rain for three years. I shall rest in the district office, boy. Tell the local officers they need not call today. I shall see them early tomorrow.

SERVANT (*calling out*): The officers and secretaries are not to call on His Excellency today. He will see them early tomorrow.

DOU: Tell the secretaries of the different departments to send all their cases here for my inspection. I shall study some under the lamp.

(*The Servant brings him the files.*)

DOU: Light the lamp for me. You have been working hard, and you may rest now. But come when I call you.

(*The Servant lights the lamp and leaves.*)

千点灯下)(天章)我将这文卷先看几宗咱。“一起犯人窦娥，将毒药致死公公。”好是奇怪也，我才看头一宗文卷，就与老夫同姓。这药死公公的罪名，犯在十恶。俺同姓之人也有不畏法度的。这是问结了的文书，不看他罢。我将这文卷压在底下，别看一宗咱。且住！不觉的一阵昏沉上来。老夫年纪高大，鞍马劳困，我搭伏定书案，歇息些儿咱。(做睡科)(旦魂上，唱)

【双调新水令】我每日哭啼啼守定望乡台，急煎煎把仇人等待。慢腾腾昏雾里走，足律律旋风儿来。则被这雾锁云埋，撺掇的鬼魂快。

(旦望空，云)门神户尉不放我进去。我是廉访使窦天章女孩儿。因我屈死，父不知，特来托一梦与他咱。(魂见，哭科)(天章亦哭科，云)端云孩儿，你在那里来？(旦虚下)(天章醒科，云)好是奇怪也！老夫恰合眼，梦见端云孩儿，恰便似在我跟前一般。我再看这文卷咱。(魂过，做弄灯科)(天章)好奇怪也！我正要看这文卷，怎生这灯忽明忽灭的。张千也睡着了，我自己剔灯咱。(往东边剔灯科)(魂翻文卷科)(天章)我剔的这灯明了也，再看几宗文卷。“一起犯人窦娥，药死公公。”好是奇怪也！这一宗文卷，我为头看过，压在文卷底下，怎生又在这上头？几时问结了的，还压在底下。我别看一宗文卷。(魂弄灯科)(天章)好是奇怪也！怎生这灯又是半明半暗的？我再自己剔这灯咱。(做

DOU: I shall go through a few cases. Here is one concering Dou E, who poisoned her father-in-law. Curious that the first culprit's surname should be the same as mine! To murder one's father-in-law is one of the unpardonable crimes; so it seems there are lawless elements among my clan. Since this case has been dealt with, I need not read it. I'll put it at the bottom of the pile and look at another. Wait, I suddenly feel drowsy. I suppose I am growing old, and am tired after travelling. I will take a short nap on the desk. (*He sleeps.*)

(*Enter Dou E's ghost.*)

DOU E:

Day after day I weep in the underworld,
Waiting impatiently for my revenge.
I pace on slowly in darkness,
Then am borne along by the whirlwind;
Enveloped by mist I come swiftly in ghostly form.

(*She looks about her.*) Now the door-gods will not let me pass. I am the daughter of Inspector Dou. Though I died unjustly, my father does not know it; so I have come to visit him in his dreams. (*She enters the room and weeps.*)

DOU (*shedding tears*): Duanyun, my child! Where have you been?

(*Dou E's spirit leaves, and Dou wakes up.*)

How odd! I fell asleep and dreamed that I saw my daughter coming towards me; but where is she now? Let me go on with these cases.

(*Dou E's spirit enters and makes the lamp burn low.*)

Strange! I was just going to read a case when the light flickered and dimmed. My servant is asleep. I must trim the wick myself. (*As he trims the lamp, Dou E's spirit re-arranges the file.*) Now the light is brighter, I can read again. "This concerns the criminal Dou E, who poisoned her father-in-law." Strange! I read this case first, and put it under the others. How has it come to the top? Since this case has already been dealt with, let me put it at the bottom again and study a different one. (*Once more Dou E's spirit makes the lamp burn low*) Strange! Why is the light flickering again? I must trim it once more.

往东边剔灯科)(魂翻文书科)(天章)我剔的这灯明了，我另拿一宗文卷看咱。"一起犯人窦娥，药死公公。"呸！好是奇怪也！我才将这文书分明压在底下，刚剔了这灯，怎生又翻在面上？莫不是扬州府后厅里有鬼么？更无鬼呵，这桩事必有冤枉。将这文卷再压在底下，我别拿一宗看咱。(魂弄灯科)(天章)实是奇怪也，怎生这灯又不明了？又这等忽明忽暗的？敢有鬼弄这灯？我再剔一剔去。(做往东边剔灯科)(慌回科)(魂翻文卷科)(做撞见科)(天章仗剑科,云)呸！呸！呸！我说有鬼！兀那鬼魂，老夫是朝廷钦差带牌走马肃政廉访使。你向前来，一剑挥之两段。张千孩儿，亏你也睡的着！都起来！有鬼了,有鬼了！兀的不吓杀老夫也！(魂旦唱)

【雁儿落】我见他疑心儿转转猜，我这里哭声儿添惊怪。哎，你个窦天章老父亲，受窦娥孩儿深深拜。

(天章)兀那鬼魂，你道窦天章是你父亲，受你孩儿窦娥拜。你敢错认了也？我的女儿叫道做端云，七岁上与了蔡婆婆为儿媳妇。你是窦娥，名字差了，怎生是我女儿？(魂旦)父亲，你将我与了蔡婆婆家，改名做窦娥。(天章)你便是端云孩儿？我不问你别的，这药死你公公，受了典刑，是你不是？(魂旦)是你孩儿来。(天

(*As Dou trims the light, Dou E's spirit once more turns over the file.*) Now the lamp is brighter, I can read another case. "This concerns the criminal Dou E, who poisoned her father-in-law." How extraordinary! I definitely put this at the bottom of the pile just before I trimmed the lamp. How has it come to the top again? Can there be ghosts in this office? Well, ghost or no ghost, an injustice must have been done. Let me put this underneath and read another. (*Dou E's spirit makes the lamp burn low again.*) Strange! The lamp is flickering again. Can there actually be a ghost here tampering with it? I'll trim it once more. (*As he trims the wick, Dou E's spirit comes up to him and he sees her. He strikes his sword on the desk.*) Ah, there's the ghost! I warn you, I am the emperor's inspector of justice. If you come near, I'll cut you in two. Hey, boy! How can you sleep so soundly? Get up at once! Ghosts! Ghosts! This is terrifying!

DOU E:

Fear is making him lose his head;
The sound of my weeping has frightend him more than ever.
Here, Dou Tianzhang, my old father,
Will you let your daughter Dou E bow to you?

DOU: You say I am your father, ghost, and offer to bow to me as my daughter. Aren't you mistaken? My daughter's name is Duanyun. When she was seven she was given to Mistress Cai as a child-bride. You call yourself by a different name, Dou E. How can you be my child?

DOU E: After you gave me to Mistresss Cai, father, she changed my name to Dou E.

DOU: So you say you are my child Duanyun. Let me ask you this: Are you the woman accused of murdering her father-in-law and executed?

DOU E: I am.

DOU: Hush, girl! I've wept for you till my eyes grew dim, and worried for you till my hair turned white. How did you come to be condemned for this most heinous of crimes? I am a high official now, whose duty it is to see that justice is done. I have come here to investigate cases and discover corrupt officials. You are my child, but you are guilty of the worst

章）禁声！你这个小贱人！老夫为你啼哭的眼也花了，忧愁的头也白了。你刬地犯下十恶大罪，受了典刑。我今日官居台省，职掌刑名，天下审囚刷卷，体察滥官污吏。你是我亲生之女，先犯下十恶大罪；老夫将你治不的，怎治他人？我将你嫁与他家呵，要你三从四德。三从者，在家从父，出嫁从夫，夫死从子。此乃为之三从！四德者，事翁姑，敬夫主，和妯娌，睦街坊。此乃为之四德！今乃三从四德全无，刬地犯了十恶大罪。常言道，事要前思，免劳后悔。我窦家三辈无犯法之男，五世无再婚之女。既将你出嫁从夫，便习学廉耻仁义。全不思九烈三贞，倒犯了十恶大罪。你辱没祖上家门，又把我清名连累。快与我细说真情，不要你虚言支对。莫说的有半厘差错，牒发你城隍祠内。我着你永世不得人身，我把你罚在阴山永做饿鬼！（魂旦）父亲停嗔息怒，暂罢虎狼之威，听你女儿慢慢的说一遍咱。我三岁上亡了母亲，七岁上离了父亲，你将我嫁与蔡婆婆家为儿媳妇，改名窦娥。至十七岁与夫配合，不幸当年儿夫亡化，我与婆婆守寡。楚州城里有个赛卢医，他本利少俺婆婆二十两白银。俺婆婆去取讨银子，被他将俺婆婆赚到城外，要将婆婆勒死。不想撞见张驴儿父子两个，救了俺婆婆性命。那老张问道："婆婆，你家里有什么人？"婆婆道："俺家无人，止有个守寡的媳妇唤做窦娥。"老张道："你家中既无人，我招与你做夫主，你意下如何？"俺婆婆坚执不肯。那老张父子两个道："你若不从，我还勒死你！"婆婆惧怕，不得已许了，实是唬吓成亲。就将他爷儿两个领到家中，过其日月。有张驴儿数次调戏你女孩儿，我坚意不肯。那一日俺婆婆身子不快，想羊肚儿

crime of all. If I could not control you, how can I control others? When I married you to the widow's son, I expected you to observe the Three Duties and Four Virtues. The Three Duties are obedience to your father before marriage, obedience to your husband after marriage, and obedience to your son after your husband's death. The Four Virtues are to serve your parents-in-law, to show respect to your husband, to remain on good terms with your sisters-in-law, and to live in peace with your neighbours. But regardless of your duties, you have committed the gravest crime of all! The proverb says: Look before you leap, or you may be sorry too late. For three generations no son of our clan has broken the law; for five generations no daughter has married again. As a married woman, you should have studied propriety and morality; but instead you perpetrated the most terrible crime. You have disgraced our ancestors and injured my good name. Tell me the whole truth at once, and nothing but the truth! If you utter one false word, I shall send you to the tutelary god; then your spirit will never re-enter human form, but remain a hungry ghost for ever in the shades.

DOU E: Don't be so angry, father. Don't threaten me like an angry wolf or tiger! Let me explain this to you. At three, I lost my mother; at seven, I was parted from my father, when you sent me to Mistress Cai as her future daughter-in-law, and my name was changed to Dou E. At seventeen, I married; but unhappily two years later my husband died, and I stayed as a widow with my mother-in-law. In Chuzhou there lived a certain Doctor Lu, who owed my mother-in-law twenty taels of silver. One day when she went to ask him for the money, he lured her outside the town and tried to strangle her; but Donkey Zhang and his father came by and saved her life. Old Zhang asked: "Whom do you have in your family, ma'am?" My mother-in-law said: "No one but a widowed daughter-in-law." Old Zhang said: "In that case, I will marry you. What do you say?" When my mother-in-law refused, the two men said: "If you don't agree, we shall strangle you again!" So she was frightened into marrying him. Donkey tried to seduce me several times, but I always resisted him. One day my mother-in-law was unwell and wanted some mutton tripe

汤吃。你女儿安排了。张驴儿言道："将来我尝一尝。"他道："好便好，只少些盐醋。"他赚的我去取盐醋，他就下了毒药，他又教我将去。俺婆婆让老张先吃，随即吃了，七窍流血，药死了老张。张驴儿便道："窦娥药死了俺老子！你要官休？要私休？"我便道："怎生是官休？怎生是私休？"他道："要官休，告到官司，你与俺老子偿命。若私休，你便与我做老婆。"你孩儿便道："俺家三辈儿无犯法之男，五世无再婚之女。好马不鞴双鞍，烈女不更二夫。我至死不与你做媳妇。我心上无事，情愿和你见官去来。"不由分说，将你孩儿拖到官中。你儿怎当他三拷六问，吊拷绷扒？那时便打死也不认。他见你孩儿不认，便要拷打俺婆婆。我怕婆婆受刑，我就屈认了。因此押赴法场，将我典刑。我到的法场，你孩儿对天发三桩誓愿：要丈二白练挂在旗枪上，若刀过去，一腔热血休落在地下，都飞在白练上；果系冤枉，如今是三伏天道，下三尺瑞雪遮了你女儿身尸；果是冤枉了你女儿，这楚州大旱三年。果然血飞上白练，六月下雪，三年不雨，寸草不生。都是为你女孩儿来。不告官司只告天，心中怨气口难言。受刑为母当行孝，尽命因夫可当贤。三尺瑞雪埋素体，一腔鲜血染白练。霜降

soup. When I prepared it, Donkey told me to let him taste it. "It's good," he said. "But there's not enough salt and vinegar." When I went to fetch more, he secretly poisoned the soup and told me to take it to her. But my mother-in-law gave it to Old Zhang. Then blood spurted from the old man's mouth, nose, ears and eyes, and he died. At that Donkey said, "Dou E, you poisoned my father. Do you want to settle this in public or in private?" "What do you mean?" I asked. "If you want it settled in public," he said, "I shall take the case to court, and you will pay for my father's death with your life. If you want it settled in private, then be my wife." "A good horse won't have two saddles," I told him. "A good woman won't remarry. For three generations no son of our clan has broken the law; for five generations no daughter has married again. I'd rather die than be your wife. I am innocent. I'll go to court with you." Then he dragged me before the prefect. I was tried again and again, stripped and tortured; but I would rather have died than make a false confession. When the prefect saw that I wouldn't confess, he threatened to have my mother-in-law tortured; and because she was too old to stand the torture, I made a false confession. Then they took me to the execution ground to kill me. I made three vows before my death. First, I asked for a twelve-foot white silk streamer and swore that, if I was innocent, when the sword struck off my head no drop of my blood would stain the ground — it would all fly up to the streamer. Next I vowed that, though it was midsummer, Heaven would send down three feet of snow to cover my body. Last, I vowed that this district would suffer three years' drought. All these vows have come true, because of the crime against me.

I complained not to any official but to Heaven,
For I could not express the injustice that was done me;
And to save my mother from torture
I confessed to a crime of which I was innocent,
And remained true to my dead husband
Three feet of snow fell on my corpse;
My hot blood gushed to the white silk streamer;

始知邹衍屈，雪飞方表窦娥冤。（唱）

【雁儿落】你孩儿是做来不曾做来？则我这冤枉无边大。我不肯顺他人，着我赴法场。不辱我祖上，把我残生坏。

【得胜令】我每日守定望乡台，一灵儿怨哀哀。父亲，你势剑吹毛快，今日个亲蒙圣主差，审问的明白。那厮乱人伦，当合败，万剐了那乔才。父亲，你将我招状儿改将过来。

（天章哭云）哎！我那屈死的儿也，则被你痛杀我也！我不问你别的，则这楚州三年不雨，可是为什么来？（魂旦）为你孩儿来。（天章）原来是为你来。不因我女儿这一件事，感起一桩故事。昔日汉朝有一孝妇守寡，其姑自缢身死。其姑女告孝妇杀姑，东阿太守将孝妇杀了。为一妇衔冤，致令得三年不雨。后于公治狱，孝妇抱卷哭于厅前。于公改正文卷，杀牛祭孝妇之墓，天乃大雨应时而降。昔汉时东海太守屈杀了贤行妇女，都则因此一妇人，致令的三年不雨，正和这事相同。到来朝我与伊做主。白头亲苦痛哀哉，屈杀了青春幼女孩儿也！天色明了，你回去。到来日我将你的文卷改正明白。（魂旦唱）

【尾声】你将那滥官污吏都杀坏，敕赐金牌势剑吹毛快。与一人分忧，万民除害。（做回身科，云）我可

Zou Yan called down frost,
And snow showed the injustice done me.
Your child committed no crime,
But suffered a great wrong:
For resisting seduction I was executed!
I would not disgrace my clan, so I lost my life!
Day after day in the shades
my spirit mourns alone.
You are sent by the emperor with authority;
Consider this case and this man's wickedness;
Cut him in pieces and avenge my wrong!

DOU (*weeping*): Ah, my wrongly slain daughter, how this wrings my heart! Let me ask you this: Is it because of you that this district has suffered for three years from drought?

DOU E: It is.

DOU: So! This reminds me of a story. In the Han Dynasty there was a virtuous widow whose mother-in-law hanged herself, and whose sister-in-law accused her of murdering the old woman. The governor of Donge had her executed, but because of her unjust death there was no rain in that district for three years. When Lord Yu came to investigate, he saw the dead woman's ghost carrying a plea and weeping before the hall; and after he changed the verdict, killed a bull and sacrificed at her grave there was a great downpour of rain. This case is rather similar to that. Tomorrow I shall right this wrong for you.

I bow my white head in sorrow
Over the innocent girl who was wrongly slain.
Now dawn is breaking, you had better leave me;
Tomorrow I shall set right this miscarriage of justice.

DOU E (*bowing*):

With sharp sword of authority and tally of gold,
You will kill all evil and corrupt officials,
To serve your sovereign and relieve the people!

(*She turns back.*) There's one thing I nearly forgot, father. My

忘了，父亲，俺婆婆年纪高大，无人侍养。（天章）好孝顺孩儿也！（魂旦）嘱付你个爷爷，迁葬了奶奶。恩养俺婆婆，可怜见他年纪高大。后将文卷舒开，将俺屈死的招伏罪名儿改。（下）

（天章）天色明了。你将那扬州府官吏——那几个是问窦娥的，都与我拿将上来！（张千）理会的。（押官吏、卜、净上。见跪科）（天章）蔡婆婆，你认的我么？（卜）不认的大人。（天章）则我便是窦天章。一行人听我下断：张驴儿谋杀亲父，欺骗良人，市曹中明正典刑；扬州官吏刑名违错，杖一百，永不叙用；赛卢医修合毒药，云阳市量决一刀；蔡婆婆我家养老；窦娥罪改正明白。为因如此，将张驴儿斩首街前，将官吏罢职除官。做一个水陆大醮，超度我女儿生天。

题目 后嫁婆婆忒心偏
守志烈女意自坚

正名 汤风冒雪没头鬼
感天动地窦娥冤

mother-in-law is old now, and has no one to look after her.

DOU: This is dutiful, my child.

DOU E:

I ask my father to care for my mother-in-law,
For she is growing old. My father now
Will reopen my case and change the unjust verdict. (*Exit.*)

DOU: Dawn is breaking. Call the local officers, and all those concerned in the case of Dou E.

SERVANT: Yes, Your Excellency.

(*The prefect, Mistress Cai, Donkey Zhang and Doctor Lu are sent in. They kneel before Dou.*)

DOU: Mistress Cai, do you recognize me?

MRS. CAI: No, Your Excellency.

DOU: I am Dou Tianzhang. Listen, all of you, to the verdict! Donkey Zhang murdered his father and blackmailed good citizens. He shall be executed in public. Let him be taken to the market-place to be killed. The prefect passed a wrong sentence. He shall be given one hundred strokes and have his name struck off the official list. Doctor Lu is guilty of selling poison. Let him be beheaded in the market-place. Mistress Cai shall be lodged in my house. The wrong sentence passed on Dou E shall be rescinded.

Let the Donkey be killed in public,
The prefect dismissed from office;
Then let us offer a great sacrifice
So that my daughter's spirit may go to heaven.

(*THE END*)

Snow in Midsummer

包待制智斩鲁斋郎

The Wife-Snatcher

第一折

（冲末扮鲁斋郎引张千上）花花太岁为第一，浪子丧门世无双。街市小民闻吾怕，则我是权豪势要鲁斋郎。小官鲁斋郎是也。方今圣人在位，四海晏然，八方无事。小官随朝数载，谢圣恩可怜，迁除授职。小官嫌官小不做，嫌马瘦不骑。但行处引的是花腿闲汉，弹弓粘竿，鲅儿小鹞。每日价飞鹰走犬，街市闲行。但见人家好的玩画，怎么他倒有，我倒无？我则借三日玩看了，第四日便还他。人家有那骏马雕鞍，我使人牵来则骑三日，第四日便还他，不坏了他的。我是个本分的人！自离了汴梁，来到许州，因街上骑着马闲行，我见个银匠铺里一个好女子。我正要看他，那马走的快，不曾得仔细看。张千，你曾听来么？（张千）比及大人有这个心，小人打听在肚里了。（鲁）你知道他是什么人家？（张）他是个银匠，姓李，排行第四。他的个浑家生的风流，长的可喜。（鲁）我如今要他，怎么能够？

ACT I

(*Enter Lu Zhailang with his servant Zhang Qian.*)

LU:

Chief of the rakes,
Unrivalled among rogues,
Feared by the townsflok —
A powerful bully!

I am Lu Zhailang. Now the empire is at peace under our sovereign's sagacious rule. After I had served at court for several years His Majesty graciously transferred me here. I will not take a small official post, just as I scorn to ride a hack. I associate with idlers and rowdies, swindlers and thieves, passing my time every day in the street or with my hawk and hounds. When others have rarities or pictures which I have not, I borrow them for three days and return them on the fourth. When they have good horses or fine saddles, I use them for three days and give them back on the fourth, none the worse for wear, for I am a decent fellow. After coming to Xuzhou from the capital, I was ambling down the street one day when I noticed a fine woman in a silversmith's shop. I wanted to take a good look, but my horse was going too fast for me to have time. Have you found out who she is, Zhang Qian?

ZHANG: Knowing you were interested, sir, I made inquiries.

LU: What is her family?

ZHANG: She is the wife of a silversmith named Li Si, a fine figure of a woman — pretty as a picture.

LU: How can I get hold of her?

（张）大人要他也不难。我如今将着一把银壶瓶去他家整理，多与他些钱钞，与他几盅酒吃，着他浑家也吃几盅，扶上马就走。推整壶瓶生巧计，拐他妻子走如飞。（鲁）此计大妙！则今日收拾鞍马，跟着我银匠铺里整理壶瓶走一遭去。（下）

（外扮李四同旦儿、俫儿上）万事分已定，浮生空自忙。小可许州人氏，姓李，排行第四，人口顺唤做银匠李四。嫡亲的四口儿：浑家张氏，一双儿女，厮儿叫做喜童，女儿叫做娇儿。全凭打银过其日月。今日早间开了这铺儿，看有什么人来。（鲁斋郎引张千上）只因李四妻娇媚，追逐张千到此间。小官鲁斋郎，因这壶瓶跌漏，去那银匠铺里整理一整理。来到门首也。左右，接了马者！将交床来。（张）理会的。（坐下科）（鲁）张千，你与我叫那银匠出来。（张）理会的。（做唤科）兀那银匠，鲁斋郎大人在门首叫你哩！（李四慌科，出门跪科）大人唤小人有何事？（鲁）兀那……你是银匠么？（李）小人是银匠。（鲁）兀那李四，你休惊休怕，你是无罪的人。你起来。（李）大人唤我做什么？

ZHANG: It shouldn't be difficult, sir. We'll take a silver kettle to his shop to be mended, give him a good sum of money and some cups of wine, and get his wife to drink too. Then grab her to horse, and we're off!

With the silver kettle as our excuse,
We'll seize the woman and make off!

LU: A magnificent idea! Saddle my horse today, and come with me to the silversmith to have that kettle mended.

(*Exeunt.*)

(*Enter Li Si with his wife and children.*)

LI:

All is settled by fate;
It is useless to toil and moil.

I am a native of Xuzhou named Li Si. I have a wife whose maiden name is Zhang, who has borne me two children. My son is called Happy Boy, and my daughter Sweet Maid. I make a living as a silversmith. I am just opening shop for the day. Is anyone coming?

(*Enter Lu with Zhang Qian.*)

LU:

Because Li Si's wife is a charmer,
I have followed Zhang Qian here.

I am Lu Zailang. This kettle had a fall and started leaking, so I am taking it to the silversmith to be mended. Here we are at the door. Take my horse, boy, and fetch me a seat.

ZHANG: Very good, sir.

LU (*sitting down*): Call the silversmith out, Zhang Qian.

ZHANG: Yes, sir.(*Calling.*) Here, silversmith! His Honour Lu Zhailang is at the door calling you.

(*Li Si comes out and kneels down fearfully.*)

LI: What are your commands, sir?

LU: Are you the silversmith?

LI: Yes, sir.

LU: Don't be afraid, Li Si. I have nothing against you. Get up.

LI: What can I do for Your Honour?

（鲁）我有把银壶瓶跌漏了，你与我整理一整理，与你十两银子。（李）不打紧。小人不敢要偌多银子。（鲁）你是个小百姓，我怎么肯亏你。与我整理的好，着银子与你买酒吃。（李四接壶整理科）整理的复旧如初，好了也。大人试看咱。（鲁）这厮真个好手段！便是新的一般。张千，有酒么？（张千）有。（鲁）将来赏他几杯。（做筛酒科。李四连饮三杯科，云）够了。（鲁）你家里再有什么人？（李四）家里有个丑媳妇，教出来见大人。大嫂，你出来拜大人。（旦出拜科）（鲁）一个好女人也！与他三盅酒吃。我也吃一盅。张千，你也吃一盅。兀那李四，这三盅酒是肯酒，银子与你做盘缠，你的浑家我要带往郑州去也。你不揀那个大衙门里告我去！（同旦下）（李四做哭科，云）清平世界，朗朗乾坤，拐了我浑家去了。更待干罢，不问那个大衙门里告他走一遭去。（下）。

（贴旦引二男女上）花有重开日，人无再少年。妾身姓李。夫主姓张，在这郑州做着个六案孔目。嫡亲的四口儿家属，一双儿女：小厮唤做金郎，女儿唤做玉姐。孔目衙门中去了，这早晚敢待来也。（李四上）一

LU: This silver kettle of mine has been knocked down and broken. If you mend it for me, I'll give you ten silver taels.

LI: That is easy. I dare not ask for so much money.

LU: You are a poor man, how could I take advantage of you? Make a good job of it. Here is some silver to buy wine.

(*Li takes the kettle and mends it.*)

LI: Now it is as good as new. It's ready. Please look, sir.

LU: Clever rascal — it really is as good as new. Zhang Qian, have you got wine there?

ZHANG: Yes, sir.

LU: Give him a few cups as a reward.

(*Wine is poured out, and Li Si has three cups.*)

LI: I have had enough.

LU: How large is your family?

LI: There is my humble wife. I will call her out to pay her respects. Wife! Come and pay your respects to His Honour.

(*Li's Wife comes out to curtsey to Lu.*)

LU: A fine woman! Give her three cups of wine. I will drink a cup too, and so shall you, Zhang Qian. Well, Li Si, these three cups of wine seal our agreement. The silver is for you, and I am taking your wife with me to Zhengzhou. Don't you dare go to the yamen to sue me! (*Exit with Li's Wife.*)

LI (*shedding tears*): In broad daylight and time of peace, he has made off with my wife! I can't let him get away with that! Let me go and lay a charge against him in some yamen. (*Exit.*)

(*Enter Zhang Gui's Wife with her son and daughter.*)

ZHANG'S WIFE:

A flower may blossom again,
But youth never returns.

My maiden name is Li. My husband's name is Zhang, and he is a clerk in Zhengzhou yamen. We are a family of four, with a son called Golden Boy and a daughter called Jade Maid. My husband is at his office, but he should be back soon.

心忙似箭，两脚走如飞。自家李四的便是。因鲁斋郎拐了我的浑家，往郑州来了。我随后赶来，到这郑州，我要告他。不认的那个是大衙门？来到这长街市上，不觉一阵心疼。我死也，却教谁人救我是好？（正末引祗从上）自家姓张，名珪，字均玉。郑州人氏。幼习儒业，后进身为吏。嫡亲的四口儿：浑家李氏，是华州华阴县人氏，他是个医士人家女儿。生下一双儿女，金郎、玉姐。我在这郑州做着个六案都孔目。今日衙门中无甚事，回家去也。见一簇人闹，祗候，你看是什么人？（祗候问云）你是什么人？倒在地上！（李四）小人急心疼，看看至死。哥哥可怜见，救小人一命咱。（祗候见末科，云）是一个人害急心疼倒在地下。（末）我试看咱。兀那君子，为什么倒在地下？（李四）小人急心疼，看看至死。怎么救小人一命！（末）那里不是积福处！我浑家善治急心疼，领他到家中，与他一服药吃，怕做什么。祗候人，扶他家里来。可早来到也。大嫂那里？（贴旦见末科）孔目来了也，安排茶饭你吃。（末）不必茶饭，我来狮子店门首，见一人急心疼，我领将来。你与他一服药吃，救他性命。那里不是积福处！（贴旦）我调药去。（做调药科）君子，你试吃这药。

(*Enter Li Si.*)

LI:

I run like an arrow,
As if my feet had wings.

I am Li Si. I have come to Zhengzhou after Lu Zhailang, because he carried off my wife. I intend to charge him, but don't know where the yamen is. Here I am in the main street. Help! What is this pain in my heart? I am dying! Who will save me?

(*Enter Zhang Gui with a Runner.*)

ZHANG: I am Zhang Gui, a native of Zhengzhou. After studying the Confucian classics in my youth, I found an official post. There are four of us in my family. My wife is the daughter of a physician named Li from Huazhou, and we have two children — Golden Boy and Jade Maid. I am a clerk in Zhengzhou yamen. As there is no work in the office today, I am going home. I see a crowd. Go and find out what has happened, man.

RUNNER (*to Li Si*): Who are you? Why are you lying on the ground?

LI: I have had a heart attack and am dying. Have pity on me, brother, and save me!

RUNNER (*to Zhang*): There is a man on the ground having a heart attack.

ZHANG: Let me have a look. Hey, you! Why are you lying there?

LI: I have had a heart attack and am dying. Save me, sir!

ZHANG: Good deeds bring their reward of happiness. My wife knows how to treat heart attacks. Why not take him home and give him a cordial? (*To the Runner.*) Help him to my house, man. Here we are. Where are you, wife?

ZHANG'S WIFE (*greeting her husband*): So you're back. Let me get you some tea and food.

ZHANG: Not just yet. When I was passing the Lion, I found a man having a heart attack, and I have brought him home. Prepare a cordial for him and you'll save his life. Good deeds bring their reward of happiness.

ZHANG'S WIFE: I'll go and brew a cordial now. (*She prepares the medicine.*) Drink this, sir.

（李四吃药科）我吃了这药。哎哟！无事了也。多谢了官人、娘子。若不是官人、娘子，哪里得我这性命来。（末）我问君子，哪里人氏，姓甚名谁？（李四）小人姓李，排行第四，人口顺都叫李四。许州人氏，打银为生。（贴旦）你也姓李，我也姓李。有心要认你做个兄弟，未知孔目心中肯不肯。我问孔目咱。（做问末科）这人也姓李，我也姓李。我有心待认他做个兄弟，孔目意下如何？（末）大嫂，你主了便罢。兀那李四，你近前来。我浑家待认你做个义兄弟，你意下如何？（李四）你救了我性命，休道是做兄弟，在你家中随驴把马也是情愿。（末）你便是我舅子，我浑家就是你亲姐姐一般。兄弟，你为什么到这里？（李四）你便是我亲姐姐、姐夫。有人欺负我来，你与我做主。（末）谁欺负你来？我便着人拿去。谁不知我张珪的名儿！（李四）不是别人，是鲁斋郎强夺了我浑家去了。姐姐、姐夫，与我做主。（末做揜口科，云）哎约，唬杀我也。早是在我这里，若在别处，性命也送了你的。我与你些盘缠，你回许州去。小舅子，你这言语也休题。

【端正好】被论人有势权，原告人无门下。你便不良会可跳塔轮铡。那一个官司敢把勾头押？题起他名儿也怕。

【幺】你不如休和他争，忍气吞声罢；别寻个家中宝，省力的浑家。说那个鲁斋郎胆有天来大，他为

LI (*taking it*): Ah, this cordial has restored me. Thank you from the bottom of my heart! If not for you both, I should have died.

ZHANG: May I ask where you are from, sir? What is your name?

LI: My name is Li, and as I am the fourth in my family they call me Li Si. I am from Xuzhou, a silversmith by trade.

ZHANG'S WIFE: Since your name is Li and my maiden name is Li too, I would like you to be my brother. Let me see if my husband is willing. (*To Zhang*.) As this gentleman and I are both named Li, I would like to call him my brother if you are willing.

ZHANG: Just as you like. Come here, Li Si. My wife wants you to be her brother. What do you say?

Li: You have saved my life. I would gladly work in your house as a stable-boy, let alone be your wife's brother.

ZHANG: Very well, now you are my brother-in-law and my wife is your sister. But what brought you to this district, brother?

LI: Someone has done me a great wrong. Now that you are my sister and brother-in-law, you must help me.

ZHANG: Who has wronged you? I'll have him arrested. Everybody knows me here!

LI: It was Lu Zhailang, who has carried off my wife. You must help me!

ZHANG (*clapping his hand to his mouth*): Heavens, what a shock you gave me! It is lucky for you you are here. If you had said that anywhere else, you wouldn't have lived to tell the tale. I'll give you some money for your journey back to Xuzhou, brother, but don't mention that name again.

The man you accuse has great power,
While you, the plaintiff, have none;
No matter how plausible you are,
What court dares issue a warrant?
The sound of his name will strike terror into them.
You had better not quarrel with him,
But swallow your anger,
And find an ugly wife
Who will not cause trouble.

臣不守法，将官府敢欺压，将妻女敢夺拿，将百姓敢踏查。赤紧的他官职大的忒稀诧。（下）

（李四）我这里近不的他，还往许州去也。（下）

（鲁斋郎上）小官鲁斋郎是也。自从许州拐了李四的浑家，起初时性命也似爱他，如今两个眼里不待见他。我今来到这郑州，时遇清明节令，家家上坟祭扫，必有生得好的女人。我领着张千一行步从，直到郊野外踏青走一遭去。（下）

（正末引贴旦上）自家张珪是也。时遇寒食，家家上坟，我今领着妻子上坟走一遭去。想俺这为吏道的多不存公道，熬的出身非同容易也呵。

【仙吕点绛唇】则俺这令史当权，案房里面，关文卷。但有半点儿牵连，那刁蹬无良善。

【混江龙】休想肯与人方便，衠一片害人心，勒掯了些养家钱。听的有件事呵！押文书心情似火，写贴子勾唤如烟。教公吏勾来衙院里，抵多少笙歌引至

Lu is high-handed as Heaven,
An officer who overrides the law
And will even threaten government offices,
Seizing men's wives and daughters
And trampling upon honest citizens.
Few officials have such power! (*Exit.*)

LI: As I cannot charge him here, I will go back to Xuzhou. (*Exit.*)

(*Enter Lu Zhailang.*)

LU: I am Lu Zhailang. I took Li Si's wife from him in Xuzhou, and at first I loved her as my own life, but now I cannot stand the sight of her. Here I am in Zhengzhou. It is the Spring Festival, when everyone sacrifices to the ancestral graves. There must be some good-looking women among these crowds. I will take Zhang Qian and my other men out to enjoy the fine weather in the country. (*Exit.*)

(*Enter Zhang Gui, leading his wife.*)

ZHANG: I am Zhang Gui. This is the Spring Festival, when each family sacrifices to the ancestral graves, and I am taking my wife to our graveyard. We government officers are usually a bad lot. It takes some doing to get these positions of ours.

A clerk such as I has great authority,
We have charge of all government files,
And if we sue a man,
We know many devices
To make things hot for him.
We never do a good turn
But try to ruin men,
Squeezing their money out of them
For ourselves.
When we have some information
We make out warrants with fiery haste
And summon the accused as quickly as smoke;
When the runners drag them to court
We feel as if some beautiful girl

画堂前。冒支国俸，滥取民财；禁持父母，冻饿妻儿。经旬间不来家，破工夫在柳陌花街串，积趱下金银富贵、花月团圆。

【油葫芦】我置下家私买下田，桃杏一二千，真是连枝带叶尽埋冤。逼的人卖了银头面，我戴着金头面。送的人典了旧宅院，我住着新宅院。有一日限满时，便想得重迁。提刑司刷出三宗卷，恁时节带铁锁、纳赃钱。

【天下乐】那其间敢卖了城南金谷园，百姓见无权，一昧里掀。泼家私如败云风乱卷。或是流二千，遮莫徒一年，恁时节则落的几度喘。

来到坟所也。是好春景也呵！

【金盏儿】觑郊原，笑声喧。古坟新土都添遍，家家慎终追远痛难言。一壁厢黄鹂声恰恰，一壁厢血

Were coming to the painted hall
Amid singing and fluting.
We embezzle state funds,
Grind the faces of the poor,
Throw parents into gaol,
Make wives and children suffer hunger and cold.
We stay away from home for weeks on end,
Spending our time with singsong girls in brothels,
Storing up wealth, living in luxury,
Amassing property and buying land:
A few thousand peach and apricot trees,
And every leaf or twig a tale of injustice!
We part men from their silver
So that we can wear ornaments of gold;
We force them to sell their old houses
So that we can live in new mansions.
When our term of office is over
And we await new appointments,
The Ministry of justice goes through our files;
Then we are fettered and fined,
Made to sell our luxurious estates;
And when the people see we have lost power,
They come down on us like a whirlwind
Which drives all clouds before it,
We are sent into exile hundreds of miles from home,
Or made to do hard labour for a year,
And have to pant for breath

Here we are at the graveyard. How lovely the country looks in spring!

Laughter is heard all over the countryside,
Fresh soil is added to the mouldering graves;
Men remember their dead and mourn them.
On one side golden orioles sing,
On the other mortal men shed bitter tears;

泪滴涟涟。正是莺啼新柳畔，人哭古坟前。

（贴旦）孔目，咱慢慢耍一会家去。（鲁斋郎引众上）你都跟着我闲游去来。所事不见？正所好坟也！树木上面一个黄莺儿，将弹弓来。（做打弹科）（俫哭云）奶奶，打破头也。（贴旦）哪个弟子孩儿，闲着那驴蹄烂爪，打过这弹子来！（末）这个村弟子孩儿无礼，我家坟院里打过弹子来，你不知我的名儿。我出去看去。

【后庭花】是谁人墙外边，直恁的没体面？我抬察望前去——（鲁）张珪，你骂谁哩？（末）唬的我行行的往后偃。（鲁）你这弟子孩儿作死也！我是谁？你骂我？（末）我恰便似履深渊，把不定心惊胆战，有这场死罪愆。我今朝遇禁烟，祖坟前来祭奠。饮金杯，语笑喧。他弓开时似月圆，弹发处又不偏，恰落在我面前。

（鲁）张珪，你要打我呵，不是寻死哩！（末）

【青哥儿】你教我如何分辩？（贴旦）是哪一个不晓事弟

Birds warble in the tender willows,
While human beings weep before ancient tombs.

ZHANG'S WIFE: Let us stay here a little, husband.

(*Enter Lu Zhailang with his men.*)

LU: Come for a stroll with me. Here is a fine graveyard, with an oriole on a tree. Give me my catapult. (*He aims at the bird.*)

GOLDEN BOY (*crying*): Mother, my head is broken!

ZHANG'S WIFE: What young donkey has hit my child with his dirty catapult?

ZHANG: How dare a lout shoot into our family graveyard? Don't you know who I am? Let me see who is there!

Who is the wretch outside the wall?
I hurry forward to see.

LU: Who do you think you are dressing down, Zhang Gui?

ZHANG:

I fall back a step in terror!

LU: Are you looking for trouble, you scoundrel? Who do you think I am? How dare you abuse me?

ZHANG:

I feel like a man
Who walks over a precipice,
Trembling in panic,
Expecting death any moment!
I came out to celebrate the Spring Festival,
And to sacrifice at my ancestral graves;
We were drinking, laughing and chatting,
When he drew his catapult,
And his shot flew past my eyes!

LU: You're going to beat me, are you, Zhang Gui? Do you want to be killed?

ZHANG:

I do not know how to answer.

ZHANG'S WIFE: What silly boy has broken my darling's head?

子孩儿打破我孩儿头？（末）省可里高声骂得胡言。（俫）打破我头也！（末）哎！你个不识忧愁小业冤。唬的我魂魄消然，言语狂颠。谁敢迟延？我只得破步撩衣，走到根前，少不的屎做糕糜咽。

（末做跪科）（鲁）张珪，你怎敢骂我？你不认的我？觑我一觑！该死！你骂我该什么罪过？（末）张珪不知道是大人，若知道是大人呵，张珪哪里死的是。（鲁）君子千言有一失，小人千言有一当。他不知是我，若知是我，怎么敢骂？我不和你一般见识。这座坟是谁家的？（末）是张珪家的。（鲁）消不的你请我坟院里坐一坐，教你祖宗都得生天。（末）请大人坟里坐一坐。（鲁）倒好一座坟院也。我听的有女人言语，是谁？（末）是张珪的丑媳妇儿。（鲁）消不得拜我一拜。（末）大嫂，你来拜大人。（贴旦）我拜他怎地？（末）你依着我。（旦上拜科）（鲁还礼科）一个好女子也！他倒有这个浑家，我倒无。张珪，你这厮该死！怎敢骂我？把你罪过且不饶

ZHANG:

Don't talk so loudly and so foolishly!

GOLDEN BOY: He's cut my head open!

ZHANG:

You little simpleton,
You don't know the meaning of worry!
I am out of my mind with terror,
And have no idea what to say;
But I dare delay no longer,
And step forward holding my gown,
Prepared to eat dirt.

(*He kneels before Lu.*)

LU: How dare you swear at me, Zhang Gui? Don't you know me? Take a look. Damn you, you shall suffer for this!

ZHANG: I had no idea it was Your Honour. I would rather have died than speak to you like that.

LU: Well, well. Even a gentleman may say one wrong word in a thousand, while even a low brute may say one right. He had no idea it was me. If he had known, of course he would not have dared. I won't take offence then. Whose graveyard is this?

ZHANG: It is my family graveyard.

LU: You might ask me in to rest for a while in that case. Then even your ancestors' spirits will go to heaven.

ZHANG: Please come inside, Your Honour.

LU: A fine place. Who is that woman I hear speaking?

ZHANG: That is my wife.

LU: You might ask her to greet me.

ZHANG: Wife, come and pay your respects to His Honour.

ZHANG'S WIFE: Why should I?

ZHANG: Do as I tell you.

(*Zhang's Wife curtseys to Lu.*)

LU (*bowing in return*): A charming woman! To think he has a wife like that, and I haven't. Damn you, Zhang Gui! How dare you swear at me? I'm

你。近前来，将耳朵来：把你媳妇明日送的我宅子里来。若来迟了，二罪俱罚。将马来，我回去也。（下）（贴旦）孔目，他是谁？你这等怕他？（末）大嫂，咱收拾回家去来。

【赚煞】巧笑倩，祸机藏。美目盼，灾星现。也是俺连年里时乖运蹇，没一个当道掘坑解倒悬。我便似没头鹅、热地上蚰蜒。恰才个马头边，附耳低言，一句话似深蒙帝主宣。（末拿弹子拜科）这弹子举贤荐贤，他来的扑头扑面。明日个你团圆，却教我不团圆。（下）

not going to let you off lightly. Come here and listen to me. Bring your wife to my house first thing tomorrow. If you don't turn up, you will pay double for it. Bring me my horse. I am going now. (*Exit.*)

ZHANG'S WIFE: Who is he, husband? Why are you so afraid of him?

ZHANG: Let's pack up, wife, and go home.

Trouble lurks in your charming smile,
Grief comes of your beautiful eyes;
For these years my luck has been bad,
And there is no one to help me.
I am a goose with its head cut off,
A worm writhing on hot ground.
His whispered order by his horse
Is like the emperor's edict.

(*He picks up the catapult pellet and bows.*)

This shot served as a go-between,
Coming like a bolt from the blue.
You will have a wife tomorrow,
But I shall have none.

(*Exeunt.*)

第二折

（鲁斋郎引张千上）着意栽花花不发，等闲插柳柳成阴。小官鲁斋郎是也。因赏玩春景，到于郊野外。张珪坟中树上歇着个黄莺儿，我拽满弹弓，谁想落下弹子来打着张珪的小的。将我千般毁骂，我要杀坏了他。不想他倒有个好媳妇。我着他今日不犯，明日送来。我一夜不曾睡着。他若来迟了，就把他杀坏。张千，门首看着，若来时报伏我知道。

（末同贴旦上）大嫂疾行动些。（贴旦）才五更天气，你敢风魔九陌？引的我那里去？（末）东庄里姑娘家有喜庆勾当，用着这个时辰。我和你行动些。大嫂，你先行。（贴旦先行科）（末）张珪，怎了也？鲁斋郎大人的言语："张珪，明日将你浑家五更你便送到我府中来。"我不送去，我也是个死。我待送去，两个孩儿久后寻他母亲，我也是个死。怎生是好也？

【南吕一枝花】全失了人伦天地心，倚仗着恶党凶徒势。活支刺母儿双折散，生各札夫妇两分离。从

ACT II

(*Enter Lu Zhailang with Zhang Qian.*)

LU:

When you plant flowers they may not bloom,
But a willow slip may grow to give shade.

I am Lu Zhailang. When I went out to enjoy the countryside in spring, in Zhang Gui's graveyard I saw an oriole on a tree, and drew my catapult. My shot went wide and hit Zhang Gui's child. He abused me roundly and I wanted to kill him, till I saw he had a pretty wife. Then I told him he need not give her to me at once, but could send her to me the next day. I have not slept all night. If he is late, I shall kill him. Go to the door, Zhang Qian, and keep a lookout. Let me know when he comes.

(*Enter Zhang with his wife.*)

ZHANG: Hurry, wife!

ZHANG'S WIFE: It is barely dawn. Are you out of your mind? Where are you taking me?

ZHANG: There is a wedding in my aunt's house in East Village. We mustn't be late. Let's walk faster. You go first, wife.

(*Zhang's Wife walks in front.*)

ZHANG: What can I do? His Honour Lu Zhailang said: "Zhang Gui, bring your wife to my house first thing tomorrow." If I do not take her, he will kill me. If I take her, the two children will cry for their mother and that will kill me too. What can I do?

He has lost all human feeling:
Relying on his roughs,
He cruelly drags a mother from her children

来有日月交蚀，几曾见夫主婚、妻招婿？今日个妻嫁人、夫做媒。自取些奁房断送陪随，那里也羊酒花红段匹。

【梁州】他凭着恶哏哏威风纠纠，全不怕碧澄澄天网恢恢。一夜间摸不着陈抟睡！不分喜怒，不辨高低。教我人离财散，宅乱家番。对浑家又不敢说是谈非，行行里没乱徘徊。你、你、你，做了个别霸王自刎虞姬，我、我、我，做了个进西施归湖范蠡，来、来、来，浑一似嫁单于出塞明妃。正青春似水，娇儿幼女成家计。无忧虑，少萦系。平地起风波二千尺，一家儿瓦解星飞。

（贴旦）俺走了这一会，在那里？（末）则那里便是。（贴

And tears husband and wife apart.
Sun and moon may be eclipsed,
But how can a husband give away his wife?
Yet today I am acting as the go-between,
And must bring wedding gifts,
While the bridegroom sends
Neither sheep, nor wine, nor silk.
Powerful and ruthless,
He fears no divine retribution.
All is dark, I am utterly lost!
I can no longer distinguish
Between joy and anger,
Between high and low.
My wife is being taken,
My family is ruined;
But I dare not tell her,
As I stumble on.
You are Lady Yu[7]
Bidding farewell to her lord,
I am Fan Li[8]
Presenting the beauty to the king;
You are Wang Zhaojun[9]
Married to the Hunnish Khan;
You are young,
With a son and daughter;
We lived free from worries and cares,
Till out of a clear sky
This storm arose;
Now our family is scattered
Like broken tiles!

ZHANG'S WIFE: We have been walking for some time. Where are we?

ZHANG: We have arrived.

旦）这个院宅便是？他做什么买卖？有这等大院宅。（末）

【牧羊关】怕不晓日楼台静，春风帘幙底，没福的怎生消得！这厮强赖人钱财，莽夺人妻室。高筑座莺花寨，斜搠面杏黄旗。梁山泊贼相似，与蓼儿洼争甚的！

大嫂，你靠后。（末见张千科）哥哥，报复一声：张珪在于门首。（张千）你这厮才来？你该死也！你则在这里，我报伏去。（鲁见张千云）兀那厮做什么？（张千）张珪两口儿在于门首。（鲁）张千，我不换衣服罢，着他过来见。（末旦施礼科）（鲁）张珪这早晚才来？（末）投到安伏下两个小的，收拾了急急走来，五更过也。（鲁）别不打紧。这个是你那浑家？近前来我看。好女人也！比夜来增十分颜色。生受你。将酒来，吃三杯。（末）

【四块玉】将一杯醇糯酒十分的吃，（贴旦）张孔目少吃，则怕你醉了。（末）更怕我酒后疏狂，落人便宜。

ZHANG'S WIFE: Is this the house? What business are they in to own such a big place?

ZHANG:

The morning sun shines upon quiet pavilions,
The spring breeze penetrates the gauzy curtains —
Happy the owner of such a property!
This man steals money,
Snatches other men's wives;
This is the brigand's castle,
And there flies his flag,
As if he were an outlaw of Liangshan.[10]

Wait here, wife. (*He greets Zhang Qian.*) Brother, please announce that Zhang Gui is at the gate.

ZHANG QIAN: At last! You deserve to die for this delay. Wait here while I announce you.

LU: What is that fellow there?

ZHANG QIAN: Zhang Gui and his wife are at the gate.

LU: I'll not stop to change, Zhang Qian. Show them in.

(*Zhang and his wife bow to Lu.*)

LU: You are late, Zhang Gui.

ZHANG: I waited till the two children were asleep, then made ready and hurried here. So it is after dawn.

LU: Never mind. Is that your wife? Come here and let me see you. A fine woman, more beautiful than when I saw her yesterday. I thank you! Bring the wine and we will have three cups.

ZHANG:

I gulp down the heady wine.

ZHANG'S WIFE: Don't drink too much, husband. I'm afraid you will get drunk.

ZHANG:

She's afraid I may get drunk
And may be cheated.

扭回身刚咽住长嘘气。我乞求得醉似痴，如烂泥，我则图别离时不记得。

（贴旦）张孔目，你为什么这般烦恼？你说么！（末）大嫂，实不相瞒：如今大人要你做夫人，我特送将你来。（贴旦）孔目也，你这般下的也！（鲁）则管里说什么！后堂中换衣服去。（贴旦）孔目，则被你痛杀我也！（末）苦痛杀我也，浑家！（鲁）张珪，你不有些烦恼，心中舍不的？（末）张珪不敢烦恼，则是家中有一双儿女，无人看管。（鲁）你早不说！你家中有两个小的无人照管他？（做唤张千科）张千，将那李四的浑家梳妆打扮得呵，与张珪。（张）使的。（鲁）张珪，你两个小的无人照管，我有一个妹子，叫做娇娥，与你看觑两个小的。你与了我你的浑家，我的妹子报酬你。你醉了骂他，便是骂我一般；你醉了打他，便是打我一般。我交付与你，我回后堂去也。（下）（末）这事可怎了也？罢，罢，罢！

【尾声】夺了我旧妻儿，却与个新佳配。我正是弃了甜桃，绕山寻醋梨。知他是甚亲戚！教喝下庭阶，转过照壁，出的宅门，扭回身体。遥望着后堂

I turn to suppress a sigh!
I want to get dead-drunk,
To be dead to the world,
So as not to remember our parting.

ZHANG'S WIFE: Tell me, husband, why do you look so sad?

ZHANG: To tell the truth, wife, His Honour wants you as his mistress. That is why I have brought you here.

ZHANG'S WIFE: Husband! How can you be so cruel!

LU: Stop talking. Go and change your clothes in the inner-room.

ZHANG'S WIFE: Husband, you have broken my heart!

ZHANG: My heart is broken too, wife.

LU: Are you feeling sad, Zhang Gui? Unwilling to leave her?

ZHANG: How dare I be, Your Honour! But I have a son and daughter at home with no one to look after them.

LU: Why didn't you say before? So you have two children at home with no one to look after them. (*He calls Zhang Qian.*) Zhang Qian, tell Li Si's wife to get dressed, and give her to Zhang Gui.

ZHANG QIAN: Yes, sir.

LU: Since your two children need someone to look after them, Zhang Gui, I will give you my sister Jiao E. You have given me your wife, and you shall have my sister in exchange. If you swear at her or beat her when you are drunk, it will be like swearing at me or beating me. I entrust this girl to you. Now I am going to the inner chamber.(*Exit.*)

ZHANG: What shall I do now? Ah!

He has seized my wife
And given me another;
I have thrown away a sweet peach
For a sour pear.
Surely she is no sister of his!
I am ushered down the steps,
Past the screen and out of the gate;
And turn to look back at my wife,

内养家的人，贤惠的妻。非是今生是宿世，我则索寡宿孤眠过年岁。几时能够再得相逢，则除是南柯梦儿里。（下）

At my good helpmate,
As if we were husband and wife
In a former life.
I must sleep alone for the rest of my days,
And never see her again except in dreams. (*Exit.*)

第三折

（李四上）自家李四。因鲁斋郎夺了我浑家，赶到郑州告不的他，又回许州来。一双儿女，不知所向，那里也难住。我且往郑州投奔我姐姐、姐夫去也。（下）

（俫儿上）我是张孔目的孩儿金郎。妹子玉姐。父亲、母亲人情去了，这早晚敢待来也。（末上）好是苦痛也！来到家了，见两个孩儿说些什么？鲁斋郎，你好狠也呵！

【中吕粉蝶儿】倚仗着恶党凶徒，害良民肆生淫欲。谁敢向他行挟细拿粗？逞凶顽，全不想他妻我妇。败坏风俗，那一个敢为敢做！

【醉春风】空立着判黎庶受官厅，理军情元帅府。父南子北各分离，端的是苦！苦！俺夫妻千死千生，百伶百俐，怎能勾一完一聚。

ACT III

(*Enter Li Si.*)

LI: I am Li Si. Because Lu Zailang snatched my wife I went to Zhengzhou to sue him, but finding that impossible, I came back to Xuzhou. Now my children have disappeared, so I cannot stay here either. I will go back to Zhengzhou to my sister and brother-in-law. (*Exit.*)

(*Enter Zhang Gui's two children.*)

GOLDEN BOY: I am Zhang Gui's son, Golden Boy. This is my sister, Jade Maid. Our father and mother are out visiting. They should be back soon.

(*Enter Zhang Gui.*)

ZHANG: Ah, was ever any man as unhappy as I? Here I am back at home, but what shall I say to my children? You brute, Lu Zhailang!

Relying on his roughs,
This lecher tramples on good citizens.
Who is bold enough to pick a quarrel with him?
He takes whatever woman strikes his fancy,
With no regard for her husband,
And flaunts morality —
But who dares stand against him?
Though there is a court of justice for civilians,
A military court for the army,
They are useless.
Now the mother is torn from her children,
And the husband and wife
Who shared so many hardships
Can never meet again.

来到家中也。（俫）爹爹，你来家也。俺奶奶在哪里？（末）孩儿，你母亲便来也。可怎了也！

【红绣鞋】怕不待打迭起忧愁思虑，怎支吾这短叹长吁？（俫）俺母亲怎生不见来了？（末）他可便一上青山化血躯。将金郎眉甲按，把玉姐手梢扶，兀的不痛杀人也儿共女！

（俫）爹爹，俺母亲端的在哪里？（末）你母亲被鲁斋郎夺去了也。（俫）兀的不气杀我也！（俫气倒科）（末救科，云）孩儿，你苏醒者！则被你痛杀我也！（张千引旦上）自家张千便是。奉着鲁斋郎大人言语，着我送小姐去。来到也，张珪在家么？（末）谁在门外？待我开门看咱。（做看科）呀！呀！你来怎么？（张千）我奉鲁斋郎言语，着我送小姐与你。休说什么。小姐，你也休说什么。我回去也。（下）（末）小姐请进家来。两个孩儿来拜你母亲。小姐，先前浑家止有这两个孩儿，小姐早晚看觑咱。（旦）孔目，你但放心，都在我身上。（末）

【迎仙客】你把孩儿亲觑付，厮抬举。这两个不肖孩儿也有什么福？便做道忒贤达，不狠毒。（旦）孔目，你放心，就是我的孩儿一般看成。（末）看成的似玉

Well, here I am home.

GOLDEN BOY: Father, you are back! Where is mother?

ZHANG: She will be home soon, child. Ah, what shall I do?

I wish I could banish sad thoughts,
But how can I hide my sighs?

GOLDEN BOY: Why hasn't mother come?

ZHANG:

She may have gone up the mountain
And turned into stone.
I pat my son's head
And hold my daughter's hand.
Ah, children, this is a sad day!

GOLDEN BOY: Father, where is mother truly?

ZHANG: Your mother has been carried off by Lu Zhailang.

GOLDEN BOY: How dare he! I could burst with rage! (*He faints.*)

ZHANG (*reviving him*): Wake up, child. Poor little creatures!

(*Enter Zhang Qian with Li's Wife.*)

ZHANG QIAN: I am Zhang Qian. By my master's order, I have brought this lady here. Is Zhang Gui in?

ZHANG: Who is that calling outside? Let me open the gate and see. (*He opens the gate.*) Ah, what are you doing here?

ZHANG QIAN: His Honour ordered me to bring you this lady. Say no more, and don't you say anything either, ma'am. I am going. (*Exit.*)

ZHANG: Please come in, ma'am. Children, come and pay your respects to your stepmother. These are my former wife's two children, ma'am. I hope you will take good care of them.

LI'S WIFE: Rest assured, sir, I shall do my best for them.

ZHANG:

Take good care of these children,
These two unfortunates.
Even if you treat them kindly,
Not cruelly —

LI'S WIFE: Make your mind easy. I shall look after them as if they were

颗神珠，终不似他娘肠肚。

（李四上）我来到郑州，这是姐姐、姐夫家，我叫门咱。（做叫门科）（末）小姐，谁叫门哩？我看去。（见科）（末）原来是小舅子，你的症候我也害了也。（李四）姐姐有好药。（末）那个症候？你姐姐被鲁斋郎夺将去了也。（李四）鲁斋郎，你早则要了俺家两个也。（末）小舅子，我可也强似你，他与了我一个娇娥。（李四）鲁斋郎，你夺了我的浑家，草鸡也不曾与一个。姐夫既没了姐姐，我回许州去。（末）小舅子，这个便是你姐姐一般，厮见一面，怕做什么？（李四）见一面我就回去。姐夫，你可休留我。（做相见科）（末）小舅子，你敢要回去也？（李四）姐夫，则这里住倒好。（末）好奇怪也！

【红绣鞋】你两个眉来眼去，不由我心内踌蹰。百般难解，哑谜难猜。那一个身无所措，那一个紧支吾，您两个其情可怪。

（粉祗候上）孔目，衙门中唤你趱文书哩。（末）舅子，

my own.

ZHANG:

Even if you treasure them
Like pearls or jewels,
You will not be like their own mother.

(*Enter Li Si.*)

LI: I have come back to Zhengzhou. Here is my sister and brother-in-law's house. I'll call at the gate. (*He calls.*)

ZHANG: There is someone at the gate, ma'am. I'll just see who it is. (*He sees Li.*) So it is my brother-in-law. I am suffering from the same trouble as you.

LI: My sister has a good cure for it.

ZHANG: Not that trouble. Your sister has been snatched by Lu Zhailang too.

LI: So, Lu Zhailang, you owe us two women!

ZHANG: I am better off than you, brother. He gave me a woman in exchange.

LI: Ha, Lu Zhailang, when you took my wife you didn't give me so much as a hen. Since my sister has gone, brother, I had better go back to Xuzhou.

ZHANG: Your new sister is here, brother. Why not let me introduce her?

LI: I will just greet her and then I must go. Don't try to keep me, brother. (*He sees his wife.*)

ZHANG: Must you really go back now, brother?

LI: I think I'd like to stay here after all.

ZHANG: Strange!

The two of them
Are exchanging significant glances,
There is some mystery here.
One looks at a loss,
The other is hiding some secret;
Their expressions are most suspicious.

(*Enter a Runner*)

RUNNER: You are wanted to write out a document, Secretary Zhang.

你和你姐姐在家中，我衙门中攒文书去也。（下）（旦与李四打悲科）（李四）浑家，则被你想杀我也！（倈上）奶奶，俺爹爹哪里去了？（旦）衙门中攒文书去了。（倈）俺两个寻俺爹爹去。（下）（李四同旦云）则被你想杀我也！（末冲上见科）（李四同旦跪科）（末）他早招了也。

【石榴花】早难道君子断其初，今日个亲者便为疏，人还害你待何如？我是你姐夫，倒做了姨夫。当初我医可了你病症还乡去，我把你太行山倚仗做亲属。我一脚的出宅门，养着俺桑新妇，我可便负你有何辜！

【斗鹌鹑】全不似管鲍分金，倒做了孙庞刖足。把恩人变做仇家，将客僧翻为寺主。自古道“无毒不丈夫”：他将了你的媳妇，不敢向鲁斋郎报恨雪冤，来俺家里尤云殢雨。

ZHANG: Stay here with your sister, brother, while I go to the office to write out a document. (*Exit.*)

(*Li Si and his wife clasp each other and weep.*)

LI: Wife, I have missed you so much!

(*Enter the children.*)

GOLDEN BOY: Where has father gone, mother?

LI'S WIFE: He has gone to his office to write a document.

GOLDEN BOY: Then we will go to look for him.

(*He and his sister go out.*)

LI and WIFE: I have missed you so much!

(*Zhang rushes in and sees them together. Li Si and his wife kneel down.*)

ZHANG: So they admit their guilt!

A gentleman should not be false,
Yet my brother has betrayed me —
What if others did this to you?
I was your sister's husband,
But you have taken her from me,
You, whom I cured of your illness,
Whom I supported
And took as my relative.
As soon as I left the house
You stole my wife.
What wrong have I done you, pray?
You are not like that friend
Who shared his gold,
But like the fellow
Who chopped off his comrade's feet.
Now friends have turned to foes,
The guest has become the host;
The hearts of some men are wicked!
He snatched your wife,
You dared not take revenge,
But instead you make love to my wife,

（李）姐夫，实不相瞒：则他便是我的浑家，改做他的妹子，与了姐夫。（末）谁这般道来？

【上小楼】谁听你胡言诈语，我这里寻根拔树。谁似你不分软弱，不识亲疏，不辨贤愚。纵是你旧媳妇、旧丈夫双双完聚，送的俺一家儿灭门绝户。

我一双孩儿在哪里？（旦）你去攒文书，他两个寻你去了。（末）眼见的所算了我那孩儿也。兀的不气杀我也！

【幺】我一时间不认的人，您两个有什么福？空教我乞留乞良、迷留没乱放声啼哭。这郑孔目拿住了萧娥胡做，知他那里去了赛娘、僧住。

罢，罢，罢！浑家又被鲁斋郎夺将去了，一双儿女不知所向；甫能得了个女人，又是银匠李四的浑家。我在这里怎生存坐？舅子，我将家缘家计都分付与你两口儿，每月斋粮、道服休少了我的，我往华山出家去也。（李四）姐夫，你怎生弃舍了铜斗儿家缘、桑麻地土？我扯住你的衣服，至死不要你去。（末）

【十二月】休把我衣服扯住，情知咱冰炭不同炉。

（李四）姐夫，这桑麻地土、宝贝珍珠，怎生割舍的？（末）管

Here in my house!

LI: Let me tell you the truth, brother. This is my wife. Lu Zhailang lied when he told you she was his sister and gave her to you.

ZHANG: That is what you say.

Who believes your wicked lies?
I must get to the bottom of this —
A fine way to carry on!
You make no difference between weak and strong,
Between friend and foe, right and wrong.
Even if you are husband and wife
Who have come together again,
You have utterly destroyed my family.

Where are my two children?

LI'S WIFE: When you went to your office they went after you.

ZHANG: So you have murdered my children. I am choking with rage!

In a moment of weakness
I made the wrong choice of a friend.
What have you done to deserve such happiness,
Leaving me to wail in misery alone?
You make love to another man's wife,
And what have you done with my children?

Well, well. My wife has been carried off by Lu Zhailang, my two children have disappeared, and this woman who was given me has turned out to be the silversmith's wife. How can I stay here? I'll leave you both my property, brother. See that I get enough food and clothing each month. I am going to be a Taoist priest in Huashan.

LI: How can you leave your fine property and your farm, brother? I'll take hold of your clothes and stop you!

ZHANG:

Let go of my clothes!
Water and fire cannot remain together.

LI: How can you give up all your land and jewels, brother?

什么桑麻地土，更问甚宝贝珍珠？（李四）姐夫，把我浑家与你罢。（末）呸！不识羞闲言长语，他须是你儿女妻夫。

（旦）孔目，你与我一纸休书咱。（末）

【尧民歌】索什么恩绝义断写休书，（李四）鲁斋郎知道，他不怪我。（末）鲁斋郎也不是我护身符。（李四）俺姐姐不知在哪里？（末）他两行红袖醉相扶，美女终须累其夫。尘俗，非是顾恋处，不如我闻早归山去。

（李四）姐夫许多家缘家计、田产物业，你怎下的撇的去了？（末）

【耍孩儿】问什么东君去了花无主，你别有了莺俦燕侣。将人间名利不关心，更问甚巧拙贤愚。浮云世态纷纷恋，秋草人情日日疏。空教我泪洒遍湘江竹！这其间心灰卓氏，干老了相如。

（李四）俺姐姐不知在哪里？（末）

【二煞】你那姐姐！这其间听一声金缕歌，看两行红

ZHANG:

Say no more of my land and jewels.

LI: Brother, I'll give you my wife!

ZHANG: Pah!

Have you no sense of shame?
You are married already.

LI'S WIFE: Then give me a divorce certificate, sir.

ZHANG:

Why do you need divorce certificate?

LI: So that when Lu Zhailang hears of this, he will not blame us.

ZHANG:

Lu Zhailang is not my patron.

LI: I wonder where my sister is.

ZHANG:

The drunken lord needs serving-maids,
A pretty woman bring trouble to her husband;
This dusty world is not worth lingering in;
Better be a hermit in the mountains.

LI: How can you give up so much property, land and other movables?

ZHANG:

Do not ask who will be the steward
When the master is gone.
You have your wife again now.
I have lost all interest
In worldly fame or profit,
In mortal wisdom or folly.
Human affairs change like the floating clouds,
Friendship is autumn grass which withers daily.
In vain my tears stain the bamboo —
I am old and disillusioned.

LI: I wonder where my sister is now.

ZHANG: Yes, indeed, your sister!

Lu is listening to music,

袖舞，笙歌缭绕丫环簇。三杯酒满金鹦鹉，六扇屏开锦鹧鸪，人心腹。那厮有拐人妻妾的器具，引人妇女的方术。

（李）一年四季衣服不打紧。姐夫，你怎么出的家？辞别了亲友去波！（末）

【尾煞】甘分向林泉下做隐君，羞见那英雄真丈夫。为什么野人自爱山中宿？幼子、娇妻，我可也做不的主。（下）

（李）姐夫去了也。我知道将斋粮不少了他的。咱往后堂中吃庆喜酒去来。（下）

Watching a woman dancing,
With flutes and maids around him.
The gold goblet is filled with wine,
The embroidered screens are spread;
He has the means
To kidnap other men's wives,
And to seduce married women.

LI: We can see to your food and clothing all the year round, brother. But how can you leave your home and bid farewell to your relatives and friends?

ZHANG:
I have resigned myself
To be a hermit in the woods;
I do not want to rival
Brave men and heroes.
It is not that I choose the mountains,
But I have lost my children and sweet wife. (*Exit.*)

LI: So my brother-in-law has gone. I shall see to it that he is well supplied with food. Now I'll go to the inner chamber to drink with my wife to our happy reunion.

(*Exeunt.*)

第四折

（孤扮包待制引从人上）冬冬衙鼓响，公吏两边排；阎王生死殿，东狱摄魂台。老夫姓包，名拯，字希文。庐州金斗郡四望乡老儿村人氏。官封龙图阁待制，正授开封府尹。奉圣人的命，差老夫五南采访。来到许州，见一儿一女，原来是银匠李四的孩儿。他母亲被鲁斋郎夺了，他爷不知所向。这两个孩儿留在身边。行到郑州，又收得两个儿女，原来是都孔目张珪的孩儿。他母亲也被鲁斋郎夺了，他爷不知去向。我将这两个孩儿也留在家中，都着学些文章。十年光景，如今都应过举，得升迁。老夫将此一事，切切于心，拳拳在念。想鲁斋郎扰害黎民，掳掠妇女，罪有百端。老夫在圣人前奏过："有一人乃是鱼齐即，苦害良民，强夺人家子女，犯法百端。"圣人大怒，即便着斩之。天子判了"斩"字，典刑此人。次日，天子宣鲁斋郎。老夫回奏道："违条，斩之。"天子大惊道："为什么斩了他？""为掳掠了百姓，强夺人家妻女，圣人判了'斩'字，杀坏了也。"天子不信："将文书来我

ACT IV

(*Enter Prefect Bao with Attendants.*)

BAO:

The court drums thunder,
The runners are ranged on two sides;
This is the judgement seat of the King of Hell,
To which all spirits are summoned.

I am Bao Zheng, a native of Laoer Village in Luzhou. I hold the posts of Academician of Longtu Pavilion and Prefect of Kaifeng. Some years ago His Majesty ordered me to make a tour of inspection. In Xuzhou I found the son and daughter of the silversmith Li Si. As their mother had been abducted by Lu Zhailang and their father had disappeared, I kept them with me. In Zhengzhou I found another boy and girl who were the children of the clerk Zhang Gui. As their mother had also been abducted by Lu Zhailang and their father had disappeared, I kept them too and made them study. Now, ten years later, the young men have passed the examinations and taken up official posts. I bore these facts in mind, well aware that Lu was oppressing innocent people, kidnapping women and committing all manner of crimes. Then I reported to His Majesty that a man named Yu Qiji[11] had been injuring good citizens, abducting women and breaking the law time and again. His Majesty was angry and issued an order for his execution. The next day, when the emperor asked for Lu, I told him: "He has been killed for his crimes." The emperor was shocked. "How could you kill him?" he asked. "As he oppressed the people and kidnapped women, Your Majesty sentenced him to death," I said. "Now he has been executed." The emperor could hardly believe his ears. "Show

看！”鱼齐即三字，鱼字下边添个日字，齐字下边添个小字，即字上边添一点。天子见了道：“苦害良民犯人鲁斋郎合该斩首。”老夫智斩了鲁斋郎，与民除害。只是银匠李四、孔目张珪不知所向。我如今着他两家孩儿各带他两家女儿，天下巡庙烧香。若认着他父母，教他父子团圆，也是老夫阴骘的勾当。两个孩儿同两个女儿明日往云台观烧香去，老夫随后便来。鲁斋郎他不遵条例疏狂，他则待强夺人妻子红妆。被我中间改做了鱼齐即，老夫用心智斩了鲁斋郎。（下）

（净扮观主上）道可道，非常道；名可名，非常名。小道姓阎，道号双梅，人口顺都叫我做阎双梅。在这云台观做着个住持。今日无事，看有什么人来。（李四同旦儿上）自家李四是也。自从与俺那儿女失散了十年光景，知他有也无？来到这云台观里，与俺姐姐、姐夫并两个孩儿做些好事咱。（做见净）兀那观主，我是许州人氏，一径的来做些好事。（净）你做什么好事，超度谁？（李四）超度姐夫张珪，姐姐李氏，一双儿女金郎、玉姐。与你这五两银子，权做经钱。（净）我出家人，要他怎么？是好银子！且收下。快看斋食。看有什么人来？（贴旦道扮上）贫姑李氏，乃张珪的浑家。被鲁斋郎夺了我去，可早十年光景。一双儿女不知去向，张珪

me the decree," he said. Then he found the name Yu Qiji changed to Lu Zhailang, and read: "The felon Lu Zhailang, who oppressed the people, is to be executed." By this trick I had Lu Zhailang killed, and rid the people of a tyrant. But the silversmith Li Si and the clerk Zhang Gui are still missing. I have told their sons to take their sisters to temples all over the country to offer sacrifice, hoping that in this way they may find their parents. If I can reunite their families, I shall have done a good deed. Today the two young men have taken their sisters to sacrifice at the Yuntai Taoist Temple. I will follow them there.

Lu Zhailang flouted the law,
And abducted other men's wives;
By writing his name as Yu Qiji,
I succeeded in having him killed. (*Exit.*)

(*Enter Yan Shuangmei, a Taoist priest.*)

YAN:

The way that can be told is not the invariable way.
The names that can be named are not invariable names.[12]

I am Yan Shuangmei, a priest in Yuntai Temple here. Today I have no duties. I will see if anyone is coming.

(*Enter Li Si and his wife.*)

LI: I am Li Si. Since I lost my children ten years have passed, and I do not know whether they are alive or dead. I have come to Yuntai Temple today to sacrifice for my sister and brother-in-law and their two children. (*He greets the priest.*) Good day, priest. I am from Xuzhou and have come here to offer sacrifice.

YAN: For whom is this sacrifice?

LI: For my brother-in-law, Zhang Gui, and his wife and two children. Here are five taels of silver for you for chanting the holy canons.

YAN: We priests have no use for money, but I will accept it for the moment and get you some food. Here is someone else coming.

(*Enter Zhang's Wife, dressed as a nun.*)

ZHANG'S WIFE: I am Zhang Gui's wife. I was seized by Lu Zailang ten yers ago, My two chilldren have disappeared and I do not know whether

未知有无。鲁斋郎被包待制斩了，我就舍俗出家。今日去这云台观，与张珪做些好事咱。早来到也。（做见净科）（净）一个姑姑也！姑姑,哪里来？（贴旦）我一径的来与丈夫张珪、孩儿金郎、玉姐做些好事。（李四）谁与张珪做好事？（贴旦）我与张珪做好事。（李四）兀的不是姐姐李氏！（相见打悲科）（贴旦）兄弟，这妇人是谁？（李四）这个便是你兄弟媳妇儿。姐姐，你怎生得出来？（贴旦）包待制斩了鲁斋郎，俺都无事释放。今日来云台观追荐你姐夫并孩儿金郎、玉姐。（李四）我也为此事来，咱同共追荐。看有什么人来？（李末同李旦上）小官李喜童，妹子娇儿。我母亲被鲁斋郎夺将去了，父亲不知所向。亏了包待制爷爷收留俺兄妹二人，训教成人。今应过举，得了头名状元。包待制爷爷言语，着俺去云台观里追荐我父母去。早来到也。兀那观主！（净）早知相公到来，只合远接；接待不着，勿令见罪。你怎生带着个小姐走？（李末）我一径的来做些好事。（净）你追荐何人？（李末）追荐我父亲银李四。（李）是谁唤银李四？（李末）兀的不是我父亲！（李四）你是谁？

my husband is alive or dead. When Lu Zhailang was executed by Prefect Bao, I renounced the world and became a nun. Today I am going to Yuntai Temple to offer a sacrifice for Zhang Gui. Here I am. (*She greets the priest.*)

YAN: Ah, a nun! Where are you from?

ZHANG'S WIFE: I have come to offer a sacrifice for my husband Zhang Gui and my children.

LI: Who is offering a sacrifice for Zhang Gui?

ZHANG'S WIFE: I am.

LI: Aren't you my sister? (*He greets her, weeping.*)

ZHANG'S WIFE: Who is this lady, brother?

LI: That is my wife. How did you escape, sister?

ZHANG'S WIFE: When Prefect Bao had Lu Zhailang executed, I was able to leave his house. So today I have come to Yuntai Temple to sacrifice for your brother-in-law and my children.

LI: I have come for the same purpose. Let us sacrifice together. But see, some others are coming.

(*Enter Li's son and daugher.*)

HAPPY BOY: I am Happy Boy and this is my sister Sweet Maid. Our mother was carried off by Lu Zhailang and our father has disappeared. Luckily for us, Prefect Bao kept us and brought us up. Now I have passed the examinations and come first in the palace test. The prefect told us to go to Yuntai Temple to offer sacrifice for our parents. Here we are. Good day, priest.

YAN: If I had known a gentleman was coming, I would have gone out to welcome you. Please excuse me. What can I do for you and this young lady?

HAPPY BOY: We have come to offer a sacrifice.

YAN: For whom?

HAPPY BOY: For my father, Li Si, the silversmith.

LI: Who is talking about Li Si?

HAPPY BOY: Isn't that my father?

LI: Who are you?

（李末）则我便是您孩儿喜童，妹子娇儿。（旦）孩儿也，你在哪里来？（李末、李旦悲科，说前事了）（李四）孩儿，拜你姑姑者。（做拜科）（贴旦）这两人是谁？（李四）这两个便是我的孩儿。（贴旦悲科）你一家儿都完聚了，只是俺那孔目并两个孩儿不知在哪里！（张末同张旦上）小官是张孔目的孩儿金郎，妹子玉姐。我母亲被鲁斋郎夺去，父亲不知所向。多亏了包待制大人收留俺兄妹二人，训教成人。应过了举，得了官也。包待制大人着俺云台观追荐俺父亲去，可早来到也。（净）又是一个官人，他也带着小娘子走。官人哪里去来？（张末）我一径的来做些好事。（净）追荐哪一个？（张末）追荐我父亲张珪，母亲李氏。（贴旦）谁唤张珪、李氏？（张末）我唤来。（贴旦）你敢是金郎么？（张末）妹子，兀的不是母亲！（做悲科）（贴旦）这十年你在哪里来？（张末）自从母亲去了，父亲不知所向。多亏了包待制爷爷将我兄妹二人训教。应过了举，得了官也。包待制爷爷着俺云台观追荐父母，不想得见母亲。不知俺父亲有也无？（做悲科）（李四）姐姐，这个既是你的儿子，我把女儿娇儿与外甥做媳妇罢。（张末）母亲，将妹子玉

HAPPY BOY: I am your son, Happy Boy, and this is my sister, Sweet Maid.

LI'S WIFE: Ah, children, where have you been?

(*Li's son and daughter weep and speak of the past.*)

LI: Now, children, pay your respects to your aunt.

(*They bow to Zhang's Wife.*)

ZHANG'S WIFE: Who are these?

LI: They are my children.

ZHANG'S WIFE (*weeping*): Now your family is reunited, but I do not know where my husband and children are.

(*Enter Zhang's son and daughter.*)

GOLDEN BOY: I am Zhang Gui's son, Golden Boy, and this is my sister, Jade Maid. My mother was carried off by Lu Zhailang and my father has disappeared. Luckily for us, Prefect Bao kept us and brought us up. I have passed the examinations and become an official. The prefect told us to go to Yuntai Temple to sacrifice for our father. Here we are.

YAN: Here is another young gentleman, who has brought a young lady too. What brings you here, sir?

GOLDEN BOY: We have come to offer a sacrifice.

YAN: For whom?

GOLDEN BOY: For my father, Zhang Gui, and my mother.

ZHANG'S WIFE: Who is talking about Zhang Gui?

GOLDEN BOY: I am.

ZHANG'S WIFE: Can you be Golden Boy?

GOLDEN BOY: Sister, isn't this our mother?

(*They weep.*)

ZHANG'S WIFE: Where have you been during the last ten years?

GOLDEN BOY: After you left, our father disappeared too. Then luckily for us, Prefect Bao brought us up, and I have passed the examinations and been appointed to an official post. Prefect Bao told us to come to Yuntai Temple to sacrifice for our parents. We never thought to meet you here, mother. I wonder if our father is alive too. (*He weeps.*)

LI: If this is your son, sister, let me give him my daughter, Sweet Maid, as his wife.

姐与兄弟为了妻罢。（贴旦）俺两家子母怕不完聚了，只是张孔目不知在哪里？（正末愚鼓简板上）身穿羊皮百衲衣，饥时化饭饱时归；虽然不得神仙做，且躲人间闲是非。

【玉交枝】猛听的山童来报，报雾锁天关未晓。采樵人鼓掌呷呷笑，笑道是雪压了蜡梅梢。舞梨花片片风乱飘，似鹅毛乱剪空中落。可知道沽酒村价高，踏雪的争些冻倒。我则见寒料峭，冻燕巢，怎敢过危桥？浩然驴怎地骑，韩退之雪拥了蓝关道。白茫茫雪满山，黑暗暗彤云罩。呀！把一带青山粉填了。

想俺出家人，好是清闲也呵！

【双调新水令】想人生平地起风波，我清闲如谢安高卧。炼丹砂似唐吕翁，制律令的汉萧何。我这里醉舞狂歌，繁华梦已参破。

【风入松】利名场上苦奔波，因甚强夺！蜗牛角上争

GOLDEN BOY: Mother, give my sister, Jade Maid, to your nephew as his wife.

ZHANG'S WIFE: Now our two families are reunited. I only wonder where Zhang Gui is.

(*Enter Zhang Gui with a clapper.*)

ZHANG:

In a patched sheepskin,
I beg for food when hungry;
Though I cannot be an immortal,
I avoid the needless troubles of the world.
Suddenly my servant-lad reports
That a fog has shut out the sun;
Wood-cutters clap their hands and laugh,
Snow falls over the winter plum
And whirls in the wind like blossoms,
Scattering in the air like feathers.
Now the village wine goes up in price,
Travellers slip on the ice,
In bitter cold the swallows' nests are frozen —
Can I cross the slippery bridge?
The poet cannot ride his donkey,
The scholar is barred from the pass,
The mountains are white with dark clouds above,
And the green hills seem covered with powder.

We hermits lead a quiet life!

In the world of men
Troubles arise from nothing.
But I rest and take my leisure like Xie An,[13]
Trying, like Lü Weng,[14] *to make the philosopher's stone,*
Wise as Xiao He, the law-maker,[15]
I drink, dance and sing with abandon,
For I have seen through worldly vanity.
Men hurry after fame and profit,

人我，梦魂中一枕南柯。不恋三公华屋，且图五柳婆娑。

俺这出家人，一年四季，春夏秋冬，好是快活也呵！

【甜水令】俺这里春夏秋冬，林泉兴味，随时且过，经夜宿山阿。有人相问，静里工夫，炼形打坐，笑指那落叶辞柯。

【折桂令】想当初向清明日共饮金波，张孔目家世坟茔，须不是风月鸣珂。想着俺挽角儿夫妻，怎知道月枕双歌。自沉吟风流过活，不曾受段匹绫罗。休只管信口开合：张孔目缘木求鱼，鲁斋郎暴虎冯河。

【雁儿落】鲁斋郎忒太过，他道："张珪，将你媳妇送将来，我要。"我道："便送来。"不是张孔目从来懦。他在那云阳市剑下分，我去那华山顶峰头卧。

我则道他一世儿荣华富贵，可怎生被包待制斩了！人皆欢悦。

【得胜令】今日个天理事如何，黎庶尽讴歌。满城

Busy with petty affairs,
While I lie and dream in peace,
Not envying noble rank or splendid mansions.

Happy the hermit's life the whole year round!

Here I pass spring and summer,
Autumn and winter,
By the fountains in the woods,
Resting at night in the mountain.
If you ask how I pass the time,
I seek the philosopher's stone
And practise yoga,
Laughing at the withered leaves
Which fall from the trees.
I remember when I drank with my wife
One Spring Festival in my ancestral graveyard;
We were a happy couple,
Not living in luxury,
But enjoying a carefree life,
With no need for silk or brocade....
But to speak of these things is as vain
As trying to catch fish up a tree.
Lu Zhailang was a reckless bully
Who had no respect for the law.

"Zhang Gui, bring me your wife," he said. "I want her." And I agreed.

It was not that I was a coward.
His head was struck off
By the executioner's sword,
But still I take my ease
On the mountain top.

I thought he would enjoy his wealth and noble rank for ever, but he was executed by Prefect Bao, and all the people rejoiced.

This proves that there is justice,
And all men praise the prefect,

中人皆喜，包龙图智慧多。鲁斋郎哥哥，自惹下亡身祸，强夺了娇娥。不想我出了家，今日先寻了安乐窠。

今日我去云台观散心咱。可早来到也。（贴旦）李四，你看那道人，好似你姐夫。我试唤他一声咱。张孔目！（末回头科）是谁叫张孔目？（做见科）兀的不是我浑家李氏也！（贴旦）你怎生撇了我出了家，劝你还俗罢！（末）你待散时我不散，悲悲切切男儿汉。从前经过旧恩情，要我还俗呵，有如曹司翻旧案。（众云）你还了俗罢！（末）我实到此际，如何肯再还俗！（众拜科）（末）

【川拨棹】不索你闹镬铎，磕着头礼拜我。（李四）姐夫，今日咱两家夫妇、儿女都完聚了，你可怎生舍的出家去？你依着我，还了俗者。（末）谁听你语话喧聒，闹似蜂窝，口似蜜钵。我若是还了俗，可未可！

For Bao Zheng is full of wisdom,
And Lu Zhailang was asking to be killed
When he seized other men's wives.
But now, as a hermit, I have found happiness.

Today I am going to enjoy myself at Yuntai Temple. Here I am.

ZHANG'S WIFE: Li Si, look at that priest! He looks like your brother-in-law. Let me call him. Zhang Gui!

ZHANG (turning): Who is calling Zhang Gui? (*He sees her.*) Isn't that my wife?

ZHANG'S WIFE: Why have you left me and become a priest? You had better leave your holy orders now.

ZHANG:

When we parted
It was against my will,
I was then your heart-broken husband;
But after all these years
Our love is over.

You want me back now, but —

Our case is settled,
It cannot be reversed.

ZHANG'S WIFE and LI: Give up your holy orders!

ZHANG: I am already a priest. How can I turn back?

(*Zhang's Wife, Li Si and Li's Wife all plead with him.*)

ZHANG:

There is no need for all this clamour,
All this bowing and begging.

LI: Brother, now our two families are reunited, how can you go away? You must do as I ask and give up your priesthood.

ZHANG:

I will not listen to such talk
Though you buzz about me like a swarm of bees
And your words are sweet as honey —
I shall not give up my orders.

（贴旦）孔目，你是受用的人。你为何出家？你怎生受的那苦？（末）

【七弟兄】你那里问我，为何受寂寞。我得过时且自随缘过，得合时且把眼来合，得卧时侧身和衣卧。

【梅花酒】不是我自间阔，趁浪逐波，落落托托，大笑呵呵。夫和妻、能摘离，儿和女、且随他。我这里自磨跎，饮香醪，醉颜酡，沉醉了卧松萝。

【收江南】抵多少南华老子鼓盆歌，任人笑我似风魔。尘寰物我不张罗，把双眉不锁，松窗一枕梦南柯。

（孤冲上）事有足濯，物有故然。老夫包拯。来到这云台观，见一簇人闹，不知为什么？（李四）大人，小人是银李四。我姐姐被鲁斋郎强夺为妻，如今姐夫张珪出了家，不肯认他。（孤）兀那张珪，你为何不认他？（末）我一双儿女不知所在，实出了家，认他做什么？（孤）张珪，你那儿女见在我跟前，李四的儿女也在我行。您都过来。将李四的女儿与张珪的孩儿为妻，张珪的女

ZHANG'S WIFE: You are used to comfort, hushand. How can you be a priest? How can you stand such a hard life?

ZHANG:

You ask me why I choose this lonely life?
It is my wish to go where fate directs me,
To close my eyes when it is time to sleep,
To lie down when I need rest.
It is not that I want to leave you,
But a man may just as well drift
And laugh at the whole of creation;
Husband and wife may part
And give no thought to their children.
Here I live free from care,
Drinking as the fancy takes me,
And sleep when drunk among the pines and creepers,
Like the ancient philosopher
Who sang at his wife's death.[16]
The world may think I am mad,
But I will not trouble myself with mundane affairs;
I will not frown,
But sleep peacefully by the window.

(*Enter Bao Zheng.*)

BAO: Events may surprise us, but there is a reason for every thing. I am Bao Zheng. I have come to Yuntai Temple and I see some people having a heated discussion. I wonder what has happened.

LI: Your Honour, I am the silversmith, Li Si. My sister was carried off by Lu Zhailang. Now my brother-in-law Zhang Gui has become a priest and will not recognize her as his wife.

BAO: Why won't you recognize her as your wife, Zhang Gui?

ZHANG: My two children have disappeared, and I have become a priest. Why then should I take a wife?

BAO: Zhang Gui, your children are here before me, and Li Si's children too. Come here, all of you. Let Li Si's daughter marry Zhang Gui's son, and

儿与李四的孩儿为妻，你两家割不断的亲。张珪快还了俗者。天下喜事无过夫妇、父子团圆，杀羊造酒、做个庆喜筵席。则为鲁斋郎倚势欺人，把人妻强占为亲；被老夫设智斩首，方表出百姓艰辛。你两家夫妻重会，把儿女各配为婚。今日个俱蒙恩泽，登金榜进士出身。两家人都皆完聚，一齐的望阙谢恩。

题目　三不知同会云台观

正名　包待制智斩鲁斋郎

Zhang Gui's daughter marry Li Si's son, to link your two households in marriage. And let Zhang Gui return to his family. For there is no greater happiness in the world than family reunions. Let us kill a sheep and heat wine to celebrate.

Lu Zhailang was a bully,
Who carried off other men's wives;
By cunning I had him killed,
Freeing the people from his tyranny.
Now husbands and wives have come together again:
Let your children marry each other.
To all of you the state has shown its favour:
The young men's names are on the golden list,
And both your families are reunited;
Then face the north and thank His Majesty!

(*THE END*)

The Wife-Snatcher

包待制三勘蝴蝶梦

The Butterfly Dream

第一折

（孛老同旦引三末上）月过十五光明少，人到中年万事休。老汉姓王，是这开封府中牟县人氏。嫡亲的五口儿家属。这是我的婆婆，生下这三个孩儿，不肯做农庄生活，只是读书写字。孩儿也，几时是那峥嵘发迹的时节也呵！（王大）父亲、母亲在上：做农庄有甚好处？您孩儿受十年苦苦孜孜，博一任欢欢喜喜。（孛老同旦云）好儿，好儿！（王二）父亲，母亲：你孩儿十年窗下无人问，一举成名天下知。（孛老同旦云）好儿，好儿！（王三）父亲在上，母亲在下。（孛老）胡说！怎么母亲在下？（王三）我小时看见俺爷在上头，俺娘在底下，一同床上睡觉来。（孛老）你看这厮！（王三）父亲，母亲：我道是文章可立身。（孛老）好儿，好儿！（旦）老子，虽然如此，你还替孩儿寻一个长久立身之计。

ACT I

(*Enter Wang, his wife and their three sons.*)

WANG:

Comes the middle of the month, and the moon grows dim:

Comes middle age, and a man is good for nothing.

My name is Wang. I am a native of Zhongmou County in the prefecture of Kaifeng. There are five in my family. This is my wife, and we have three sons. They will not work on the land because they prefer to study. When will you show your worth, boys, and become famous?

BIG WANG: What good is farming, father? When I have studied hard for ten years I shall become an official and make you all happy.

WANG and WIFE: Good lad, good lad!

MIDDLE WANG: I may study for ten years by the window without receiving any recognition, father, but when I pass the examination and win fame, then the whole world will know me.

WANG and WIFE: Good lad, good lad!

LITTLE WANG: Father above and mother underneath....

WANG: What's that? Why "mother underneath"?

LITTLE WANG: When I was small I saw you in bed together, with mother underneath father.

WANG: You rascal!

LITTLE WANG: Father and mother, all I mean is that scholarship leads to a good career.

WANG: Good lad, good lad!

WIFE: Still, husband, you must find some way to set our boys up for life.

【赏花时】且休说文章可立身，争奈家私时下窘。枉了寒窗下受辛勤，如今街市上小民，宜假不宜真。

【幺】子敬衣衫不敬人，我言语从来无向顺。若三个儿到开春，有什么实诚定准，怎生便都能够跳龙门？（同下）

（孛老上）老汉来到这长街市上，替孩儿买些纸笔。走的乏了，且歇一歇咱。（净上）将相本无种，男儿当自强。自家葛彪是也。我是个权豪势要之家，我打死人不偿命，如常的则是坐牢。今日无甚事，长街市上闲耍去咱。（做撞孛老科）（净）这老子是什么人？敢冲着我马头？好打这老驴！（做打科。孛老死科。下）（净）这老子诈死赖我。马咬，马咬！马踢，马踢！马合，马合！（下）

（副末上）王大、王二、王三在家么？（三人上）叫怎的？（付末云）我是地方。不知什么人打死你父亲在长街上里！（三人云）是真实？母亲，祸事了也！（众哭科。王三）我那儿也！打死俺老子。母亲，你来。（旦）孩儿、为什么大惊小怪的？（王三）不知是谁打死了俺父亲也。（旦）嗨，可是怎地来。

Don't tell me scholarship leads to a good career —
We are short of money now.
What use is your hard study by the frosty window?
In this world rogues do better than honest men,
The clothes — not the men — are respected.
I always speak my mind:
What guarantee is there that our three sons
Will pass their test next spring?
How can they enter the dragon gate of officialdom?

(*Exeunt.*)

(*Enter Wang.*)

WANG: I have come to the main street to buy paper and pens for the boys. Walking has tired me. Let me rest here.

(*Enter Ge Biao.*)

GE:

Generals and ministers come from common stock:
Men should carve out their own career.

I am Ge Biao. Mine is a powerful family. When I kill men I do not have to pay with my life, but at most go to gaol for it. Today I am free, so I may as well take a ride (*He knocks into Wang.*) Who is this old fellow who dares get in my horse's way? Beat the old ass! (*He beats and kills Wang.*) The old man is shamming dead in order to blackmail me. I'll let my horse kick and trample him. (*Exit.*)

(*Enter the Bailiff.*)

BAILIFF: Big Wang, Middle Wang, Little Wang! Are you there?

(*Enter the three sons.*)

SONS: What do you want?

BAILIFF: I am the bailiff. Somebody has killed your father in the street.

SONS: What! Mother, a fearful thing has happened! (*They weep.*)

LITTLE WANG: Someone has killed our father! Mother, come here!

WIFE: What are you shouting about?

LITTLE WANG: Someone has killed our father.

WIFE: What! Never!

【仙吕点绛唇】仔细寻思，两回三次，这场蹊跷事。走的我气咽声丝，恨不的两肋生双翅。

【混江龙】俺男儿负天何事？拿住那杀人贼，我乞个罪名儿。他又不曾时连外境，又无甚过犯公私。若是俺软弱男儿有些死活，索共那倚势的乔才打会官司。我这里过六街、穿三市，行行里挠腮撧耳，抹泪揉眵。

（旦做行见尸科）

【油葫芦】你觑那着伤处，一埚儿青间紫，可早停着死尸。你可便从来忧念俺家私，昨朝怎晓今朝死，今日不知来日事。血模糊污了一身，软答剌冷了四肢，黄甘甘面色如金纸。干叫了一炊时！

【天下乐】救不活将咱没乱死！咱家私，自三思：到明朝若是出殡时，又没他一陌纸，空排着三个儿。这正是家贫也显孝子。

（三人云）母亲，人说是葛彪杀了俺父亲来。俺如今寻见那厮，扯到官偿命来。（下）（旦）

I puzzle my head over this terrible news,
Running till I am out of breath
And my voice is just a croak.
I wish I had wings!
What wrong had my husband done?
When I catch his murderer
I shall demand and answer.
He never plotted with the enemy,
Never harmed any man or the state.
If my poor husband is really dead,
I shall sue that wicked scoundrel.
I run through the streets and market,
Wiping my tears.

(*She sees the corpse.*)

Look at those angry wounds!
Here he lies, black and blue.
So devoted a husband and father —
Who could have thought you would die like this?
None knows what will happen from one day to the next.
Covered with blood,
You lie here cold and limp,
Your face like yellow paper.
For an hour I call your name,
But to my horror you will not wake;
And you know how it is at home —
How can we afford a sacrifice
When we bury you tomorrow?
All I have left is these three boys;
It is true that a poor family has good sons.

SONS: Mother, they all say it was Ge Biao who killed our father. We are going to find him and take him to court, to make him pay with his life. (*Exeunt.*)

【那吒令】他本是太学中殿试，怎想他拳头上便死，今日个则落得长街上检尸！更做道见职官，俺是个穷儒士，也索称词。

（净上）自家葛彪是也。饮了几杯酒，无甚事，且回家中去来。（三人上）兀的不是那凶徒！拿住这厮！（做拿住科）是你打死俺父亲来？（净）就是我来，我不怕你！（旦）

【鹊踏枝】若是俺到官时，更做您一枝儿。使不着国戚皇亲，玉叶金枝，便是他龙孙帝子，打杀人也吃官司。

（三人打科，净死科，三人云）这凶徒妆醉不起来。（旦）我试问他。（旦问科）哥哥，俺老的怎生撞着你，你就打死他？你如何推醉，睡在地下不起来？则这般干罢了？你起来，你起来。呀，你三人可不打杀他也！（王三）好也！我并不曾动手。（旦）可怎了也！

【寄生草】你可便斟量着做，似这般有甚意思？你三人非是闲周次，你三人打死虽然是，你三人到惹下刑名事。则被这清风明月两闲人，送了你玉堂金马三学士。

WIFE:

Ge Biao is a scholar of the Imperial College,
Why should he strike a man dead?
Now I must take the corpse home.
He is an official and we are poor,
Yet still I mean to sue him.

(*Enter Ge Biao.*)

GE: I am Ge Biao. I have had a few cups of wine. Now there's nothing to do, I may as well go home.

(*Enter Wang's three sons.*)

SONS: There is the murderer! Catch him! (*They seize Ge.*) You beat our father to death!

GE: What if I did? I am not afraid of you.

WIFE:

I shall charge you in the court!
What does it matter if you are a noble,
Related to the imperial house?
Even the emperor's own sons and grandsons
Must go to court for murder!

(*The three sons set on Ge Biao and kill him.*)

SONS: This murderer is shamming drunk and won't get up.

WIFE: Let me speak to him. (*To Ge.*) See here, what harm did my husband do you that you should beat him to death? And why should you sham drunk on the ground and refuse to get up? You can't escape like that! Get up, get up! Ah! Have you three killed him?

LITTLE WANG: Lucky I didn't hit him!

WIFE: Now what shall we do?

You should have been more careful;
What was the use of beating him like that?
Although you did not pick a quarrel for nothing,
And it was not wrong to kill him,
You will have to go to court.
Your careers are ruined.

（旦指净唱）

【金盏儿】想当时，你可也不三思，这一还一报从来是。想皇天报应不容私，则道你长街上妆好汉，谁想你血泊内也停尸！正是“将军着痛箭，还似射人时”。

（三人）咱家无有钱钞，打这官司使些什么？（旦）

【醉中天】咱每日一瓢饮、一箪食，有几双箸、几张匙。若到官司使钞时，则除典当了闲文字。便这等也不济事。你合死呵今朝便死；虽道是杀人公事，也落个孝顺名儿。

（祗候上）休教走了！拿住这杀人贼者！（旦）

【金盏儿】苦孜孜，泪丝丝，这场烦恼由天赐。把俺横拖倒拽怎推辞！一壁厢磣可可停着老子，一壁厢眼睁睁送了孩儿。可知道福无重受日，祸有并来时。

（祗候）杀人事不同小可，咱见官去来。（旦悲科）

【后庭花】想天公不受私，正是一还一报时。恨小非

(*She points to Ge's corpse.*)

You did not stop to think either
That force would be met by force.
Heaven is just and impartial,
You acted the bully in the street
And now you too lie here a bloody corpse.
A general can be pierced by an arrow too,
Though he likes to shoot at others.

SONS: We have no money. How can we go to court?

WIFE:

Each day one ladle of soup, one single dish —
How many spare chopsticks have we?
We need money to go to court,
But all we have to pawn is a few old books,
And they will not bring us much.
It must be your fate to die;
But though you have killed a man
You are good sons.

(*Enter the Runners.*)

RUNNFRS: Don't let them get away! Catch those murderers!

WIFE:

Bitterness in my heart, tears in my eyes!
Ruin has come down from Heaven!
We are dragged away and cannot even protest.
There lies my husband dead,
And here before my eyes my sons are ruined;
Good fortune never repeats itself,
But troubles come thick and fast.

RUNNERS: Murder is no small offence. Come to the court!

WIFE (*weeping*):

Surely Heaven will not tolerate injustice.
Evil must be repaid,
And all men long for revenge,

君子，无毒不丈夫。你好不寻思，这场公事。你三人痛莫支。你集贤为秀士，跳龙门，折桂枝。为亲爷遭横死，须当是报怨私。若官司拿住尔，审情真，问口词；下脑箍，使拶子。

【柳叶儿】不想这场祸从天至，你可打得来血泊停尸。你为亲爷雪恨合当是，便当刑死赴阴司，也得个孝顺名儿。

（祗候）见官去罢。（旦）孩儿，你每做下这事，可怎了也？（三人）母亲，可怎了也？（旦）

【赚煞】为甚我教你看诗书，习经史，俺待学孟母当时教子。不能够金榜上分明题姓字，则落得犯由牌书写名儿。想当时也是不得已而为之。止不过罪若当刑奏过圣旨，不过是一人处死；须断不了王家宗祀，且不致灭门绝户了俺一家儿。（同下）

But alas! that the three of you shlould be involved,
Three scholars about to pass the dragon gate
And pluck the cassia bough.[17]
Because you took revenge
On your murdered father,
You will be arrested and tried,
Tortured with rack and thumbscrews;
I never knew that we were so ill-starred,
Never knew that you would kill him.
It was right to avenge your father;
Though you are executed
And go to the nether regions,
Your name will be remembered as filial sons.

RUNNERS: Come to the court!

WIFE: Now you have done this, boys, what shall we do?

SONS: Ah, mother, what can we do?

WIFE:

I made you study the classics and history,
As the mother of Mencius taught her son;
But your names will never appear on the golden list,[18]
Instead they will be in the list of felons!
Yet this was no premeditated murder,
And if punishment is decreed
At most only one of you should pay with his life —
How can all my sons be killed?
This will not be the end of our family.

(*Exeunt.*)

第二折

（张千领祇候排衙走科）（张）在衙人马平安，喏！（孤扮包待制上）咚咚衙鼓响，公吏两边排；阎王生死殿，东岳摄魂台。老夫姓包，名拯，字希文。庐州金斗郡四望乡老儿村人也。官拜龙图阁待制学士，正授开封府府尹。今日升厅，坐起早衙。张千，有合佥押的文书，将来老夫佥押。（张）六房吏典，有什么合佥押的文书？（内应科）（张）可不早说？早是我问你。喏！酸枣县解到一起偷马贼赵顽驴。（孤）与我领过来。（祇候押犯人跪科）（孤）开了那行枷者。兀那小厮，你是赵顽驴？是你偷马来？（赵）是小的偷马来。（孤）张千，上了长枷，下在死囚牢里去。（押下）（孤）老夫这一会儿困

ACT II

(*Enter Zhang Qian with Runners.*)

ZHANG: All is ready to open court.

(*Enter Bao Zheng.*)

BAO:

The court drums thunder,
The runners are ranged on two sides;
This is the judgement seat of the King of Hell,
To which all spirits are summoned.

I am Bao Zheng, a native of Laoer Village in Luzhou. I hold the posts of Academician of Longtu Pavilion and Prefect of Kaifeng. I am now going to preside over the morning session in my court. Zhang Qian, bring me whatever documents await my signature.

ZHANG: Secretaries and clerks! Have you any documents for His Honour to sign?

(*There is an answer off.*)

ZHANG: Why didn't you report this before? Your Honour, Suanzao County has sent us a horse thief, Donkey Zhao.

BAO: Bring him in.

(*The Runners bring in Donkey Zhao, who kneels before the prefect.*)

BAO: Remove the cangue. You there, are you Donkey Zhao and did you steal horses?

DONKEY ZHAO: Yes, Your Honour, I did.

BAO: Zhang Qian, fasten the cangue on him and have him sent to the condemned cell.

(*Donkey Zhao is led away.*)

倦，张千，你与六房吏典休要大惊小怪的，老夫暂时歇息咱。（张）大小属官、两廊吏典，休要大惊小怪的，大人歇息哩。（孤做伏案睡做梦科）老夫公事操心，哪里睡的到眼里？老夫闲游玩咱。来到这开封府厅后，一个小角门。我推开这门，我试看则，是一个好花园也。你看那百花烂熳，春景融和。兀那花丛里一个撮角亭子，亭子上结下个蜘蛛罗网。花间飞将一个蝴蝶儿来，正打在罗网中。包拯暗暗伤怀，蝴蝶曾打飞来；休道人无生死，草虫也有非灾。呀！蠢动含灵，皆有佛性。飞将一个大蝴蝶来，救出这蝴蝶去了。呀！又飞了一个蝴蝶，打在罗网中。那大蝴蝶必定来救他。好奇怪也！那大蝴蝶两次三番，只在花丛上飞，不救那小蝴蝶，佯常飞去了。圣人道："恻隐之心，人皆有之。"你不救，等我救。（做放科）（张）喏！午时了也。（孤醒科，云）草虫之蝴蝶，一命在参差。撒然梦惊觉，张千报午时。张千，有什么应审的罪囚？将来我看问。（张）两房吏典，有什么合审的罪囚？领来勘问。（内应科）（张）喏！中牟县解到一起犯人：弟兄三人打死平人葛彪。解至也。（孤）小县中百姓怎敢打死平人！解到也未？（张）解到也。（孤）与我一步一棍打上厅来。（解子押三人上）（旦上，唱）

BAO: I feel a little tired, Zhang Qian. Tell the secretaries to make no noise. I want to take a nap.

ZHANG: Now, gentlemen, no noise! His Honour is resting.

(*The prefect dozes off at the table.*)

BAO: (*talking in his sleep*): Worried by affairs of state, how can I sleep? I have strolled to the back of the hall and found a small gate. Let me open it and have a look. What a beautiful garden! All the flowers are blooming in the warm spring weather. Set among the flowers is a pavilion, with a spider's web on it. A butterfly fluttering from the flowers is caught in the web. The sight makes me sad. Man may die at any hour, and even insects are exposed to danger. Ah, even insects have intelligence! A big butterfly has come to rescue the smaller. Ah, another butterfly has been caught in the web. No doubt the big butterfly will save it again.... How strange! The big butterfly is simply fluttering around the flowers. Instead of saving the smaller one, it has flown off. Well, as the sage said, all men have a sense of pity. Since it will not save the butterfly, let me do so. (*He makes a gesture as if releasing the butterfly.*)

ZHANG: Your Honour, it is noon.

BAO: (*waking*):

In my dream a butterfly's life
Was hanging in the balance,
When I woke to hear Zhang Qian
Announcing that it is noon.

Well, Zhang Qian, are there any culprits awaiting trial? Send them in.

ZHANG: Secretries, are there any culprits awaiting trial? Send them in.

(*There is a shout off.*)

ZHANG: Your Honour, some felons have been sent from Zhongmou County. They are three brothers who beat the noble Ge Biao to death.

BAO: How dare men of a small county kill a noble? Are they here?

ZHANG: They are.

BAO: Bring them into court, beating them.

(*A Runner brings in the three sons and their mother.*)

WIFE:

【南吕一枝花】解到这无人情御史台，早来到有官法开封府。把三个未发迹小秀士，生扭做吃勘问死囚徒。空教我意下惆惕，把不定心惊惧。赤紧的贼儿胆底虚，教我把罪犯私下招伏，不比那小处官司孔目。

【梁州】这开封府王条清正，不比那中牟县官吏糊涂。扑咚咚阶下升衙鼓，唬的我手忙脚乱，使不得胆大心粗，惊的我魂飞魄丧，走的我力尽筋舒。这公事不比寻俗，就中间担负公徒。嗨，嗨，嗨！一壁厢老夫主在地停尸。更，更，更，赤紧地子母每坐牢系狱。呀，呀，呀！眼见的弟兄每受刃遭诛。早是怕怖！我向这屏墙边侧耳偷睛觑，谁曾见这官府！则今日当厅定祸福，别辨个实虚。

（旦同众见官跪科）（张）犯人当面。（孤）张千，开了行枷，与那解子批回去。（做开枷科）（王三）母亲、哥哥，咱家去来。（孤）哪里去？这里比你那中牟县那！张千，这三个小厮是打死人的，那婆子是什么人？必定是证见人。若不是呵，敢与这小厮关亲？兀那婆子，这两个是你什么人？（旦）这两个是大孩儿。（孤）这个小的呢？（旦）是我第三的孩儿。（孤）噤声！你可甚治家有法？

We are brought to this cruel yamen in Kaifeng,
Where the emperor's justice is administered.
Three scholars, who have not yet made their name,
Dragged here and tried as criminals.
Trembling and fearful,
Knowing our guilt,
We shall have to confess our crime.
This is not the county court;
Here in Kaifeng they are strict,
With none of our easy-going country ways.
The drum thunders beneath the steps;
Awe-struck and terrified,
I have lost my head and am utterly exhausted.
This is no light offence but a serious crime.
There my old man lies dead on the ground,
And here mother and sons are arrested.
My eyes shall see my own children executed.
I peep fearfully at this court
Which I never entered before.
Today our fate will be decided here,
The prefect will decide between right and wrong.

(*She and her sons kneel before the prefect.*)

ZHANG: The felons are here, Your Honour.

BAO: Remove their cangues, Zhang Qian, and dismiss the runner.

(*The cangues are removed.*)

LITTLE WANG: Let's go home now, mother.

BAO: Where do you think you are going? This is not your county office. Zhang Qian, I take it these three young men are the murderers, but who is the old woman? Is she a witness or some relation? Speak up, woman. Are these two young men related to you?

WIFE: They are my sons.

BAO: And the boy?

WIFE: He is my youngest.

想当日：孟母教子，居必择邻；陶母教子，剪发待宾；陈母教子，衣紫腰金。你个村妇教子，打死平人。从实招了者！（旦）

【贺新郎】孩儿每万千死罪犯公徒。那厮每情理难容，俺孩儿杀人可恕。俺穷滴滴寒贱为黎庶，告爷爷与孩儿每做主。这三个自小来攻考文书，他子会依文典、习礼义，那里会定计策、厮亏图。百般的拷打难分诉。岂不闻“三人误大事，六耳不通谋。”

（孤）不打不招。张千，与我加力打者！（旦悲唱）

【隔尾】俺孩儿犯着徒流绞斩萧何律，枉读了恭俭温良孔圣书。拷打的浑身上怎生觑！打的来伤筋动骨，更疼似悬头刺股。他每爷饭娘羹，何曾受这般苦！

（孤）三个人必有一个为首的。是谁先打死人来？（王大）也不干母亲事，也不干两个兄弟事，是孩儿打死人来。（王二）爷爷，也不干母亲事，也不干哥哥、兄弟

BAO: So this is the way you taught your sons! In ancient times the mother of Mencius moved house in order to find good neighbours for her son. The mother of Tao made him cut his hair before seeing guests, and the mother of Chen taught her son until he wore the official purple and golden belt. But you, a village woman, have taught your sons to kill a noble. Confess the truth now!

WIFE:

I am wretched to think my sons have broken the law,
But that scoundrel's crime was more than they could bear,
And they should be forgiven for killing him.
We are poor, humble folk,
Your Honour must protect us!
These three lads are all diligent students,
Whose conduct has always been guided by the classics —
How could they have plotted to kill him?
Tortured and beaten, they cannot put their case,
But how could three of them have made this plot?

BAO: You will not confess without a beating. Zhang Qian, give them a good beating.

WIFE (*weeping*):

My sons have broken the law:
Was it for this they studied the Confucian classics?
The poor lads are beaten black and blue,
Their flesh is torn, their bones splintered —
Much worse than self-inflicted pain during study.[19]
Brought up by loving parents,
They never knew such agony before.

BAO: One of these three youths must be the ringleader. Which of you was responsible for that man's death?

BIG WANG: My mother and brothers had nothing to do with this. I killed him.

MIDDLE WANG: Your Honour, my mother and brothers had nothing to do with this. I killed him.

事，是孩儿打死人来。（王三）大人爷爷，也不干母亲事，也不干两个哥哥事，也不干我事。（旦）并不干三个孩儿事。当时是皇亲葛彪先打死妾身夫主，妾身疼忍不过，一时乘忿争斗，将他打死。委的是妾身来。（孤）胡说！你也招承，我也招承，想是串定的。必须要一人抵命。张千，与我着实打者！（旦）

【斗虾蟆】静巉巉无人救，眼睁睁活受苦。孩儿每索与他招状，官人跟前拜覆：那厮将人欺负，打死咱家丈夫。官人监收媳妇，公人如狼似虎。相公停嗔息怒，休说麻槌脑箍。六问三推，刑狱勘问，有甚数目？打的浑身血污。大哥声冤叫屈，官人不由分诉。二哥活受地狱，疼痛如何担负？三哥打的更毒，老身牵肠割肚。这壁厢、那壁厢：由由忬忬，眼眼厮觑，来来去去，啼啼哭哭。则被你打杀人也待制龙图。暗想当初老子，可不儿孙自有儿孙福。难吞吐，没气路。短叹长吁，愁肠似火，泪雨如珠。

（孤）我试看看这来文咱。（做看科）中牟县官好生不才也，如何这文书上写着“王大、王二、王三打死平人

LITTLE WANG: Your Honour, my mother and brothers had nothing to do with this, and neither had I.

WIFE: My three sons had nothing to do with this. When that noble, Ge Biao, beat my husband to death, I could not choke back my anger. So I fought with him and killed him. It was my doing.

BAO: Nonsense! You all admit to murder — this is a plot. We must find the true murderer to make him pay with his life. Zhang Qian, give them another beating.

WIFE:

No one will speak up to save them;
I have to look on, helpless.
Make a clean breast of things, sons!
I will plead again with the prefect.
That bully murdered my husband,
Yet Your Honour had me arrested
By runners as fierce as tigers and wolves.
Do not be angry, Your Honour!
You have instruments of torture, hammer and screws,
And you question these lads again and again,
Beating them till the blood streams from their wounds.
My eldest boy cries out at this injustice,
But Your Honour turns a deaf ear;
My second is suffering the torments of hell —
How can he bear such torture?
My third is beaten even more cruelly,
And the sight makes my heart bleed.
We gaze at each other, weeping.
You are killing them, Your Honour!
Their father thought his sons would do well;
Now we cannot put our case, we can only sigh;
My heart is broken, my tears stream down like rain.

BAO: Let me read the charge. (*He looks at it.*) What a fool the magistrate of Zhongmou County must be! This charge says that Big Wang, Middle

葛彪"?这县里就无个排房吏典?这三个小厮必有名讳。更不呵,也有个小名儿。兀那婆子,你大小厮叫做什么?(旦)叫做金和。(孤)第二的小厮叫做什么?(旦)叫做铁和。(孤)这第三个呢?(旦)叫做石和。(王三)尚。(孤)什么尚?(王三)石和尚。(孤)嗨。可知打死人哩,庶民人家取这等刚硬名字。敢是金和打死人来?(旦)

【牧羊关】这个是金呵,有什么难镕处。(孤)敢是石和打死人来?(旦)这个是石呵,怎做的虚。(孤)敢是铁和打死人来?(旦)这个便是铁呵,怎当那官法如炉。(孤)打这赖肉顽皮!(旦)非干是孩儿每赖肉顽皮,委的衔冤负屈。(孤)张千,便好道:"杀人的偿命,欠债的还钱。"把那大的小厮拿出去与人偿命。(旦)眼睁睁难搭救,簇拥着下阶基。教我两下里难顾瞻,百般里无是处。

包待制爷爷好葫芦提也!(孤)我着那大的儿子偿命,兀

Wang and Little Wang beat to death the noble Ge Biao. Hasn't he got a proper secretary? These three lads must have names, or at least nicknames. What is your eldest son's name, woman?

WIFE: Gold.

BAO: And your second son's?

WIFE: Iron.

BAO: And the third?

WIFE: Stone.

LITTLE WANG: Broke.

BAO: What do you mean, broke?

LITTLE WANG: Stony broke.

BAO: Stop cracking jokes. This is a murder case. Why should common citizens choose such unusual names? Did Gold Wang kill this man?

WIFE:

Gold is not hard to refine.

BAO: Did Stone Wang kill this man?

WIFE:

Stone is strong and true.

BAO: Did Iron Wang kill this man?

WIFE:

Even iron would melt in the furnace of the law.

BAO: Have these stubborn scoundrels beaten!

WIFE:

They are not being stubborn:
They are unjustly accused!

BAO: You know the proverb: A murderer must pay with his life, a debtor must pay his debt. Have the eldest taken out and executed, Zhang Qian.

WIFE:

I look on and cannot save him —
He is being dragged down the steps!
I am at my wit's end!

What a fool this prefect is!

BAO: What did that woman say just now when I ordered her eldest son to

那婆子说什么？（张）那婆子手扳定枷梢说，包待制爷爷葫芦提。（孤）那婆子他道我葫芦提，与我拿过来。（旦跪科）（孤）着你大儿子偿命，你怎生说我葫芦提？（旦）老婆子怎敢说大人葫芦提？则是我孩儿孝顺，不争杀坏了他，教谁人养活老身？（孤）既是他母亲说大小厮孝顺，又多邻家保举，这是老夫差了。留着大的养活他。张千，着第二的偿命。（旦）

【隔尾】一壁厢大哥行牵挂着亲肠肚，一壁厢二哥行关连着痛肺腑。要偿命留下孩儿，宁可将婆子去。似这般狠毒，又无处告诉，手扳定枷稍叫声“屈”！

包待制爷爷好葫芦提！（孤）又做什么大惊小怪的？（张）那婆子又说大人葫芦提。（孤）与我拿过来。（旦跪科）（孤）兀那婆子，将你第二的小厮偿命，怎生又说我葫芦提？（旦）怎敢说大人葫芦提？则是第二的小厮会营运生理，不争着他偿命，谁养活老婆子？（孤）着大的偿命，你说他孝顺。着第二的偿命，你说他营运生理，却着谁去偿命？（王三自带枷科）（孤）兀那厮做什么？（王

be executed?

ZHANG: She clutched the cangue and called Your Honour a fool.

BAO: So she called me a fool, did she? Bring her over here.

(*She kneels before the prefect.*)

BAO: I decreed that your eldest son should pay with his life. Why did you call me a fool?

WIFE: How dare I call Your Honour such a name? But this boy is a good son. If you kill him, who will support me?

BAO: Since his mother says the eldest is a good son, and the neighbours will vouch for him, I must be wrong. Let the eldest live to support her. Zhang Qian, take the second son to be executed.

WIFE:

I cannot bear to give up Gold,
Yet Iron's death would also break my heart.
If we must pay with a life,
Let my boys be spared
And let me die in their place.
This cruel prefect will not listen to reason,
So I cling to the cangue and cry that injustice is done!

What a fool this prefect is!

BAO: What did that woman call out this time?

ZHANG: Your Honour, she called you a fool again.

BAO: Bring her over here.

(*She kneels before the prefect.*)

BAO: See here, woman, I have just sentenced your second son instead. Why did you call me a fool again?

WIFE: How dare I call Your Honour such a name? But my second son has a good head for business. If you kill him, who will support me?

BAO: When I sentence your eldest to death,you say he is a good son. When I sentence your second to death, you say he has a good head for business. Who is to pay for the crime then?

(*Little Wang puts on a cangue himself.*)

BAO: What is that boy doing?

三）大哥又不偿命，二哥又不偿命，眼见的是我了。不如早做个人情。（孤）也罢！张千，拿那小的出去偿命。（做推转科）（孤）兀那婆子，这第三的小厮偿命，可中么？（旦）是了。可不道"三人同行小的苦"，他偿命的是。（孤）我不葫芦提？（旦）大人爷爷不葫芦提。（孤）噤声！张千，拿回来。争些着婆子瞒过老夫。眼前放着个前房后继：这两个小厮必是你亲生的；这一个小厮必是你乞养过房螟蛉之子，不着疼热，所以着他偿命。兀那婆子，说的是呵，我自有个主意。说的不是呵，我不道饶了你哩！（旦）三个都是我的孩儿，着我说些什么？（孤）你若不实说，张千，与我打着者！（旦）大哥、二哥、三哥，我说则说，你则休生分了。（孤）这大小厮是你的亲儿么？（旦）

【牧羊关】这孩儿虽不曾亲生养，却须是咱乳哺。（孤）这第二的呢？（旦）这一个偌大小是老婆子抬举。（孤）兀那小的呢？（旦打悲科）这一个是我的亲儿，这两个我是他的继母。（孤）兀那婆子近前来，你差了也。前家儿着一个偿命，留着你亲生孩儿养活你，可不好哪？（旦）大人差了也。不争着前家儿偿了命，显得后尧婆忒心毒。我若学嫉妒的桑新妇，不羞见那贤达的鲁义姑。

LITTLE WANG: Since my eldest brother is not to die, nor my second brother either, it looks as if it will be me. So I may as well make a noble gesture.

BAO: All right. Zhang Qian, take the youngest to be executed.

(*Little Wang is pushed away.*)

BAO: Well, woman, do you agree to let your youngest pay for the crime?

WIFE: Yes. The proverb says: When there are three partners, the youngest shoulders the hardships. He is the one who should pay.

BAO: Am I a fool or not?

WIFE: Your Honour is not.

BAO: Wait! Zhang Qian, bring him back. I was nearly taken in by this woman. I see now that this is a case of different treatment for one's own children and those adopted. These two older lads must be your own sons, while the youngest is adopted. As you have no fondness for him, you want him to pay for the crime. Speak up, woman. If you tell the truth, I shall take steps accordingly. If you lie, I shall not spare you.

WIFE: All three are my sons. What do you want me to confess?

BAO: Since she won't tell the truth, Zhang Qian, beat them!

WIFE: Sons, I shall have to tell the truth. Don't hold it against me.

BAO: Is the eldest boy your own?

WIFE:

He is not my son, but I nurse him.

BAO: How about the second?

WIFE:

I tended him as a child.

BAO: And the youngest?

WIFE (*weeping*): He is my own. The others are adopted.

BAO: Now look here, woman, aren't you making a mistake? Wouldn't it be better to let one of the adopted sons pay for this crime, and keep your own child to support you?

WIFE: That would not be right, Your Honour. If I let the first wife's son die, it would look as if I were a heartless stepmother. If I took advantage of these boys, I should blush to remember those virtuous mothers of old.

（孤）兀那婆子，你还着他三人心服。果是谁打死人来？

（旦）

【红芍药】浑身是口怎支吾？恰似个没口的葫芦。打的来皮开肉绽损肌肤，鲜血模糊，恰浑似活地狱。三个儿都教死去。你都官官相为倚亲属，更做道国戚皇族。

（旦打悲科）

【菩萨梁州】大哥罪犯遭诛，二哥死生别路，三哥身归地府，干闪下我这老业身躯。大哥孝顺识亲疏，二哥留下着当门户。第三个哥哥休言语，你偿命正合去。常言道“三人同行小的苦”，公人每大叫高呼。

（孤）听了这婆子所言，始信道：良贾深藏若虚，君子盛德，容貌若愚。这件事，老夫见为母者大贤，为子者至孝。为母者与陶、孟同列，为子者与曾、闵无二。适间老夫昼寐，梦见一个蝴蝶坠在蛛网中，一个大蝴蝶来救出。次者亦然。后来一小蝴蝶亦坠网中，大蝴蝶虽见不救，飞腾而去。老夫心存恻隐，救小蝴蝶出离罗网。天使老夫预知先兆之事，救这小的之

BAO: Well, woman, to be fair to them, you must tell the truth. Who killed that man?

WIFE:

How can I make reply?
I will not answer this question.
Their flesh is in shreds,
They stream with blood,
This is a living hell!
All my three boys may be killed,
For officials are all related,
And the prefect takes the side of the dead noble.

(*She weeps.*)

Now if my eldest son dies for this crime,
My second forfeits his life as well,
And my third becomes a shade too,
I shall be left alone, a poor old woman.
Gold is good to his mother,
Iron, if set free, will support the family:
So say no more, Stony,
It is right you should pay with your life;
The third of three partners is always the one to suffer,
And now the runners are shouting again.

BAO: Hearing this woman, I realize the truth of the saying: A clever merchant will apear to have no goods, and a worthy gentleman will look like a fool. I see what fine people this mother and her sons are — they stand comparison with the men of old. As I was dozing just now, I dreamed that a butterfly caught in a spider's web was rescued by a big butterfly. When this had happened twice, another small butterfly was caught, but instead of saving it the large one flew away. As my heart was touched, I saved the little creature myself. In fact, Heaven was forewarning me of this case so that I might save the boy's life.

I weighed the case according to the law,
But this suit is most involved.

命。恰才我依条犯法分轻重，不想这分外却有别词讼。杀死平人怎干休？莫言罪犯难轻纵。先教长男赴云阳，为言孝顺能供奉。后教次子去餐刀，又言营运充日用。我着那最小的幼男去当刑，他欢喜紧将儿发送。他将那前家儿子苦哀矜，自见亲儿不悲痛。似这等三从四德可褒封，贞烈贤达宜请俸。忽然一事上心来，天使游魂先惊动：三个草虫伤蛛丝，便和那子母官司都一等。三番继母弃亲儿，正应着午时一枕蝴蝶梦。张千，把一干人都下在死囚牢中去。（旦慌向前扯科，唱）

【水仙子】则见他前推后拥厮揪捽，我与你扳住枷梢高叫屈。眼睁睁有去路无回路，好教我百般的没是处。这祸儿便死待何如！好和弱随将去，死共活拦当住，我这里紧攥住衣服。

（张千推旦科，押三人下）（旦唱）

【收尾】包龙图往常断事会着数，今日为官不大古。枉教你坐黄堂，带虎符；受荣华，请俸禄。俺孩儿，忒冤屈。不睹事，下牢狱。割舍了，待泼

The murder of a noble cannot be pardoned,
Nor the culprit go unpunished.
First I sentenced the eldest lad to death,
But she said he was a good son;
When I sentenced the second,
She said he must support her;
When I sentenced the third,
She was pleased and let him go.
She showed most kindness to the adopted sons,
And hardened her heart against her own flesh and blood.
Such virtuous conduct is most praiseworthy,
Such a good mother deserves to be rewarded.
This flashed into my mind
Because Heaven had given me warning
Through the dream of three butterflies caught in a web.
That was precisely the case of this mother and sons:
Three times she spoke, and abandoned her own child,
Exactly as I saw in my dream at noon.

Zhang Qian, take all three of them to the condemned cell.

WIFE (*trying desperately to stop them*):

They are dragging and pushing them off;
I seize the cangue and cry out against such injustice!
They are going, never to return.
I am distracted. What if I die with them?
Yes, best to share their death:
Let me catch hold of their clothes.

(*Zhang Qian pushes her away and takes the three sons off.*)

WIFE:

This prefect has a reputation for justice,
But today he passed wrong judgement.
He sits in the court with his insignia of office,
And draws a high salary — but all for what?
My sons are unjustly condemned and thrown into gaol.

做：告都堂，诉省部；撅皇城，打怨鼓；见銮舆，便唐突。呆老婆唱今古，又无人肯做主，则不如觅死处。眼不见鳏寡孤独，也强如没归着。痛煞煞、哭啼啼、活受苦。（下）

（孤）张千，你近前来。可是恁的……（张）可是中也不中？（孤）贼禽兽！我的言语可是中也不中？我扶立当今圣明主，欲播清风千万古。这些公事断不开，怎坐南衙开封府！（同下）

I am desperate — I must act.
Shall I appeal to the provincial governor,
Beat the court drum in the capital,
Or call aloud before the imperial carriage?
No, who would pay any heed to a foolish woman?
To die would be better than to live on alone
With no one to support me,
Weeping and wretched to the end of my days. (*Exit.*)

BAO: Come here, Zhang Qian! What do you think of all this?

ZHANG: Are you sure you are right, Your Honour?

BAO: Do you question my orders, you rascal?

Well I serve my sagacious sovereign,
My fame will endure through the ages;
Unless I pass just sentence on this case,
How can I be the prefect of Kaifeng?

(*Exeunt.*)

第三折

（张千上）手执无情棒，怀揣滴泪钱；晓行狼虎路，夜伴死尸眠。自家张千便是。有王大、王二、王三下在死囚牢中，与我拿将他三个出来。（王大、王二上）哥哥可怜见。（张）别过枷梢来，打三下杀威棒。（打三下科）（张）那第三个在哪里？（王三上）我先来了。（张）李万，抬过押床来。丢过这滚肚索去，扯紧着。（做扯科）（三人叫科）（张）李万，你家去吃饭。我看着，则怕提牢官来。（旦上）我三个孩儿都下在死囚牢中，我叫化了些残汤剩饭，送与孩儿每吃去。

【正宫端正好】遥望着死囚牢，恰离了悲天院。谁敢道半步俄延？排门儿叫化都寻遍，讨了些泼剩饭和杂面。

ACT III

(*Enter Zhang Qian.*)

ZHANG:

A pitiless club in my hands,
Tear-stained money in my pockets;
A tiger or wolf by day,
At night I sleep beside corpses.

I am Zhang Qian. Now the three Wang brothers are in the condemned cell. Let me have them in.

(*Enter Big and Middle Wang.*)

BOTH: Have pity on us, brother!

ZHANG: Turn those cangues round, and let me give you three strokes apiece. (*He beats them.*) Where is the third?

(*Enter Little Wang.*)

LITTLE WANG: Here I am.

(*Enter Li Wan.*)

ZHANG: Li Wan, bring that bed over and pass me the rope. Let's truss them up tight. (*He pulls the rope and the boys groan.*) Now, Li Wan, go and have your meal while I look after them. I hope the gaoler doesn't turn up.

(*Exit Li Wan. Enter Wang's Wife.*)

WIFE: All my three sons are in the condemned cell. I have been begging and got some scraps of food for them.

Coming from the alms-house to the prison,
Not daring to lose a second,
I have begged from door to door
And got some left-overs — noodles and dumplings.

【滚绣球】俺孩儿本待做状元，坐琴堂、请俸钱。谁曾遭这般刑宪？又不曾犯五刑之属三千。我不肯吃、不肯穿，烧地卧、炙地眠。谁曾受这般贫贱？正按着陈婆婆古语常言：他须不求金玉重重贵，却甚儿孙个个贤？受煞熬煎。

（做到牢门科）早来到也。我拽动这铃索则。（张）则怕是提牢官来，我开开这门，看看是谁拽动铃索来？（旦）是我拽来。（张打科）老村婆子！这是你家里？你来做什么？（旦）我与三个孩儿送饭来。（张）灯油钱也无，冤苦钱也无。俺吃着死囚的衣饭，有钞将些来使。（旦）哥哥怜悯！可怜见一个老的被人打死了，三个孩儿又在死囚牢内；老身吃了早晨，无有晚夕，前街后巷叫化了些残汤剩饭，与孩儿每充饥。哥哥，可怜见。

【倘秀才】叫化的剩饭重煎再煎，补衲的破袄儿翻穿了正穿。哥哥，则这件旧衣服送你罢。有这个旧褐袖与哥哥且做些冤苦钱。（张）我也不要你的。（旦）谢哥哥相觑当，厮周全，把孩儿每可怜。

（张）罪已问定也，救不的了。（旦）

【脱布衫】争奈一家一计肠肚萦牵，一上一下语话

My sons were going to pass the examination,
Sit in courtrooms and draw high pay;
But instead they got into this trouble!
They have done nothing wrong,
We skimped and scraped,
And slept on the bare ground —
No one ever put up with such poverty.
As the proverb says: Good sons
Are better than riches and rank.
For this I put up with much.

(*She reaches the gaol gate.*) Here I am. I'll pull the bell.

ZHANG: I'm afraid the gaoler is here. Let me open the gate and see who it is.

WIFE: It is me.

ZHANG (*striking her*): Is this your home, old crone? What are you doing here?

WIFE: I've brought some food for my three sons.

ZHANG: They have paid me nothing for the lamp oil and this thankless job. I have to live on these gaol-birds, so give me what money you have.

WIFE: Have a heart, brother! My old man was beaten to death and my three sons are here in gaol. I can barely keep going myself, and have simply begged some scraps for my hungry children. Don't be hard on us!

Beggars' scraps heated up again,
Rags I have mended;
Take this tattered coat, brother,
And this old sleeve as a tip.

ZHANG: I don't want them.

WIFE:

Please keep an eye on these wretches;
Have pity on them, brother.

ZHANG: Sentence has already been passed. I can't help them now.

WIFE:

We are one loving family,

熬煎。一左一右把孩儿顾恋，一捋一把雨泪涟涟。

【醉太平】数说起罪愆，委实的衔冤，我这里烦烦恼恼怨青天。告哥哥可怜，他三个足丢没乱眼脑剔抽秃刷转，依柔乞煞手脚滴羞笃速战，迷留没乱救。他叫破咽喉，气的我前合后偃。

（张）放你进来，我掩上这门。（旦进见科）兀的不是我孩儿！（众悲科）（王大）母亲,你做什么来？（旦）我与你送饭来。（旦向张千云）哥哥，怎生放我孩儿吃些饭也好？（张）你没手？兀那婆子,喂你那孩儿！（旦喂王大、王二科）

【笑和尚】我、我、我，两三步走向前，将、将、将，把饭食从头劝；我、我、我，一匙匙都抄遍。你、你、你，胡噎饥，你、你、你，润喉咽。（王三）娘也，我也吃些儿！（旦）石和尚好共歹一口口刚刚咽。

（旦将饭都倾在地上科，云）大哥，这里有个烧饼，你吃，休教石和看见。兀二哥，这里有个烧饼，你吃，休叫石和看见。

【叨叨令】叫化的些残汤剩饭，那里有重罗面！你不想堂食玉酒琼林宴。想当初长枷钉出中牟县，却不道布衣走上黄金殿。兀的不苦杀人也么哥！兀的不苦杀人也么哥！告你个提牢押狱休埋怨。

大哥，我去也。你有什么说话？（王大）母亲，家中有一

My heart bleeds for these boys,
My tears rain down.
It is unjust to accuse them of a crime;
I call on Heaven, and beg you to have pity.
There they lie, rolling their eyes,
Trembling in every limb.
I have cried myself hoarse to save them,
And despair has bent me double.

ZHANG: All right. Come in. Let me close the gate.

WIFE (*entering the gaol*): My poor children!

(*The three boys weep.*)

BIG WANG: Mother, what are you doing here?

WIFE: I've brought you food. (*She turns to Zhang.*) Could you set them free, brother, to eat?

ZHANG: Haven't you got hands, woman? Feed them yourself.

WIFE (*feeding her two elder sons*):

I stumble forward to feed my boys.
Spoon after spoon I satisfy their hunger,
Drop after drop I quench their thirst

LITTLE WANG: Give me a little, mother.

WIFE:

Here's a mouthful for you, boy.

(*She puts the food on the ground.*)

Here is some bread for you, Gold. Don't let Stony see it.

Here is some bread for you, Iron. Don't let Stony see it.

Beggars' leavings, no rich fare,
No scholars' feast in the imperial hall.
You were hauled here from the county court in cangues,
Not walking as candidates to the golden palace.
Ah, this will be the death of me!
But it is useless to murmur against the gaol.

I am going, Gold. Have you anything to say?

BIG WANG: There is a volume of the *Four Books* at home, mother. Sell it

本《四书》，卖了替父亲买些纸烧。（旦）二哥有什么话说？（王二）母亲，我有一本《孟子》，卖了替父亲做些经忏。（王三哭云）我也没的分付你，你把你的头来我捞一捞。（旦出科）（张千云）兀那婆子，你要欢喜么？（旦）我可知要欢喜哩。（张千入牢科，云）那个是大的？（王大）小人是大的。（张）放水火！（王大做出科）（张）兀那婆子，你这大的孝顺，保领出去养活你。你见了这大的儿子，你欢喜么？（旦）我可知欢喜哩。（张）我着你大欢喜。（做入牢科，云）那个是第二的？（王二）小人便是。（张）起来，放水火！（做放出科）（张）兀那婆子，再与你这第二的，能营运养活你。（旦）哥哥，那第三个孩儿呢？（张）把他盆吊死，替葛彪偿命去。明日早墙底下来认尸。（旦）

【上小楼】将两个哥哥放免，把第三的孩儿推转。想着我咽苦吞甘，十月怀耽，乳哺三年。不争教大哥哥、二哥哥身遭刑宪，教人道桑新妇不分良善。

【幺】你本待冤报冤，到做了颠倒颠。岂不闻杀人

to buy paper money for father's sacrifice.

WIFE: Have you anything to say, Iron?

MIDDLE WANG: I have a volume of Mencius, mother. Sell it to pay for father's sacrifice.

LITTLE WANG (*weeping*): I have nothing. Let me stroke your head a moment.

(*Their mother goes out.*)

ZHANG: Hey, woman! Do you want some good news?

WIFE: Indeed I do.

ZHANG (*entering the gaol*): Where is the eldest son?

BIG WANG: Here.

ZHANG: You can go. (*Big Wang leaves the gaol.*) Hey, woman, since this eldest boy is a good son, you can take him back to look after you. Are you glad to see him?

WIFE: Indeed I am!

ZHANG: I'll give you some more good news. (*He enters the gaol again.*) Where is the second son?

MIDDLE WANG: Here.

ZHANG: Get up, you can go too. (*He lets Middle Wang out.*) Hey, woman! As your second boy has a good head for business, you can take him back to support you.

WIFE: How about my youngest?

ZHANG: He will be hanged till he is dead, to pay for the death of Ge Biao. Come first thing tomorrow to pick up his corpse outside the wall.

WIFE:

The two elder boys are free,
But the third is a prisoner still.
After all that I went through,
Carrying and nursing him!
But if I let his elder brothers be killed,
They will call me a heartless stepmother.
This is unjust — you are bearing the brunt for others;
Still, a life must pay for a life,

偿命，罪而当刑，死而无怨。（做看王三科）若是我两三番将他留恋，教人道后尧婆两头三面。

（王大、王二）母亲，我怎舍得兄弟也！（旦）大哥、二哥，家去来，休烦恼。

【快活三】教他死去煞可怜，教你小兄弟丧黄泉。（做觑王三悲科）教我扭回身，忍不住泪涟涟。（王大、王二悲科）（旦）罢，罢！咱回去来。教他便死而无怨。

【朝天子】我可便可怜，孩儿忒少年。何日得重相见？不争将前家儿一命掩黄泉，枉惹得后代人埋怨。我这里自揣自推到三十余遍，畅好是苦痛也么天！到来日一刀两段，尸横在市廛，再不见石和面。

【尾声】做爷的不曾烧一陌纸钱，做儿的又当了罪愆，爷和儿要见何时见？若要再相逢一面，则除是梦儿中咱子母团圆。（下）（王大、王二随下）

（王三云）张千哥哥，我大哥、二哥都哪里去了？（张）大人的言语，你大哥、二哥都饶了，着养活你母亲去了。只着你替葛彪偿命。（王三）饶了我两个哥哥，着我偿命去？把这两面枷我都带上。虽然我死，正是三家厮靠。哥哥，我明日怎么死？（张）把你盆吊死！三十板

So die content!

(*She looks back at Little Wang.*)

If I keep turning back again and again,
They will say I am faint-hearted.

BIG and MIDDLE WANG: Mother, how can we leave our brother to die?

WIFE: Come home with me, children. Don't grieve for him.

Your unhappy younger brother will be killed
And go to the nether regions.

(*She gazes at Little Wang and weeps.*)

I turn back and shed tears.

(*The two brothers weep.*)

All right, let us go.

He will die content.
Poor child, so young in years,
We shall never meet again.
I cannot let the sons of others be killed,
Or later generations will reproach me,.
I stamp my foot in despair three dozen times.
Tomorrow he will lie dead in the market-place;
I shall never see Stony again.
Before I have burned the paper money for my husband,
My child is found guilty too.
When will son and. father meet?
In dreams alone
Shall I see my son again.

(*She goes out, followed by Big Wang and Middle Wang.*)

LITTLE WANG: Where are my brothers?

ZHANG: By His Honour's orders, your two brothers have been pardoned and sent home to support your mother. You alone will pay for Ge Biao's death.

LITTLE WANG: So my two brothers are spared. and I must pay with my life. Put the two other cangues on me then. Though I alone am to die, the three of us are one. How shall I die tomorrow, brother?

高墙丢过去。(王三)哥哥，你丢我时放仔细些，我肚子上有个疖子哩！（张）你性命也不保哩！（王三）

【端正好】腹揽五车书，(张)你怎么唱？（王三）是曲尾。学成《礼记》和《周易》。眼睁睁死限相随！指望待为官为相身荣贵，今日个毕罢了名和利。

【滚绣球】包待制比问牛的省气力，俺父亲比那教子的少见识，俺秀才每比那题桥人无那五陵豪气。眼睁睁棍棒淋漓，包待制又葫芦提，令史每装不知。两边厢列着祗候人役，貌堂堂都是一火洒日娘的。隔牢撺彻墙头去，却甚一举成名天下知？张千，得我日你奶奶歪屁！（下）(张千随下)

ZHANG: You will be hanged till you are dead, then thrown over this thirty-foot wall.

LITTLE WANG: Be careful when you throw me, brother. I have a boil on my belly.

ZHANG: You'll be dead by then.

LITTLE WANG:

A bellyful of learning....

ZHANG: So you still want to sing, eh?

LITTLE WANG: Yes, my last song.

...is no use to me at all.
I studied the Book of Rites, the Book of Change,
But death has caught up with me.
My ambition was to be a high official,
But now all fame and wealth have passed me by.
This prefect is an irresponsible judge,
My father was a fool to make me study,
And I am no brilliant scholar after all,
To get myself beaten with a bastinado.
The prefect is a foolish bureaucrat,
The clerks pretend to know nothing,
And the runners ranged in the court
Are a worthless bunch of fellows.
By being thrown over the wall
I shall win renown throughout the empire,
And a curse on you, Zhang Qian!

(*He goes out, followed by Zhang Qian.*)

第四折

（王三背赵顽驴尸上，伏定）（王大，王二上）咱同母亲寻三哥尸首去来。母亲，行动些。（旦上）听的说石和孩儿盆吊死了，他两个哥哥抬尸首去了。我叫化了些纸钱，将着柴火烧埋孩儿去。

【双调新水令】我从未拔白悄悄出城来，恐怕外人知大惊小怪。我叫化的乱烘烘一陌纸，拾得粗坌坌几根柴。俺孩儿落不得席卷椽抬，谁想有这一解。

（打悲科）

【驻马听】孩儿呵！你那报怨心怀，和那横死爷相逢在分界牌。若相见时呵，您两个施呈手策，把那杀人贼推下望乡台。黑洞洞天色恰拔白，静巉巉迥野荒郊外，隐隐似有人来，觑绝时教我添惊骇。

ACT IV

(*Little Wang carries in Donkey Zhao's corpse, and crouches on the ground. Enter Big Wang and Middle Wang.*)

BIG and MIDDLE WANG: We have come with our mother to look for Stony's body. This way, mother!

(*Enter Wang's Wife.*)

WIFE: We hear that Little Wang has been hanged, so his two brothers have gone to fetch the corpse. I have begged some cash to buy sacrificial paper money. I have also brought some firewood to burn and bury his body.

Before dawn I slipped out of the city,
Fearful lest folk should find out
And make trouble for me.
I have bought some paper with money I begged,
And picked up a few sticks of firewood.
To think that my son should die like this —
Without a mat to cover him or a coffin.

(*She weeps.*)

Ah, my son, unjustly killed,
You will meet your father at the dividing line,
Where you must work together
To push the wicked murderer down to hell!
The dark sky is turning white,
All is quiet in this lonely stretch of country,
At a distance some men are approaching,

（王大,王二背尸上）母亲哪里？这不是三哥尸首！（旦做认悲科）

【夜行船】慌急列教咱观了面色，血模糊污尽尸骸。我与你慌解下麻绳，急松开衣带，你疾忙向前来扶策。

【挂玉钩】你与我揪住头心掐下颏，我与你高阜处招魂魄。石和，哎！贪慌处孩儿落了鞋，唤着越不揪采。闷转加，愁无奈，空教我哭哭啼啼，怨怨哀哀。

石和孩儿呵！

【沽美酒】我将这老精神强打拍，小名儿叫的明白：你个孝顺的石和安在哉？则被他抛杀您奶奶，教我空没乱把地皮掴。

【太平令】空教我哭啼啼自敦自摔，百般的唤不回来。越教我自生残害，急煎煎不宁不耐。石和孩儿呵！（王三上，应云）我在这里。（旦）教我左猜右猜，不知是那里应来，莫不是山精水怪？

And watching their shadowy forms, I tremble with fear.

(*Big Wang and Middle Wang approach, carrying a corpse.*)

BOTH: Where are you, mother? Here is our brother's body.

WIFE (*glancing at it and weeping*):

I look hastily at the body,
A corpse bespattered with blood!
With haste I undo the rope
And swiftly loosen the straps.
Come quickly and help me!
Take his head, holding the chin,
While from high ground I call back his spirit.

Ah, my child!

In your haste you have lost your shoes;
I call, but you do not answer.
I weep and mourn in vain.

Ah, Stony, my son!

I call you with all the strength in my old body,
Calling your pet name clearly —
Where is my good son Stony?
Why have you left your mother?
In vain I beat the ground,
In vain I sob and stamp;
I cannot call back your spirit;
This will drive me out of my mind.

Stony, child!

LITTLE WANG (*standing up*): Here I am!

WIFE:

What is that answering voice?
Where could it come from?
Can it be some mountain goblin?

LITTLE WANG: I am here, mother.

WIFE: A ghost! A ghost!

（王三上）母亲，孩儿来了。（旦慌科）有鬼！有鬼！（王三）母亲休怕，是石和孩儿。（旦）

【风入松】我前行，他随后赶将来，唬的我捲耳扫腮。教我战笃速忙把孩儿拜，我与你收拾垒七修斋。（王三）母亲，我是人！（旦）不是鬼疾言个皂白，怎地得却回来？

（王三）大人把偷马贼赵顽驴盆吊死，着我拖出来。饶了你孩儿也。（旦）

【川拨棹】这场灾，一时间命运衰。早则解放愁怀，喜笑盈腮。我则道石沉大海！大哥、二哥，休怨我！您两个管什么？这言语休见责。

你两个不仔细，抬这尸首来做甚？

【小妇孩儿】你也合把眼睁开，却把谁家尸首背将来？也不是提鱼穿柳欢心大，也不是鬼使神差。你小名儿上把命该，为甚你无妨碍？（王三）孩儿知道没事。（旦）常言道"老实的终须在"。把错抬的尸

LITTLE WANG: Don't be afraid, mother. I am your son Stony.

WIFE:

He follows me as I run,
I am at my wit's end in terror.
Trembling, I bow before my dead son —
I shall make good sacrifice to you.

LITTLE WANG: Mother, I am flesh and blood.

WIFE:

If you are not a ghost,
Tell me quickly
How you escaped.

LITTLE WANG: His Honour hanged that horse thief, Donkey Zhao, and told me to carry his corpse out. Me he spared.

WIFE:

So all our troubles are over!
My sorrow ended, I laugh.
I thought you were gone
Like a pebble in the ocean.

But my elder sons deserve a scolding.

What were you about?
Don't grumble if I blame you.

How could you be so offhand as to carry another's corpse here?

You should have kept your eyes open,
Instead of bringing me a stranger's corpse.
Yet what happiness this is,
What a miracle wrought by fairies!
You, the youngest, were sentenced to death —
How was it you were spared?

LITTLE WANG: I knew I should be all right.

WIFE:

So it is true that honesty prevails!
Let us bury this corpse

首，你与我土内藏埋。

（孤冲上，云）你怎生又打死人？（旦众慌科）（孤）你休慌！他是偷马贼赵顽驴，替你偿葛彪之命。你一家听圣人的命，你本是龙袖娇民，堪可为报国贤臣。大儿去随朝勾当，第二的冠带荣身，石和做中牟县令，母亲做贤德夫人。国家重义夫节妇，更爱那孝子顺孙。圣明主加官赐赏，一齐的望阙谢恩。（众云）万岁，万岁，万万岁！（旦）

【水仙子】九重天飞下纸赦书来，您三下里休将招状责。一齐的望阙疾参拜，愿的圣明君千万载，更胜如枯树花开。捱了些脓血债，受彻了牢狱灾，今日个苦尽甘来。

【尾煞】不甫能还了恓惶债，黑漫漫打出迷魂寨。愿待制位列三公，日转千阶。唱道娘加做贤德夫

Which was carried here by mistake.

(*Enter the prefect.*)

BAO: What! Are you committing another murder?

(*Wang's Wife and her sons are frightened.*)

BAO: Don't be alarmed. That is the corpse of the horse thief, Donkey Zhao. He has paid in your place for the death of Ge Biao. Now listen to His Majesty's orders:

You are the sovereign's good subjects,
Worthy to serve the state as officers.
The eldest son shall have a post at court,
The second son shall be a high official,
The third shall be Magistrate of Zhongmou County,
And their mother shall be a lady;
For the court sets store by virtuous wives and mothers,
And values those who are good sons to their parents.
So our sage emperor rewards you all.
Face the capital and thank His Majesty!

ALL: Long live the emperor!

WIFE:

An amnesty has come down from highest Heaven,
And we no longer complain about the verdict,
But face the capital and bow our thanks,
Hoping our emperor will live for ever.
Like a withered tree which blooms again,
After beating and imprisonment
Our sadness has turned to joy,
Our debt of sorrow is paid,
We have left the castle of darkness.
May Your Honour rise to be chief minister,
With fresh promotion each day.
Now the mother has a lady's rank,
And her son is made Magistrate of Zhongmou.

人，儿加做中牟县宰。赦得俺子母每今后无妨碍，大小无灾，则愿得龙椅上君王万万载！

题目　葛皇亲挟势行凶横
　　　　赵顽驴偷马残生送
正名　王婆婆贤德抚前儿
　　　　包待制三勘蝴蝶梦

So mother and son will live together in peace,
Free from all calamities, great and small.
May our gracious sovereign reign on his throne for ever!

(*THE END*)

The Butterfly Dream

赵盼儿风月救风尘

Rescued by a Coquette

第一折

（冲末周舍上）酒肉场中三十载，花星整照二十年；一生不识柴米价，只少花钱共酒钱。自家郑州人氏，周同知的孩儿周舍是也。自小上花台，做子弟。这汴梁城中有一歌者，乃是宋引章。他一心待嫁我，我一心待娶他，争奈他母亲不肯。我今做买卖回来，今日是吉日良辰，一来探望他母亲，二来提这门亲事，走一遭去。（下）

（卜儿同外旦上）花有重开日，人无再少年。老身汴梁人氏，自身姓李。夫主姓宋，早年亡化已过。止有这个女孩儿，名做宋引章。俺孩儿拆白道字，顶真续麻，无般不晓，无般不会。有郑州周舍与孩儿作伴，一个待要娶，一个待要嫁。只是老身谎彻梢虚，则怕久后受苦。（外旦）奶奶，不妨事，我一心则待要嫁

ACT I

(*Enter Zhou She.*)

ZHOU:

Thirty years I've been a glutton,
Twenty years I've been lucky with girls.
I never know the price of rice or firewood,
For all my money goes on wine and women.

I am Zhou She, son of a sub-prefect and a native of Zhengzhou. Since boyhood I've haunted bawdy-houses. Now here in Bianliang is a sing-song girl called Song Yinzhang. We want to marry each other, but her mother won't give her consent. I'm just back from a business trip. Today is a lucky day, so I'm going to their house to say "How do you do?" to her mother and propose this match. Here I go.

(*Enter Mistress Song and her daughter.*)

MRS. SONG:

A flower may blossom again,
But youth never returns.

I am a native of Bianliang. My family name is Li, but I married a man named Song. My husband died early and I have only this daughter Yinzhang. She's clever at jokes and puns and a good hand at quips and pranks. Zhou She of Zhengzhou has been her admirer for several years, and they want to marry each other; but I keep putting it off, afraid she might suffer for it later.

YINZHANG: Don't worry about that, mother. I've set my heart on having him.

他。（卜）随你，随你。（周舍上）自家周舍。来到这门首也，只索进去。（做见科）（外旦）周舍，你来了也？（周）我一径的来问亲事。母亲如何？（外旦）母亲许了亲事也。（周）我见母亲去。（做见科）母亲，我一径的来问这亲事哩！（卜）则今日好日辰，我许了你，则休欺负俺孩儿。（周）我并不敢欺负大姐。母亲，把你那姊妹弟兄都请下者，我便收拾来取则。（下）（卜）大姐，你在家执料，我去请那一般的老姊妹去。（下）（外旦）母亲去了，看有什么人来？（安秀实上）屈子投江千古恨，颜回乐道一生贫。小生姓安，名秀实，洛阳人氏。平生以花酒为念。到此汴梁，有一歌者宋引章和小生作伴。当初他要嫁我来，如今却嫁了周舍。他有个八拜交的姐姐，是赵盼儿，我如今央他劝他一劝。早来到也。赵大姐在家么？（正旦上）妾身赵盼儿是也。恰待做些针指生活，只听的有人叫门。我开开这门试看则。（见科）我道是谁，原来是妹夫。你那里去来？（安）我一径的来相烦你。当初姨姨引章要嫁我来，如今却要嫁

MRS. SONG: Have it your own way then.

(*Enter Zhou She.*)

ZHOU: Here comes Zhou She. This is their house. I'll go in. (*He greets Yinzhang.*)

YINZHANG: So it's you, Zhou She.

ZHOU: I have come about our marriage. What does your mother say?

YINZHANG: Mother is willing.

ZHOU: Then let me speak to her. (*He greets Mistress Song.*) I have come about this marriage, ma'am.

MRS. SONG: Today is a lucky day: I give my consent. But mind you don't ill-treat my child.

ZHOU: How dare I ill-treat her? Invite all our friends, ma'am, and I'll make myself ready and come.

MRS. SONG: Keep an eye on the house, child, while I go to invite my old friends.

(*Exeunt.*)

YINZHANG: Mother has gone. Let me see who is coming now. (*Exit.*)

(*Enter the scholar An Xiushi.*)

AN:

Qu Yuan drowned himself, leaving eternal sorrow;
All his life, poor Yan Hui remained steadfast in his aim.

I am An Xiushi, a native of Luoyang. I have always enjoyed women and wine. Here in Bianliang is a singsong girl called Song Yinzhang, who is my sweetheart. She promised to marry me, but now she is marrying Zhou She. She has a sworn sister, Zhao Paner. And I'm on my way to ask Paner for help. Here I am. Are you at home, sister?

(*Enter Paner.*)

PANER: I am Zhao Paner. I was going to do some needlework, but I hear someone calling. Let me open the door and see who it is. (*She greets An.*) I was wondring who it was. So it's my sister's betrothed. Where have you come from?

AN: I have come to ask you a favour. Your sister Yinzhang promised to marry me, but now she's agreed to marry Zhou She instead. I want you

周舍。我央你劝他一劝。（正旦）当初这亲事不许你来？如今又要嫁别人。姻缘事非同容易也呵。

【仙吕点绛唇】妓女追陪，觅钱一世；临收计，怎做的百纵千随，知重咱风流婿。

【混江龙】我想这姻缘匹配，少一时一刻强难为。如何可意？怎的相知？怕不便脚搭着脑勺成事早，久以后手拍着胸脯悔时迟！寻前程，觅下稍，恰便似黑海也似难寻觅。人心料的不问，天理何为？

【油葫芦】姻缘簿全凭我共你，谁不待拣一个聪俊的！他每都拣来拣去转一回：待嫁一个老实的，又怕尽世儿难相配；待嫁一个聪俊的，又怕半路里相抛弃。遮莫向狗溺处藏，遮莫向牛屎里堆，忽地便吃了一个合扑地。那时节睁着眼怨他谁！

【天下乐】我想这先嫁人一般女伴每，折倒的容仪瘦似鬼，受了些难分说难告诉闲气息。我看了寻前程俊女娘，我判了这几日，我一世没男儿直甚颓！

妹夫，我可也待嫁个客人。有个比喻。（安）喻将何比？（旦）

【那吒令】待装一个老实，学三从四德；争奈是匪妓，都三心二意。端的是那的是三梢末尾？俺虽居

to speak to her!

PANER: Yes, she gave you her promise, didn't she? But now she wants to marry someone else. Really, getting married is a difficult business!

Though we singsong girls make money by pleasing men,
We can find no devoted admirers in the end.
No match should be made by force,
Or hurried through before the time is ripe.
If two people marry as soon as they fall in love,
A day will come when they repent their rashness.
The future is dark as the never-fathomed ocean;
Men's hearts are a riddle which Heaven alone can make out.
To marry, you need a couple,
And each one hopes to find a perfect mate;
We make our choice a hundred, thousand times,
Seeking an honest man — but can we find one?
Seeking a clever fellow — but will he prove constant?
As it is, we are thrown away on curs and swine;
We fall suddenly to the ground,
And wake to find we have only ourselves to blame.
I have known young brides in my time,
But a few days of harsh treatment
Make haggard ghosts of them;
Yet they cannot express their despair
Or tell their sorrow.
I have seen ambitious beauties fare like that.
I would rather sleep alone the whole of my life!

Brother, I am going to get married myself, so I know what these would-be brides are like.

AN: What are they like?

PANER:

They want to be honest and learn the wifely virtues,
But all singsong girls are considered light and giddy:
This is really the lowest trade;

在柳陌中，花街内，可是那件儿便宜？

【鹊踏枝】俺说是卖虚脾，他可得逞狂为；一个个败坏人伦，不辨贤愚，出来一个个绰皮。但来两三遭，不问那厮要钱。他便道："这弟子敲谩儿哩。"倒说俺女娘每不省越着迷。

【寄生草】他每有人爱为娼妓，有人爱作次妻。干家的落取些虚名利，买虚的看取些羊羔利，嫁人的见放着傍州例。他正是"南头做了北头开，东行不见西行例"。

妹夫，你且坐一坐，我去劝他。劝的省时，你休欢喜；劝不省时，休烦恼。（安）我不必坐，我且回家去等信罢。大姐留心者。（下）（旦见外旦云）鹿牙这科子糙手！他撇着坐。你那里人情去哩？（外旦）我不人情去，我待嫁人哩。（旦）正来与你保亲来。（外旦）你保谁？（旦）保安秀才。（外旦怒云）我嫁了安秀才呵，一对儿好打莲花落！（旦）你待嫁谁？（外旦）我嫁周舍。（旦）你如今嫁人，莫不还早哩？（外旦）有什么早不早？今日

Though I live in luxury, what good does it do me?
We live by cheating others,
But men torment us too,
In wicked, unnatural ways.
Each mother's son is a scoundrel.

If a fellow comes two or three times and we don't ask him for money, the wretch says we have designs on him.

Yet we won't see through him,
But fall in love with him.
Some women envy singsong girls,
Some envy concubines;
But the girl who wants to marry
Is out for wealth and a good reputation,
While the girl who simply pretends to want to marry
Is hoping to marry money.
Though the girl who marries is bound to be deceived,
Others still tread in her steps,
Instead of learning a lesson from her despair.

Take a seat, brother, while I go to persuade her. Don't be too pleased if she takes my advice, and don't be too sad if she doesn't.

AN: I won't stay, but go home to wait for your news. Please do your best for me, sister! (*Exit.*)

(*Enter Yinzhang.*)

PANER (*meeting Yinzhang*): That's a stag with sharp antlers. Whom are you going to call on, sister?

YINZHANG: I'm not calling on anyone. I'm getting married.

PANER: I've just come to propose a match to you.

YINZHANG: With whom?

PANER: The scholar An.

YINZHANG (*crossly*): If I marry him, we'll have to go begging together.

PANER: Well, whom do you mean to marry?

YINZHANG: I'm going to marry Zhou She.

PANER: Aren't you too young to marry?

也大姐，明日也大姐，出了一包儿脓。我嫁了一个张郎家妇、李郎家妻，立个妇名，我做鬼也风流。（旦）

【村里迓鼓】你也合三思，然后再思可矣。你如今年纪小哩，我与你慢慢的别寻个姻配，你可便宜。守着铜斗儿家缘家计。则你歹姐姐衷肠话劝妹妹，则怕受不过男儿气息。

那做丈夫的做的子弟，做子弟的做不的丈夫。（外旦）你说我听咱。（旦）

【元和令】做丈夫的做子弟，他终不解其意。做子弟的他影儿里会虚脾，那做丈夫的忒老实。（外旦）那周舍穿着一架子衣服，可也堪爱也。（旦）那厮虽穿着几件蛇螂皮，人伦事晓的甚的！

妹子也，你为什么就要嫁他？（外旦）则为他知重您妹子，因此要嫁他。（旦）他怎么知重你？（外旦）一年四季：夏天我好的一觉晌睡，他替你妹子打着扇。冬天替你妹子温的铺盖儿暖了，着你妹子歇息。但你妹子哪里人情去，你妹子穿哪一套衣服，戴哪一副头面，替你妹子提领系、整钗环。只为他这等知重你妹子，因此上我要嫁他。（旦）你原来为这般嫁他！

【上马娇】我听的说就里，你原来为这的，引的我忍不住笑微微。你道是暑月间扇子扇着你睡，冬月间着炭火煨，烘炙着绵衣。

【游四门】吃饭处把匙头挑了筋共皮，出门去提领

YINZHANG: Why? Singsong girl today, singsong girl tomorrow: this is a wretched life. If I marry some Zhang or Li and become a respectable woman, I can hold my head up even when I'm a ghost.

PANER:

You had better think again! You are still quite young;
Why not wait until I find you a good husband
With whom you can live in comfort all your life?
Your elder sister is telling you the truth:
You won't be able to stand a husband long.

Some good husbands make good lovers too, sister. But good lovers may not make good husbands.

YINZHANG: What do you mean?

PANER:

Though some husbands make poor lovers,
The lovers are false, while the husbands at least are honest!

YINZHANG: But Zhou She looks so handsome in his fine clothes!

PANER:

Though he decks himself out in fine feathers,
What does he know of how to treat a wife?

Why do you want to marry him, sister?

YINZHANG: Because he's so good to me.

PANER: In what way is he good to you?

YINZHANG: He cares for me all the year round. In summer, when I take a nap he fans me. In winter, he warms the quilt for me. When I dress to go out, he helps me straighten my clothes. When I put on my trinkets, he helps me pin them on. It's because he's so good to me that I want to marry him.

PANER: So that's the reason!

I can hardly keep from laughing!
In summer, you say, he fans you to sleep,
Warms your padded clothes
And your quilt at the brazier in winter.
At table he takes his spoon

系整衣袂，戴插头面整梳篦。衠一味是虚脾，女娘每不省越着迷。

【胜葫芦】休想这子弟道求食，娶到他家里，多无半载相抛弃。又不敢把他禁害，着拳椎脚踢，打的你哭啼啼。

【幺】恁时节船到江心补漏迟，烦恼怨他谁？事要前思，免劳后悔。我也劝你不得，有朝一日，准备着搭救你块望夫石。

久以后你受苦呵，休来告我。（外旦）我便有那该死的罪，我也不来央告你。（周舍上）小的每，把这礼物摆的好看些！（旦）来的敢是周郎？那厮不言语便罢，他若但言，着他吃我几嘴好的。（周）那壁姨姨敢是赵盼儿么？（旦）然也。（周）请姨姨吃些茶饭波。（旦）你请我？家里饿皮脸也，揭了锅儿底也！窨子里秋月——不曾见这等食！（周）央及姨姨保门亲事。（旦）你着我保谁？（周）保宋引章。（旦）你着我保宋引章那些儿？保他那针指油面、刺绣铺房、大裁小剪、生儿长女？（周）这婆娘

To remove the skin and gristle from your meat;
And when you go out he straightens the folds of your dress,
Pins on your trinkets and places the combs in your hair.
All this is done to deceive you;
Yet you won't see through him, but fall in love with him!
You say your lover is good to you;
But once you marry him and go to his house
Within a few months he will cast you off,
And you will be quite helpless.
He'll kick you and punch you until you burst into tears:
But by then, with the boat in mid-stream,
It will be too late for you to stop the leak,
And whom will you have to blame?
So look before you leap!
I know, if I can't convince you,
That some fine day I shall have to rescue you!

Don't come running to me when he starts ill-treating you!

YINZHANG: Even if I'm condemned to death, I shan't ask for your help! (*Enter Zhou She with porters.*)

ZHOU: Display the presents, men.

PANER: So Zhou She is coming. If he says nothing, well and good. If he speaks, I shall give him a tongue-lashing!

ZHOU: Is that Sister Zhao?

PANER: It is.

ZHOU: Won't you have some tea and food with us?

PANER: Are you asking me home to a meal? You serve hungry guests from an empty pan — what food can I expect from you?

ZHOU: I want you to act as voucher.

PANER: As voucher for whom?

ZHOU: For Yinzhang here.

PANER: So you want me to vouch for her? You want me to vouch that she'll do all a housewife's work — sew, cook, embroider, make clothes and bear you children?

好歹嘴也。我已成了事了，不索央你。（旦）我去罢。（做出门科）（安冲上，云）姨姨，劝的引章如何？（旦）不济事了也！（安）这等呵，我上朝求官应举去也。（旦）你且休去，我有用你处哩。（安）依着姨姨说，我去客店中安下去。（下）（旦）

【赚煞】这妮子是狐魅人女妖精，缠郎君天魔祟。则他那裤儿里休猜做有腿，吐下鲜红血则当做苏木水。耳边休采那等闲食，那的是最容易剜眼睛嫌的，则除是亲近随着他便欢喜。着他疾省呵，哎！你个双郎子弟安排下金冠霞帔，一个夫人也，来到手里，自家了却。则为三千张茶引嫁了冯魁。（下）

（周）去辞了母亲，着大姐上轿，咱回郑州去来。（同外旦下）

ZHOU: Oh, what a tongue you have! Well, since I've succeeded already, I can do without your help.

PANER: I'll be going then. (*She walks out.*)

(*Enter An.*)

AN: Well, sister, how did your talk with Yinzhang go?

PANER: It made no impression at all.

AN: In that case, I'd better go to the capital to sit for the examination.

PANER: Don't go yet. I need you here.

AN: Whatever you say. I'll stay on in the inn, and see what you can do for me. (*Exit.*)

PANER:

She's a fox-fairy, witch, a vampire who sucks men's blood,
With no human legs in her trousers!
Though you spit out blood for her, ah,
She thinks nothing of it!
You must sow no more wild oats,
For it's easy to make her jealous,
But must stick to her side to please her.

Look out, An Xiushi, I warn you!

You have made ready wedding robes and a gold tiara.

You think you have won a wife.

But she's marrying another for his money! (*Exit.*)

ZHOU: When you've said goodbye to your mother, my dear, get in the sedan-chair and we'll set off to Zhengzhou.

(*Exeunt.*)

第二折

（周舍上）自家周舍是也。我骑马一世，驴背上失了一脚。我为娶这妇人呵，磨了半截舌头。今日是吉日良辰，着这妇人上了轿先行，我骑了马，离了汴京，来到郑州。让他轿子先行，怕那一般的舍人说："周舍娶了宋引章。"怕人笑话。则见那轿子一晃一晃的，我向前打那抬轿的小厮，道："你这等欺辱人！"举起鞭子就打。问他道："你走便走，晃怎么？"那小厮道："不干我事，奶奶在里边不知做什么？"我着鞭子挑起轿帘一看，则见他精赤条条地在里面打斤斗。来到家中，我说："你套一床被我盖。"我到房里，只见被子倒高似床。我便叫那妇人："在哪里？"则听的被子里答应道："周舍，我在被子里面哩！"我道："被子里面做什么？"他道："我套绵被，把我翻在里头了！"我拿起棍来，恰待要打，他道："周舍，打我不打紧，休打了隔壁王婆婆。"我道："好也！把邻舍都翻在被里面！"我褡护上掉了一根带儿，着他缀一缀。他道："我缀了。"我道："在哪里？"他道："我缀的牢牢的哩！"着我衣裳高处看，无有。可哪里去了？拿过镜子则一照，把根带儿缀在肩头上。兀的是你的生活！兀那妇人，我手里有打杀的，无有买休卖休的。我吃酒去也，回来慢慢的打

ACT II

(*Enter Zhou She.*)

ZHOU: I am Zhou She. After riding horses all my life, I've ended up on a donkey. I practically wore out my tongue to get this woman. On a lucky day I managed at last to mount her in a sedan and ride out of Bianliang with her towards Zhengzhou. I let her travel by chair in front so that people wouldn't laugh at me for marrying a singsong girl. But when I saw the chair tossing up and down, I rode across to beat the bearers. "How dare you make fun of me like this?" I asked. And I raised my whip to beat them. "Just carry the chair," I said. "Why toss it up and down?" "It's not us," said the bearers. "It's the lady inside." When I lifted the curtain with my whip, what do you think I saw? She had stripped herself naked and was turning somersaults! When we got home I told her to sew me a quilt; but when I went in, there was the quilt standing up as high as the bedposts. "Yinzhang! Where are you?" I shouted. "I'm in here, Zhou She!" she called from inside the quilt. "What are you doing in there?" "When I put in the cotton, I sewed myself in by mistake." I took up a stick to beat her. "You can beat me, Zhou She," she said. "But mind you don't beat our neighbour, Mistress Wang." "A fine thing!" said I. "So you've sewn up the neighbour too!" When the belt on my coat got loose, I told her to sew it on. "I've done it," she said. "Where is it?" I asked. "I've sewn it strongly," she answerd. I looked all round, but couldn't find it. Where could it be? When I picked up a mirror to look at myself, I found it sewn on my shoulder. That's the way you behave, you slut. I may beat you or kill you, but I won't sell you or let you go. I'm going out now for a drink. When I come back, I'll give you a proper

你。（下）

（外旦上）不信好人言，必有恓惶事。当初赵家姐姐劝我不信，进的门来，打了我五十杀威棒。我这隔壁有个王货郎，他如今去汴梁做买卖。我写一封书稍将去，着俺母亲和赵家姐姐来救我；若来迟了，我无那活的人也。天也，只被你打杀我也！（下）

（卜儿哭上）满怀心腹事，尽在不言中。自家宋引章的母亲是也。有我女孩儿从嫁了周舍，昨日王货郎寄信来，上写着道："从到他家，进门打了五十杀威棒，如今朝打暮骂。急急央赵家姐姐来救我。"我拿着书去与赵家姐姐说知，怎生救他去？引章孩儿，则被你痛杀我也！（下）

（旦上）自家赵盼儿是也。这门衣饭几时是了也呵，我也待寻个前程，这些时消息也甚好。

【商调集贤宾】咱收心待嫁人，早引起那话头：听的道谁揭债，谁买休。他每待强巴劫深宅大院，便待折摧了舞榭歌楼。一个个眼张狂似漏了网的游鱼，一个个嘴卢都似跌了弹的斑鸠。御园中可不道是栽路柳，好人家怎容这等娼优！他便初间时有些

hiding. (*Exit.*)

(*Enter Yinzhang.*)

YINZHANG: Ignore good advice, and you're bound to get into trouble! When Paner warned me against him, I wouldn't listen to her. But the moment I crossed his threshold he gave me fifty strokes to be going on with. There's a pedlar in this neighbourhood named Wang, who is going to Bianliang on business. I'll ask him to take a note to my mother, so that she and Paner can rescue me. If they don't come soon, they'll find me dead. Heaven knows, I'm likely to be beaten to death! (*Exit.*)

(*Enter Mistress Song, crying.*)

MRS. SONG:

My heart is full of grief,
But I am silent.

I'm the mother of Yinzhang who married Zhou She. Yesterday Pedlar Wang brought me a letter from her in which she said: "The moment I crossed Zhou's threshold he gave me fifty strokes to be going on with; since when he's been beating and cursing me day and night. Please ask Paner to come at once to save me." I'm taking this letter now to show Paner, to ask her how we can rescue my unfortunate daughter. Ah, child, you'll be the death of your poor mother! (*Exit.*)

(*Enter Paner.*)

PANER: I am Zhao Paner. When shall I be able to leave this wretched profession, I wonder? I want to find a husband too, and now is a good time.

I'm longing to marry and settle down,
But I've never heard of a man
Willing to clear a singsong girl's debts and redeem her.
All they do is to fawn on the rich in their splendid mansions,
Not caring if they ruin the courtesans' quarters,
Floundering like fish escaping from a net,
Or flapping, if something goes wrong, like wounded pigeons.
We girls are roadside willows,
And good families will not take in courtesans;

志诚，临老也没来由。

【逍遥乐】那一个不因循成就，那一个不顷刻前程，那一个不等闲罢手。他每一做一个水上浮沤。和爷娘结下不断见的冤仇，恰便似日和月参辰卯酉，正中那男儿机彀。他使那千般贞烈、万种恩情，到如今一笔都勾。

看有什么人来？（卜儿上）可早来到也，我索过去。（做见科。云）大姐，烦恼杀我也！（旦）奶奶，你为什么哭哭啼啼？（卜）好教大姐知道：引章不听你劝，嫁了周舍。进门去，打了五十杀威棒。如今打的看看至死，不久身亡。姐姐，怎生是好？（旦）引章吃打也！

【金菊香】想当日他暗成公事，今日决成仇。我当初作念你的言词，今日都应口。则你那说着去时恰便似去秋。似这般燕侣莺俦，畅好是容易恩爱结绸缪。

【醋葫芦】你铺排着天长和地久，指望并肩携素手；蓦入门知滋味便合休，几番家眼睁睁打干净待离了我这手。赵盼儿！你做的今见死不救，羞见这桃园中杀白马宰乌牛。

你道当初这般呵，谁着你嫁来？（卜）大姐，周舍说誓

Our lovers seem sincere in the beginning,
But as they grow old they forget their former sweethearts.
They take pleasure for a time,
Then swiftly go their way,
Leaving us all too quickly
Like foam on the waves.
For them we offend our master and our mistress
Till we are as far apart as sun and moon,
Yet we let ourselves be taken in
By their ardent looks and ten thousand vows of love.
How soon all these are forgotten!

Let me see who is coming.

(*Enter Mistress Song.*)

MRS. SONG: This is her door. Let me go in. (*Greeting her.*) Paner, I am so worried!

PANER: Why are you crying so bitterly, mother?

MRS. SONG: Let me tell you. Though you warned her against him, Yinzhang would marry Zhou She; but the moment she crossed his threshold he gave her fifty strokes to be going on with. And now he is beating her so cruelly he'll soon kill her. What shall I do, Paner?

PANER: Oh, Yinzhang, have you been beaten?

I remember how you arranged your marriage in secret,
And today you are enemies:
My warnings have come true!
You left here only last autumn,
Thinking you had found a good husband,
Hoping his love for you would last for ever,
Clinging fondly to his hand;
But as soon as you crossed his threshold it was over!
He is beating you every day, and you want to escape;
If I do not save your life,
I shall be ashamed when I think of our former friendship.

Ah, why did she marry a man like this?

来。（旦）

【醋葫芦】那一个不嗲可可道横死亡，那一个不实丕丕拔了短筹？则你这亚仙子母老实头！普天下爱女娘的子弟口，奶奶，不则周舍说谎也，那一个不掉麻各般说咒？恰似秋风过耳休休。

（卜）姐姐，怎生搭救引章孩儿？（旦）奶奶，我有两个压被的银子，咱两个拿着买休去来。（卜）他说来："则有打死的，无有买休卖休的。"（旦寻思科，做与卜耳语科，云）则除是这般。（卜）可是中也不中？（旦）不妨事，将书来我看。（卜递书科，旦念云）"引章拜上姐姐并奶奶：自别之后，果应其言。当初不信好人言，果有恓惶事。进他门来，打我五十杀威棒。如今朝打暮骂。你来的早，还得见我；来得迟呵，不能勾见我面了。只此拜上。"妹子也，当初谁教你这等来！

【醋葫芦】想当初有忧呵同共忧，有愁呵一处愁。他道是残生早晚丧荒丘，做了个游街野巷村务酒。你道是"百年之后——"妹子也，你不道来"这个也大姐，那个也大姐，出了一包脓。不如嫁个张郎妇、李郎

MRS. SONG: Zhou She swore he would be true, Paner.

PANER:

All of them swear they will die before they stop loving;
All of them break their word.
You were too simple, mother,
To believe a young man who was courting a girl.

Zhou She is not the only liar, mother.

All of them swear great oaths,
But like wind that brushes your ear their vows are lost.

MRS. SONG: But tell me, Paner, how can I rescue my child?

PANER: I have two silver ingots I've saved, mother. Let's use them to buy her back.

MRS. SONG: He said he would beat her to death, but never sell her.

(*Paner reflects, then whispers something to Mistress Song.*)

PANER: This is the only way.

MRS. SONG: But will it work?

PANER: Don't worry. May I see her letter?

(*Mistress Song passes her the note, and Paner reads it.*)

PANER: "Yinzhang greets her sister Paner and her mother. It has happened just as you said. Because I wouldn't listen to good advice, I am having a terrible time. The moment I crossed his threshold he gave me fifty strokes to be going on with; since when he's been beating and cursing me day and night. If you come soon, you will still be able to see me; but if you don't come soon, you'll find me dead." Ah, sister! Who told you to do such a foolish thing?

We used to share all our troubles;
Now she says she may die
And become a homeless ghost,
While I do nothing to help her.

Ah, sister, didn't you say, "What's the good of being a singsong girl all my life? If I marry some Zhang or Li —

And become a respectable woman,
I can hold my head up

妻，立一个妇名儿做鬼也风流”？

奶奶，那寄书的去了不曾？（卜）还不曾去哩。（旦）我写一封书，寄与引章去。（做写科）

【后庭花】我将这知心书亲自修，教他把天机休泄漏。“传示与休莽戆收心女，拜上你浑身疼的歹事头。”写就了也，到那里呵！我则索再梳头，身穿上些锦绣。那厮每日家不住手，无情的棍棒丢，浑身上鲜血流，逐朝家如暴囚。扭捏的身分儿抯，贴翠钿上额颅，绕珍珠衔凤口，梳妆的我不见丑。

【双雁儿】我着这粉脸儿搭救你个女眷牛，割舍了一不做二不休，拚了由他咒也波咒。不是我说大口，怎出我烟月手！

奶奶，你放心。（卜）姐姐，到那里仔细着。烦恼杀了我也！（旦）

【浪里来煞】不须你心内忧，你可便莫僝愁，我直着花叶不损觅归秋。那厮爱女娘的心，见的便似驴共狗，卖弄他那玲珑剔透。我到那里，三言两句，肯

Even when I'm a ghost."

Mother, has the messenger left?

MRS. SONG: Not yet.

PANER: I'll write a letter to her. (*She writes.*)

I am writing this letter myself
To bid her keep my plan secret,
And to send my greetings to the rash, foolish creature —
Poor girl, she must be aching all over now!
Now the letter is written. When I go there,
I shall dress my hair again,
And wear rich embroidery.
That fellow beats her all day long,
Under his savage rods her red blood flows;
And he treats her like a criminal.
But I shall show him my figure,
And wear emerald leaves on my forehead,
With pearls and a phoenix design.
I shall be beautifully turned out,
And with a powdered face I'll rescue her!
I've made up my mind, and mean to go through with it;
He can curse me as much as he likes when it is done!
This is no idle boast:
I shan't let the scoundrel slip through my delicate fingers!

Don't you worry, mother.

MRS. SONG: Be careful, Paner, when you get there. Ah, child, you are worrying me to death!

PANER:

Set your heart at rest, mother,
And smooth that wrinkled forehead;
I promise to bring her home to you safe and sound.
That dangler after women
Is like a dog or donkey;
I know he'll be up to all his tricks to please me.

写休书，万事俱休。若是不肯写休书，我将他掐一掐，拈一拈，搂一搂，抱一抱，着那厮通身酥，遍体麻。鼻凹上抹上一块砂糖，着那厮舔又舔不着，吃又吃不着。赚得那厮写了休书，引章将的休书来，淹的撇了。我这里出的门儿，可不是一场风月，我着那汉一时休。（下）

When I reach Zhengzhou, I shall speak to him. If he's willing to divorce her, well and good. If not, I'll pinch him and stroke him, hug him and cuddle him, till he's completely distracted. I'll put sugar under his nose that he can't lick and can't eat until he divorces Yinzhang. But when she has her divorce paper and leaves him, I'll walk out on him too!

I'll charm him into losing both of us!

(*Exeunt.*)

第三折

（周舍同店小二上）万事分已定，浮生空自忙。店小二，你开着客店，我那里希罕你那房钱养家！有那等好科子来你这客店里，你便来叫我。（小二）我知道。一时哪里寻你去？（周）你来粉房里寻我。（小二）粉房里没有呵？（周）赌房里来寻。（小二）赌房里没有呵？（周）牢房里来寻！（下）（小闲挑笼上）钉靴雨伞为活计，偷寒送暖作营生，自家小闲的便是。平生做不的买卖，止是与歌者姐姐每叫些人，两头往来传消寄信都是我。这里有个大姐赵盼儿，着我收拾两箱子衣服行李往郑州去。都收拾了，请姐姐上马。（旦上）小闲，我这等打扮可冲动那厮么？（小闲倒科）（旦）你做什么哩？（小闲）休道冲动那厮，这一会儿连小闲也酥倒了。（旦）

ACT III

(*Enter Zhou She and a Waiter.*)

ZHOU:

If all that happens is fated,
Why should men toil and moil?

It wasn't to make money that I let you open this inn, waiter. But if any attractive girls come here, call me over at once.

WAITER: All right. But how am Ito find you?

ZHOU: Look for me in the courtesans' quarters.

WAITER: And if I can't find you there?

ZHOU: Then look for me in the gambling dens.

WAITER: And if I can't find you there?

ZHOU: Then look for me in gaol. (*Exit.*)

(*Enter Zhang, the errand boy, carrying cases.*)

ZHANG:

Nailed boots and umbrella:
My job is to deliver billets-doux.

I'm Zhang the errand boy. My job is to run errands for the singsong girls. I deliver their chits and bring back messages for them. Now Zhao Paner wants me to rope two chests of clothes and bedding to take to Zhengzhou, They're all ready, sister. Please mount your horse.

(*Enter Paner.*)

PANER: Boy, am I well enough tricked out to make that fellow fall for me?

(*Zhang falls to the ground.*)

PANER: What are you doing?

ZHANG: Don't talk about *him* falling for you. I've just fallen badly myself.

【正宫端正好】则为他满怀愁，心间闷，做的个进退无门。那婆娘家一涌性，无思忖，我可也强打入迷魂阵。

【滚绣球】我这里微微把气喷，输个姓因，怎不教那厮背槽抛粪！更做道普天下无他这等郎君。想着容易情，忒献勤，几番家待要不问；第一来我则是可怜见无主娘亲，第二来是我惯曾为旅偏怜客，第三来也是我自已贪杯惜醉人。到那里呵！也索费些精神。

早来到郑州地方了。小闲，接了马者。且在柳阴下歇一歇咱。（小闲）我知道。（旦）小闲，咱闲口论闲话：这好人家好举止，恶人家恶家法。（小闲）姐姐，你说我听。（旦）

【倘秀才】县君的则是县君，妓人的则是妓人。怕不扭捏着身子驀入他门，怎禁他使数的到支分，背地里暗忍。

【滚绣球】那好人家将粉扑儿浅淡匀，那里像咱干茨腊手抢着粉。好人家将那篦梳儿慢慢地铺鬓，那里像咱解了那襻胸带下颏上勒一道深痕。好人家知个远近，觑个向顺，那些个好人家风韵；那里像咱门，恰便似空房锁定个胡孙：有那千般不实乔躯

PANER:

Yinzhang is in such a tight corner,
She doesn't know what to do.
The silly child acted so rashly
That I shall have to use all my charms to save her.
I must wheedle that donkey and coax him,
Till he leaves his stable to trot after me,
While I act as if there's no better man in the world.
This may sound easy, but it takes an effort,
And several times I've felt like giving up;
But I pity her poor, helpless mother,
And because I've no home of my own
I can sympathize with others,
Just as a drinker sympathizes with drunkards.
So I mean to spare no pains.

Now we've arrived at Zhengzhou. Take the horse, boy. We'll rest for a while in the willow's shade.

ZHANG: Very good.

PANER: You know, boy, people from good families have good manners, and people from bad families bad manners.

ZHANG: What do you mean, sister?

PANER:

A lady is always a lady,
A singsong girl is always a singsong girl.
I may mince along in my husband's house,
But I'll find it hard to keep all the household rules.
Young ladies simply dust their faces with powder,
They don't plaster it on the way we do.
Young ladies comb their hair slowly and modestly,
They don't loosen their clothes like us, and half choke themselves.
Young ladies know how to act in a seemly way,
Not like us, who run wild like monkeys locked in a room.
So in spite of my tricks and wiles,

老，有万种虚嚣歹议论，断不了风尘。

（小闲）这里一个客店，姐姐好住下罢。（旦）叫店家来。（店小二见科）（旦）小二哥，你打扫一间干净房儿，放下行李。你与我请将周舍来，说我在这里久等多时也。（小二）我知道。（做行科）小哥在哪里？（周舍上）店小二,有什么事？（小二）店里有个好女子请你哩！（周）咱去来。（做见科）是好一个科子也。（旦）周舍来了也。

【滚绣球】俺那妹子儿有见闻，可有福分，抬举的个丈夫俊上添俊，年纪儿恰正青春。（周）我那里曾见你来？我在客火里，你弹着一架筝，我不与了你个褐紬段儿？（旦）小的不知道？（小闲）不是他与褐紬。（周）早起杭州散了，赶到陕西。客火里吃酒，我不与了大姐一分饭来？（旦）小的每不曾见。你则是忒现新，忒忘昏，更做道你眼钝。那唱词话的有两句留文：“咱也曾武陵溪畔曾相识，今日佯推不认人。”我为你断梦劳魂。

（周）我想起来了，你敢是赵盼儿么？（旦）然也。（周）然你奶奶那耳根！当初破亲也是你来。关了店门，则打这

In spite of all my fine talk,

I can't hide the fact that I'm a singsong girl.

ZHANG: Here's an inn, sister. Let's put up here.

PANER: Call the waiter.

(*The Waiter greets her.*)

PANER: Clean out a room for me, boy, and put our luggage there; then go to ask Zhou She over. Tell him I've been waiting for him a long time.

WAITER: All right. (*He walks out.*) Master Zhou, where are you?

(*Enter Zhou She.*)

ZHOU: Why are you calling me, boy?

WAITER: There's a beautiful girl in the inn, who is asking for you.

ZHOU: Let's go! (*He greets Paner.*) She certainly is a fine-looking singsong girl!

PANER: So, Zhou She, you've come!

How clever my sister is and how lucky,

To marry the handsomest man I've ever seen,

And such a young man too!

ZHOU: Haven't I seen you before? Was it in that inn where you were playing a harp, and I gave you a length of brown silk?

PANRE: I don't know about that.

ZHANG: No, I never saw any brown silk.

ZHOU: I have it! When I left Hangzhou for Shaanxi and was drinking in an inn, didn't I invite you to a meal?

PANER: No, I never saw that.

You're so forgetful you don't recognize me,

Just like the man in the story.

We met by Peach Blossom Stream,

But today, when we meet again, you pretend not to know me,

While I have been thinking so fondly of you all this time!

ZHOU: Ah, I remember now, Aren't you Zhao Paner?

PANER: That's right!

ZHOU: Well, well! You were the one who tried to break up my marriage. Here, waiter! Close the gate, and beat up that boy!

小闲！（小闲）你休要打我。俺姐姐将着锦绣衣服、一房一卧来嫁你，你倒打我？（旦）周舍，你坐的。你听我说。你在南京时，人说个周舍名字，说的我耳满鼻满的，则是不曾见你。自见了你呵，我不茶不饭。听的你娶了宋引章，我待嫁你，你却着我保亲！

【倘秀才】我当初倚大呵妆儇主婚，须是我火性起特故里破亲。你这厮外相儿通疏就里村！你今日结婚姻，咱罢论。

我好意将着车辆鞍马奁房来断送，你刬地将我打骂！小闲，拦回车儿，咱家去来。（周）早知姐姐来嫁我，怎肯打舅舅！（旦）你真个不知道？你既不知，你休出店门，只守着我坐的。（周）休说一两日，就是一两年，您儿也坐的将去。（外旦上）周舍两三日不家去，我寻到这店门首，我试看则：原来是赵盼儿和周舍坐的。兀那老弟子不识羞，直赶到这里来！周舍，你放心。等你来家呵，我拿一把刀子，你拿一把刀子，和你一递一刀子截哩！（下）（周）我和你抢生吃哩！不是奶奶在这里，我打杀你！（旦）

【脱布衫】我更是的不待饶人，我为甚不敢明闻。肋底下插柴自忍，不忍你便打他一顿。

ZHANG: Don't beat me! My sister has come with silk dresses and bedding to marry you. Why should you want to beat me?

PANER: Sit down, Zhou She, and listen to me. When you were in the southern capital, I heard everyone talk of you, but never met you. Later, after meeting you , I couldn't take a bite or sup for thinking of you. Then I heard you were going to marry Yinzhang. I wanted to marry you, Zhou She, yet you asked me to vouch for her!

As an elder sister, I had to pretend to be pleased,
Though I was jealous and wanted to break up your match;
You look intelligent, but you must be stupid,
If you think, because you're married, I'll give you up!

I come with carriage and horses and a dowry to give you; yet for no reason at all you curse and beat us! Boy, turn the carriage round. We're going home.

ZHOU: If I'd known you had come to marry me, of course I wouldn't have beaten your boy.

PANER: Do you mean it? Well, if you really didn't know, don't leave this inn but stay a few days with me.

ZHOU: I'm willing to stay a couple of years here with you, not just a few days.

(*Enter Yinzhang.*)

YINZHANG: Zhou She hasn't been home for several days, and now I've traced him to this inn. Let me have a look. Why, there he is, sitting with Sister Zhao! You shameless lecher, you! I've followed you all the way here. Just try to come home, Zhou She! If you do, I'll take a knife and you can take a knife, and we'll fight it out between us! (*Exit.*)

ZHOU (*seizing a stick*): I'll deal with you presently. If not for this lady's presence, I'd beat you to death!

PANER:

I never forget a grudge either;
But instead of losing my temper
I keep my feelings to myself.
Why should you beat her here?

【小梁州】可不道一夜夫妻百夜恩，你可便息怒停嗔。你村时节背地里使些村，对着我合思忖：那一个双同叔打杀麒麟？

【幺】则见他恶哏哏摸按着无情棍，有火性的不似你个郎君。你拿着偌粗的棍棒，倘或打杀他呵，可怎了？（周）丈夫打杀老婆，不该偿命！（旦）这等说，谁敢嫁你！（背唱）我假意瞒，虚科儿喷，着这厮有家难奔。妹子，你试看风月救风尘。

周舍，你好道儿！你这里坐着，点的你媳妇来骂我这一场。小闲，拦回车儿，咱回去来。（周）好奶奶，请坐。我不知道他来，我若知道他来，我就该死！（旦）你真个不曾使他来？这妮子不贤惠。打一棒快毬子，你舍的宋引章，我一发嫁你。（周）我到家里就休了他。（背云）且慢着！那个妇人是我打怕了的，与他一纸休书，那妇人便去了。这女子他可不嫁，不弄的"尖担两头脱"了？休的容易！把这女子摇撼的实着。（向旦云）奶奶，您孩儿肚肠是驴马的见识，我今家去把媳妇休了呵，奶奶，你把肉吊窗儿放下来，"可不嫁你！"做的个尖担两头脱。奶奶，你说下个誓。（旦）周舍，你真个教我赌咒？你若休了媳妇，我不嫁你呵，我着堂子里马踏杀，灯草打折臁儿骨。你逼的我赌这般重咒也！（周）将酒来。（旦）休买酒，我车儿上有十瓶酒哩。

One night of love is worth a hundred of friendship,
So stop your angry fuming;
And if you must be rough, be rough in private.
In front of me you ought to be more careful —
What lover will beat a pretty girl to death?
He's still glaring and brandishing his cruel stick;
Other hot-tempered men don't behave like this.

That's a big stick you're holding. What will happen if you beat her to death?

ZHOU: If a husband kills his wife, he need not pay with his life.

PANER: If you talk like that, who will dare to marry you?

I pretend not to understand, and play the coquette,
So that soon he'll have no home left;
For with my charms I can rescue poor Yinzhang.

A fine friend you are, Zhou She! Sitting here, and sending for your wife to come and abuse me! Boy, turn the carriage round. We're going home.

ZHOU: Please sit down, ma'am. I didn't know she was coming. May I die if I knew of it!

PANER: Are you sure? That woman is no good. If you'll get rid of her at once, I'll marry you.

ZHOU: I'll divorce her as soon as I get home. (*Aside.*) Wait a bit, though! I've scared Yinzhang by beating her every day. If I give her a divorce, she'll dash off like a streak of smoke. And then suppose Paner backs out? Won't I be losing at both ends? I mustn't do anything rash, but get Paner to promise to marry me. (*To Paner.*) Excuse me, ma'am, I'm as stupid as a donkey or a horse. If I go home today and divorce my wife, suppose you let me down, won't I be losing at both ends? Will you make an oath, ma'am?

PANER: So you want me to make an oath? Very well, if you divorce your wife and I refuse you, may I be trampled to death by a horse in the hall, or have my legs crushed by a lampwick. See what fearful oaths I've sworn for you!

ZHOU: Boy, bring wine!

(周)买羊来。(旦)休买羊，我车上有个熟羊哩。(周)买红去。(旦)休买红，我箱子里有一对大红罗。周舍，争什么哪？你的便是我的，我的就是你的。

【煞尾】则这紧的到头终是紧，亲的原来只是亲。凭着我花朵儿身躯，笋条般年纪，为这锦片也似前程，倒陪了十万贯家缘。十米九糠，问什么两妇三妻！受了些万苦千辛，我着人头上气忍，不枉了一世做郎君。

【尾声】你穷杀呵甘心受分捱贫困，你富呵休笑我饱暖生淫惹人议论。您中心觑个意顺，休了你门内人，教的钱财不使半文。领将来人到陪了几定银。家业家私待你六亲，肥马轻裘待你一身，倒陪了家缘和你为眷姻。我若还嫁了你，我不比宋引章针指油面、刺绣铺房、大裁小剪。我将你写了的休书正了本。(同下)

PANER: There's no need to buy wine. I've ten bottles in my carrige.

ZHOU: Then I'll buy a sheep.

PANER: There's no need. I have one cooked already.

ZHOU: At least let me buy the red silk.

PANER: There's no need. I have two lengths of red silk in my chest. What difference does it make? What's yours is mine, and what's mine is yours.

Near and dear will always be near and dear.
I give you my body as lovely as a flower,
And my youth like a tender shoot,
In order to share your distinguished career.
I bring a dowry of hundreds of thousands of cash;
I don't mind risking coarse food,
And I don't ask how many other wives you have;
For I'm willing to suffer hardships,
And put up with anything to marry you.
If you go hungry, I'll share your poverty;
If you grow rich, don't discard me as a wanton!
I want you because you please me.
I want you to divorce your present wife,
But not to spend a single cent on me;
I have come to you myself,
Making over my estate to your family,
Making over my good horses and furs to you,
And paying for the wedding into the bargain!

After our marriage you won't find me like Song Yinzhang, who has no idea of wifely duties and knows nothing about cooking, embroidery or sewing.

I'll see that you don't lose out if you divorce her!

(*Exeunt.*)

第四折

（外旦上）周舍敢待来也。（周舍上，见科）（外旦）周舍，你吃什么茶饭？（周怒云）好也！将纸笔来，写与你一纸休书，你快走！（外旦接休书科，云）我有什么不是,你休了我？（周）你还在这里？你快走！（外旦）你真个休了我也？（出门科，云）我出的这门来。周舍也，你好痴也！赵盼儿姐姐，你好强也！我将着这休书，直至店肆中去望姐姐去也。（下）（周）我却去店肆中娶那妇人去来。（下）

（店小二上）这早晚不见周小哥来？（周舍上）店小二,恰才成的那妇人在那里？（小二）你刚出门，他也上马去了。（周）倒着他道儿了。将马来，我赶将他去。（小二）马揣驹了。（周）鞴骡子。（小二）骡子思粪。（周）鞴驴子。（小二）驴子漏蹄。（周）我步行赶将他去。（下）

ACT IV

(*Enter Yinzhang.*)

YINZHANG: Zhou She may be back any time now. (*Enter Zhou She.*) Do you want anything to eat or drink?

ZHOU: (*angrily*): A fine wife you are! Here, bring me paper and brush, and I'll write you out a divorce paper. There! Now be off with you.

YINZHANG: (*takes the paper:*) What have I done wrong that you should divorce me?

ZHOU: Are you still here? Get out!

YINZHANG: So you're really divorcing me! (*She goes out.*) At last I've escaped from his clutches. Ah, Zhou She, what a fool you are! And Paner, how clever you are! I shall take this paper straight to the inn to my sister. (*Exit.*)

ZHOU: Now I shall go straight to the inn to marry Paner. (*Exit.*)

(*Enter the Waiter.*)

WAITER: Why is Zhou She not here yet?

(*Enter Zhou She.*)

ZHOU: Boy, where is the girl who arrived not long ago?

WAITER: She left with her carriage just after you went out.

ZHOU: She must have been fooling me! Bring me the mare.I shall catch her up.

WAITER: The mare is foaling.

ZHOU: Bring me the mule.

WAITER: The mule is lame.

ZHOU: Bring me the donkey.

WAITER: The donkey needs to be shod.

（小二）我也赶将他去。（下）

（旦同卜儿、外旦上）（卜云）若不是姐姐，怎能够出的这门也！（旦）走，走，走！

【双调新水令】笑吟吟案板似写着休书，则俺脱空故人何处？卖弄他能爱女，有权术，怎禁他得胜葫芦说到有九千句。

引章，你再要嫁人呵，我将这休书与周舍去。将那休书来，我试看咱。再嫁人呵，只来问我。（周舍赶上科）那里去？宋引章，你是我的老婆。（外旦）周舍，你与了我休书，赶出我来了。（周）休书上手模印五个指头，哪里四个指头是休书？（外旦展看科）（周夺科）（外旦不与科）（周咬碎科）（外旦）姐姐，周舍咬了我的也。（旦上救科）（周）你也是我的老婆。（旦）我怎么是你的老婆？（周）你吃了我的酒来。（旦）我车上有十瓶好酒，怎么是你的？（周）你可受我的羊来。（旦）我自有一只熟羊，怎么是你的？（周）你受了我的红定来。（旦）我自有大红罗，怎么是你的？

【乔牌儿】酒和羊车上物，大红罗自将去。你一心

ZHOU: Then I'll go after her on foot. (*Exit.*)

WAITER: I'll go, too. (*Exit.*)

(*Enter Paner and Yinzhang.*)

YINZHANG: If not for you, sister, I could never have got away.

PANER: Let's go.

I smile with pleasure now the divorce is granted.
Where is our crafty friend now?
He thinks the world of his charm and cleverness;
But he is no match for me.

If you want to marry again, I shall give this divorce paper back to Zhou She. Show me your divorce paper, Yinzhang. When you want to marry, ask for my advice.

(*Zhou She runs in.*)

ZHOU (*shouting*): Stop, you slut! Song Yinzhang, you are my wife! How dare you run away?

YINZHANG: You gave me a divorce paper, Zhou She, and drove me out.

ZHOU: There should be five finger-prints on the paper. How can one with four finger-prints be valid?

(*Yinzhang takes the paper out to examine it. Zhou snatches it from her, stuffs it into his mouth, and chews it up.*)

YINZHANG: He's swallowing my certificate, sister!

(*Paner comes back to help her.*)

ZHOU: You are my wife too.

PANER: How can I be your wife?

ZHOU: You've drunk my wine.

PANER: I had ten bottles of good wine in my carriage. It was none of yours.

ZHOU: Well, you accepted my sheep.

PANER: I had my own cooked sheep. It was none of yours.

ZHOU: Well, you took my red silk.

PANER: I had my own red silk. It was none of yours.

You can have the wine and the sheep from my carriage,
And the red silk that I brought;

淫滥无是处，要将人白赖取。

（周）你说了誓嫁我来。（旦）

【庆东原】俺须是卖空虚，凭着那说来了言咒誓为活路。怕你不信呵！走遍花街请妓女，道“死了全家”誓，说道无重数。论报应全无；若依着咒盟言，死的来灭门户。

引章妹子，你跟将他去。（外旦怕科，云）姐姐，跟了他去就是死！（旦）

【落梅风】则为你无重数，恰模糊。（周）休书已毁了，你不跟我去待怎么？（外旦怕科）（旦）妹子，休慌莫怕，咬碎的是假休书。我特故抄与你个休书题目，我跟前见放着你亲模。（周夺休书科）（旦）便有九头牛也拽不出去。

（周扯二旦云）明有王法，我和你告官去来！（同下）

（孤一行上）声名德化九重闻，良夜家家不闭门；雨后

But lust has made you mad
If you think you can win a wife by such a trick.

ZHOU: Well, you swore an oath to marry me.

PANER:

That was simply to fool you.
We singsong girls live by such oaths.

If you don't believe me,

Ask all the other girls in the courtesans' quarters.
There's not one who will not take a solemn oath,
Calling on Heaven to wipe out her whole clan,
Swearing again and again.
If such oaths came true,
Why, all of us would have perished!

Yinzhang, you must go with him.

YINZHANG (*frightened*): If I go with him, sister, he'll kill me.

PANER:

How could you be
So thoughtless and so foolish?

ZHOU: I've destroyed the certificate. Can you refuse to go back with me?

(*Yinzhang looks terrified.*)

PANER: Don't be afraid, sister. The one he chewed up was a forgery.

That was a copy I gave you
But here is the paper itself.

(*Zhou tries to snatch it from her.*)

Even nine strong bulls couldn't get it away from me!

ZHOU (*seizing the two girls*): We'll see what the law says. Come with me to the court!

(*Exeunt.*)

(*Enter the Prefect of Zhengzhou with Attendants.*)

PREFECT:

My noble reputation has reached heaven;
At night no household needs to close its doors,
The peasants plough their fields after the rain,

有人耕绿野，月明无犬吠花村。小官郑州守李公弼是也。今日升起早衙，看有什么人来。张千，喝撺箱。（张）理会的。（周舍同二旦、卜儿上）（周云）冤屈！（孤）告什么事？（周）大人可怜见，混赖我媳妇。（孤）谁混赖你的媳妇？（周）是赵盼儿设计混赖我媳妇宋引章。（孤）那妇人，怎么说？（旦）

【雁儿落】这厮心狠毒，这厮家豪富，衠一味虚肚肠，不干些实活路。

【得胜令】宋引章有亲夫，他强占作妻室。淫乱心情歹，凶顽胆气粗。无徒！到处里胡为做。见放着休书，望恩官明鉴取。

大人，宋引章是有丈夫的，被周舍强占为妻，昨日又与了休书了。（孤）他丈夫是谁？（旦）是安秀才。（孤）周舍，他是有丈夫的，你怎生还赖是你的妻？这桩事我尽知也。若不看你父亲面上，送你有司问罪。您一行人听我下断：周舍杖六十，与民一体当差。宋引章仍归安秀才为妻。赵盼儿等宁家住坐。只为老虔婆爱贿贪

And no dogs bark under the silver moon.

I am Li Gongbi, Prefect of Zhengzhou. Today I am holding a morning session, and shall see what cases there are. Attendants, summon the court!

ATTENDANTS: Yes, Your Honour!

(*Enter Zhou She with the two girls and Mistress Song.*)

ZHOU (*shouting*): Avenge my wrong, Your Honour!

PREFECT: What is your complaint?

ZHOU: Your Honour, she has tricked me of my wife.

PREFECT: Who has?

ZHOU: Zhao Paner played a trick to get my wife Song Yinzhang away from me.

PREFECT: What have you to say, woman?

PANER:

That cruel scoundrel counts on his wealth,
That false-hearted wretch won't tread the path of virtue.
Yinzhang was betrothed, but he forced her to be his wife!
Bold, wicked lecherous man,
He does many lawless things wherever he goes.
But here is the deed of divorce. Please read it, Your Honour!

Your Honour, Song Yinzhang was already betrothed, but Zhou She forced her to marry him. Yesterday he gave her a divorce certificate.

PREFECT: Who was her betrothed?

PANER: A scholar named An.

PREFECT: Zhou She, Song Yinzhang has her own husband. How could you claim she was your wife? This case is very clear. If not for your father's sake, I would send you to gaol. Listen, all of you, to my verdict. Zhou She shall be given sixty strokes with the bastinado, and in future shall be liable to labour conscription like a common citizen. Song Yinzhang shall go back to marry the scholar An. Zhao Paner and the others may go home.

This trouble was caused by the mother's avarice;
Zhao Paner made all things clear;

钱，赵盼儿细说根原。呆周舍不安本业，安秀才夫妇团圆。（旦）

【收尾】对恩官一一说详细，分剖开贪夫怨女。面糊盆再休说死生交，风月所别寻莺燕侣。

题目 念彼观音力
还着于本人
正名 虚脾瞒俏倬
风月救风尘

Zhou She was convicted of gross impropriety;
But the scholar An and his wife are reunited.
(*They kowtow to thank the Prefect.*)

PANER:

Now all has been explained to His Honour,
And the ill-assorted couple part company;
Do not say that, once married, they should remain together;
But let the love-birds find their mates again!

(*THE END*)

Rescued by a Coquette

望江亭中秋切鲙旦

The Riverside Pavilion

第一折

（冲末净扮白姑姑上，云）道可道，非常道；名可名，非常名。贫姑乃白姑姑是也。在这庵观里做着个住持。幼年舍俗出家。此处有一女人，乃是谭记儿，生的模样过人，不幸夫主亡逝已过。此个女人家中守寡，逐朝每日来俺这清庵观里与贫姑攀话。贫姑有一个侄儿，姓白，是白士中。数年不见，音信皆无。近来闻知得了官也，未能相会。今日无甚事，看有什么人来？（白士中上，云）万般皆下品，惟有读书高；一自登科甲，金榜姓名标。小官白士中。前往潭州为理，路打清庵观过。观中有我的姑娘，是白姑姑，在此观中做住持。小官今日与白姑姑相见一面，便索履任。来到门首也。无人报复，我自过去。（做见科，云）姑姑，你侄儿除授潭州为理，一径的来望姑姑来。（姑姑云）白士中孩儿也，喜得美除。我恰才道罢，孩儿果然

ACT I

(*Enter Abbess Bai.*)

ABBESS:

The law that can be told is not the invarible law;

The names that can be named are not invariable names.

I am Abbess Bai. I entered holy orders as a girl and am now abbess of the Convent of Pure Tranquillity. There's a young woman here called Tan Jier who's as pretty as a picture. But the poor thing's husband has died, leaving her a widow. She comes here every day for a chat. For some years I neither saw nor heard of my nephew Bai Shizhong. Not long ago I was told he'd been made an official, but I haven't seen him yet. Well, we've nothing on today. Let me see who is coming.

(*Enter Bai Shizhong.*)

BAI:

All other qualifications count as nothing:

Only scholarship wins respect.

I have passed the examinations:

My name has figured on the Golden List.

I am Bai Shizhong, on my way to Tanzhou to take up office. Since my road passes the Convent of Pure Tranquillity, where my aunt is abbess, I shall pay her a call before going on to my post. Here I am at the gate. There is no one to announce me. I may as well go straight in. (*He greets the Abbess.*) Aunty, I have been appointed magistrate of Tanzhou, and have broken my journey to pay my respects to you.

ABBESS: Congratulations, dear nephew! I was just this moment thinking of

来了也。孩儿，你媳妇儿好么？（白士中云）不瞒姑姑说，媳妇儿亡逝已过了也！（姑姑云）侄儿也，这里有个女人，乃是谭记儿，大有颜色。逐朝每日在我这庵里与我攀话。等他来时，我圆成与你做个夫人。意下如何？（白士中云）姑姑,莫非不中么？（姑姑云）不妨事，都在我身上。你壁衣后头躲者，我咳嗽为令，你便出来。（白士中云）理会的。（虚下）（姑姑云）这早晚夫人敢待来也。（正旦上，云）妾身乃学士李希颜的夫人，姓谭，小字记儿。不幸夫主亡化，过了三年光景也。我每日在清庵观和白姑姑闲攀话。今日无什么事，望白姑姑走一遭去。我想这妇人身无主也呵！

【仙吕点绛唇】则为这凤只鸾单，绣衾香散，身归晚，粉淡香残，我日暮愁无限。

【混江龙】我为甚一声长叹？玉容寂寞泪栏杆。则这落花里外，竹影中间，气吁的纷纷花似雨，泪洒的珊珊青竹滴残斑。但生三分颜色，有一点聪明，把儿夫不顾，守服三年。这愁烦恰便似海来深，忧和闷却兀的无边岸。那厮每荒淫好欲，一个个钻懒帮闲。

（正旦云）可早来到也。这观门首无人报复，我自过去。（做见姑姑科，云）姑姑万福。（姑姑云）夫人请

you, and here you are! How is your wife?

BAI: Why, aunty, my wife is dead.

ABBESS: Well, nephew, there's a young lady here called Tan Jier who's a real beauty. She comes every day for a chat. By and by, when she arrives, I'll get her to marry you. What do you say to that?

BAI: Suppose she isn't willing, aunty?

ABBESS: Don't worry! you can count on me. Just stay behind the curtain till you hear me cough, then come out.

BAI: Very well, aunty. (*Exit.*)

ABBESS: Jier should be coming soon.

(*Enter Tan Jier.*)

TAN: My name is Tan Jier. I was married to a scholar, Li Xiyan, who died three years ago. I come to this convent every day to see Abbess Bai. Today I have nothing to do, so I will call on her. Ah, it's hard for a woman when she has no one to turn to.

The phoenix has lost her mate,
Fragrance has fled my embroidered quilts,
And dusk filled my quiet chamber.
My cheeks bare of rouge and powder,
I grieve through the long, long twilight;
I sigh alone and shed tears
By falling flowers or in the bamboo's shade;
My sighs like a spring breeze make the petals fall,
And my tears stain the emerald rushes.
With my good looks and quick wit
I have mourned for three years as a widow,
My wretchedness as deep as the fathomless sea!
My sorrow knows no bounds:
All men are licentious and lustful,
All out to seduce and trick women.

Here I am at the convent. There is no one to announce me, so I may as well go straight in. (*She greets the Abbess.*) Ten thousand blessing, mother!

ABBESS: Please sit down.

坐。（正旦云）我每日定害姑姑，多承雅意。妾身有心跟的姑姑出家，姑姑意下如何？（姑姑云）夫人，你哪里出的家！这出家的要餐松啗柏，熬齑受淡。如此般凄凉！白日犹闲可，到晚来独自一个孤栖。不如嫁一个丈夫，可不好？（正旦云）姑姑，你差矣也！

【村里迓鼓】我待学恁这出家儿清静，到大来一身散袒，难熬他这日月韶光似相随相伴。怕不俺这世间，无危难，俺便多曾经惯。则我这玉鬓环，黄粱饭，则是一梦间。姑姑也，都来与您烧药炼丹。

（姑姑云）夫人，你怎生熬的这一顿素斋食？你不可出家也呵！

【元和令】则您那素斋食则一餐，休道我粗米饭几曾惯。把心猿意马紧牢拴，将繁华不挂眼。（姑姑云）姐姐，常言道："雨里孤村雪里山，看时容易画时难。当初不解俗人意，多买胭脂画牡丹。"你出不的家也。这的是"看时容易画时难"，虽不烧药不炼丹，不住山

TAN: It is good of you to let me take up your time every day like this. Now I would like to enter holy orders myself. Are you willing to have me?

ABBESS: How can you become a nun, my dear? Plain clothes and poor fare — ours is a hard life. It is not so bad in the day time, but when evening comes the loneliness is unbearable. You'd do better to marry again.

TAN: No, mother, you are wrong.

I long for this quiet life,
For then I shall know freedom.
It is hard to live all alone;
I have had my fill of the world
And its many changes of fortune;
All beauty and comfort are nothing but a dream:
Let me join you to seek for the philosopher's stone.

ABBESS: My dear, I'm afraid you couldn't stomach our vegetarian diet. No, you can't join holy orders.

TAN:

What hardship is there in that?
I am used to plain food.
I shall keep a check on my passionate, mischievous heart,
And renounce all earthly splendour.

ABBESS: Remember that verse, my dear —

A lonely village in the rain,
A mountain in the snow,
Although they seem such simple things
Are hard to paint, you know;
And had I guessed such scenes would not
Be popular today,
I would have bought some crimson paint
And painted posies gay!

No, my dear, how can you take orders?

TAN:

You say it is harder than it looks,
But how do you know I cannot live as a nun,

不坐圜。

（姑姑云）比似这般受苦呵，放着这一表人物，嫁个丈夫可不好？（正旦云）若有似俺男儿知重我的，便嫁他。（姑姑做咳嗽科）（白士中上，见正旦科，云）祗揖。（正旦云）万福。姑姑，兀的不有人来也？我索回去也。（姑姑云）你哪里去？他便是你的夫主。（正旦云）姑姑，什么言语哪？

【上马娇】咱则是因语间，好是干。姑姑倒做了曹仙嫁撮合山。（姑姑云）你夫妇之礼多曾经惯也。你道我"鸾交凤友从来惯"。（姑姑云）关了门者，我不放你出去！把门来关了，将人来厮邀拦。

【游四门】你却便引的人来心恶烦。你可甚撒手不为奸！你暗埋伏隐藏着谁家汉？将我来紧遮拦。畅好是奸！相待数年间，语话儿拴，则今日索分颜。

【胜葫芦】姑姑，抵多少"雨里前村雪里山"。（姑姑云）您两个今日成就了这夫妇罢。枉展污了你七星坛。你自做的着人下眼看。依本分明窗纸帐，药炉经

Cannot practise yoga and seek
The philosopher's stone?

ABBESS: With your looks, my dear, you can easily find a man you fancy and marry him. Why choose such a hard life?

TAN: If I could find a man who would love me as much as my last husband, I would consider it.

(*The Abbess coughs. Bai comes in and greets the girl.*)

BAI: Good day!

(*Tan returns his greeting.*)

TAN: Since you have a guest, mother, I will leave you now.

ABBESS: Don't go, my dear! What do you say to taking this man as your husband?

TAN: Mother, what a thing to say!

How could you take a chance remark so seriously?
We have scarcely met, yet you talk like a go-between!

ABBESS: After all, you have been married once.

TAN: How can you imply that I would take a lover?

ABBESS: The gate is shut and I won't let you go!

TAN:

So now you shut me in!
You dare bring this stranger to vex me!
Do you think me a loose woman,
That you hide this man in your convent
And stop me from leaving?
For three years we have been friends,
But this is the end of our friendship.
You have been an abbess all these years for nothing.

ABBESS: Why shouldn't the two of you become man and wife?

TAN:

You will spoil the reputation of your convent;
People will start to despise you,
You ought to keep this nunnery clean and chaste,
Attend to your stove and sutras,

卷。姑姑，抵多少叉手告人难。

（姑姑云）兀那君子！谁着你来这里来？（白士中云）这小娘子来着我来。（正旦云）什么言语！我至死也不随顺你！（姑姑云）你要官休也私休？（正旦云）怎生是官休？怎生是私休？（姑姑云）你要官休呵，我这里是个祝寿的道院，你不守志，领着人来打搅。我告到官中，三推六问，枉打坏了你。若是私休呵，你又青春，他又年少，我与你做个落花的媒人，成合了您两口儿，可不省事也！（正旦云）姑姑，等我自寻思咱。（姑姑云）“千求不如一吓”。（正旦云）哪个出家儿的放刁来！姑姑，他依的我两桩事，我便就随顺他。他若不依着我呵，我断然是不肯随顺他。（白士中云）休道两桩事，十桩我也依的。

【后庭花】依着他休离了我行坐间。则这十个字不放闲。岂不闻“法正天心顺”，则他这“官清民自安”。姑姑，着他看今番，我着他实实称赞。姑姑，你念经处不放闲，闲管处手段奔。你东山里做谢安，南山南指弱兰。

【柳叶儿】姑姑，你若题着这桩儿公案，则他那观名儿唤做清庵。你道是“鸾交凤友从来惯”。怕有人担疾患，来你行求丸散，则你与他这一服灵丹。姑

And not complain so much of your lonely life!

ABBESS: Who told you to come here, sir?

BAI: This young lady.

TAN: How dare you! I would rather die than marry you!

ABBESS: Do you want this settled in court or out of court?

TAN: What do you mean?

ABBESS: If you want it settled in court, I'll report it to the authorities. You've no right to carry on like this in our convent, bring a man here to drag our name through the mud. You'll be tried and given a beating. If you want it settled out of court — you are a girl, he is a young man, and I am your go-between. That is much the better way.

TAN: Let me think it over, mother.

ABBESS: So a thousand prayers are less use than one threat!

TAN: What a fine abbess — so good at blackmail! I'll marry him on two conditions, mother. Not otherwise.

BAI: I'd agree to ten conditions, let alone two.

TAN:

I'll agree to marry him
If he promises never to leave me,
And to remember the saying:
A just rule accords with Heaven,
A good official gives the people peace.
Let him live up to this!
And I must congratulate you
For finding time to make matches between your sutras;
Remaining in the hills like a statesman of old,
You manage affairs outside from your quiet retreat.
Well, mother, let me say this —
Though your convent's name is Pure Tranquillity,
You seem an experienced matchmaker!
All the love-sick and lonely
Should come to you for medicine,
And you can give them this treatment;

姑，你专医那枕冷衾寒。

（正旦云）罢，罢，罢！我依着姑姑，成就了这门亲事罢。（姑姑云）白士中，这桩事亏了我么？（白士中云）“你专医人枕冷衾寒”！亏了姑姑。您孩儿履任罢，便来相谢也。（正旦云）相公也，你就辞了姑姑，咱便索长行也。（白士中云）夫人说的是也。（姑姑云）白士中，你一路上小心在意者。您两口儿正是“郎才女貌”皆相配也。

【赚煞尾】这行程则宜疾不宜晚，休想我着那别人绊翻。不用追求相趁赶，则他这等闲，怎得见我这容颜。姑姑，你放心安，不索恁语话相关。收了缆，撅了桩，跳踏板，挂起这秋风布帆。试看那碧云梯两岸，端的他比“轻舟已过万重山”。（同白士中下）

（姑姑云）谁想成合了我侄儿白士中这门亲事也！我心中甚是欢喜。今朝无甚事，施主人家化些道粮走一遭去。非是贫姑乱主张，只因谭记守空房。观中怕惹风情事，故使机关配俊郎。（下）

For surely you are an expert
In curing loneliness and sleeplessness!

Very well, mother. I'll do as you say and accept his offer.

ABBESS: Well, nephew, you ought to thank me for this.

BAI: Yes, surely you are an expert in curing loneliness and sleeplessness! I do thank you, aunty. After I've been to my new post, I'll thank you properly.

TAN: Since you have to go to your post, let us say goodbye now and set out.

BAI: Very well, ma'am.

ABBESS: Take good care of yourself on the journey, dear nephew. You make a capital pair — a talented scholar and a beautiful girl.

TAN:

Let us start with no more delay,
Lest pursuers overtake us;
But if any man pursues me
He shall not see my face.
You need not warn us, aunty. Rest assured!
Pull in the boat, pull out the stake, step aboard!
Hoist sail and scud before the autumn wind!
As clouds alight upon the river banks,
Our light craft races past ten thousand hills.

(*Exeunt Tan and Bai.*)

ABBESS: Well! Today I have found my nephew an excellent wife! I am pleased! I've nothing to do now — I may as well go and ask our patrons for alms.

I didn't impose on her,
But feared trouble might come to my convent
If she remained a young widow;
That's why I tricked her into taking my nephew! (*Exit.*)

第二折

（杨衙内上，云）花花太岁为第一，浪子丧门世无对；街下小民闻吾怕，则我是势力并行杨衙内。某乃杨衙内是也。闻知有亡过了的李希颜夫人谭记儿，大有颜色，我一心要他做个小夫人。颇奈白士中无理，他在潭州为官，不期他倒娶了谭记儿做夫人。便好道："恨小非君子，无毒不丈夫。"量他到我哪里？你妒我为冤，我妒你为仇。小官今日奏知圣人："有白士中贪花恋酒，不理公事。"奉着圣人的命："差人去摽了白士中首级。"小官道："别人去不会干事，小官亲自到潭州取白士中首级。"张千，你说与亲随张稍："驾起小舟，直到潭州，取白士中首级走一遭去。"某已心下自寻思，一准要娶谭记儿。不期做了别人妇，我摽他首级在片时！（下）

（白士中上，云）小官白士中。自到任以来，一郡黎民

ACT II

(*Enter Lord Yang.*)

YANG:

I am the rake of rakes,
First among profligates.
All citizens fear me —
The powerful Lord Yang!

I am Lord Yang. When I heard of the beauty of Li Xiyan's widow, Tan Jier, I tried to make her my concubine. But now that dog Bai Shizhong has married her on his way to Tanzhou, where he is magistrate. The abbess of the Convent of Pure Tranquillity was their go-between. Well, a gentleman knows how to hate. A stout fellow does nothing by halves. I am not going to stand for this. He has no call to envy me, but I envy him. So I told the emperor today that Bai neglects public business for wine and women. When His Majesty issued an order for his execution, I immediately urged him not to send anyone else, but to let me go in person to cut off Bai's head — then there could be no mistake. His Majesty has agreed and given me the sword of authority and gold tally. Now, attendant, tell my two men to get the boat ready. We're going straight to Tanzhou to cut off Bai's head.

I weigh this matter well:
I meant Tan Jier to be mine
But she married another man.
Well, soon I shall cut off his head! (*Exit.*)

(*Enter Bai.*)

BAI: Since I came to this post, I have won the people's heart and every man

各安其业，颇得民心。托赖我夫人大贤。我别无甚勾当，当日有杨衙内要图他为妾，不期我娶了做夫人。谁想此女子十分贤达，聪明智慧。是佳人的领袖，美女的班头，天然聪明。闻知杨衙内十分怀恨我，我也恐怕他害我，每日悬悬在心。今朝无甚事，衙门中已回。在于前厅上闲坐，看有什么人来？（院公上，云）老汉最殷勤，答应在白门。谨遵老母命，持言见大人。老汉是白士中家的老院公。有俺白士中大人在潭州为理，杨衙内暗奏圣人，摽取首级。俺老夫人得知，差我先至潭州报知大人去。可早来到潭州也。我将着这封书见相公去。不必报复，我自过去。（见科，云）相公将息的好也！（拜科）（白士中云）院公，你来做什么来？（院公云）相公的老母着我将着这书来与相公，不知有甚事？（白士中云）有母亲的书呵，将来我看。（院公递书，云）书在此。（白士中看书科，云）书中的意，我知道了也。果中此贼之计！院公，你吃饭去。（院公云）理会的。（下）（白士中云）谁想杨衙内为我娶了谭记儿，挟这仇气，奏了圣人，要枭取我首级。似此如之奈何！我在前厅上纳闷，看有什么人来。

（正旦上，云）妾身谭记儿。自从相公履任以来，颇得

under my jurisdiction can go about his work in peace. My wife is very able, and has proved a great help to me. Lord Yang wanted to make her his concubine, but instead she became my wife. Beside being so virtuous, she is most brilliant and accomplished — I have never seen another woman like her. But I hear Lord Yang bears me a grudge, and I am afraid he means to harm me. This is preying on my mind. This morning's court session is over and I have nothing to do. I will rest a little here in the front hall, so that my wife does not see how worried I am.

(*Enter an old Steward.*)

STEWARD:

An old servant, I work hard
For the house of Bai.
The old lady has ordered me
To warn the young master.

I am an old steward of the Bai family. My master, Bai Shizhong, is magistrate of Tanzhou, but Lord Yang has slandered him to the emperor, who has ordered Lord Yang to cut off my master's head. Our old mistress got word of this, and has sent me to Tanzhou to warn her son. Here I am at last. I must give him the letter. I won't wait to be announced, but go straight in. (*He bows to Bai.*) Greetings, sir.

BAI: What brings you here?

STEWARD: The old lady ordered me to bring you this letter.

BAI: A letter from my mother? Let me see it.

STEWARD (*handing him the letter*): Here it is.

(*Bai reads the letter.*)

BAI: Very well, I understand. So that scoundrel is plotting against me as I suspected. Go in and have a meal.

STEWARD: Thank you, sir. (*Exit.*)

BAI: So Lord Yang bears me such a grudge for marrying Tan Jier that he has slandered me to the emperor in order to have me killed. What can I do? Let me think this over. Ah, I hear someone coming.

(*Enter Tan.*)

TAN: Since my husband came to this post he has won the people's heart.

民心。俺在这衙门后面居住，相公每日坐罢早衙，便与妾身闲攀话。今日这早晚不见来，我亲自望相公走一遭去。

【中吕粉蝶儿】不听的报喏声齐，待道是坐衙来恁时节不退，多管是接新官通报咱知。又无甚紧文书、忙公事，可着我心儿里不会。转过这影壁观窥，可怎生独自个死临侵地？

（正旦云）我且不过去，我试看咱。相公手里拿着一张纸，我也猜着了也呵。

【醉春风】常言道“人死不知心”，则他这海深也须见底。多管是前妻将书至，知他娶了新妻。他心儿里悔，悔。你做的个弃旧怜新。他则是见咱有意，使这巧谋之计。

（正旦云）无人报复，我自过去。（做见科，云）相公。（白士中云）夫人，有什么勾当，自来前厅上来？（正旦云）敢问相公，为什么不回后堂中去？敢是前妻寄书来哪？（白士中云）夫人，并无什么“前妻”寄书来。我自有两桩公事也。（正旦云）相公，不可瞒着妾身。你定有夫人在家，今日捎书来也。（白士中云）夫人不要多心！小官并不敢欺心也。

【红绣鞋】把似你守着一家一计。谁着你收拾下两妇三妻？你常好是七八下里不伶俐。堪相守留着相

After each morning court he usually comes to me in the inner hall. He is late today. I must go and see what has happened.

I hear no runners shouting —
Can he still be holding court?
I should have heard of an official visit,
And I doubt if there is any emergency.
I wonder what this means.
I step to the screen to have a look —
There he is, alone and dejected.

I had better have a look before going in. Ah, he has a sheet of paper in his hand and is poring over it. Now I understand.

Though the proverb says: Men's secrets die with them,
Even the ocean bed lies revealed at last.
He must have another wife,
Who has learned of his marriage to me
And sent him this letter.
He left his old wife for a new one,
Marrying me by a trick!

Since there is no one to announce me, I'll go straight in. (*She greets Bai.*) Sir!

BAI: Why have you come here, my love?

TAN: Why didn't you join me? Has your first wife written to you?

BAI: How can you suspect such a thing, my dear! No, I am worried by some public business.

TAN: Don't try to deceive me. You must have another wife at home, who has written to you now.

BAI: How can you be so suspicious? I would never deceive you.

TAN:

You must be faithful to your wife;
Why should you take more women than one?
So now you are in a quandary.
Well, keep the one you prefer
And abandon the other.

守，可别离与个别离。这公事合行的不在你！

（白士中云）我若无这些公事呵，与夫人白头相守。小官之心，惟天可表，并无前妻也！（正旦云）我见相公手中将着一张纸，必然是在家夫人寄来的书。相公休瞒妾身，我试猜这书中的意咱。（白士中云）夫人，你试猜咱。

【普天乐】弃旧的委实难，迎新的终容易。新的是半路里姻眷，旧的是绾角儿夫妻。我须是个妇女身，我须是个裙钗辈。见别人瞅眼抬头，我早先知来意。不是我卖弄所事精细！（正旦云）相公，妾身若不依命呵，直等的恩断意绝，眉南面北，恁时节水尽鹅飞。

（白士中云）夫人，小官不是负心的人，哪得那前妻来？（正旦云）相公，你说也不说？（白士中云）夫人，我无前妻，你着我说什么？（正旦云）既然真个不说，我觅个死处也！（白士中云）住！住！住！夫人，你死了，哪里发付我哪？我说则说，夫人休烦恼。（正旦云）相公，你说，我不烦恼。（白士中云）夫人不知……今有杨衙内要图谋你为妾，不期我娶了你做夫人。他恨小官，他在圣人前妄奏，说我“贪花恋酒，不理正事”，要摽我首级。这个是家中老院公，奉我老母的命捎此书来，着

It is you who must make the decision.

BAI: It really is public business, and I hope it will not prevent my living to a great age with you. I swear before Heaven I shall always be true to you, and I have no other wife.

TAN: What was that paper I saw in your hand? It must be a letter from your wife at home. Don't try to deceive me. I can guess what is in it.

BAI: Well, what is your guess?

TAN:

It is hard to abandon your first wife,
But easy to deal with the second,
For she is simply a casual love,
While the first is your wife betrothed to you in childhood.
Though merely a simple woman,
I can guess what is in a man's mind
By the slightest movement of his eyes or head.
I am not trying to display my intelligence!

Ah, sir, I will leave you when you tell me to,

Without waiting till our love burns out,
Till we turn our faces away from each other;
Till the lake dries up and the wild geese fly apart.

BAI: I am not so heartless, my dear. How could I have another wife?

TAN: Why won't you tell me the truth?

BAI: I have no other wife — what do you expect me to say?

TAN: If you won't tell me, I shall kill myself.

BAI: Wait! Wait! What should I do without you? I'll tell you if you insist, but you must promise not to worry.

TAN: If you tell me the truth, I shan't worry.

BAI: Very well. You know Lord Yang wanted to have you as his concubine, but I married you instead. Because he bears me a grudge, he has slandered me to the emperor, saying I neglect public business for wine and women. Now His Majesty has given him the sword of authority and gold tally, and he is coming to Tanzhou to cut off my head. An old steward brought this letter from my mother to warn me of my danger. That is

我知会。我因此上烦恼。(正旦云)原来是为这般!相公,你怕他做什么哪?(白士中云)夫人,休要惹他,则他是"花花太岁"!

【十二月】你道他是"花花太岁",敢也他怎生强要人为妻?全不学知文达礼,则待要雨约云期!这句话专心儿记者:我怎肯和他步步相随。

【尧民歌】呀!着那厮得便宜翻做了落便宜,着那厮满船空载月明归。休那里乞留乞良堆跌谩伤悲,你看我淡扫梳妆画蛾眉。今日、今日,我亲身到那里,着那厮有备应无备。

(白士中云)似这般如之奈何也!(正旦云)相公,不妨事。你将耳朵来!……则除是恁的……(白士中云)则怕落在他彀中么?(正旦云)相公,不妨事。

【煞尾】我着那厮磕着头见一番,恰便是神羊儿忙跪膝。着他此一来船横缆断在江心里,我可便智赚了金牌,着他便去不得!(下)

(白士中云)夫人去了也。据着夫人的机谋见识,休说一个杨衙内,一百个杨衙内也出不得我夫人之手也。我眼观旌节旗,耳听好消息。(下)

what was on my mind.

TAN: So that is it! Why should you be afraid of him?

BAI: The scoundrel is a powerful man, my dear.

TAN:

What if he is?
He can hardly take another man's wife by force.
The fellow has no sense of propriety,
But only tries to gratify his lust.
So mark my words:
I shall never yield to him;
His advantages will work to his disadvantage;
He will have to slink back empty-handed.
Stop beating your breast and lamenting!
I shall go in plain costume
With unlacquered eyebrows,
I shall go today
And see what he means to do.

BAI: No, no! You mustn't go.

TAN: Don't worry, sir. Listen! (*She whispers to him.*) What do you say to that?

BAI: But you may fall into his trap.

TAN: Don't be afraid.

I shall make him kowtow to me
Like a bleating lamb.
On his boat in midstream
I shall steal his gold tally from him
And leave him no way out! (*Exit.*)

BAI: So my wife has gone. She is so intelligent that a hundred Lord Yangs could not escape her, let alone one!

The army has gone into battle,
And I wait here for good tidings. (*Exit.*)

第三折

（衙内领亲随、净张稍上）（衙内云）小官杨衙内是也。颇奈白士中无礼，量你到的哪里！我举保你为官，单为谭记儿。谁想此人背我之恩，他娶了谭记儿为妻。此恨非浅！小官亲身到潭州取白士中首级。别的人为什么不带的来？这个是亲随，这个是张稍。这两个小的聪明乖乖，则是我心腹人；我因此上只带的这两个人来。（亲随去衙内鬓边做拿科）（衙内云）嗯！亲随，你做什么？（亲随云）相公鬓边一个虱子。（衙内云）这厮倒也说的是。我在这舡只上个月期程，也不曾梳篦的头。好儿乖乖也！（张稍去衙内鬓边做拿科）（衙内云）张稍，你也怎的？（张稍云）相公鬓上一个狗鳖！（衙内云）你看这厮！（亲随、张稍同去衙内鬓边做拿科）（衙内云）弟子孩儿！直恁般多！（张稍云）亲随，今日是八月十五日中秋节令，我每安排些酒果与大人玩月，可不好？（亲随云）你说的是也，等我和你禀一禀大人。（亲随同张稍做见科）（衙内云）您两个做什么？（张稍云）大人，今日是八月十五日中秋节令，对着如此般月色，俺与大人把一

ACT III

(*Enter Lord Yang with Zhang Shao and another servant.*)

YANG: I am Lord Yang. Let's see you escape me now, Bai Shizhong — curse you! I recommended you for this post, but I wanted Tan Jier for my concubine. How could I tell that he would turn against me and marry her behind my back? That was too much! I have come to Tanzhou to cut off his head. Why did I only bring Zhang Shao and one other man with me? Because they're clever rogues who can be trusted. That's why I brought them.

(*The Servant plucks at Lord Yang's hair.*)

YANG: Hey, what are you doing?

SERVANT: There was a louse in your hair, sir.

YANG: The fellow may be right. I have been on this boat for a month and not combed my hair. Good lad!

(*Zhang plucks at Lord Yang's hair.*)

YANG: Hey, Zhang Shao, what are you doing?

ZHANG: Sir, there was a tick in your hair.

YANG: Devil take it!

(*The Servant and Zhang both snatch at Lord Yang's hair.*)

YANG: Steady on, boys. How can there be so many?

ZHANG: I say! Today is the fifteenth of the eighth month — the Moon Festival. Let's prepare some wine and sweetmeats so that our master can enjoy the moonlight. How about it?

SERVANT: Right. Let's suggest it to him. (*They bow to Yang.*)

YANG: What do you want?

ZHANG: Sir, today is the Moon Festival and there is bright moonlight. We

杯赏月也。（衙内做怒科，云）嗯！这个弟子孩儿什么言语！我来干事来，怎么教我吃酒？（亲随云）大人，您孩儿并无歹意，是孝顺的心肠。大人便食用，孩儿一点不敢吃。（衙内云）亲随，你若吃酒呵呢？（亲随云）我若吃一点酒，吃血！（衙内云）正是休要吃酒。张稍，你若吃酒呵呢？（张稍云）我若吃酒呵，害疔疮！（衙内云）既是你两个不敢吃酒，也罢，也罢，我则饮三杯。安排酒果来！（亲随云）张稍，抬果桌，将酒来！（张稍做抬果桌科，云）果桌在此。我执壶，你递酒。（亲随云）我儿，酾满着！（递酒科，云）大人饮一杯。（衙内做接酒科）（亲随倒褪自饮科）（衙内云）亲随，你怎么自吃了？（亲随云）大人，这个是摄毒的盏儿。这酒不是家童带来的酒；大人吃下去，若有些好歹，药杀了大人，我可怎么了？（衙内云）说的是，你是我心腹人。（张稍做递酒科，云）你说嘴儿，你则是要吃酒！大人满饮一杯。（衙内接科）（张稍自饮科）（衙内云）张稍也，怎的了？（张稍云）大人，他吃的，我也吃的。（衙内云）你看这厮！我和你慢慢的饮酒。把船赶开。看有什么人来。

（正旦拿鱼上，云）这里也无人——妾身白士中的夫人谭记儿是也。妆扮做个卖鱼的，见杨衙内去也。好鱼也！这鱼在那江波游戏，趁浪寻食。我驾一孤舟，撒网

want to prepare a little wine to celebrate the festival.

YANG (*angrily*): Are you raving? I am here on public business — how can you expect me to drink?

SERVANT: We meant well, sir. We just wanted to show our respect. You drink. We won't touch a drop.

YANG: Ha! What if you break your word?

SERVANT: If I drink so much as a drop, may the wine turn to blood!

YANG: Good. You mustn't drink. How about you, Zhang Shao?

ZHANG: If I drink, may I break out in boils!

YANG: All right, since the two of you aren't going to drink, I'll have a few cups. Get the wine and sweetmeats ready.

SERVANT: Bring out the tray, Zhang Shao.

ZHANG (*fetching the tray*): Here it is. I'll hold the wine pot while you pass the wine.

SERVANT: Yes, fill the cup. (*He holds out the cup.*) Drink up, sir. (*As Lord Yang reaches for the cup, the Servant turns away and drinks the wine himself.*)

YANG: What do you think you're doing?

SERVANT: I'm testing it for poison, sir. We didn't bring this wine with us but bought it outside. If you were to drink it and get poisoned, what should we do?

YANG: Quite right. You're a good fellow.

ZHANG (*passing the wine*): You made that up because you wanted a drink. Sir, have a cup of wine. (*Before Lord Yang can take the cup, Zhang drains it.*)

YANG: Hey! Why are *you* drinking it now?

ZHANG: If he can drink, sir, so can I.

YANG: Curse you! Let me have a few cups now in peace while you drive away the other boats. There is someone coming.

(*Enter Tan carrying a fish.*)

TAN: There is no one here. I am Tan Jier, the wife of Bai Shizhong. I have dressed myself like a fishwife to see Lord Yang. A fine fish this is! It was frisking along with the waves looking for food, when I launched my

打出三尺锦鳞，细切着拖泥新鲜有味！绝好鱼也！

【越调斗鹌鹑】则这今晚开筵，宜时按节。饮味歌欢，花残月缺。见了的珍奇，不消的咱说。则这鱼更鲜滋味别，这鱼不宜那水煮油煎，则是那薄批细切。

（正旦云）我这一来，非同容易也！

【紫花儿序】俺则待稍关打节，怕有那惯施舍的经商的请言赊。则俺这盘中鱼尾，又不比那岸上罗列，活计全别。俺则是一撒网、一蓑衣、一蔓笠。俺则是先图些打捏，怕有那惯买的哥哥照顾些些。

（正旦云）我缆住这舡，上的岸来。（做见张稍云）哥哥万福。（张稍云）这个阿娘，我有些面熟也。（正旦云）你道我是谁？（张稍云）阿娘敢是张二娘？（正旦云）我便是张二嫂。你怎么不认的我了？你是谁？（张稍云）则我便是张阿鳖。（正旦云）你是张阿鳖？（正旦做打科，云）儿子，这些儿吃的好了。我想你来！（张稍云）阿娘，你见我亲么？（正旦云）儿子，我见了你，可知亲哩。你如今过去和相公说一声，着我过去切鲙。得些钱钞，养活娘也。（张稍云）我知道了。亲随，你来。（亲随云）弟子孩儿！唤我做什么？（张稍云）我有个张阿娘要与大人切鲙。（亲随云）什么张阿娘？（正旦见亲随科，云）媳妇孝顺的心肠，将这一尾金色鲤鱼特献新，望与相公

boat, cast my net and caught it. Glittering scales, three feet long! It will be very tasty, sliced. A beautiful fish!

Tonight is a festival,
There should be singing and drinking
Before the flowers fade and the moon wanes;
The tables are spread with dainties,
But nothing is so delicious as this fish;
No need to boil or fry it —
Simply cut it into thin slices.

It is not easy to come here.

I am using this fish to approach;
May some generous customer buy it.
This is not the usual fish sold in the market;
With one net, straw coat and straw hat,
I have come on special business;
May I find good customers!

I moor my boat and step ashore. (*She greets Zhang.*) Good evening.

ZHANG: I seem to know you, sister.

TAN: Who do you think I am?

ZHANG: Aren't you Mrs. Zhang?

TAN: Of course. How could you forget me? But who are you?

ZHANG: I'm Tortoise Zhang, of course.

TAN: That's it! (*She slaps him.*) Darling boy! These days I can see you have been eating well. I often think of you.

ZHANG: Do you love me, sister?

TAN: Of course, son. Now go and tell your master that I'm going to slice some fish for him, so that I can make a little money.

ZHANG: Sure. Here, you!

SERVANT: What do you want?

ZHANG: There's a Mrs. Zhang here who wants to slice some fish for our master.

SERVANT: What Mrs. Zhang?

TAN (*greeting the Servant*): To show my respect, I have brought a golden

说一声咱。（亲随云）也罢，也罢。我与你说去。得的钱钞与我些买酒吃。你身背后跟着我走。（做见衙内科，云）大人，有个张二嫂要与大人切鲙。（衙内云）什么张二嫂？（正旦见科，云）相公万福！（衙内做意儿科，云）一个妇人也！（亲随云）一个娘子也！（张稍云）一个好妈儿也！（衙内云）小娘子，你来做什么？（正旦云）媳妇孝顺的心肠，将这尾金色鲤鱼一径的来切鲙来。将砧板、刀子来，我切鲙。（衙内云）着小娘子如此般用心！怎敢着小娘子切鲙，村了手？张稍，拿了去。与我姜辣煎爨了来。（张稍云）大人，你就村了！（衙内云）多谢小娘子来意。抬过果桌来，我和小娘子饮三杯。将酒来，娘子满饮一杯。（亲随做吃酒科）（衙内云）你怎的？（亲随云）吃，不吃。请，请，请！（衙内云）你看这厮！靠后！将酒来！小娘子，满饮此一杯。（正旦云）相公请。（亲随云）你吃便吃，不吃我便来也。（正旦做跪科）（衙内扯正旦科，云）小娘子，请起，请起！我受了礼呵，做不的夫妻了。（正旦云）媳妇来到这里，受了礼也做的夫妻。（亲随同张稍云）相公，你此一来，妙哉！（衙内云）小娘子请坐。（正旦云）相公何往？（衙内

carp to give your master. Please put in a word for me.

SERVANT: All right, I will, if you'll give me some of the money to buy a drink. Come on. (*To Lord Yang.*) Sir. a Mrs. Zhang here wants to slice some fish for you.

YANG: What Mrs. Zhang?

TAN (*greeting Lord Yang*): Good evening, Your Honour.

YANG (*admiring her*): A fine-looking woman!

SERVANT: A nice lady!

ZHANG: A real bitch!

YANG: What brought you here, ma'am?

TAN: To show my respect, I have brought you this golden carp. If you'll let me have a knife and chopping board, I'll slice it for you.

YANG: That's very good of you, but I can't have you soiling your hands with that. Zhang Shao, take it and fry it with ginger and pepper.

ZHANG: Better let her do it, sir.

YANG: Thank you for coming here, my good woman. Here, fellow, bring some sweetmeats. I'll drink a few cups with this young woman. Pour out the wine. Drink it, ma'am!

(*The Servant drinks the wine.*)

YANG: What are you doing?

SERVANT: Are you going to drink or not? You just press each other.

YANG: Hold your tongue and get out of the way. Bring more wine. (*To Tan.*) Drink this cup.

TAN: After you, Your Honour!

SERVANT: Go on! If you won't drink, I will.

(*Tan kneels to Lord Yang, who helps her up.*)

YANG: Please sit down, ma'am. If I let you kneel to me, how can we be lovers?

TAN: Now that I'm here, even if you let me kneel to you we can still be lovers.

ZHANG and SERVANT: Wonderful, wonderful!

YANG: Please be seated, ma'am.

TAN: Where are you going, Your Honour?

云）小官有公差事。（张稍云）阿娘，杀白士中来！（衙内云）你说的什么哪？（正旦云）相公若拿了白士中呵，也除潭州一害。为甚的不着人来接待相公？（衙内云）小娘子，你不知，我怕人知道。

【金蕉叶】相公，你道是报一声，着官人远接，这船儿上有五十座笙歌间别。你为公差事来到这些，不知你怎生做兀的关节？

（衙内云）小娘子早是来的早，若来的迟呵，小官歇息了。

【调笑令】若是贱妾晚些来，相公船儿上黑鼾鼾的熟睡者。则你那金牌虎符旁边列，见官人远离一舍。索甚用从人拦当者，俺这里拖狗皮的考断他腰截。

（衙内云）张稍，我央及你！你替我做个落花媒人。你和张二嫂说："大夫人不许他，做第二个夫人。包髻、团衫、绣手帕，都是他受用。（张稍云）相公放心，都在我身上。（做见正旦科，云）阿娘，你有福也！相公说来："大夫人不许你，做第二个夫人。包髻、团衫、袖绣项帕……"（正旦云）敢是绣手帕？（张稍云）是绣手帕，绣手帕。（正旦云）我不信，我问相公去。（正旦见衙内，云）相公，恰才张稍说的那话，说道是相公说

YANG: I am travelling on public business.

ZHANG: He's here to kill Bai Shizhong, Mrs. Zhang.

YANG: Hold your tongue!

TAN: If Your Honour arrests Bai Shizhong, that will be one rogue the less. But how is it the prefecture hasn't sent men to welcome you?

YANG: You don't understand — I don't want word to leak out.

TAN:

Had you announced your arrival,
You could have feasted on board
With dozens of musicians.
Coming on government business,
Why need you travel in secret?

YANG: It's a good thing you came early, ma'am. If you'd come any later, I should have gone to bed.

TAN:

Yes, had I come any later,
You would have been sound asleep
With your sword of authority and gold tally by you.
All seeing an official would have kept away
With no need for attendants to guard you.
And I, who came to do business,
Would surely have had a stick broken across my back!

YANG: Zhang Shao, do me a favour and be my go-between. Tell Mrs. Zhang she can't be my wife, but I'll take her as my concubine. She shall have a shawl, silk smock and embroidered handkerchief.

ZHANG: Don't worry, sir. You can depend on me. (*To Tan.*) Mrs. Zhang, you are in luck. You heard what our master said. You can't be his wife, but he'll take you as his concubine, and give you a shawl, silk smock and border chief....

TAN: You mean an embroidered handkerchief.

ZHANG: That's right.

TAN: I can't believe it. I'll ask him for myself. (*To Yang.*) Sir, is what Zhang Shao said just now true?

来。（衙内云）是小官说来。（正旦云）量媳妇有何才能，着相公如此般错爱也。（衙内云）不敢，不敢。小娘子，靠着小官坐一坐，可也无伤也。（正旦云）妾身不敢。

【鬼三台】不是我夸贞烈，世不曾心肠趄。我丑则丑刁决古懒，不由我见官人便心邪，我也立不的志节。官人你救黎民为人须为彻，拿滥官杀人须见血。我和你雨约云期，（正旦与衙内做意儿科）使不着冰清玉洁。

（衙内做喜科，云）吻！吻！吻！（亲随同张稍做喜科，云）吻！吻！吻！（衙内云）你两个怎的？（张稍云）大家耍一会！

【圣药王】珠冠儿怎生戴者？霞帔是那里挂者？这三檐伞下怎向顶门上遮？唤侍妾，引领者。我来打鱼舡上身子儿扭的来别，替你稳坐七香车。

（衙内云）我出一对你对：罗袖半翻鹦鹉盏。（正旦云）妾对个：玉纤重整凤凰杯。（亲随同张稍做拍桌子科，云）妙也！妙也！（衙内云）小娘子莫非识字么？（正旦云）妾身须识个撇、竖、点、划。（衙内云）小娘子原来识

YANG: Yes, that's what I said.

TAN: Who am I to deserve such an honour?

YANG: All right, all right. Won't you sit next to me? It doesn't matter.

TAN: You are doing me a great honour.

I will not boast of my chastity,
But this is the first time I have fallen in love.
Though I am plain, and a little rude and stubborn,
At the sight of you I cannot hold myself back
Or put up any resistance.
You have come, sir, to rescue the people,
Take no half measures then —
When you catch that wicked magistrate
You must see that blood is spilt!
I am longing to share your bed:
I cannot be pure as snow or cold as ice.

(Tan Jier glances at him significantly.)

YANG (*pleased*): Well, well!

ZHANG and SERVANT (*echoing him*): Well, well!

YANG: What are you two doing?

ZHANG: Joining in the fun.

TAN:

I shall have a pearl-decked head-dress,
Bright silks, gay canopy,
And maids to wait on me!
My bones ache from rowing a boat,
But now I shall enjoy a comfortable carriage.

YANG: Let us compose a couplet together, ma'am.

Her silk sleeve overturns the cockatoo cup.

TAN:

My slender fingers fold the phoenix bedding.

SERVANT and ZHANG (*banging the table*): Wonderful, wonderful!

YANG: I suppose you can read and write?

TAN: A little.

字！小官出一题：鸡头个个不舒头。（正旦云）妾对个：龙眼团团不转眼。（亲随同张稍做拍桌子科，云）妙！妙！妙！（正旦云）张稍，我和你出个对句。（张稍云）我正好和你对哩！（正旦云）我是阿娘，休胡说！天上仙鹤对对飞。（张稍云）地下夫妻对对儿。（正旦云）相公，告珠玉。（衙内云）张稍，将纸、墨、笔、砚来。（张稍做拿笔砚科，云）理会的。相公，纸、墨、笔、砚在此。（衙内云）我写就了也。词寄是"西江月"。（正旦云）相公表白一遍咱。（衙内做念科，云）夜月一天秋露，冷风万里江湖。好花须有美人扶，情意不堪会处。　似仙子初离月浦，姮娥忽下云衢。小词仓卒对君书，付与你个知心人物。（正旦云）好高才也！我回一首，词寄是"夜行船"。（衙内云）小娘子，你表白一遍咱。（正旦做念科，云）花底双双莺燕语，也胜如凤只鸾孤。一霎儿恩情，片时云雨，关连着宿缘前注。　天保今生为眷属，但则愿似水如鱼。冷落江湖，团圞人月，相连着夜行船去。（衙内云）如此高才也！小娘子，俺慢慢的饮几杯。（正旦云）敢问衙内，因

YANG: Then let's compose another couplet.

The cock-head[20] seed cannot stretch its neck.

TAN:

The dragon-eye[21] fruit cannot turn its glance.

ZHANG and SERVANT (*banging the table*): Wonderful, wonderful!

TAN: Zhang Shao, let me make a couplet with you.

ZHANG: Of course! We'd make a fine couple.

TAN: Hold your tongue!

Storks fly in pairs through the sky —

ZHANG:

Lovers sleep together on earth.

TAN: Your Honour, may I ask you to write a poem?

YANG: All right. Zhang Shao, bring pen, paper and ink.

ZHANG (*bringing them*): Here they are, sir.

YANG: It is done. This is to the tune "Moonlight on the Western River."

TAN: Do read it to me, Your Honour!

YANG (*reading*):

The chill dew falls, the moonlight gleams,
The autumn wind sweeps lakes and streams.
Let lovely maid a blossom hold,
My inmost thoughts cannot be told;
Descended from the sky by night,
She knows my heart — for her I write.

TAN: What genius! I shall reply with another poem to the tune of "Sailing at Night."

YANG: Read it to me, ma'am.

TAN (*reading*):

Two birds beneath the blooms are better than a lonely phoenix:
This sudden romance of ours was surely predestined.
Like the fish and water we,
The lake is cold but, with the moon as companion,
We sail our boat through the night.

YANG: Wonderful, wonderful! Let's drink a few more cups, ma'am.

甚杀白士中也？（衙内云）你休问他，小娘子。（张稍云）小娘子，有势剑！（衙内云）休与他看。（正旦云）这个是势剑？衙内见爱媳妇，借与我持三日鱼。（衙内云）借与他。（亲随云）还有金牌哩！（正旦云）这个是金牌？衙内见爱我，与我打戒指儿带罢。再有什么也？（张稍云）这个是文书。（正旦云）这个便是买卖的合同？（正旦做袖文书科，云）相公，再饮一杯。（衙内云）酒够了也。小娘子，休唱前篇，则唱幺篇。（做醉科）（正旦云）冷落江湖，团圞人物，相随着夜行船去。（亲随同张稍做睡科）（正旦云）这厮都睡着了也。

【秃厮儿】那厮着懵懂玉山低趄，有鬼祟醉眼横斜。我将这金牌虎符袖褪者，我唤相公，"快疾些，来者"。

【络丝娘】我且回身将杨衙内深深拜谢：您娘回向他急飐飐船儿上去也。到家对儿夫尽说那一场欢悦。

（正旦云）惭愧也。

【尾】两口儿在玩月楼不放金杯歇，携素手怀揣着趔趄。两口儿吃的醉醺醺紧相偎，向他那冷清清船

TAN: Why do you want to kill Bai Shizhong, Your Honour?

YANG: You mustn't ask me that.

ZHANG: Mrs. Zhang, our master has the sword of authority here.

YANG: Don't show it!

TAN: So this is the sword of authority. Will you lend it to me for a couple of days to slice fish?

YANG: All right.

SERVANT: And here is the gold tally.

TAN: So this is the gold tally. Will you give it me to make gold rings? What else have you got?

ZHANG: Here is the imperial edict.

TAN: This is only a business contract. (*She slips it into her sleeve.*) Drink another cup, Your Honour.

YANG: I've had enough. Just sing the last part of your poem, ma'am. (*He falls into a drunken stupor.*)

TAN:

The lake is cold but, with the moon as companion,
We sail our boat through the night.

(*Zhang and the Servant fall asleep too.*)

Now, they are all asleep.

Fools, there they lie in a heap,
Their eyes heavy with sleep and wine;
Tucking the tally in my sleeve,
I wish them a rude awakening.
And make a deep bow to Lord Yang.
My skiff will soon take me home
To tell my husband all that has happened here,
And this will make him glad.

What a stroke of luck!

Holding gold goblets,
We shall enjoy the moon;
Hand in hand we shall drink,
Leaning close to each other,

儿上觉来也。(下)

(衙内云)张二嫂,张二嫂!(做失惊科,云)张稍,张二嫂那里去了?看我的势剑金牌也!(亲随云)就不见了金牌,还有势剑共文书哩!(张稍唱)

【马鞍儿】想着想着跌脚儿熬!(亲随唱)想着想着我难熬!(衙内唱)酩子里愁肠酩子里焦!(众合唱)又不敢傍人知道。则把他这好香烧,咒的他热肉儿跳!

(张稍云)黄昏无旅店,(亲随云)今夜宿谁家?(衙内云)这厮每扮南戏哪!(众同下)

While Lord Yang sleeps alone in his boat. (*Exit.*)

YANG: Where is Mrs. Zhang? (*Startled.*)

ZHANG: Where has she gone? Where is the gold tally?

SERVANT: The gold tally isn't the only thing that has gone. The sword and edict have disappeared too.

ZHANG: I stamp my feet in dismay!

SERVANT: Here's a fine to-do!

YANG: I am burning with secret rage!

TOGETHER:

But we dare not let anyone know.
Let us go to offer incense,
And lay a curse on that woman!

ZHANG: The sun has set and we have nowhere to go.

SERVANT: Where shall I sleep tonight?

YANG: These rogues are singing southern opera![22]

(*Exeunt.*)

第四折

（白士中领张千上，云）民无争讼差徭减，四野欢声乐太平。小官白士中。今日无其事，在衙门闲坐，看有什么人来。（衙内同净亲随、张稍上）（衙内云）小官杨衙内是也。如今取白士中的首级去。可早来到门首也，我自过去。（做见白士中科，云）令人与我拿下白士中去！（亲随做拿科）理会的。（白士中云）你凭什么文书来拿我？（衙内云）我有文书，我念与你听。（衙内做读文书科，云）词寄“西江月”……（白末做抢科，云）这个是淫词！这个不是，还别有哩？（衙内做读文书科，云）词寄“夜行船”……（白末做抢文书科，云）这个又是淫词！（衙内云）这厮倒挟制我！不妨事，又无原告，怕他做什么！（白士中云）怎么得个原告人可也好也！（正旦冲上，云）妾身白士中的夫人谭记儿是也。颇奈这杨衙内无礼也呵！

【双调新水令】有这等倚权豪贪酒色滥官员，将俺

ACT IV

(*Enter Bai Shizhong with his Attendant.*)

BAI:

Here are no quarrels, and little conscript labour;
All my people are happy and live at peace.

I am Bai Shizhong. There is no public business today. Let me see who is coming.

(*Enter Lord Yang with his Servant and Zhang Shao.*)

YANG: I am Lord Yang. I am going to get Bai Shizhong's head. Here is the gate. Let's go in. (*He sees Bai.*) Men, arrest Bai Shizhong.

SERVANT (*going to seize Bai*): Yes, Your Honour.

BAI: Where is your warrant for my arrest?

YANG: I have an imperial edict. Let me read it to you. (*Reading.*) To the tune of "Moonlight on the Western River."...

BAI (*snatching the paper*): This is an indecent poem!

YANG: That's not the one. Here it is. (*Reading.*) To the tune of "Sailing by Night."

BAI (*snatching the paper*): Another indecent poem!

YANG: This wretch has turned the tables on me. Well, never mind. As there is no charge against me, I have nothing to fear.

BAI: I wish someone would come and lay a charge against him.

(*Enter Tan dressed as a fisherwoman.*)

TAN: I am Tan Jier, Bai Shizhong's wife. That scoundrel Lord Yang has done me a great wrong.

Was there ever official so corrupt
As this bully, so inflamed by wine and women!

这有儿夫的媳妇来欺骗。使官府逼临的连理枝，倚势力唬吓的并头莲。我其实负屈衔冤，将俺这穷百姓可怜见！

（正旦做见跪科，云）大人可怜见！有杨衙内在半江心里欺骗我来，告大人与我做主。（白士中云）司房里责口词去。（旦云）理会的。（下）（白士中云）杨衙内，有人告你哩。你如今怎么说？（衙内云）可怎么了！我则索央及你。相公，我有说的话。（白士中云）你有什么话说？（衙内云）相公，如今你的罪过我也饶了你，你也饶过我罢。又一件，则说你有个好夫人，请出来我见一面。（白士中云）也罢，也罢。张千，请出夫人来。（张千云）理会的。夫人，相公有请哩。（正旦上，云）妾身乃是白士中的夫人是也。我如今过去，看那厮怎生意儿也。

【雁儿落】唬的他口不开怎的言？脚不离花街串，数年闻姓名，今日重相见。

【得胜令】请你个杨衙内恕生面。（衙内云）这个小娘子好面熟也！（张稍云）则他便是张二嫂。（衙内云）你又来也！你好见识，被你瞒过小官也。唬的他半晌家口难言。又无那人挟十棒罪，止不过三交两句言。这一只鱼

He wanted to seduce a married woman,
And tried to use his power
To separate husband and wife.
He has used me most unjustly —
Protect the poor, Your Honour!

(*She kneels to Bai.*) Have pity, Your Honour! Lord Yang tried to seduce me on the river. I demand justice.

BAI: Go to the clerks' office and write down your plea.

TAN: Yes, Your Honour. (*Exit.*)

BAI: So there is a charge against you after all, Lord Yang. Now what do you say?

YANG: What ever shall I do? I'll try to get on the good side of him. Sir, listen to me.

BAI: What is it?

YANG: I am willing to let you off, if you will let me off. But I have one request to make. I have heard much praise of your wife — I should like to meet her.

BAI: Very well. Attendant, ask my lady to come out.

ATTENDANT: Yes, Your Honour. Madam, His Honour wants you.

(*Enter Tan in different dress.*)

TAN: Now I shall see what that fellow will do.

He is too stunned to speak.
I have heard of your fame as a profligate,
And am honoured to meet you today.
Accept my greetings, my lord.

YANG: I seem to have seen this lady before.

ZHANG: Isn't she Mrs. Zhang?

YANG: Ah, madam, that was a fine trick you played. You took me in completely!

TAN:

He is speechless with surprise.
We cannot have him beaten or thrown into gaol,
For between him and me

船，半夜工夫缠；俺两个今年，一个中秋人月圆。

（李秉忠冲上，云）紧骤青骢马，星火赴潭州。小官乃府官李秉忠是也。因为杨衙内妄奏不实，奉上司台旨，着小官亲身体察。可早来到也。白士中，杨衙内，您这桩事小官尽知也，听我下断：杨衙内依势挟权，栋梁材负屈衔冤；谭记儿聪明智慧，赚金牌搭救英贤。奉上司差吾问理，将衙内削职身闲。做一个庆喜筵会，白士中夫妇团圆。

题目　洞庭湖半夜赚金牌
正名　望江亭中秋切鲙旦

There passed simply a few words.
Half a night on a fishing-boat
Has won us joy at this Moon Festival.

(*Enter Li Bingzhong the prefect.*)

PREFECT:

On my black charger
I gallop to Tanzbou.

I am Li Bingzhong, the prefect. After Lord Yang made a false report, the government sent me here to find out the truth. Now I have come to Tanzhou and learned all about you both — Bai Shizhong and Lord Yang. Listen now to my verdict!

Lord Yang abused his power
And accused a good officer wrongly;
Tan Jier is a clever woman,
Who tricked him out of the tally to save her husband.
I was sent by the government to investigate.
Lord Yang shall lose his official post;
Let a feast be spread to celebrate,
And may Bai Shizhong and his wife
Live happily hereafter!

(*THE END*)

The Riverside Pavilion

温太真玉镜台

The Jade Mirror-Stand

第一折

（老夫人引梅香上）花有重开日，人无再少年；休道黄金贵，安乐最值钱。老身姓温，夫主姓刘，早年辞世；别无儿男，止生得一个女儿，小字倩英，年长一十八岁，未曾许聘他人。夫主在日，教孩儿读书写字，未至精妙。老身有意教孩儿写字抚琴，无个要好明师。我有个从侄温峤，见任翰林学士，今将老身子母搬取来京旧宅居住。说道来拜望老身，争奈侄儿公事忙，不得空便。昨夜灯花爆，今朝喜鹊噪，梅香门首觑着，看有什么人来。（梅香）理会的。（正末扮温峤上）小官姓温，名峤，字太真。官拜翰林学士。小官别无亲眷，止有一个从姑，年老寡居，近日取来京师居住。连日公衙事冗，不曾拜候，今日稍闲，姑娘是尊行，须索拜候一遭。我想方今贤臣登用，际遇圣主，

ACT I

(*Enter Mistress Liu with Meixiang.*)

MRS. LIU:

Flowers may bloom again,
But youth will never return.
Do not count gold a treasure:
Happiness is more precious.

My maiden name is Wen. My husband's name was Liu. He died before his time, leaving me with no son but with one daughter — Qianying. She is eighteen now, but not yet engaged. When my husband was alive he taught her to read and write, but she is not very accomplished yet. Now I want her to learn calligraphy and the lyre. She needs a good tutor though. My nephew Wen Jiao, who is a member of the Hanlin Academy, has invited us to move into his old house in the capital and promised to call; but so far his work has kept him too busy. Last night the lamp sputtered, and this morning I heard magpies cry.[23] Keep your eye on the gate, girl, and let me know who is coming.

MEIXIANG: Yes, ma'am.

(*Enter Wen Jiao.*)

WEN: I am Wen Jiao, a scholar of the Hanlin Academy. My only relative is an old aunt who is a widow, whom I recently asked to come and live in the capital. These last few days I have been too busy with public affairs to call, but today I have time to pay my respects to her. Now that we have a wise ruler, men of talent are promoted, and wealth and official rank seem easy to win. But it has always been the way that some

觑的富贵容易。自古及今，那得志与不得志的多有不齐。我先将这得志的说一遍则个。

【仙吕点绛唇】车盖轩昂，诣门稽颡，来咨访。剖决条章，出语言无让。

【混江龙】食前方丈，望尘遮拜路途傍。出则高牙大纛，入则峻宇雕墙。万里雷霆驱号令，一天星斗焕文章。武夫前喝，从者塞途；无欲不得，无求不成。喜则鹓鸾并进，怒则虎豹平驱。生前不惧獬豸冠，死后图画麒麟像。分茅列土，拜将封王。

却说那不得志的也有一等。

【油葫芦】一个白发书生无伎俩，一年一度等选场，守着那聚萤积雪看书窗；几时得出为破虏三军将，入为治国头厅相？上古佐着舜尧，立着禹汤。黄金结作漫天网，收俊杰，揽贤良。

【天下乐】当日天下谁家得凤凰？为甚成汤基业昌？

scholars have realized their ambitions while others have failed. As for those who succeed —

High carriages throng their gates,
Humble visitors wait at their doors,
They discuss affairs of state,
And their word is law.
They feast in sumptuous style,
And such is their fame that strangers
Bow to them in the street;
They travel with a handsome èquipage,
Live in magnificent mansions,
Give orders potent as the thunderbolt,
Write with the brilliance of the stars in heaven;
Armed guards precede them, servants go behind,
And everything they may desire is theirs.
Their smile makes sparrows flaunt like phoenixes,
Their frown makes tigers cringe;
In life they are beyond the reach of the law,
In death their portraits hang for all to see;
Theirs are many fiefs and titles,
Generals they are, and princes.

And then there are the failures —

White-haired, ineffectual scholars
Year after year take the examinations,
And study by the window in poor light.
Will they never be appointed
A minister or commander?
They long for a sage monarch's properous reign,
When gold nets are cast far and wide
To gather in all good men.
In ancient times the sovereign sought for talent,
And King Tang had a happy reign
Because he went to Youxin to find ministers.

就商岩有莘求宰相，傅说版筑里生，伊尹稼穑中长，做的朝为田舍郎。

自古来有德的好难说也呵。

【那吒令】孔子为素王，训一人万邦；门生每受讲，立三纲五常；轩车离故乡，走四面八方。他是万代天子师，为四海生灵望，划地到陈国绝粮。

【鹊踏枝】孟子亦荒荒，走齐梁。更不算纣剖桀诛比干龙逢，屈原投大江。周公祷上苍，直到启金縢，才感悟成王。

非我自己矜夸也。

【寄生草】我正行功名运，我正在富贵乡。俺祖宗入世高名望，伯兄万人无诽谤，孩儿累代为卿相。俺帽檐相接御楼前，俺靴踪不离金阶上。

【幺】不枉了开着金屋、空着画堂，酒醒梦觉无情况，好天良夜成虚旷，临风对月空惆怅。不见可情

Fu Yue was a humble mason,
Yi Yin a peasant working in the fields,
Country fellows both of them.
And not all good men do well.
Confucius was a king without a throne,
Whose teachings influenced the entire world.
From him his disciples learned
The rules of morality.
He travelled from his native place
By carriage to different states;
He was a teacher of kings,
The guide of all men —
But in the State of Chen he nearly starved.
Mencius also had to wander
Through the States of Qi and Liang,
And all men know how the kings Zhou and Jie
Killed the wise Bi Gan and Long Peng.
Qu Yuan was driven to drown himself,
The Duke of Zhou prayed to Heaven,
But not till they opened the golden casket
Did King Cheng know his loyalty.[24]
I would not say I am boastful.
I am now enjoying fame,
Wealth and nobility;
My forbears were eminent men,
The elders of my clan have a good name,
And the younger members serve as ministers.
We are constantly at court,
Continually beside the golden steps;
But my gilded chamber and painted hall are empty,
I wake lonely after drinking
And pass the spring days in boredom,
Saddened by the breeze and the moon.

受锦屋凤凰衾，堪消在玉枕鸳鸯帐。

行说着话，来到姑姑门首。报复去，说温峤在于门首。（梅香）理会得。（报科）报的奶奶得知：有温峤在于门首。（夫人）老身恰才说罢，哥哥真个来了。道有请！（梅香）有请！（正末做见夫人拜科）（夫人）哥哥王事勤劳，将坐儿来，教哥哥稳便；将酒来，与学士递一杯。（梅香）有酒在此。（夫人）学士满饮一杯。（末接酒饮科）（夫人）梅香，绣房中叫小姐来拜哥哥者。（梅香）理会的。小姐，有请。（旦扮倩英上）妾身倩英。正在房中习针指，梅香说母亲在前厅呼唤。不知有甚事？须索走一遭去。（旦见科）母亲叫孩儿有甚事？（夫人）孩儿，唤你来无别事，把体面拜哥哥。（旦）理会的。（夫人）且住者，休拜！梅香，前厅上将老相公坐的栲栳圈银交椅来，请学士坐着，小姐拜。（末）老相公的交椅，侄儿如何敢坐？（夫人）学士休谦，"恭敬不如从命"。（末）谨依尊命。（夫人）小姐，把体面拜哥哥。（旦）理会的。（旦做拜科）（末做欠身科）（夫人）妹拜兄

Shall I never hold a bride in my arms,
And drown all my cares in the pleasures
Of the curtained wedding bed?

While talking to myself, I have reached my aunt's house. Girl! Go and tell your mistress that Wen Jiao is at the gate.

MEIXIANG: Yes, sir. (*Announcing him.*) The academician is at the gate, ma'am.

MRS. LIU: I was just talking of him, and here he is. Ask him to come in.

MEIXIANG: Please come in, sir.

(*Wen greets Mistress Liu.*)

MRS. LIU: You must be very busy with affairs of state. Draw up a seat, girl, and ask the gentleman to sit down. Then pour him some wine.

MEIXIANG: Here is the wine, sir.

MRS. LIU: Please drink one cup.

(*Wen drinks the wine.*)

MRS. LIU: Meixiang, tell your young mistress to come out and meet our guest.

MEIXIANG: Yes, ma'am. You are wanted, young mistress!

(*Enter Qianying.*)

QIANYING: I was sewing in my room when Meixiang told me my mother wanted me in the front hall. What can she want me for? Let me go and find out. (*She greets Mistress Liu.*) Why did you send for me, mother?

MRS. LIU: I want you to pay your respects to your cousin, child.

QIANYING: Yes, mother.

MRS. LIU: Wait one minute. Meixiang, fetch the master's silver-inlaid armchair from the front, and ask the gentleman to sit in it while the young mistress pays her respects.

WEN: How can I presume to sit in my uncle's chair?

MRS. LIU: Please don't stand on ceremony, but do as I say.

WEN: Very well, aunt.

MRS. LIU: Now, Qianying, pay your respects to your cousin.

QIANYING: Yes, mother.

(*Qianying curtseys, and Wen bows from his seat.*)

岂有欠身之理？（末）礼无不答，焉可坐受？（夫人）好一个有道理的人。（末背云）一个好女子也！

【六幺序】兀的不消人魂魄，绰人眼光？说神仙那的是天上？则见脂粉馨香，环佩丁当，藕丝嫩新织仙裳，但风流都在他身上，添分毫便不停当。见他的不动情，你便都休强，则除是铁石肝胆，也索恼断柔肠。

【幺】我这里端详他那模样：花比腮庞，花不成妆；玉比肌肪，玉不生光。宋玉襄王，想像高唐，止不过蝶梦悠扬，朝朝暮暮阳台上，害的他病在膏肓；若还来此相亲傍，形消骨化，命丧身亡。

（夫人）梅香，将酒来，小姐与哥哥把盏。（旦）将酒来，哥哥，满饮一杯。（做递酒科）（末）

【醉扶归】虽是副轻抬盏无斤两，则他这手纤细怎擎将？久立着神仙也不当。你待把我做真个的哥哥

MRS. LIU: When your younger cousin pays her respects, why should you bow to her?

WEN: All courtesies should be returned. How can I sit here and make no acknowledgement?

MRS. LIU: What a charming man!

WEN (*aside*): What a beautiful girl!

My soul is taking flight,
My eyes are dazzled!
She is an angel from heaven,
Powdered, rouged and scented,
With tinkling pendants of jade,
And gauzy, new, heavenly garments,
Yet her charm is still her own.
Nothing can add to it; no one
Could remain unmoved by her;
Even a heart of iron
She would surely break!
I devour her with my eyes —
Flowers are not so lovely as her cheeks,
Jade not so fair as her skin.
When the poet Song Yu wrote
Of King Xiang and his dream of the goddess,
Imagined delights in the tower day and night
Made him fall mortally ill;
Were he here beside her now
His bones would melt —
He would perish utterly.

MRS. LIU: Bring the wine, Meixiang. Offer your cousin a cup, Qianying.

QIANYING (*presenting the wine*): Cousin, please drink some wine.

WEN (*taking the cup*):

Though the cup is light, how can
Such slender fingers hold it?
I should not keep a fairy standing so long!

讲，我欲说话别无甚伎俩，把一盏酒淹一半在阶基上。

（夫人）老身欲教小姐写字弹琴，争奈无个明师。学士肯看老身薄面，教你妹子弹琴写字？（末）姑娘在上，据你侄儿所学，怎生教的小姐？（夫人）哥哥休谦。梅香，取历日来，教哥哥选个好日子，教小姐弹琴写字。（末）温峤今日出来时有别勾当，也曾选日子，来日是个好日辰。

【金盏儿】来日不空亡，恰相当。天生壬申癸酉全家旺，这长星交语不相妨。大纲来选好日子，何必开个学堂。岂不闻成开皆大吉，闭破莫商量。

（夫人）哥哥休谦。（末）谨依尊命！来日温峤自来。但温峤无学，怎生教得小姐？（夫人）老身无面皮，且看你下世姑夫的面皮。（末）

【醉中天】白日短，无时晌，兼夜教，正更长，便误了翰林院编修有甚忙？我待做师为学长，只得一件后十分应当，离了天堂上，别收拾个幽静书房。

（夫人）教小姐辞别了哥哥，回绣房去。（旦）理会的。（拜科，下）（夫人）多谢哥哥不违阻，是必明日早来。

Treated as her elder brother,
I am too confused to reply,
And spill half my wine on the steps.

MRS. LIU: I want her to learn calligraphy and to play the lyre, but I cannot find a good tutor. I hope, for my sake, you will teach her to write and play.

WEN: Why, aunty, unskilled as I am, how can I teach her?

MRS. LIU: Don't be over-modest. Meixiang, fetch the calendar, and let the gentleman choose a lucky day to begin lessons.

WEN: When I came out today I looked up the calendar for other reasons, and found that tomorrow is an auspicious day.

There is nothing amiss tomorrow;
It is an auspicious day for our family,
Not a day of evil comets to be avoided.
The calendar is a sure guide —
Some days are propitious,
Others ill-starred and unlucky.

MRS. LIU: Don't be too modest.

WEN: Certainly, ma'am, I shall come tomorrow. But I do not know enough to teach the young lady.

MRS. LIU: Don't refuse now. Teach her for her father's sake if not for mine.

WEN:

The days are so short,
Would I could teach her all night!
I would gladly abandon my post
In order to be her teacher.
Only one thing is needed —
Let a quiet study be prepared for us!

MRS. LIU: Child, you may go back to your chamber after you have said goodbye to your cousin.

QIANYING: Yes, mother. (*She curtseys and goes out.*)

MRS. LIU: It is very good of you to accept her as your pupil. I hope you will

（末）随姑娘尊意。

【赚煞】恰才立一朵海棠娇，捧一盏梨花酿。把我双送入愁乡醉乡。我这里下得阶基无个顿放，画堂中别是风光。恰才则挂垂杨一抹斜阳，改变了黯黯阴云蔽了上苍。眼见得人倚绿窗，又则怕灯昏罗帐，天那，休添上画檐间疏雨，滴愁肠。（下）

（夫人）梅香，便收拾了万卷堂，来日是吉日良辰，请学士来教你姐姐弹琴写字。收拾的停当，可教我知道。（下）（梅香）奉老夫人言语，便与姐姐说知，收拾万卷堂去。（下）

come early tomorrow.

WEN: Indeed I will, ma'am.

She stood there like a spray of cherry blossom,
Holding the fragrant wine,
Filling my heart with sorrow
And making me drunk with her beauty.
I walk down the steps in a daze,
Leaving the wonders of the painted hall;
Just now the setting sun hung over the willows,
Now dark clouds cover the sky;
We shall sit together by the green gauze window,
But when night falls I shall lie alone in the gloom;
And rain dripping from the eaves
Will only increase my despair. (*Exit.*)

MRS. LIU: Get the library ready, Meixiang. Tomorrow is a lucky day, and we have asked the academician to teach the young mistress to play the lyre and write. When you have cleaned the room out, let me know. (*Exit.*)

MEIXIANG: I must do as I am told. Let me go to tell my young lady and to get the study ready. (*Exit.*)

第二折

（老夫人上）昨日选定今日是吉日良辰。梅香，门首觑者，则怕哥哥来。（梅香）理会的。（正末上）姑娘选定今日好日辰，不曾衙门里去。肯分的姑娘又来请；便不来请，我也索去。可早来到门首也。报伏去，道温峤在门首。（梅香）理会的。温学士来了也。（夫人）道有请。（梅香）有请。（末做见科）（夫人）今日哥哥怎生来的早？（末）领尊命教小姐琴书，就不曾赴公衙去。（夫人）因为老身薄面，误了学士公事，老身知感不尽。快教小姐出来拜哥哥。（梅香）理会的。小姐，有请。（旦上）妾身正在绣房中，听的母亲呼唤，说哥哥来了，须索见去。（做见拜科）（夫人）倩英，你拜哥哥！今日为始，便是你师父了也。（旦）理会的。（做拜科）（末背云）小姐比昨日打扮的又别了，真神仙中人也。

ACT II

(*Enter Mistress Liu.*)

MRS. LIU: Yesterday we decided that this was a lucky day. Go and watch at the gate, Meixiang. Let me know when the tutor comes.

MEIXIANG: Yes, ma'am.

(*Enter Wen.*)

WEN: As my aunt decided I should start teaching today, I did not go to my office. She sent again to remind me, but I should have come in any case. Here is her gate. Please announce me, girl.

MEIXIANG: Yes, sir. Academician Wen is here.

MRS. LIU: Ask him to come in.

MEIXIANG: Please come in, sir.

(*Wen greets Mistress Liu.*)

MRS. LIU: You have come very early today.

WEN: As you asked me to teach the young lady music and calligraphy, I did not go to my office today.

MRS. LIU: So you have set aside your public business for our sake! How very good you are to us! Meixiang, call your young mistress at once — her tutor is here.

MEIXIANG: Yes, ma'am. Mistress Qianying, you are wanted!

QIANYING: I was in my room when I heard my mother call. I must go to her. (*She curtseys to her mother.*)

MRS. LIU: Pay your respects to your cousin, child. From today on, he is your tutor.

QIANYING: Yes, mother. (*She curtseys to Wen.*)

WEN (*aside*): In this dress she looks even lovelier than yesterday — a

【南吕一枝花】藕丝翡翠裙，玉腻蝤蛴颈。妲己空破国，西子枉倾城。天上飞琼，散下风流病。若是寝正浓，梦乍醒，且休问斜月残灯，直睡到东窗日影。

将琴来，教小姐操一曲。

【梁州】兀的不可喜煞罗帏绣幕，风流煞金屋银屏！这七条弦兴亡祸福都相应，圣贤可对，神鬼堪惊，俗怀顿爽，尘虑皆清。一弄儿指法非轻，不比那出塞鹤鸣。金徽弹流水潺湲，冰弦打余声齐整，玉纤点逸韵轻盈。聪明，怎生得口诀手未到心先应！海棠色、蕙兰性，天地气都将来结秀成，一团儿智巧心灵。

（夫人）再操一曲，则怕有不是处，教哥哥听，有不是处再教。（末）

goddess!

Her lotus skirt is flecked with kingfisher blue,
Her soft neck is white as jade;
Fairer than Daji who caused a kingdom's fall,
Or Xishi who ruined a state,
She is the angel who scatters lovesickness,
And could I see this fair vision in my dreams
I should not dread even the approach of dawn;
The moon might sink and the lamp burn low,
But I should sleep on till the sun
Shone through my eastern window.

Bring a lyre, and let the young lady play.

Beside embroidered silk curtains
In the gilded chamber,
By screens inlaid with silver,
What delight to listen to the seven strings
As they echo joy and sorrow!
This stately, unearthly music
Sweeps away all worldly thoughts
And banishes mundane cares;
Her touch is light, and the music
Is like the cry of wild storks in northern lands.
Resonance ripples from the golden stop-key,
Sweet harmonies from the chilly strings,
And the touch of her slender fingers is exquisite
In this art she has mastered superbly.
Most subtle in perception,
Pretty as cherry blossom,
Pure as the orchid,
She embodies the rarest virtues
Of earth and heaven!

MRS. LIU: Play that again. Then your tutor can point out any mistakes you still make.

【牧羊关】纵然道肌如雪、腕似冰，虽是一段玉，却是几样磨成：指头是三节儿琼瑶，指甲似十颗水晶。稳坐的有那稳坐堪人爱，但举动有那举动可人憎。他兀自未揎起金衫袖，我又早先听的玉钏鸣。

（夫人）小姐，弹不打紧；装香来，请哥哥在相公抱角床上坐着，小姐拜哥哥。一日为师，终身为父。哥哥教小姐写字。（旦写字科）（末）腕平着，笔直着。小姐，不是这等。（末起身把笔科。搭旦手科）（旦）是何道理？妹子跟前捻手捻腕！（末）小生岂有他意？（夫人）小鬼头，但得哥哥拿手搭腕，你早十分有福也。（旦）“男女七岁，不可同席。”（夫人）哥哥跟前调书带儿。（末）

【隔尾】女孩儿更温柔，起手里须当硬。我呆想望迎头儿撇会清，尽教我恰才轻搭着春纤算有幸。似这等酥蜜般抢白。折莫发作半生，我也忍得四星，也强如编修院里书生每壮厮挺。

小姐，不是了也，腕平着，笔直着。（旦怒云）哥哥，

WEN:

Skin white as snow,
Hands like jade
And fingernails like crystal,
She sits with charm and distinction,
Grace in her every movement,
And her jade bracelets tinkle
Before her gilded sleeves flutter.

MRS. LIU: That's enough of the lyre, child. Now prepare the incense, and let your cousin sit on your father's couch while you pay your respects. For since he is your tutor you must treat him as your father. Now, nephew, will you help her with her writing?

(*Qianying writes.*)

WEN: Keep your wrist down and your pen straight. No, not like that. (*He shows her how to hold the pen, and squeezes her hand.*)

QIANYING: Where are your manners? How dare you hold my hand?

WEN: I meant no harm.

MRS. LIU: You should think yourself very lucky, child. to have your cousin take your hand.

QIANYING: "After the age of seven, boys and girls should not share one seat."[25]

MRS. LIU: Now you're showing off your book-learning to your cousin.

WEN:

A gentle girl may appear stubborn at first;
I hope she is just being coy.
I congratulate myself on my good fortune —
What happiness to touch those tapering fingers!

How sweetly she flashed back at me!

However long she complains
I shall put up with it gladly,
This is better than being refuted
By the academy scholars!

No, that is not right. Keep your wrist down and your pen straight.

你又来也。（末）

【四块玉】兀的紫霜毫烧甚香，斑竹管有余庆，倒能够柔荑般指尖擎。你那双勾手腕儿先索平正，我不曾将你玉笋汤，他又早星眼睁，好打我这没气性。

（夫人）小姐，辞了哥哥回绣房去。（旦）理会的。（旦拜科下）（末）温峤更衣去咱。（做行科）见小姐下的阶基，往这里去了。见小姐中柱模样，不曾见小姐脚儿大小。沙土上印下小姐脚踪儿，早是我来的早，若来的迟了呵，一阵风吹了这脚踪儿，怎能够见小姐生的十全也呵！

【牧羊关】妇女每鞋袜里多藏着病，塘土儿没面情，除底外四周围并无余剩。几般儿窄窄狭狭，几般儿周周正正。几时迤逗的独强性，引逗的把人憎。几时得使性气由他跐，恶心烦自在蹬。

小姐去了也。几时得见着？小官撇不下也呵！

【贺新郎】你便是醉中茶，一啜瞟然醒。都为他皓齿明眸，不由我使心作倖。待寻条妙计无踪影。姑姑手把着头稍自领，索什么嘱付丁宁，似取水垂辘轳，用酒打猩猩。到这里惜甚廉耻，敢倾人命。

QIANYING (*angrily*): There you go again!

WEN:

Oh, lucky brush
Of rabbit's hair and bamboo,
Caressed by such tender fingers!
Do keep down your slender wrist!
Her eyes flash again as I touch her,
Reproaching me for playing such a trick on her.

MRS. LIU: Take your leave of your cousin now, child, and go back to your room.

QIANYING: Yes, mother. (*She curtseys and goes out.*)

WEN: Excuse me for a moment, aunty. (*He walks after Qianying.*) I saw her walk down the steps and go this way, but all I noticed was her face and figure — not her feet. She has left footprints in the sand. How lucky that I followed her so quickly! Had I waited, a breeze might have blown these prints away, and I should not have seen how utterly perfect she is.

Most slippers hide some lack of symmetry,
The candid sand shows no mercy;
But her footprints are flawless —
Slender, well-formed and bewitching.
She is charming in a passion,
When she stamps her feet in anger.

Now she has gone. When shall I see her again? How can I forget her?

Tea will sober a drunkard,
But I am intoxicated
By her white teeth and bright eyes.
I rack my brains for a good plan to win her,
But my old aunt is watchful.
I need no warning: this will be as hard
As drawing water from a deep, deep well,
Or catching gorillas with wine;
But love deadens me to shame;
I am willing to risk my life,

休、休，做一头海来深不本分，使一场天来大昧前程。

【隔尾】他藉妆颜色花难并，宜环珮腰肢柳笑轻，一对不倒踏窄小金莲尚古自剩。天公是怎生？这世情，教他独占人间第一等。

（末回科）（夫人）哥哥稳便。老身有句话：想小姐年长一十八岁，不曾许聘他人，翰林院有一般学士，烦哥哥保一门亲事。（末背云）小官暗想来，只得如此，若不恁的呵，不济事。（做向夫人云）姑娘，翰林院有个学士，才学文章不在侄儿之下。（夫人）似你这般才学少有。那学士多大年纪？怎生模样？哥哥你说一遍。（末）

【红芍药】年纪和温峤不多争，和温峤一样身形；据文学比温峤更聪明，温峤怎及他豪英？保亲的堪信凭，答配的两下里相应。不提防对面说才能，远不出门庭。

【菩萨梁州】古人亲事，把闺门礼正，人心至诚，更休问礼物微轻。点灯吃饭两分明：缑山无梦碧瑶笙，玉台有主菱花镜。更有场大厮併，月夜高烧绛

With cunning deep as the ocean,
Daring great as the sky.
Flowers fall short of her charm,
Willows of her slender waist,
And her tiny feet are like the golden lotus.
How could Heaven conceive such beauty,
Matchless in the world of men?

(*He turns back.*)

MRS. LIU: Excuse me, nephew, I would like to ask you a favour. My daughter has turned eighteen, but she isn't engaged yet. Your academy is full of fine scholars. Will you find a good match for her?

WEN (*aside*): I must play a trick if I want to have my way. (*To Mistress Liu.*) I know a scholar there, aunty, no less gifted and learned than I am.

MRS. LIU: Few scholars are your equal, I'll be bound. How old is this gentleman? What does he look like?

WEN:

He is my age, my build,
But a better scholar,
A bolder, more dashing man.
Take my word for it,
They will make a well-matched pair;

(*Aside.*)

You do not know
That he is here before you!
Though the custom is to wed with ceremony,
If both sides are sincere
You need no extravagant dowry.

(*Aside.*)

Light lamps and spread the feast,
Then for a dreamless sleep in fairyland!
A jade mirror-stand shall be the betrothal gift.
A tussle lies ahead
By crimson candles on a moonlit night;

蜡灯，只愁那烦扰非轻！

温峤与那学士说成，择定日子同来。（夫人）多劳哥哥用心。（末做出门笑科）温峤，你早则人生三事皆全了也。（末下、将砌末上科。做见夫人科）告的姑娘得知，恁侄儿径去与那学士说了。今日是吉日良辰，将这玉镜台权为定物；别使官媒人来通信，央您侄儿替那学士谢了亲者。

【煞尾】俺待麝兰腮、粉香臂、鸳鸯颈，由你水银渍、朱砂斑、翡翠青。到春来小重楼策杖登，曲阑边把臂行，闲寻芳、闷选胜。到夏来秋千院、斗草亭，碧纱厨、绿窗净，针穿珠、扇扑萤。到秋来霜天凉、雪气晴，入兰堂、开画屏，看银河、牛女星，伴添香、拜月亭。到冬来摘疏梅、浸古瓶，欢寻常、乐余剩，那时节、趁心性，由他娇痴、尽他索憎，善也偏宜、恶也相称。朝至暮不转我这眼睛，孜孜觑定，端的寒忘热、饥忘饱、冻忘冷。（下）

（夫人）侄儿去了也。梅香，门首觑者，看有什么人

And I foresee

That my work is cut out for me!

After I have spoken to him and arranged a date for the marriage, I shall bring him here.

MRS. LIU: It is very good of you to help.

(*Wen starts off, laughing to himself.*)

WEN: Now, Wen Jiao, your greatest wish will come true. (*He goes out, to return very shortly with something in his hand.*) Aunty, I have spoken to that scholar. Today is an auspicious day, and this jade mirror-stand is his betrothal gift. He will send a matchmaker to arrange the affair, but asked me to thank his future mother-in-law for him first.

Her sweet cheeks, snowy arms and downy neck
Shall be scented, powdered and tinged with cinnabar;
In spring we shall climb pagodas,
Walk arm in arm along winding corridors,
And search for new beauty spots.
In summer we shall haunt cool courts and pavilions,
Or rest by the immaculate green gauze window,
Threading pearls or catching glowworms with our fans.
In autumn when the frosty sky is clear
We will rest by painted screens
In halls fragrant with orchids;
We shall watch the stars of love
And burn incense to the moon.
In winter we shall pluck plum blossom
To set in antique vases,
And seek other pleasures too.
Then her slightest wish shall be law,
She may smile or frown,
For in every mood she is lovely.
I shall feast my eyes on her day and night,
Forgetting hunger, cold and all else beside. (*Exit.*)

MRS. LIU: He has gone. Watch the gate, Meixiang, and tell me if anyone

来。（媒人上）全凭说合为活计，一生作媒做营生。老身是个官媒人。温学士着我去老夫人家说知，选吉日良辰，娶小姐过门。可早来到也。无人报伏，我自过去。（做见科）老夫人万福！（夫人）媒人何来？（媒）奉学士言语，着我见老夫人，选日辰娶小姐过门。（夫人）是那个学士？（媒）是温学士。（夫人）他是保亲人。（媒）他不是保亲人，则他是女婿。（夫人）何为定物？（媒）玉镜台便是定礼。（夫人）我把这玉镜台摔碎了罢！（媒）住，住！这玉镜台不打紧，是圣人御赐之物，不争你摔碎了，做的个不敬上来。（夫人）嗨，吃他瞒过了我也！梅香，便说与小姐知道，收拾停当，选定吉日送小姐过门去。我且回后堂中去来。（下）

comes.

(*Enter the Matchmaker.*)

MATCHMAKER:

Introducing couples is my job,
Making matches is my trade.

I am a matchmaker. Academician Wen has sent me to Mrs. Liu's house to fix a lucky day for his wedding. Here I am. As there's no one to announce me, I'll go straight in. (*She greets Mistress Liu.*) My respects, ma'am!

MRS. LIU: Who sent you here?

MATCHMAKER: The academician sent me to you to arrange the day for the young lady's marriage.

MRS. LIU: Which academician?

MATCHMAKER: Academician Wen.

MRS. LIU: But he is the guarantor.

MATCHMAKER: No, no! Not the guarantor, but your future son-in-law.

MRS. LIU: What betrothal gift did he give?

MATCHMAKER: The jade mirror-stand was his gift.

MRS. LIU: The wretch! I'll smash it to pieces!

MATCHMAKER: Stop! That mirror-stand was a present from the emperor. To break it would be most disrespectful, and the cosequences might be very serious.

MRS. LIU: Well! So he has deceived me. Meixiang, tell your young mistress to get ready. When we have fixed on a lucky day, we shall send her to her husband's house. Now I must go to the back.

(*Exeunt.*)

第三折

（正末引媒人扶旦鼓乐迎上）（鼓乐住）（末）

【中吕粉蝶儿】怕不动的鼓乐声齐，若是女孩儿不谐鱼水，我自索自拖拽这一场出丑扬疾，安排下丹方一味：他若是皱一对双眉，我则索牙床前告他一会。

媒人，你遮我一遮，我试看咱。（媒）我遮着，你看。（末做看科）（旦）这老子好是无礼也！（末）

【红绣鞋】则见他无发付氤氲恶气，急节里不能够步步相随。我那五言诗作上天梯，首榜上标了名姓，当殿下脱了白衣，今夜管洞房中抓了面皮。

媒人，咱都过去来。

【迎仙客】到这里论甚使数，问甚官媒？紧皱定一团

ACT III

(*Enter Wen and Qianying escorted by the Matchmaker. Music sounds.*)

WFN:

Now drums and flutes are played:
If the girl won't have me,
Then I must take her by force.
Prepared for an awkward scene,
I put on a bold front;
If she frowns I shall plead with her
Before the ivory couch.

(*To the Matchmaker.*) Stand in front of me, ma'am, while I have a look at her.

MATCHMAKER: All right. Now you can peep.

(*Wen gazes at the girl.*)

QIANYING: What a boor!

WEN:

She is fuming with rage,
She will not submit to me.
As a poet I won preferment,
Passed first in the imperial examinations,
And at court wear official robes;
But tonight I shall have my face scratched by my bride.

I must screw up my courage and go up to her.

Enough of these fears,
I'll ignore the matchmaker
And stay close by my bride.

儿休厮离。和他守何亲，等甚喜？一发的走到跟底，大家吃一会没滋味。

（旦）兀那老子，若近前来，我抓了你那脸！教他外边去。媒人，你来，我和你说，这老子当初来时节，俺母亲言道，教小姐拜哥哥，他曾受我的礼来。（媒）学士，小姐说起初时你曾受他礼来。（末）我哪里受他礼来？你与小姐说去。（媒）小姐，学士说哪里受你礼来。（旦）在俺先父银椅栳圈交椅上坐着，受我的礼来。（媒）小姐说学士在他父亲银交椅上受他礼来。（末）

【醉高歌】我见他姿姿媚媚容仪，我几曾稳稳安安坐地？向傍边踢开一把银交椅，我则是靠着个椅栳圈轧坯。

（旦）媒人，你来，他又受我的礼来。（媒）学士，小姐说你又受他的礼来。（末）我哪里又受他礼来？（媒）小姐，学士说他哪里受你的礼来？（旦）这老子！俺母亲着我弹琴写字，他坐在俺先父抱角床上，我拜他为师来。（媒）学士，小姐说你在老相公抱角床上受礼，拜你为师来。（末）

Why stand on ceremony?
I must step forward
Even if she makes a scene.

QIANYING: If that fellow comes near me, I'll scratch his face! Make him go away! Come here, ma'am. I've something to tell you. When this fellow first turned up, my mother told me to pay my respects to him, and he accepted my curtsey.

MATCHMAKER: Sir, the bride says that when she first met you she paid her respects to you, and you accepted her curtsey.

WEN: I did not accept. Tell her that.

MATCHMAKER: He says he did not accept, ma'am.

QIANYING: He sat on my father's silver-inlaid armchair and accepted my curtsey.

MATCHMAKER: She says you sat on her father's silver-inlaid armchair and accepted her curtsey.

WEN:

The sight of her sweet face
Would not let me sit unmoved;
I kicked aside the chair
And stood beside it.

QIANYING: Come here, ma'am. He let me pay my respects to him another time too.

MATCHMAKER: Sir, she says you let her pay her respects to you another time too.

WEN: Never!

MATCHMAKER: He says never, ma'am.

QIANYING: When my mother told me to play the lyre and practise my calligraphy, he sat on my fathers couch while I bowed to him as his pupil.

MATCHMAKER: Sir, she says that before playing the lyre and practising calligraphy she bowed to you as her teacher, and seated on her father's couch, you accepted her bow.

【醉春风】我坐着窄窄半边床，受了怯怯两拜礼，我这里磕头礼拜却回席。怎地须还了你，你，便得些欢娱，便谈些好话，却有那般福气。

（旦）媒人，你说与他去：我在正堂中做卧房，教他休来我跟前来；若是他来，我抓了他那老脸皮，从他哪房里去。（媒）学士，小姐说来，他在正堂中做卧房，教你休来他跟前；若是你来，他抓了你老脸皮，从你哪房里去。（末）

【红绣鞋】正堂里夫人寝睡，小官在书房中依旧孤恓，遮莫待尽世儿不能够到他这罗帏；人说道谁家女被温峤娶为妻，落得个虚名儿则是美！

将酒来，我与小姐把盏咱。（末把酒科）（旦）我不吃。（媒）小姐接酒。（末）

【普天乐】初相见玉堂中，则想在天宫内，则索空闲中偷觑，怎生敢整顿观窥？得如今伏侍他，情愿待为奴婢。厨房中水陆烹炮珍羞味，箱柜内无限锦绣珠翠，但能够与你插戴些首饰，执料些饮食，则

WEN:

I simply sat on the edge of the couch,
And accepted two bows from her.
Now I bow back to you,
Returning your curtsey.
You have received what is your due,
And if I am honoured and pleased
That is my good luck.

QIANYING: Tell him this! I am going to bed, and I don't want him to come near me. If he does, I shall scratch his ugly face so that he won't dare show it to anyone.

MATCHMAKER: Sir, your bride says she is going to bed, and you must keep away. If you go near her, she will scratch your face so that you won't dare show it to anyone.

WEN:

My wife will sleep in the inner room
And I in the study, all alone as before.
But though I may never share her bed,
When it is said that Wen Jiao has married Qianying,
I shall still take pride in this!

Bring wine. Let me pour a cup for her. (*He pours out some wine.*)

QIANYING: I won't drink it.

MATCHMAKER: Take one cup, ma'am.

WEN:

When I first saw her in the stately hall
I thought I was in heaven,
And dared steal glances only,
Not look her in the face.
Now I can wait on her,
I'd gladly be her slave.
My larder holds rare dainties,
My chests are crammed with silks and embroideries!
If I can put on your trinkets

这的我早福共天齐。

（旦做潑酒科）我不吃。（末）

【满庭芳】量这个直得甚的？忒斟的金杯潋滟，因此上宫锦淋漓。大人家展污了何须计，恶心烦弃嫌他更衣，尽教温夫人潑到一两瓮香醪在地，浇到百十个袄子须心回！今夜我先知人来意，酒淹得袖湿，几时花压帽檐低。

（媒）这小姐则管不就亲，做的个违宣抗敕。（末）媒人，休说这般话。

【上小楼】休题着违宣抗敕，越逗的他烦天恼地。你则说迟了燕尔，过了新婚，误了时刻；你说领着省事，掌着军权，居着高位；又道会亲处倚官挟势。

我则索哀告你个媒人。（末跪科）（媒）学士，你为何在老身跟前下礼？（末）

【幺】我求灶头不如告灶尾。为甚我今日媒人跟前

And wait on you hand and foot,
I shall be in paradise.

QIANYING (*spilling the wine*): I won't drink!

WEN:
This is nothing.
I filled the gold cup too full,
So my court robe is wet;
But a little stain is of no account;
I can go and change my dress.
I do not mind if whole casks of wine are spilt
Or a hundred court robes stained,
If my lady will relent.
Tonight I know her plan,
My sleeve is wet with wine —
When will flowers deck my cap?

MATCHMAKER: If the young lady goes on scorning her husband like this, she will be disobeying His Majesty's decree.

WEN: Don't say such things, ma'am!
Don't talk of imperial decrees;
That will only enrage her more.
Beg her not to tarry,
Not to hesitate,
For the time is slipping away;
But if you speak of high position
Or of authority,
It will sound as if I am putting pressure on her.

But I beg you, ma'am, to help me! (*He kneels to the Matchmaker.*)

MATCHMAKER: Why do you kneel to me, sir?

WEN:
To ask the tail
Serves better than asking the head.
I bow to the matchmaker
To ask her to reason gently with my bride,

做小伏低？教他疑慢里劝谏的俺夫妻和会，兀的是罗帏中用人之际。

（媒）天色明了也。学士，你先往衙门中去，我投夫人跟前回话去也。（末）夫人，你的心事我已知道了，你听我说。

【耍孩儿】你这少年心则想着青春配，不知这争岁数男儿甚味？我心中常印着个不相宜，你便万般乖，我则索百纵千随：你便独强性，我则满面儿相陪笑；与些好气呵，我浑身儿都是喜。把你看承的家宅土地，本命神祇。

【六煞】且论咱、休说谁，娶得个幼年娇艳为妻室。久以后拿动针则是乞巧楼穿珠网，蘸手湿则除是芙蓉盆洗面水；宰相人家合当礼，张口吃饭，舒手穿衣。

【五煞】我将驾车马也选下，把车人也准备。打的辆细车子样制都无比：着绿絛结穗头，内金铎子银裹钉，雕轮上漆壤泥。无大人在车箱内，绾搭得异样，装裹得希奇。

【四煞】你便有王侯将相孙，穿着虚器谎诈衣，走的匹马汗如汤洗。这厮每黄昏鸾凤团圞寝，清晓鸳

So that husband and wife can live in happiness.
This is a time when a third party is needed.

MATCHMAKER: It is dawn now, sir, and you must go to your office. I shall report this to the old lady.

WEN: I know what is in your heart, my dear, but listen to me —

You are young and want to marry a handsome youth,
Yet what is there in a few years?
I shall always know that you are too good for me;
You may be difficult to please,
But I shall always obey you.
You may sulk, but I shall beam;
You may be angry and swear at me,
But I shall still be happy,
For I look on you as my goddess and guiding star.
Just consider my position.
As my young and pretty wife,
You will not use your needle
Except to show your skill by stringing pearls;
You will not wet your hands
Except to wash them in warm, scented water.
Married to a minister,
You will have all the food and clothes you need;
I have carriage, horses and drivers ready for you;
Your equipage is handsomely turned out
With green tassels, gilded axle, silver nails,
And brightly painted wheels,
And no one else will share
Your smart, distinguished carriage.
If you marry some young noble,
Dishonest and full of deceit,
He will go riding all day;
At night he and his wife are lovebirds together,
But at dawn the husband flies;

鸯各自飞。觑的你如儿戏；把你千金体似粪堆般看待，泥土般抛掷。

【三煞】你攒着眉熬夜阑，侧着耳听马嘶，闷心欲睡何曾睡。灯昏锦帐郎何在？香尽金炉人未归，渐渐不成器。攸得你一年半载，他可早两妇三妻。

【二煞】今日咱守定伊，休道近前使唤丫环辈，便有王母瑶池无心觑，月殿嫦娥不欲窥。俺也别无意，为甚千般惧怕？只为几岁年纪。

【煞尾】我都得知、都得知，你休执迷、休执迷，你若外事得个年少轻狂婿，不似我这般看承敬重你。（同下）

He considers her a toy,
Treats her as rubbish to be tossed aside.
You may knit your brows through the night,
And turn to listen to the horses neighing
When loneliness keeps you from sleep.
The lamp grows dim but still he does not come
The incense burns away — no sign of him!
So in a few short years you pine away,
While he enjoys himself with concubines.
But I shall be true to you:
I shall not lay hands on the maids,
And even if fairies came down from the moon
I should not look at them.
Being slightly your senior
Make me afraid of you —
That is how I know your thoughts.
So do not hanker after other men:
If you took a younger husband,
He would not treat you so well.

(*Exeunt.*)

第四折

（孤扮府尹引祗从上）龙楼凤阁九重城，新筑沙堤宰相行；我贵我荣君莫羡，十年前是一书生。老夫王府尹是也。今有温学士亲事一节，老夫设一会是玳瑁筵，请学士同夫人赴鸳鸯会。筵宴中间，则教他两口和会。等学士夫人来了，自有主意。这早晚敢待来也。（末同旦上）今日府尹相公设宴请双客，不知何意，须索走一遭去来也呵！

【双调新水令】则为凤鸾失配送了苍鹘，府尹设鸳鸯会请俺绾角儿夫妇。前面我骑着三领马，背后他坐着七香车；人道是村里夫妻，直这般似水如鱼，两口儿不肯离了一步。

ACT IV

(*Enter Prefect Wang with Attendants.*)

PREFECT:

In this lofty capital
With dragon and phoenix pavilions,
A new sanded avenue
Is built for the minister.
But do not envy
My high estate and splendour;
Ten years ago
I was still a mere civilian.

I am Prefect Wang. Trouble has arisen over Academician Wen's marriage. I have invited Wen and his wife to a special feast at which I shall try to reconcile them. I shall put my plan into action when they arrive. They should be here now.

(*Enter Wen and Qianying.*)

WEN: Today the prefect has asked us to a feast. I do not know what he means by this, but we are going to see.

When husband and wife are estranged,
A third party's help is needed.
Today the prefect asks us both to a feast;
I ride my charger in front,
She sits in the carriage behind;
They say this country couple
Is as close as the fish to the water;
Man and wife refuse to be parted.

【驻马听】想当日沽酒当垆，捹了个三不归白头卓氏女；今日膝行肘步，招了个百般嫌皓首汉相如。不肯好头好面，驾香车我懒古，没牙没口题桥柱。谁跟前敢告诉，兀的是自招自揽风流苦！

可早来到也。报伏去，道温学士来了也。（祗从）理会的。（报科）温学士来了也。（府尹）道有请。（见科）（府尹）小官奉圣人的命，设此玳瑁筵，请学士夫人吟诗作赋。有诗的，学士金钟饮酒，夫人插金凤钗，搽官定粉；无诗的，学士瓦盆里饮水，夫人头戴草花，墨乌面皮。（旦）学士，你听者，大人说，你若有诗便吃酒，无诗便吃冷水。你用心着。（末）

【乔牌儿】自从不应举，对不的两字句。昨日会宾朋，饮到瑶天暮，今日酒渴的我没是处。

【挂玉钩】恨不的巴得咽喉中咽下去。井坠着朱砂玉，与咱更压瘴气，凉心经，解大毒。夫人他自有规画处，至如肿了面皮，疮生眉目，也索蘸笔挥

When Sima Xiangru sold wine
He had a young wife by the name of Zhuo;
But I had to go on my knees to mine,
For she was disgusted by her white-haired husband
And would not go quietly with me.
I write listlessly on the bridge
With none to complain to.
This is love's sweet sorrow which I brought on myself.

Here we are. (*To the Attendants.*) Go and announce that Academician Wen and his wife have arrived.

ATTENDANT: Yes, sir. (*Announcing.*) Academician Wen and his wife are here.

PREFECT: Ask them to come in.

(*They greet each other.*)

PREFECT: By His Majesty's order I have prepared this feast to ask you to write a poem. If your poem is good, you shall drink wine from a gold goblet and your lady shall put a gold-phoenix pin in her hair and powder on her face. If your poem is bad, you shall drink water from an earthenware pitcher and your lady shall put straw in her hair and paint her face black.

QIANYING: Do you hear that, sir? His Excellency says if you write a good poem, you will have wine. If you don't write a good one, you will have to drink cold water. Do take care!

WEN:

I have not written a couplet
Since I passed the examinations,
And after drinking all last night with friends
Today my throat is parched—
I would like a drink of water to quench my thirst.
Well-water from an earthenware pot
Will cool the passions, damp down noxious fumes,
And counteract any poison.
Water is a wonderful drink;

毫，咒水书符。

（府尹）无诗呵罚水，夫人墨乌面皮。（末）

【川拨棹】这官人待须臾，第一名走脏毒。你道是傅粉涂朱，妖艳妆梳，貌赛过神仙洛浦，把紫罗襕权当住。

（旦）学士着心吟诗，无诗的吃水，墨乌面皮，什么模样！（末）休叫学士，你叫我丈夫。（旦）无计所奈，则索唤丈夫。（末）

【豆叶黄】正是黑屹落里欺你男儿，你这里却不指斥銮舆，也有禁住你限时、降了你乖处！两个月今日方才唤了我个丈夫，虽不曾彻胆欢娱，汤着皮肤，听的叫了一声儿夫，教我浑身麻木。

（旦）丈夫，你着心吟诗。你见末，倘或罚水，乌墨搽面，教我怎了？（末）

【乔牌儿】如今面上笔落处，则是浮抹不生住，咱那新合来细香澡豆天生楚，到家银盆中洗面去。

（旦）丈夫，着心在意吟诗。（末）

You can cure a boil or swollen face
With water and an incantation.

PREFECT: If there is no poem, the academician must drink water and the lady must paint her face with ink.

WEN:

The prefect must wait:
I need a draught to cool the passions first.
My lady is charmingly gowned,
Beautifully painted and powdered,
Fairer than a river nymph —
And she thinks herself more than a match for me.

QIANYING: Do apply your mind to your poem, sir! If you don't write one, you will have to drink water and my face will be painted black — that would be too bad!

WEN: You should address me as "husband," not as "sir."

QIANYING: Very well, I'll call you "husband." Do concentrate, husband!

WEN:

You plague your husband in private,
But you cannot disobey the emperor's order —
There is something at least to control you.
It has taken you two months to call me "husband."
I have not yet enjoyed you,
Not yet touched your skin;
But when you call me "husband,"
You throw me into raptures!

QIANYING: Husband! Do concentrate! Otherwise you will be punished with water; and if my face is painted black, what shall I do?

WEN:

Even if your face is painted,
It will not be black for long;
We have freshly-made, fragrant soap —
Once home again you can wash in a silver basin.

QIANYING: Husband, do give your attention to your poem!

【挂玉钩】我从小里文章不大古，到今日甚日辰见言语？年纪大也，如今老模糊，自今日我也有妆幺处。见他害恐惧，我且身无措。且等指的他着忙，放出诗题句。

（府尹）教学士吟诗者。（末）小官吟诗。（旦）丈夫着意者。（末）夫人放心。

【水仙子】你须闻得温峤不尘俗，明知道鲰生饱看书；我可甚书中有女颜如玉，嫌的我无地缝钻入去！少什么年少妻夫；丈夫眼灌的白邓邓，媳妇脸抹的黑突突，空这般绿鬓何如？

（旦）学士吟诗波，休似吃凉水的。（末）夫人，我吟的诗好呵，你肯随顺我么？（旦）你若吟得诗好，我插金钗、饮御酒，我便依随你。（末）夫人，你放心。

【甜水令】我如今先取纸墨，拿将笔砚，收拾完聚。我则待依例饮一银盂；这一盆凉水醒酒清神，自家看觑、看觑得浑似无物。

【折桂令】则我这秀才每胸卷江湖，不爱我这穷酸

WEN:

I have never been much of a poet,
What verses can I write
Now that I am old and dull-witted?
Today I am acting a part;
Her alarm is rather touching,
But I shall leave her in suspense
Before I start to write.

PREFECT: Please write your poem, sir.

WEN: Very well.

QIANYING: Husband, do give your mind to it!

WEN: There is no cause for alarm, ma'am.

You should understand that Wen Jiao is no common scholar,
But has read a great many books.
Yet my learning won me no beauty,
For you treated me with such disdain
That I longed to sink through the earth.
But though young men are easy to find,
If a youth has to drink cold water
And your face is painted black,
What use are his handsome looks?

QIANYING: Please, husband, write that poem! I don't want you to drink cold water.

WEN: If I write a good poem, my dear, will you be kind to me?

QIANYING: If you write a good poem, and I can wear a gold pin and drink the emperor's wine, then I promise to love you.

WEN: In that case, my dear, you need not worry.

I take paper and ink; my brush is ready at hand;
I shall drink from the silver cup.
A glance at the pitcher of water does not dismay me —
It will sober me after drinking.
I am not in the least alarmed.
My knowledge is all-embracing as rivers and lakes,

者也之乎，翰林院编修。把小生觑的似有如无！则被你欺负得我千足万足，我但轻还着早无情无绪。恰才款移莲步，似三谒茅庐；为咱不言不语，不曾承伏。醋支刺走向前来，恶支煞倒褪回去。

（末吟诗科）翰林学士坐华堂，挥笔吟诗动四方。御酒饮来花插帽，当今天子重贤良。（府尹）温学士不枉了，好高才大手，吟得好诗！教夫人插凤钗、饮御酒。（旦喜科）学士，多亏了你也！（末）夫人，你又早欢喜了也。（府尹）夫人，你肯依随学士么？（旦）妾身愿随学士。（府尹）既然夫人一心成其夫妇，老夫与学士准备做一个庆喜的筵席。（末）

【雁儿落】你常好是吃嬴不吃输，你又索还报相思苦，你番悔了我告处，这篇诗勒揩的情和睦。

【得胜令】不弱如韩信吓蛮书，一字也不差误。他着宝钗簪云髻，我着金杯饮酥醑，把金珠，车载的还家去。娇姝早则不嫌你老丈夫。

But my wife despises my scholarship
And considers me as useless;
She has tormented me so
That I will pose as befuddled.
Now she moves forward, a suppliant,
But I pay no attention to her.
She is all meekness now,
A shrew no more!

(*He chants his poem.*)

When the academician sits down in the hall
And composes a verse, he dumbfounds one and all;
He has won royal wine and renown by his pen,
For the emperor honours all talented men.

PREFECT: You certainly have genius, sir, to throw off such an excellent poem. Let his lady put on the gold hairpin and drink the royal wine.

QIANYING (*delighted*): I thank you with all my heart, sir!

WEN: You seem rather pleased with me now, ma'am.

PREFECT: Are you willing to be his wife now, ma'am?

QIANYING: Yes, I am willing.

PREFECT: In that case I shall prepare another feast to congratulate you both.

WEN:

You fear the strong and torment the weak,
But now you must repay my love
And repent of what you did.
With this poem I made you love me.
This is like the famous reply to the foreign envoy —
Each word completely correct.[26]
She has a gold pin in her hair,
I drink from the gold goblet,
And we will carry many gifts away.
No more will the lovely bride
Despise her elderly husband.

（府尹）人间喜事无过夫妇会合。杀羊造酒，安排庆喜筵席。金尊酒泛会宾筵，一派笙歌启玳筵；庆喜今朝全四美，夫荣妻贵永团圆。（末）多感盛情。

【鸳鸯煞】冰人完月老姻缘簿，巫娥全宋玉相思苦。今日个锦帐欢娱，索强如绣幕孤独。胜道执酒的相如，怎肯把驾车女文君负？从今后琴趣诗篇吟和处，风流句，则我这意见功夫，会合了朝云共暮雨。

题目　王府尹水墨宴

正名　温太真玉镜台

PREFECT: There is no happier occasion than a reconciliation between a husband and wife. We shall kill sheep and prepare wine for a congratulatory feast.

We feast with gold goblets brimming with wine;
Fluting and singing accompany the banquet;
Today their joy is complete;
The distinguished husband and wife will live happy for ever.

(*Wen bows to the Prefect.*)

WEN: I thank you, sir, for your help.

Now our marriage is a true one,
The sorrows of love are ended,
We shall take delight in each other —
This is better than sleeping alone.
Sima Xiangru in his tavern
Would not give up Lady Zhuo.
From now on we shall live in harmony —
By my own exertions I have won my love.

(*THE END*)

The Jade Mirror–Stand

关大王独赴单刀会

Lord Guan Goes to the Feast

第一折

（冲末鲁肃上）（云）三尺龙泉万卷书，皇天生我意何如；山东宰相山西将，彼丈夫兮我丈夫。小官姓鲁，名肃，字子敬。见在吴王麾下为中大夫之职。想当日俺主公孙仲谋占了江东，魏王曹操占了中原，蜀王刘备占了西川。有我荆州乃四冲用武之地，保守无虞，分天下为鼎足之形。想当日周瑜死于江陵，小官为保，劝主公以荆州借与刘备，共拒曹操。主公又以妹妻刘备。不料此人外亲内疏，挟诈而取益州，遂并汉中，有霸业兴隆之志。我今欲取索荆州，料关公在那里镇守，必不肯还我。今差守将黄文，先设下三计。启过主公，说关公韬略过人，有兼并之心，且居国之上游，不如取索荆州。今据长江形势，第一计：趁今日孙刘结亲，已为唇齿，就江下排宴设乐，修一书以

ACT I

(*Enter Lu Su, Huang Wen and Soldiers.*)

LU:

Three feet of steel, ten thousand books —
For what am I destined by Heaven?
Statesmen of the east, generals of the west —
What were they?
I am the equal of them all.

I am Lu Su, Minister to the King of Wu. My master, Sun Quan, rules over the Changjiang River Valley, while Cao Cao, King of Wei, holds the north, and Liu Bei, King of Shu, the west. Formerly we controlled the strategic province of Jingzhou, and by holding it securely kept the empire divided into three. But when Zhou Yu died at Jiangling I urged our king to let Liu Bei occupy Jingzhou for a time, so that we could join forces against Cao Cao. I acted as guarantor for that. Then our master gave his younger sister to Liu Bei. However, the scoundrel's friendship was false — he tricked us by seizing Yizhou, and annexed Hanzhong, hoping to set himself up as emperor. Now I want to take Jingzhou back, but Lord Guan who is governor there will certainly not return it. I have therefore sent General Huang Wen with a memorial to our king proposing three plans, in which I urge that since Lord Guan is so able, is determined to annex our territory, and holds the upper reaches of the river, we should demand the return of Jingzhou, so that we may control the whole Changjiang River Valley. My plans are: First, since the kings of both our states are related by marriage, we can prepare a feast with music by the

贺近退曹兵，玄德称主于汉中，赞其功美。邀请关公江下赴会为庆。此人必无所疑。若渡江赴宴，就于饮酒席中间，以礼取索荆州。如还，此为万全之计。倘若不还，第二计：将江上应有战舡，尽行拘收，不放关公渡江回去。淹留日久，自知中计，默然有悔，诚心献还。更不与呵，第三计：壁衣内暗藏甲士。酒酣之际，击金钟为号，伏兵尽举，擒住关公，囚于江下。此人是刘备股肱之臣。若将荆州复还江东，则放关公还益州；如其不然，主将既失，孤兵必乱，乘势大举，觑荆州一鼓而下，有何难哉！虽则三计已定，先交黄文请的乔公来商议则个。

（正末乔公上，云）老夫乔公是也。想三分鼎足已定：曹操占了中原，孙仲谋占了江东，刘玄德占了西蜀。想玄德未济时，曾问俺东吴家借荆州为本，至今未还。鲁子敬常有索取之心，沉疑未发。今日令人来请老夫，不知有甚事？须索走一遭去。我想汉家天下，谁想变乱到此也呵！（唱）

【仙吕点绛唇】俺本是汉国臣僚。汉皇软弱；兴心闹，惹起那五处兵刀，并董卓，诛袁绍。

【混江龙】止留下孙刘曹操，平分一国作三朝。不

Changjiang River, and write to congratulate Lord Guan on Liu Bei's recent victory over Cao Cao, the establishment of his rule in Hanzhong, and the great achievements of the Kingdom of Shu. We will invite Lord Guan to cross the river to our feast, and he will hardly suspect us. Should he come, during the banquet we will ask him courteously for the return of Jingzhou. If he agrees, well and good. If not, we can carry out our second plan — seize all his ships and detain him. Once this is done and he knows he is caught in a trap, he should think better of it and return us our province. If he still refuses, we can resort to our third plan — conceal armed men behind the arras, and signal to them during the drinking to come out and take him captive. Lord Guan is Lui Bei's right hand. We shall let him go back to Yizhou only after he agrees to return us Jingzhou. In any case, the commander's absence will throw his troops into disorder, and by seizing this opportunity we should have no difficulty in recapturing Jingzhou in one battle. These are the three plans which I gave to Huang Wen. I have asked Qiao Gong here to discuss them.

(*Enter Qiao Gong.*)

QIAO: I am Qiao Gong. Now the empire is divided into three, with Cao Cao in the north, Sun Quan in the Changjiang River Valley and Liu Bei in the west. Before Liu Bei scored such successes, our king gave him the use of Jingzhou as a base, but he has not yet returned it. Though Lu Su has determined to win it back, he has not yet taken any action. Today he has sent for me. I must go and see what he wants. Who could have foreseen this break-up of the Han Empire?

I was a subject of Han,
But the emperor was a weakling,
Discontent was rife,
And five rebellions broke out.
Two warlords were killed, leaving only
Sun Quan, Liu Bei and Cao Cao,
Who divided one state into three.
Now the world is at peace again,
The wind and waves are calmed

付能河清海晏，雨顺风调。兵器改为农器用，征旗不动酒旗摇。军罢战，马添膘。杀气散，阵云高。为将帅，作臣僚；脱金甲，着罗袍。则他这帐前旗卷虎潜竿，腰间剑插龙归鞘。人强马壮，将老兵骄。

（云）可早来到也。左右报伏去，道：乔公来了也。（卒子报云）报的大夫得知：有乔公来到了也。（鲁云）道：有请。（卒云）老相公，有请。（末见鲁云）大夫今日请老夫来，有何事干？（鲁云）今日请老相公别无甚事，商量取索荆州之事。（末云）这荆州断然不可取！想关云长好生勇猛，你索荆州呵，他弟兄怎肯和你甘罢？（鲁云）他弟兄虽多，兵微将寡。（末唱）

【油葫芦】你道“他弟兄虽多兵将少”。（云）大夫，你知博望烧屯那一事么？（鲁云）小官不知，老相公试说则。（末唱）赤紧的将夏侯惇先困了。（云）这隔江斗智你知么？（鲁云）隔江斗智小官知便知道，不得详细。老相公试说

And the rain propitious;
Swords are turned into ploughshares,
Martial banners are furled,
But signs hang from every tavern;
Fighting has ceased, horses grow sleek,
Hatred is at an end, the air is clear,
And generals turn into ministers,
Changing their gleaming armour for silken robes.
Here at headquarters flags remain furled,
Swords remain in their sheaths,
Our troops are strong, our horses mettlesome,
The officers grow old, the conscripts swagger.

Now I have arrived. Report that Qiao Gong is here, man.

SOLDIER (*announcing him*): Your Honour, Qiao Gong has come.

LU: Invite him in.

SOLDIER: His Honour asks you to go in.

(*Qiao Gong greets Lu.*)

QIAO: Your Honour sent for me. May I know your wishes?

LU: I asked you to come today, sir, to discuss the recovery of Jingzhou.

QIAO: You will never recapture Jingzhou. Lord Guan is as brave as a tiger. Even if you make such a request, he and his sworn brothers will certainly refuse you.

LU: Though he has many sworn brothers, his force is a small one.

QIAO:

You say he has many friends
But not many troops.

Do you know, Your Honour, how he burned the camp at Bowang?

LU: No. I should like to hear, sir.

QIAO:

He hemmed the enemy general in.

And have you heard of his tactics in the river battle?

LU: I heard some talk of that. I should like to know more.

则。（末唱）则他那周瑜蒋干是布衣交。那一个股肱臣诸葛施韬略，亏杀那苦肉计黄盖添粮草。（云）赤壁鏖兵那场好厮杀也！（鲁云）小官知道，老相公再说一遍则。（末云）烧折弓弩如残苇，燎尽旗幡似乱柴；半明半暗花腔鼓，横着扑着伏兽牌；带鞍带辔烧死马，有袍有铠死尸骸；哀哉百万曹军败，个个难逃水火灾！（唱）那军多半向火内烧，三停在水上漂。若不是天交有道伐无道，这其间吴国尽属曹。

（鲁云）曹操英雄智略高，削平僭窃篡刘朝；永安宫里擒刘备，铜雀宫中锁二乔。（末）

【天下乐】你道是"铜雀春深锁二乔"，这三朝恰定交。不争咱一日错便是一世错。（鲁云）俺这里有雄兵百万、战将千员，量他到的哪里！（末唱）你则待要行霸

QIAO:

Zhou Yu and Jiang Gan were old friends,
Zhuge Liang made a crafty plan,
Huang Gai had himself beaten
And offered grain to the enemy.[27]

That was a fine battle at Red Cliff![28]

LU: I have some recollection of it, but should like to hear the tale again.

QIAO:

Snapped bows burned like dry reeds,
Banners flared up like fuel,
Drums rolled and then fell silent,
Carved shields littered the field,
Steeds smouldered in their harness,
And corpses lay in their battle-dresses and helmets
As Cao Cao's million were routed.
Not a single man escaped —
All perished by fire or water;
Either burned in the flames
Or drowned in the rushing river.
Had not Heaven defended the just
Our kingdom would have fallen to Cao Cao!

LU: Cao Cao is a mighty warrior and a shrewd one. He overthrew his rivals and seized the throne. He may imprison Liu Bei in Yongan Palace and hold both your daughters in the Tower of Bronze Sparrows.

QIAO:

Even if my daughters are captive
We are allies now,
And one false move
Would cause irreparable harm.

LU: We have a million fine troops here and a thousand officers. What can he do to us?

QIAO:

Do you mean to use brute force?

道，你待要起战讨。（鲁云）我料关云长年迈，虽勇无能。（末唱）你休欺负关云长年纪老。

（云）收西川一事我说与你听。（鲁云）收西川一事我不得知，你试说一遍。（末唱）

【那吒令】收西川白帝城，将周瑜来送了。汉江边张翼德，将尸骸来当着。舡头上鲁大夫，几乎间唬倒。你待将荆州地面来争，关云长听的闹，他可便乱下风雹。

（鲁云）他便有甚本事？（末唱）

【鹊踏枝】他诛文丑逞粗躁，刺颜良显英豪。他去那百万军中，他将那首级轻枭。（鲁云）想赤壁之战，我与刘备有恩来。（末唱）那时间相看的是好，他可便喜孜孜笑里藏刀。

（鲁云）他若与我荆州，万事罢论；若不与荆州呵，我将他一鼓而下。（末云）不争你举兵呵！（唱）

【寄生草】幸然是天无祸，是咱这人自招。全不肯

To provoke a war?

LU: Lord Guan is growing old. He has more courage than ability.

QIAO:

You will not get the better of him,
Though he is old.

Let me tell you how General Zhou Yu went to collect grain in Sichuan.

LU: I have not heard that. Go on.

QIAO:

Collecting grain in the west,
Zhou Yu lost his life;
Zhang Fei by the River Han
Stopped the men bearing home his corpse,
And standing in the prow
You nearly fell over with fright —
Yet you want to recover Jingzhou!
When Lord Guan knows of this
He will rain down blows like hailstones.

LU: What can he do?

QIAO:

He killed one general in a fit of rage,
Another to show his skill;
Galloping through a million men,
He strikes off enemy heads as if in sport.

LU: Speaking of the battle of the Red Cliff, Liu Bei ought to be grateful to us.

QIAO:

You were outwardly on good terms,
But his smile hid daggers.

LU: If he gives me back Jingzhou, well and good. If not, I shall take it by storm.

QIAO: If you unleash a war,

You cannot blame Heaven for the calamity
When you brought it on yourself,

施恩布德行王道，怎比那多谋足智雄曹操。你须知南阳诸葛应难料。（鲁云）他若不与呵，我大势军马好歹夺了荆州！（末唱）你则待千军万马恶相持，全不想生灵百万遭残暴。

（鲁云）小官不曾与此人相会。老相公，你细说关公威猛如何。（末云）想关云长但上阵处，凭着他坐下马、手中刀、鞍上将，有万夫不当之勇。（唱）

【金盏儿】他上阵处赤力力三绺美髯飘，雄纠纠一丈虎躯摇。恰便似六丁神簇捧定一个活神道。那敌军若是见了，唬的他七魄散，五魂消。（云）你若和他厮杀呵，（唱）你则索多披上几副甲，剩穿上几层袍。便有百万军，当不住他不剌剌千里追风骑。你便有千员将，闪不过明明偃月三停刀。

（鲁云）老相公不知，我有三条妙计索取荆州。（末云）是那三条妙计？（鲁云）第一计：趁今日孙刘结亲，以为唇齿，就于江下排宴设乐，作书一封，以贺近退曹兵，玄德称主于汉中，赞其功美。邀关公江下赴会为庆。此人必无所疑。若渡江赴宴，就于饮酒中间，以礼索取荆州。如还，此为万全之计。如不还，第二

By acting without any faith or kindness.
And how do you compare with crafty Cao Cao
Who is no match for the wily Zhuge Liang?

LU: If he will not return Jingzhou, I shall take it by force.

QIAO:

You will throw your troops into a bloody battle,
Not caring if thousands are killed.

LU: I have never met this Lord Guan, sir. How good a soldier is he?

QIAO: When Lord Guan rides into battle whirling his sword, ten thousand men cannot withstand him.

His tufted beard streams in the wind,
With his huge frame he is a tiger,
Or like a god among lesser deities.
His enemies blench at the sight
And take leave of their senses.

If you pit yourself against him —

Put on all your armour
All your battle-dresses;
For even a million men
Cannot check his galloping horse;
Even a thousand generals
Are no match for his scimitar.

LU: Let me tell you something, sir. I have three good plans for recovering Jingzhou.

QIAO: What are they?

LU: The first plan is this: since the kings of both our states are related by marriage, we can prepare a feast with music by the Changjiang River, and write to congratulate Lord Guan on Liu Bei's recent victory over Cao Cao, the establishment of his rule in Hanzhong, and the great achievements of the Kingdom of Shu. We will invite Lord Guan to cross the river to our feast, and he will hardly suspect us. Should he come, during the banquet we will ask him courteously for the return of Jingzhou. If he agrees, well and good. If not, we can carry out our second plan — seize

计：将江上应有战舡尽行拘收，不放关公回还。淹留日久，自知中计，默然有悔，诚心献还。更不与呵，第三条计：壁衣内暗藏甲士。酒酣之际，击金钟为号，伏兵尽举，擒住关公，囚于江下。此人乃是刘备股肱之臣。若将荆州复江东，则放关公归益州；如其不然，主将既失，孤兵必乱，领兵大举，乘机而行，觑荆州一鼓而下，有何难哉！这三条决难逃。（末云）休道是三条计，就是千条计也近不的他。（唱）

【金盏儿】你道是“三条计决难逃”，一句话不相饶。使不的武官粗慥文官狡。（鲁云）关公酒性如何？（末唱）那汉酒中劣性显英豪！圪塔的揪住宝带，没揣的举起钢刀。（鲁云）我把岸边战舡拘了。（末唱）你道是岸边厢拘了战舡，（云）他若要回去呵，（唱）你则索水面上搭座浮桥。

（鲁云）老相公不必展转议论，小官自有妙策神机。乘此机会，荆州不可不取也。（末云）大夫，你这三条计比曹公在灞陵桥上三条计如何？到了出不的关云长之手。（鲁云）小官不知，老相公试说一遍我听咱。（末唱）

【尾声】曹丞相将送路酒手中擎，饯行礼盘中托，

all his ships and detain him. Once this is done and he knows he is caught in a trap, he should think better of it and return us our province. If he still refuses, we can resort to our third plan — conceal armed men behind the arras, and signal to them during the drinking to come out and take him captive. Lord Guan is Liu Bei's right hand. We shall let him go back to Yizhou only after he agrees to return us Jingzhou. In any case, the commander's absence will throw his troops into disorder, and by seizing this opportunity we should have no difficulty in recapturing Jingzhou in one battle. These are my three plans, which will leave him no way out.

QIAO: A thousand plans will not trap him, let alone three.

You say these three plans will outwit him,
But bear in mind —
If you offend Lord Guan,
Your brave soldiers and crafty scholars
Will be no match for him.

LU: What sort of drinker is Lord Guan?

QIAO:

In his cups he shows his daring,
He will suddenly grasp your jade belt
And whirl his sword over your head.

LU: I shall seize his warships at the shore.

QIAO:

You may seize his warships at the shore.
But if he wants to go back —
You will have to make a floating bridge for him.

LU: Stop trying to dissuade me, sir. I have my well-laid plans and the time has come — Jingzhou must be re-taken.

QIAO: Your Honour, how do you think your plans compare with the three Cao Cao made on Baling Bridge? You will end by falling into Lord Guan's hands.

LU: I never heard that story. Please tell it me, sir.

QIAO:

Cao Cao was holding the stirrup-cup

没乱杀侄儿和嫂嫂。曹孟德心多能做小，关云长善与人交。早来到灞陵桥，险唬杀许褚张辽。他勒着追风骑，轻抡动偃月刀。曹操有千般计较，则落的一场谈笑。（云）关云长道：“丞相勿罪，某不下马了也。”（唱）他把那刀尖儿斜挑锦征袍。（下）

（鲁云）黄文，你见乔公说关公如此威风，未可深信。俺这江下有一贤士，复姓司马，名徽，字德操。此人与关公有一面之交。就请司马先生为伴客，就问关公平昔知勇谋略、酒中德性如何。黄文，就跟着我去司马庵中相访一遭去。（下）

And the parting gifts were ready;
His nephew and sisters-in-law were in a panic,
For he is full of cunning and acts with caution.
But Lord Guan, who was also a friend,
Came early to Baling Bridge,
Striking terror into all the generals there.
When he reined in his wind-swift steed
And swung his crescent-shaped sword,
Cao Cao, for all his plans,
Became a laughing-stock.

Lord Guan simply said: "Excuse me, Your Honour, if I do not alight."

And with the point of his sword
He picked up the silk battle-dress. (*Exit.*)

LU: Qiao Gong has said a great deal about Lord Guan's might, but I find it hard to believe him, Huang Wen. By the river bank there lives another talented scholar, Sima Hui, who once knew Lord Guan. I shall invite him to a feast to question him about Lord Guan's courage and cunning and his temper after drinking. Come with me now to his hermitage to find him.

(*Exeunt.*)

第二折

（正末扮司马徽领道童上，末云）贫道复姓司马，名徽，字德操，道号水鉴先生。想汉家天下，鼎足三分。贫道自刘皇叔相别之后，又是数载。贫道在此江下结一草庵，修行办道，是好幽哉也呵。（唱）

【正宫端正好】本是个钓鳌人，倒做了扶犁叟。笑英布、彭越、韩侯。我如今紧抄定两只拿云手，再不出麻袍袖。

【滚绣球】我则待要聚村叟，会诗友，受用的活鱼新酒，问什么瓦钵磁瓯。推台不换盏，高歌自掴手。任从他阴晴昏昼，醉时节衲被蒙头。我向这矮窗睡彻三竿日，端的是傲杀人间万户侯，自在优游。

（云）道童，门首觑者，看有什么人来。（道童云）理会的。（鲁肃上，云）可早来到也，接了马者。（见道童

ACT II

(*Enter Sima Hui with a Boy.*)

SIMA: I am Sima Hui. Now the Han Empire is divided into three kingdoms. Several years have passed since Liu Bei left me, and I have built a thatched cottage by the river, where I study the holy law. It is very peaceful here.

The proud angler for huge sea-monsters
Has become a simple ploughman;
Scorning Ying Bu, Peng Yue and Han Xin,[29]
I keep my hands, which once reached for the stars,
Folded in hempen sleeves,
Gathering country folk
And rustic poets round me
To enjoy fresh fish and wine;
Drinking from a single cup
Of earthenware or porcelain,
We sing aloud and clap hands,
Not caring if the day be foul or fair;
When drunk I curl up in my quilt
And sleep till the sun comes shining through my low window.
I am prouder than any great noble,
Free to do as I please.

Boy, go and see who that is at the gate.

BOY: Yes, master.

(*Enter Lu Su.*)

LU: Here we are. See to my horse. (*He catches sight of the Boy.*) Is your master in, lad?

科，鲁云）道童，先生有么？（童云）俺师父有。（鲁云）你去说："鲁子敬特来相访。"（童云）你是子敬？你和那松木在一答里！我报师父去。（见末云）师父弟子孩儿……（末云）这厮怎么骂我？（童云）不是骂。师父是师父；弟子是徒弟，就是孩儿一般。师父弟子孩儿。（末云）这厮泼说！有谁在门首？（童云）有鲁子敬特来相访。（末云）道：有请。（童云）理会的。（童出见鲁云）有请。（鲁见末科）（末云）稽首。（鲁云）区区俗冗，久不听教。（末云）数年不见，今日何往？（鲁云）小官无事不来，特请先生江下一会。（末云）贫道在此江下修行，方外之士，有何德能，敢劳大夫置酒张筵？（唱）

【倘秀才】我又不曾垂钓在磻溪岸口，大夫也，我可也无福吃你那堂食玉酒，我则待溪山学许由。（云）大夫请我呵，再有何人？（鲁云）别无他客，止有先生故友寿亭侯关云长一人。（末唱）你道是旧相识寿亭侯，和咱是故友。

（云）若有关公，贫道风疾举发，去不的，去不的。（鲁云）先生初闻鲁肃相邀，慨然许诺。今知有关公，力辞不往。是何故也？想先生与关公有一面之交，则是筵间劝几杯酒。（末唱）

BOY: He is.

LU: Go and tell him Lu Su has come to pay his respects.

BOY: Lousy, are you? I'll tell him. (*He goes up to Sima Hui.*) Master, me son.

SIMA: How dare you call me your son?

BOY: I didn't mean that. You are my master, I am your desciple, and a desciple is like son. That's what I meant by "master, me son."

SIMA: Stop talking nonsense. Who is at the door?

BOY: Lu Su has come to pay his respects.

SIMA: Ask him in.

BOY: Very good. (*He goes out to Lu Su.*) Please come in.

(*Lu Su greets Sima Hui.*)

SIMA: Good day, Your Honour.

LU: The press of worldly affairs has long prevented me from seeking your instructions.

SIMA: Yes, we have not met for several years. What brings you here today?

LU: I have come to invite you to a feast by the river.

SIMA: I am living a hermit's life here. Out of touch as I am with all that goes on in the world, of what use can I be to you? Why should Your Honour trouble to prepare a feast?

I am not the fisherman Lu Shang at the Pan Stream;[30]
I should cut a sorry figure at a banquet,
For I live by hills and streams like Xu You[31] *of old.*

What other guests have you asked?

LU: Only your old friend Guan Yu, Marquis of Shouting. No one else.

SIMA:

My old friend, Marquis of Shouting?

Oh, no! If Lord Guan is coming, I am ill. I cannot go.

LU: First you accept my invitation, but when you hear Lord Guan will be there you decline. Why is this, sir? You have met Lord Guan. All I want you to do is to drink a cup with him.

【滚绣球】大夫，你着我筵前劝几瓯，那汉劣性怎肯道折了半筹！（鲁云）将酒央人，终无恶意。（末唱）你便休提安排着酒肉，他怒时节目前见鲜血交流。你为汉上九座州，我为筵前一醉酒，（云）大夫，你和贫道——（唱）咱两个都落不的完全尸首。（鲁云）先生是客，怕做什么！（末唱）我做伴客的少不的和你同病同忧。（鲁云）我有三条计取索荆州。（末唱）只为你千年勋业三条计，我可甚一醉能消万古愁，提起来魂魄悠悠。

（鲁云）既是先生故友，同席饮酒何妨？（末云）大夫既坚意要请云长，若依的贫道两三桩儿，你便请他。若依不得，便休请他。（鲁云）你说来，小官听者。（末云）依着贫道说，云长下的马时节，（唱）

【倘秀才】你与我躬着身将他来问候。（云）你依的么？（鲁云）关云长下的马来，我躬着身问候。不打紧，也依的。（末唱）大夫，你与我跪着膝连忙的劝酒。饮则饮，吃则吃，受则受。道东呵，随着东去；说西去，随着西流。（云）这一桩儿最要紧也：（唱）他醉了

SIMA:

You want me to drink with him,

But will he keep his temper?

LU: If you ask him to drink, he can hardly take it amiss.

SIMA:

It is no use preparing wine and meat,

Once Lord Guan is in a rage, blood will be spilt.

Will you risk your life for that province across the river?

Shall I risk mine for a feast?

No, Your Honour, the two of us

Would end as headless corpses.

LU: But as a guest what have you to be afraid of?

SIMA:

As a guest I might share your misfortune.

LU: I have three plans for recovering Jingzhou.

SIMA:

You have three plans to achieve undying fame,

But why should I risk my life for one cup of wine?

The mere thought of it appals me!

LU: As old friends, what harm is there in having a drink together?

SIMA: I see you are set on asking him. Well, if you listen to me no harm will be done. If not, you had better not ask him.

LU: Go on. I am listening.

SIMA: This is it. When Lord Guan alights from his horse —

Bow and greet him courteously.

Will you do that?

LU: When Lord Guan alights I should bow and greet him? Certainly, I agree.

SIMA:

On bent knees offer him wine,

Let him eat and drink his fill,

Go east or west as he wills,

And, most important of all —

The moment he is drunk

呵，你索与我便走。

（鲁云）先生，关公酒后德性如何？（末唱）

【滚绣球】他尊前有一句言，筵前带二分酒。他酒性躁不中撩斗，你则绽口儿休题着索取荆州。（鲁云）我便索荆州有何妨？（末云）他听的你索荆州呵，(唱）他圆睁开丹凤眸，轻舒出捉将手，他将那卧蚕眉紧皱，五云山烈火难收。他若是玉山低趄，你安排着走。他若是宝剑离匣，准备着头。枉送了你那八十一座军州。

（鲁云）先生不须多虑！鲁肃料关公勇有余而智不足。到来日，我壁间暗藏甲士，擒住关公，便插翅也飞不过大江去。我待要“先下手为强”。（末云）大夫，量你怎生近的那关云长！

【倘秀才】比及你东吴国鲁大夫仁兄下手，则消得西蜀国诸葛亮先生举口，奏与那有德行仁慈汉皇叔。那先生抚琴霜雪降，弹剑鬼神愁。则怕你急难措手。

（鲁云）我观诸葛亮也小可，除他一人也再无用武之人。（末云）关云长他弟兄五个，他若是知道呵，怎肯

We must slip away!

LU: How does he behave after drinking, sir?

SIMA:

He is wild enough when sober,
But full of fight after wine;
You must keep a watch on your tongue,
And not let the name of Jingzhou pass your lips.

LU: What if I do?

SIMA: If you mention Jingzhou,

He will flash his phoenix eyes,
Stretch out his death-dealing hands,
And furrow his shaggy brows
Like a mountain ablaze.
If he stoops from his towering height
Prepare to leave!
If he draws his sword
Be ready to lose your head!
You will never recover Jingzhou.

LU: You need not worry, sir. Lord Guan may be brave, but I fancy he lacks cunning. When the time comes I shall hide armed men behind the arras to seize him. Then even if he has wings, he will not be able to fly across the river. The first to strike will win.

SIMA: You will not be able to touch him.

Before you can lay hands on him
Zhuge Liang will report the matter
To the good and great-hearted Liu Bei.
Zhuge Liang with his lyre can bring snow,
And his sword frightens ghosts and demons;
You have no hope of succeeding.

LU: I do not share your high opinion of Zhuge Liang. And apart from him, Liu Bei has no mighty warriors.

SIMA: Lord Guan has four sworn brothers. When they hear of this, they will not let you off lightly.

和你甘罢！（鲁云）可是哪五个？（末唱）

【滚绣球】有一个黄汉升猛似彪。有一个赵子龙胆大如斗。有一个马孟起，他是个杀人的领袖。有一个莽张飞，虎牢关力战了十八路诸侯。骑一匹闭月乌，使一条丈八矛。他在那当阳坂有如雷吼，喝退了曹丞相一百万铁甲貔貅。他瞅一瞅漫天尘土桥先断，喝一声拍岸惊涛水逆流。那一伙怎肯干休！

（鲁云）先生若肯赴席呵，就与关公一会何妨！（末云）大夫，不中！不中！休说贫道不曾劝你。（唱）

【尾声】我则怕刀尖儿触抹着轻劈了你手，树叶儿提防打破我头。关云长千里独行觅二友，匹马单刀镇九州。人似巴山越岭彪，马跨翻江混海兽。轻举龙泉杀车胄，怒扯昆吾坏文丑。麾盖下颜良剑标了首，蔡阳英雄立取头。这一个躲是非的先生决应了口。那一个杀人的云长——（云）稽首！（唱）我更怕他下不的手。（末下）

（道童云）鲁子敬，你愚眉肉眼不识贫道。你要取索荆

LU: Who are they?

SIMA:

General Huang Zhong, fierce as a leopard;
Zhao Yun, a tiger for courage;
Ma Chao, that great slayer of men;
And stout Zhang Fei, who at Hulao Pass
Fought the barons single-handed;
He rides on a coal-black charger
With a lance more than ten feet long;
When he thundered at Dangyang Slope,
He scattered Cao Cao's million;
When he glared, a dust storm sprang up
And the bridge was shattered;
When he shouted, great waves reared high
And the river flowed backwards.
These men will not stay their hands.

LU: I beg you to come to my feast, sir. What does it matter if Lord Guan is there too?

SIMA: No, no, Your Honour. And don't complain that I didn't warn you.

The point of his sword may scratch your hand,
Leaves may fall and break my head.
When Lord Guan went out alone to find two comrades,
With one horse and sword he awed the entire land,
For he was like a tiger roaming the hills,
His horse was like a sea-monster wreaking havoc;
With raised blade he killed Che Zhou,
Then made an end of Wen Chou.
Struck off Yan Liang's head beneath his flag,
And slaughtered brave Cai Yang.
If I accept — I who want a quiet life —

Farewell!

Will that executioner spare me? (*Exit.*)

BOY: Lu Su, You are too dense to see my worth. If you want Jingzhou,

州，不来问我。关云长是我酒肉朋友，我交他两只手送与你那荆州来。（鲁云）道童，你师父不去，你去走一遭去罢。（童云）我下山赴会走一遭去，我着老关两手送你那荆州。（唱）

【隔尾】我则待拖条藜杖家家走，着对麻鞋处处游。（云）我这一去，（唱）恼犯云长歹事头。周仓哥哥快争斗，轮起刀来劈破了头。唬的我恰便似缩了头的乌龟则向那汴河里走。（下）

（鲁云）我听那先生说了这一会，教我也怕上来了！我想三条计已定了，怕他怎的！黄文，你与我持这一封请书，直至荆州请关公去来，着我知道。疾去早来者。（下）

why not ask me? Lord Guan is my boon companion. I'll get him to hand over Jingzhou.

LU: Since your master will not go, boy, you had better come to my feast.

BOY: Yes, I'll go down the hill and attend your feast. I'll tell him to hand the place back.

I shall go to different houses trailing my stick,
And wander everywhere in my hempen shoes.

If I go —

When I offend Lord Guan, that will be too bad!
Brother Zhou Cang will come after me
And his sword will split my skull!
Tucking my head in like a frightened tortoise,
I shall scuttle for safety into the River Bian. (*Exit.*)

LU: I am beginning to be alarmed myself by all this talk. Still, with my three plans why should I be afraid? Huang Wen, take this invitation for me to Jingzhou to Lord Guan, then bring me his reply. Make all the speed you can.

(*Exeunt.*)

第三折

（正末扮关公领关平、关兴、周仓上，云）某姓关，名羽，字云长，蒲州解良人也。见随刘玄德，为其上将。自天下三分，形如鼎足：曹操占了中原，孙策占了江东，我哥哥玄德公占了西蜀。着某镇守荆州，久镇无虞。我想当初楚汉争锋，我汉皇仁义用三杰，霸主英雄凭一勇。三杰者，乃萧何、韩信、张良。一勇者，喑呜叱咤，举鼎拔山。大小七十余战，逼霸主自刎乌江。后来高祖登基，传到如今；国步艰难，一至于此！（唱）

【中吕粉蝶儿】那时节天下荒荒，恰周秦早属了刘项，分君臣先到咸阳。一个力拔山，一个量容海，他两个一时开创。想当日黄阁乌江，一个用了三杰，一个诛了八将。

【醉春风】一个短剑下一身亡，一个静鞭三下响。

ACT III

(*Enter Lord Guan with his sons Guan Ping and Guan Xing and Zhou Cang.*)

LORD: I am Guan Yu, a native of Xieliang in Puzhou. I serve Liu Bei as his chief general. Since the empire split into three, Cao Cao has occupied the north, Sun Quan has occupied the land south of the Changjiang River, and my sworn brother Liu Bei has occupied Sichuan and ordered me to govern Jingzhou and defend it well. Many years ago, when the armies of Chu and Han contended together, Liu Bang in his goodness and justice relied on three able men — Xiao He, Han Xin and Zhang Liang — while Xiang Yu relied on his own courage and might. Xiang Yu the Conqueror could lift a huge cauldron or tear down a mountain boulder; yet after more than seventy battles, great and small, he was forced to take his own life at Wujiang. Then Liu Bang ascended the throne and the Han Dynasty was established. But now the country is in turmoil again.

The whole empire was in tumult
In the hands of Xiang Yu and Liu Bang,
And the first to enter Xianyang would win the day.
One had strength to tear down mountains,
One had generosity as deep as the sea.
The two of them started equal,
But Liu Bang reigned in state
While Xiang Yu died at Wujiang.
One relied on three able men,
One killed his eight lieutenants;
So one perished at his own hands,

祖宗传授与儿孙，到今日享、享。献帝又无靠无依，董卓又不仁不义，吕布又一冲一撞。

（云）某想当日俺弟兄三人在桃园中结义，宰白马祭天，宰乌牛祭地。不求同日生，只愿同日死。（唱）

【十二月】那时节兄弟在范阳，兄长在楼桑，关某在蒲州解良，更有诸葛在南阳。一时出英雄四方，结义了皇叔、关、张。

【尧民歌】一年三谒卧龙冈，却又早鼎分三足汉家邦。俺哥哥称孤道寡世无双，我关某匹马单刀镇荆襄。长江，今经几战场，却正是后浪催前浪。

（云）孩儿，门首觑者，看什么人来。（关平云）理会的。（黄文上，云）某乃黄文是也。将着这一封请书来到荆州，请关公赴会。早来到也。左右，报伏去：有江下鲁子敬差上将拖地胆黄文持请书在此。（平云）你则在这里者，等我报伏去。（平见正末，云）报的父亲得知：今有江东鲁子敬差一员首将持请书来见。（正

The other ascended the throne in a hushed court.
Generation after generation
The rule was handed down and homage paid,
Till Emperor Xian lost support,
Dong Zhuo was neither good nor just,
And rough Lü Bu ran wild.

When Zhang Fei, Liu Bei and I became sworn brothers in the peach orchard, we sacrificed a white horse to heaven and a black ox to the earth, and swore that though born on different days we would choose to die together.

Zhang Fei came from Fanyang,
Liu Bei from Lousang,
I myself from Puzhou,
And at Nanyang was Zhuge Liang;
So heroes arose on all sides,
And we became sworn brothers, Liu, Guan and Zhang.
Three times we climbed the Sleeping-Dragon Mount
To invite Zhuge Liang to join us,
And at last the empire was carved into three.
Liu Bei has no match as a monarch,
And alone I govern Jingzhou.
No end to the battles on the river,
Waves impelling each other on!

Son, go to the door and see who is there.

GUAN PING: Yes, father.

(*Enter Huang Wen.*)

HUANG: I am Huang Wen. I have brought a letter to Jingzhou inviting Lord Guan to a feast. Now I have arrived. Guards, kindly announce that Lu Su from across the river has sent Huang Wen the Dauntless here with an invitation.

GUAN PING: Wait here while I announce you. (*He goes in to Lord Guan.*) Father, Lu Su from across the river has sent a general here with an invitation.

云）着他过来。（平云）着你过去哩！（黄文见科）（正末）兀那厮什么人？（黄荒云）小将黄文，江东鲁子敬差我下请书在此。（正云）你先回去，我随后便来也。（黄文云）我出的这门来。看了关公英雄一相个神道！鲁子敬，我替你愁哩！小将是黄文，特来请关公。髯长一尺八，面如挣枣红。青龙偃月刀，九九八十斤；脖子里着一下，哪里寻黄文？来便吃筵席，不来豆腐酒吃三盅。（下）（正末云）孩儿，鲁子敬请我赴单刀会走一遭去。（平云）父亲，他那里筵无好会，则怕不中么？（正云）不妨事。（唱）

【石榴花】两朝相隔汉阳江，上写着道"鲁肃请云长"。安排筵宴不寻常，休想道是画堂别是风光。那里有凤凰杯满捧琼花酿，他安排着巴豆砒霜；玳筵前摆列着英雄将，休想肯开宴出红妆。

【斗鹌鹑】安排下打凤牢龙，准备着天罗地网。也

LORD: Let him come in.

GUAN PING: Come in.

(*Huang Wen greets Lord Guan.*)

LORD: Who is this fellow?

HUANG (*nervously*): I am Huang Wen. Lu Su from across the river sent me here with an invitation. Here it is.

LORD: You may go back first. I shall be coming soon.

HUANG: I see Lord Guan looks as brave as a god. I tremble for you, Lu Su!

I, General Huang Wen,
Have come to invite Lord Guan.
His beard is two feet long,
His face is crimson,
His gleaming scimitar
Weighs eighty pounds;
If once that touches my neck —
Goodbye to Huang Wen!
If he comes, we shall feast;
If not, I may drink alone. (*Exit.*)

LORD: Son, Lu Su has asked me to a feast. I mean to go.

GUAN PING: That will not be a friendly feast, father. You had better not go.

LORD: That does not matter.

The river divides our two kingdoms,
And now Lu Su has invited me to a feast.
This is no common banquet,
No gay affair in a painted hall
With foaming wine in phoenix cups —
No, he is preparing arsenic and hemlock;
And instead of girls, painted and powdered,
There will be pitiless warriors.
He wants to entrap the dragon
By spreading cunning snares;
This is no entertainment;

不是待客筵席，则是个杀人、杀人的战场！若说那重意诚心更休想，全不怕后人讲。既然谨谨相邀，我则索亲身便往。

（平云）那鲁子敬是个足智多谋的人，他又兵多将广，人强马壮，则怕父亲去呵，落在他彀中。（正唱）

【上小楼】你道他“兵多将广，人强马壮”。大丈夫敢勇当先，一人拚命，万夫难当！（平云）许来大江面，俺接应的人可怎生接应？（正唱）你道是隔着江起战场，急难亲傍。我着那厮鞠躬，鞠躬送我到舡上。

（平云）你孩儿到那江东，旱路里摆着马军，水路里摆着战舡，直杀一个血胡同。我想来，先下手的为强。（正唱）

【幺】你道是“先下手强，后下手殃”。我一只手攥住宝带，臂展猿猱，剑掣秋霜。（平云）父亲，则怕他那里有埋伏。（正唱）他那里暗暗的藏，我须索紧紧的防，都是些狐朋狗党！（云）单刀会不去呵，（唱）小可如

But a gory field of war.
Do not speak of honour and integrity,
He cares nothing for the verdict of posterity;
But since he has invited me,
I must go.

GUAN PING: That fellow Lu Su is a clever, crafty man, with many troops and officers — good fighters with sturdy steeds. If you go, I am afraid you may be trapped.

LORD:

What if he has many officers, men and good horses?
When a hero marches forward and braves death,
Even ten thousand foes cannot stand against him.

GUAN PING: The river is so wide, how are my men to come to your rescue?

LORD:

You think when the battle rages across the river
You will not be able to reach me;
But I shall get that rogue to escort me back,
Bowing as I go aboard.

GUAN PING: I mean to cross the river with horsemen and warships, carving out a way with my sword. It is better to strike the first blow.

LORD:

So you think the first to strike will win
While the one who delays will be lost?
But I shall seize his belt,
And boldly draw my bright sword.

GUAN PING: But what if he has laid an ambush, father?

LORD:

He may have laid an ambush in the dark,
But I know how to take precautions.
They are merely foxes and jackals!
Why shouldn't I go to his feast?
I have travelled hundreds of miles alone,

千里独行，五关斩将。

（云）孩儿，量他到的哪里！（平云）想父亲私出许昌一事，您孩儿不知。父亲慢慢说一遍。（正唱）

【快活三】小可如我携亲侄访冀王，引阿嫂觅刘皇。灞陵桥上气昂昂，侧坐在雕鞍上。

【鲍老儿】俺也曾挝鼓三冬斩蔡阳，血溅在杀场上。刀挑征袍出许昌，险唬杀曹丞相。向单刀会上，对两班文武，小可如三月襄阳。

（平云）父亲，他那里雄纠纠排着战场。（正唱）

【剔银灯】折莫他雄纠纠排着战场，威凛凛兵屯虎帐；大将军智在孙吴上，马如龙人似金刚。不是我十分强，硬主张，但提起厮杀呵磨拳擦掌。排戈甲，列旗枪，各分战场。我是三国英雄汉云长，端的是豪气有三千丈。

And killed generals at five passes.

Let us see what he can do, son.

GUNA PING: I never heard how you escaped from Xuchang. Will you tell me the story, father?

LORD:

That was no more than when
I took my nephew to Yuan Shao,
Or Liu Bei's wife to him;
Fearless on Baling Bridge,
On my well-made saddle,
Before the drum rolled three times
I killed Cai Yang.
After shedding blood in battle,
Catching up the gift robe with my sword
I left Xuchang,
Striking terror into Cao Cao.
Now I am going to the banquet alone,
To face their ministers and warriors —
This is no more than that banquet at Xiangyang.

GUAN PING: They have a great force ready, father.

LORD:

What if they have?
They may have fierce troops
Stationed ready at their camp,
But my strategy is superior.
With a marvellous horse.
Invulnerable as a god —
Not that I am unduly confident —
At talk of battle my hands begin to itch!
Make ready spears, armour and banners;
Prepare for the fight!
I am Lord Guan, champion of the three kingdoms,
And my valour knows no bounds!

（云）孩儿与我准备下舡只，领周仓赴单刀会走一遭去。（平云）父亲去呵，小心在意者！（正唱）

【尾声】须无那临潼会秦穆公，又无那鸿门会楚霸王。折么他满筵人列着先锋将，小可如百万军刺颜良时那一场攘。（下）

（周仓云）关公赴单刀会，我也走一遭去。志气凌云贯九霄，周仓今日逞英豪；人人开弓并蹬弩，个个贯甲与披袍；旌旗闪闪龙蛇动，恶战英雄胆气高；假饶鲁肃千条计，怎胜关公这口刀！赴单刀会走一遭去也。（下）

（关兴云）哥哥，父亲赴单刀会去了，我和你接应一遭去。大小三军，跟着我接应父亲去。到那里古刺刺彩磨征旗，扑冬冬画鼓凯征鼙，齐臻臻枪刀如流水，密匝匝人似朔风疾；直杀的苦淹淹尸骸遍郊野，哭啼啼父子两分离；恁时节喜孜孜鞭敲金镫响，笑吟吟齐和凯歌回。（下）

（关平云）父亲、兄弟都去也，我随后接应走一遭去。大小三军，听吾将令：甲马不许驰骤，金鼓不许乱鸣。不许交头接耳，不许语笑喧哗。弓弩上弦，刀剑出鞘。十分人人敢勇战，个个威风。我到那里：一刃

Prepare a boat, son. I shall take Zhou Cang to the banquet.

GUAN PING: Take good care of yourself, father!

LORD:

This is not like the meeting with Duke Mu at Lintong,[32]
Nor the meeting with Xiang Yu at Hongmen;[33]
What if their foremost generals attend the feast?
I killed Yan Liang amid a million men. (*Exit.*)

ZHOU: Lord Guan has left for the feast. I had better go too.

My brave spirit aspires to the skies,
Today I shall show my prowess;
Let all prepare bows and arrows,
Put on armour and battle-dress;
Flags shall wave like writhing dragons,
As our men display their courage in the fight;
Though Lu Su has a thousand plans,
He will be no match for Lord Guan!

Well, I am off to the banquet. (*Exit.*)

GUAN XING: Father has gone to the feast, brother. Let us go to his aid. Follow me, men!

Let embroidered banners flutter,
And painted drums sound the charge;
Let lances and swords surge forward like a river,
And troops charge swift as the wind,
Till unhappy corpses cover the whole plain
And, torn apart, the sons and fathers weep.
Then with gay whips beating our gilded stirrups,
Laughing and singing, we shall ride back in triumph. (*Exit.*)

GUAN PING: Both my father and brother have gone. I must follow to help them. Listen to my orders, men. Rein in your steeds, muffle your drums. There is to be no whispering, talking or din. Keep your bows and arrows ready and your swords unsheathed. We must all acquit ourselves like men.

Sabres and two-edged swords

刀、两刃剑，齐排雁翅；三股叉、四楞炼，耀日争光；五方旗、六沉枪，遮天映日；七稍弓、八楞棒，打碎天灵；九股索、红绵套，漫头便起；十分战、十分杀，显耀高强。俺这里雄兵浩浩渡长江，汉阳两岸列刀枪；水军不怕江心浪，旱军岂惧铁衣郎！关公杀入单刀会，显耀英雄战一场；匹马横枪诛鲁肃，胜如亲父刺颜良。大小三军，跟着我接应父亲走一遭去。（下）

Will whirl like swans in flight,
Tridents and maces will glitter in the sun;
Banners and lances will obscure the sky,
Crossbows and clubs will smash our enemy's skulls,
While ropes and red cotton halters fly overhead —
So we battle to show our might!
Now with a mighty force I cross the river,
A forest of swords and spears on either bank.
Our sailors do not fear the tossing waves,
Our soldiers do not fear the iron-clad foe;
Lord Guan will fight his way into the feast,
And show what a hero is made of.
Alone on horseback he will smite Lu Su
As he once killed Yan Liang.

Come with me, men, to your commander's assistance!
(*Exit.*)

第四折

（鲁肃上，云）欢来不似今朝，喜来那逢今日！小官鲁子敬是也。我使黄文持书去请关公，欣喜许今日赴会，荆襄地合归还俺江东。英雄甲士已暗藏壁衣之后，令江上相候，见舡到便来报我知道。

（正末关公引周仓上，云）周仓，将到那里也？（周云）来到大江中流也。（正云）看了这大江，是一派好水也呵！（唱）

【双调新水令】大江东去浪千叠，引着这数十人驾着这小舟一叶。又不比九重龙凤阙，可正是千丈虎狼穴。大丈夫心别，我觑这单刀会似赛村社。

（云）好一派江景也呵！（唱）

【驻马听】水涌山叠，年少周郎何处也？不觉的灰飞烟灭。可怜黄盖转伤嗟。破曹的樯橹一时绝，鏖兵的江水犹然热。好教我情惨切！（云）这也不是江水，

ACT IV

(*Enter Lu Su.*)

LU: There can be no day as happy as today. I am Lu Su. I dispatched Huang Wen with an invitation to Lord Guan, who consented readily to come to the feast today. So Jingzhou will be ours again! My brave armed men are hidden behind the arras. I have sent scouts to watch the river. When his boat comes, they will report to me.

(*Enter Lord Guan and Zhou Cang.*)

LORD: Where are we now, Zhou Cang?

ZHOU: We are in the middle of the stream.

LORD: This great river is a noble sight!

A thousand billows flow eastwards,
A few dozen rowers are with me in this small craft;
I go to no nine-storeyed dragon-and-phoenix palace,
But a lair, ten thousand feet deep, of tigers and wolves.
A stout fellow is never afraid,
I go to this feast as if to a country fair.

What a magnificent river!

Tossing waves, hill after hill —
Where is young Zhou Yu today?
He has turned to dust.
General Huang Gai suffered much;
The warships that conquered Cao Cao are no more,
But the waves are still warm from past battles —
This wrings my heart!

This is no river water,

（唱）二十年流不尽的英雄血！

（云）却早来到也，报伏去。（卒报科）（做相见科）（鲁云）江下小会，酒非洞里之长春，乐乃尘中之菲艺。猥劳君侯屈高就下，降尊临卑，实乃鲁肃之万幸也。（正云）量某有何德能，着大夫置酒张筵。既请必至。（鲁云）黄文，将酒来。二公子满饮一杯。（正云）大夫饮此杯。（把盏科）（正云）想古今咱这人过日月好疾也呵！（鲁云）过日月是好疾也。光阴似骏马加鞭，浮世似落花流水。（正唱）

【胡十八】想古今立勋业，那里也舜五人汉三杰？两朝相隔数年别，不付能见者，却又早老也。开怀的饮数杯，（云）将酒来，（唱）尽心儿待醉一夜。

（把盏科）（正云）你知"以德报德，以直报怨"么？（鲁云）既然将军言"以德报德，以直报怨"，借物不还者，为之"怨"。想君侯文武全材，通练兵书，习《春秋》《左传》。济拔颠危，匡扶社稷，可不谓之仁乎？待玄德如骨肉，觑曹操若仇雠，可不谓之义乎？辞

But the blood of heroes
Shed for these twenty years!
Here we are. Announce my arrival.
(*An Attendant announces Lord Guan.*)
(*Lu Su greets him.*)

LU: This is simply a small gathering by the river. Our wine is no elixir, and our music just the poor tunes of this dusty world. It was good of Your Lordship to condescend to come.

LORD: I have done nothing to deserve this honour. Of course I was glad to come.

LU: Bring wine, Huang Wen. Let me offer Your Lordship a cup.

LORD: Your health, Your Honour! (*They drink.*) When you think back, the time has passed very quickly.

LU: Yes, indeed. The years gallop by like swift horses, and worldly affairs pass like fallen flowers or the water of a flowing stream.

LORD:
Think of the heroes of old —
Where are King Shun's five ministers
Or the three able men of Han?
Living in two different kingdoms,
We have not met for many years;
Now face to face again,
We are both growing old.
Let us drink to our hearts' content,
More wine!
Let us drink our fill this night.
(*They drink.*)

LORD: Both the just and the unjust, you know, should be requited.

LU: Since you mention it, I think it unjust to borrow without returning. Your Lordship is well versed in the arts of peace and war; you have mastered the books of military strategy, as well as the history of the Spring and Autumn Period.[34] You have aided those in distress and defended the state — this shows your humanity. You treat Liu Bei as your

曹归汉，弃印封金，可不谓之礼乎？坐服于禁，水渰七军，可不谓之智乎？且将军仁、义、礼、智俱足。惜乎止少个“信”字，欠缺未完。再若得全个“信”字，无出君侯之右也！（正云）我怎生失信？（鲁云）非将军失信，皆因令兄玄德公失信。（正云）我哥哥怎生失信来？（鲁云）想昔日玄德公败于当阳之上，身无所归，因鲁肃之故，屯军三江夏口。鲁肃又与孔明同见我主公，即日兴师拜将，破曹兵于赤壁之间。江东所费巨万，又折了首将黄盖。因将军贤昆玉无尺寸地，暂借荆州以为养军之资，数年不还。今日鲁肃低情曲意，暂取荆州以为救民之急。待仓廪丰盈，然后再献与将军掌领。鲁肃不敢自专，君侯台鉴不错。（正云）你请我吃筵席来那，是索荆州来？（鲁云）没，没，没……我则这般道：孙刘结亲，以为唇齿，两国正好和谐。（正唱）

【庆东原】你把我真心儿待将筵宴设，你这般攀今览古，分甚枝叶？我跟前使不着你“之乎者也”、“诗云”、“子曰”，早该豁口截舌！有意说孙刘，你休目下翻成吴越！

（鲁云）将军原来傲物轻信！（正云）我怎么“傲物轻信”？（鲁云）当日孔明亲言：“破曹之后，荆州即还江

brother, and Cao Cao as your enemy — this shows your sense of justice. You left Cao Cao for Liu Bei, giving up high office and gold — this shows your probity. You vanquished Yu Jin without a fight, simply by drowning his army — this shows your wisdom. The only pity is that you break your word, so you lack one of the five virtues. If only you kept faith, no one could compare with Your Lordship.

LORD: How do I break my word?

LU: It is not your fault — your brother Liu Bei is faithless.

LORD: In what way?

LU: When Liu Bei was defeated at Dangyang and had nowhere to turn, I arranged for him to station his troops at Xiakou and elsewhere. Then I went with Zhuge Liang to our sovereign, and lost no time in mobilizing our troops and defeating Cao Cao at Red Cliff. The expedition was a costly one, and we lost General Huang Gai in the course of it. Because your brother had not a single inch of territory, we lent him Jingzhou as a base for his army. He has not yet returned it after all these years. Today I humbly beg to have Jingzhou back for a time to relieve our people. Once we have an ample reserve of grain, we may hand it back to you to govern. I shall not presume to decide on this matter. I hope Your Lordship will not take offence.

LORD: Are you inviting me to a feast, or are you demanding Jingzhou?

LU: No, no! Don't misunderstand me. Our rulers are bound by marriage. We desire to live at peace.

LORD:

You ought to be sincere when you play host,
What is all this talk of the past?
I have no patience with your high-flown phrases;
Such a glib tongue should be cut off.
You talk of our kingdoms' friendship,
But treat us as enemies.

LU: So Your Lordship is overbearing and lacking in faith.

LORD: Just why am I overbearing and lacking in faith?

LU: Zhuge Liang himself promised that after Cao Cao was defeated he

东。”鲁肃亲为代保。不思旧日之恩，今日恩变为仇；犹自说“以德报德，以直报怨”。圣人道：“信近于义，言可复也。去食去兵，不可去信。大车无輗，小车无軏，其何以行之哉？”今将军全无仁义之心，枉作英雄之辈。荆州久借不还，却不道“人无信不立”！（正云）鲁子敬,你听的这剑界么？（鲁云）剑界怎么？（正云）我这剑界，头一遭诛了文丑，第二遭斩了蔡阳。鲁肃呵，莫不第三遭到你也？（鲁云）没，没……我则这般道来。（正云）这荆州是谁的？（鲁云）这荆州是俺的。（正云）你不知，听我说：（唱）

【沉醉东风】想着俺汉高皇图王霸业，汉光武秉正除邪，汉献帝将董卓诛，汉皇叔把温侯灭。俺哥哥合情受汉家基业。则你这东吴国的孙权，和俺刘家却是甚枝叶？请你个不克己先生自说！

（鲁云）那里什么响？（正云）这剑界二次也！（鲁云）却怎么说？（正云）这剑：按天地之灵，金火之精，阴阳之气，日月之形。藏之则鬼神遁迹，出之则魑魅潜踪。喜则恋鞘，沉沉而不动；怒则跃匣，铮铮而有声。今

would return Jingzhou to us, and I acted as guarantor. But instead of remembering past obligations, today you have turned against us; yet you speak of requiting both the just and unjust. The sage said: When agreements are made in accordance with what is right, the words spoken can be made good. One can do without food or troops, but not without faith, any more than a carriage can do without a cross-bar. Now although you are so great a hero, Your Lordship, you have absolutely no sense of right. You have kept Jingzhou all this time, and refuse to return it. Yet a gentleman must keep faith.

LORD: Lu Su, do you hear my sword clang?

LU: What does it mean?

LORD: The first time my sword clanged, I killed Wen Chou. the second time Cai Yang. Now I fear your turn has come.

LU: No, no! You must not take it like that.

LORD: To whom does Jingzhou belong?

LU: Jingzhou is ours.

LORD: You are wrong there. Listen to me.

Our first emperor built up the empire;
Emperor Guang Wu set right a wrong,
And Emperor Xian killed the usurper Dong Zhuo;
Liu Bei followed in their steps and killed Lü Bu,
So that the Han throne should be his.
What relationship has the King of Wu
To the royal house of Han?
Answer me this, if you can, sir.

LU: What is that sound?

LORD: My sword has sounded for a second time.

LU: What does it mean this time?

LORD: This sword was forged with the spirit of the universe, the essence of fire and metal, the dual elements of nature, and the forms of the sun and the moon. Sheathed, it keeps ghosts away; unsheathed, it makes spirits scatter in fright. When it is happy, it rests still in the sheath; when

朝席上，倘有争锋。恐君不信，拔剑施呈。吾当摄剑，鲁肃休惊！这剑：果有神威不可当，庙堂之器岂寻常！今朝索取荆州事，一剑先交鲁肃亡！（唱）

【雁儿落】则为你三寸不烂舌，恼犯我三尺无情铁。这剑饥飡上将头，渴饮仇人血。

【得胜令】则是条龙向鞘中蛰，虎在坐间踅。今日故友每才相见，休着俺弟兄每相间别。鲁子敬听者：你心内休乔怯，畅好是随邪。吾当酒醉也！

（鲁云）臧宫动乐。（臧宫上，云）天有五星，地攒五岳。人有五德，乐按五音。五星者：金、木、水、火、土。五岳者：常、恒、泰、华、嵩。五德者：温、良、恭、俭、让。五音者：宫、商、角、徵、羽。（甲士拥上科）（鲁云）埋伏了者！（正击案，怒云）有埋伏也无埋伏？（鲁云）并无埋伏。（正云）若有埋伏，

it is angry, it leaps in its scabbard with a clang. There seems to be trouble brewing at your feast today. If you do not believe me I can show you my sword. Now I will sheathe it again. Don't lose your head.

This sword has irresistible might,
It is not a common weapon.
If you ask again for Jingzhou,
It will strike you dead at once.
For your wagging tongue
Has incensed my ruthless blade,
Which sups on generals' heads
And drinks the blood of foes.
It is a dragon hidden in its sheath,
A tiger couched between our seats;
We are meeting as old friends,
Let us have no quarrel.
Then listen well, Lu Su!
You have no cause for fear,
Set your mind at rest —
I am drunk.

LU: Call for music, Zang Gong.

(*Enter Zang Gong.*)

ZANG: There are five planets in heaven, five great mountains on earth, five *virtues in men, and five notes in music. The five planets are those of gold, wood, water, fire and earth. The five mountains are Changshan, Hengshan, Taishan, Huashan and Songshan. The five virtues are gentleness, goodness, courtesy, frugality and modesty. The five notes in music are kong, shang, jiao, zhi and yu.*

(*Enter Lu Su's Troops.*)

LU: Remain concealed, men!

LORD (*banging the table in rage*): Is this an ambush?

LU: No, this is no ambush.

LORD: If it is, with one stroke I shall chop you into two!

一剑挥之两断！（做击案科）（鲁云）你击碎菱花……（正云）我特来破镜！（唱）

【搅筝琶】却怎生闹炒炒军兵列？休把我当拦者！（云）当着我的，呵呵！（唱）我着他剑下身亡，目前流血。便有那张仪口、蒯通舌，休那里躲闪藏遮。好生的送我到船上者，我和你慢慢的相别。

（鲁云）你去了倒是一场伶俐。（黄文云）将军，有埋伏哩！（鲁云）迟了我的也！（关平领众将上，云）请父亲上舡，孩儿每来迎接哩。（正云）鲁肃，休惜殿后。（唱）

【离亭宴带歇指煞】我则见紫袍银带公人列，晚天凉风冷芦花谢，我心中喜悦。昏惨惨晚霞收，冷飕飕江风起，急飐飐帆招惹。承管待，承管待。多承谢，多承谢。唤梢公慢者，缆解开岸边龙，舡分开

(*He smashes his fist on the table.*)

LU: You have broken the mirror.

LORD: I am here to make a break.

Why should your soldiers make such a noise?
Mind they keep out of my way.

If anyone crosses me — ha!

He shall perish by my sword,
His blood will spurt out!
Even men as eloquent as Zhang Yi and Kuai Tong[35]
Would do well not to waste their breath.
Escort me instead to my boat,
And I shall take a leisurely leave of you.

LU: It will certainly be quieter if you leave.

HUANG: The ambush is ready, Your Honour.

LU: It is too late now.

(*Enter Guan Ping with his troops.*)

GUAN PING: Father, please board your boat. We have come to meet you.

LORD: I will trouble you to escort us, Lu Su.

I see my officers waiting
In purple robes and silver belts;
The evening breeze is cool,
The reeds are withering
And my heart is well content.
Dark evening clouds are gathering,
The wind on the river is chill,
And sails flap in the breeze.
I thank you for your hospitality,
We are much obliged to you.
The boatman need not hurry;
Wait till the hawser is loosened.
Then let the prow cleave the waves,
And oars break the moon reflected in the water —

波中浪，棹搅碎江心月。正欢娱有甚进退？且谈笑不分明夜。说与你两件事先生记者：百忙里趁不了老兄心，急切里倒不了俺汉家节。

题目 孙仲谋独占江东地
请乔公言定三条计
正名 鲁子敬设宴索荆州
关大王独赴单刀会

Go slowly, for we are merry;
We shall laugh and chat all night.
There are two things I would remind you of:
You could not gain your end, for all your art;
For none shall overpower my loyal heart!

(*THE END*)

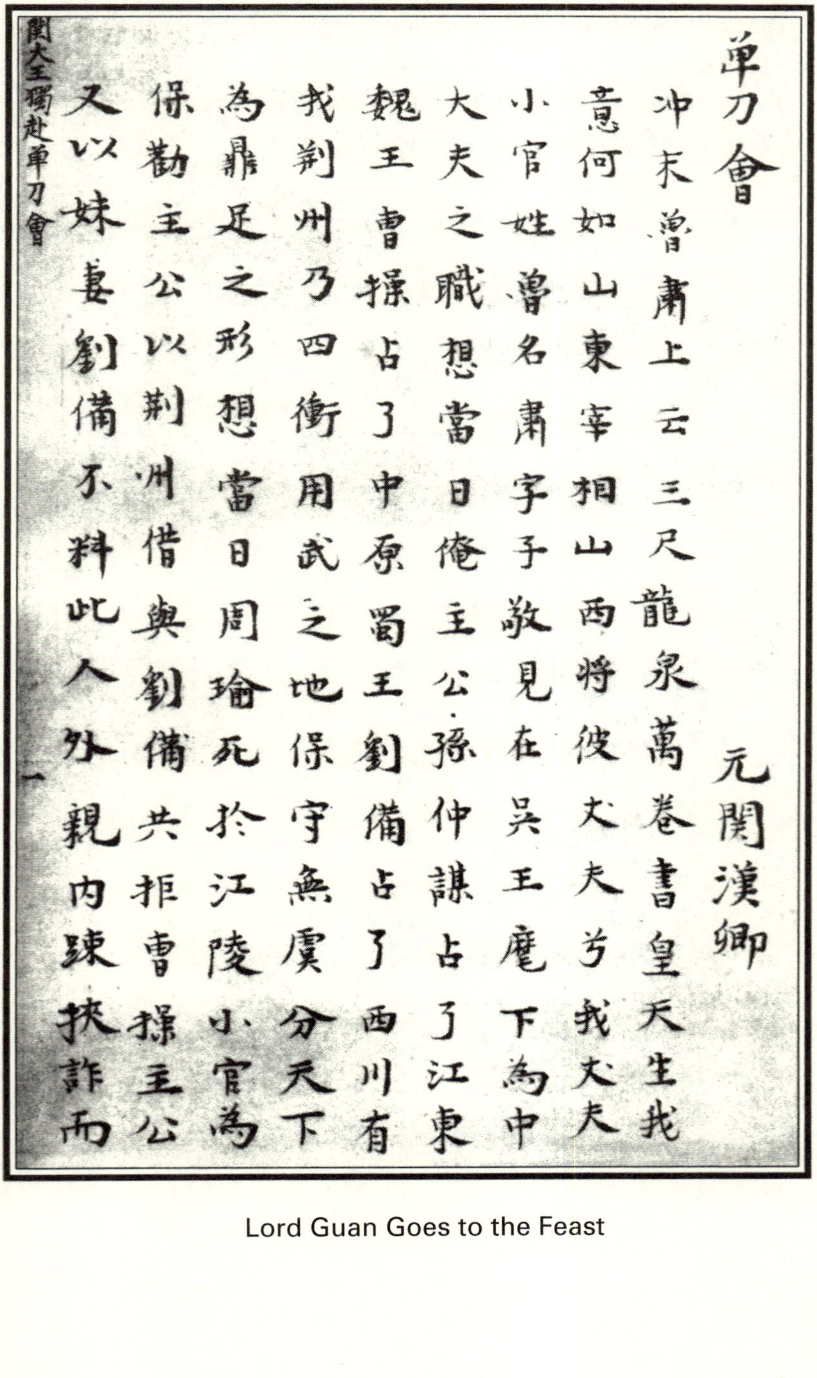

單刀會

元 關漢卿

冲末魯肅上云 三尺龍泉萬卷書皇天生我意何如山東宰相山西將彼丈夫兮我丈夫小官姓魯名肅字子敬見在吳王麾下為中大夫之職想當日俺主公孫仲謀占了江東魏王曹操占了中原蜀王劉備占了西川有我荊州乃四衝用武之地保守無虞分天下為鼎足之形想當日周瑜死於江陵小官為保勸主公以荊州借與劉備共拒曹操主公又以妹妻劉備不料此人外親內踈挾詐而

Lord Guan Goes to the Feast

邓夫人苦痛哭存孝

Death of the Winged-Tiger General

第一折

（冲末净李存信同康君立上）（李存信云）米罕整斤吞，抹邻不会骑。弩门并速门，弓箭怎的射？撒因答剌孙，见了抢着吃。喝的莎塔八，跌倒就是睡。若说我姓名，家将不能记。一对忽剌孩，都是狗养的。自家李存信的便是，这个是康君立。俺两个不会开弓蹬弩，也不会厮杀相持；哥哥会唱，我便能舞。俺父亲是李克用，阿妈喜欢掩两个。无俺两个呵，酒也不吃，肉也不吃；若见俺两个呵，便吃酒肉。好生的爱俺两个！自破黄巢之后，太平无事，阿妈复夺的城池地面，着俺五百义儿家将，各处镇守。阿妈的言语：将邢州与俺两个镇守。那里是朱温家后门，他与俺父亲两个不和；他知俺在邢州镇守，他和俺相持厮杀，俺两个武艺不会，则会吃酒肉，倘或着他拿将去了，杀坏了俺

ACT I

(*Enter Li Cunxin and Kang Junli.*)

CUNXIN:

We gulp down pounds of mutton,
But cannot ride;
We know nothing of archery,
And cannot shoot.
At the sight of good wine
We start to swill,
Until we end up
In a drunken stupor.
Even our officers
Forget our names;
We are a pair of rogues,
A couple of curs.

I am Li Cunxin and this is Kang Junli. We cannot draw a bow or fight, but he can sing and I can dance. We are the adopted sons of Li Keyong, who dotes on us. When we are away he takes neither meat nor wine, but when we are there he takes both — that shows how he loves us. Since Huang Chao[36] was defeated the empire has been at peace, and the old man has seized many cities and districts which are garrisoned by his five hundred adopted sons and officers. Now he has ordered us to garrison Xiangzhou, but that is Zhu Wen's back door, and he is on bad terms with our father. When Zhu Wen knows we are there he will attack us, but we don't know how to fight — all we're good for is eating and drinking.

两个怎了？（康君立云）如今阿妈将潞州天党郡与存孝镇守，潞州地面吃好酒好肉去。如今我和你两个，安排酒席，则说辞别阿妈，灌的阿妈醉了，咱两个便说："邢州是朱温家后门，他与阿妈不和，倘若索战，俺两个死不打紧，着人知道呵，不坏了阿妈的名声！着李存孝镇守邢州去，可不好么？"（李存信云）俺两个则今日安排酒席，辞别父亲去走一遭来。我是李存信，他是康君立；两个真油嘴，实然是一对。（同下）

（李克用同刘夫人领番卒子上）（李克用云）番番番，地恶人奔，骑宝马，坐雕鞍。飞鹰走犬，野水荒山。渴饮羊酥酒，饥飧鹿脯干。凤翎箭手中施展，宝雕弓臂上斜弯。林间酒阑胡旋舞呵者，丹青写入画图间。某乃李克用是也。某袭封鳌州节度使，因带酒打了段文楚，贬某在沙陀地面，已经十年。因黄巢作乱，奉圣人的命，加某为忻、代、石、岚都招讨使，破黄巢天

What if he captures us and decides to kill us?

JUNLI: The old man has made Cunxiao garrison commander of Luzhou, a place where you can enjoy good wine and good meat. Let us prepare a farewell feast now for the old man. When we have made him drunk, we can tell him that Xingzhou is Zhu Wen's back door, and Zhu is on bad terms with father. If he attacks us it won't matter our being killed, but when others hear of it the old man's good name will suffer. So he had better let Cunxiao garrison Xingzhou.

CUNXIN: Right, let's prepare a farewell feast. Come on!

I am Li Cunxin,
He is Kang Junli —
A pair of plausible
Rascals we!

(*Exeunt.*)

(*Enter Li Keyong and his wife Madam Liu, with Tartar Soldiers.*)

LI:

Tartars! Tartars!
Wild country breeds rough fellows.
Thorough-bred horses,
Ornamented saddles,
Falcons and hounds,
Torrents and barren hills!
We slake our thirst with koumiss,
Our hunger with dried venison;
Our arrows have phoenix feathers,
Carved bows are slung on our arms;
Drunk in the forest
We whirl in Hunnish dances —
This is a truthful picture of Tartary.

I am Li Keyong. I was once governor of Binzhou, but when I was drunk I beat Duan Wenchu, and was banished for ten years to Tartary. Then Huang Chao revolted, and the emperor made me commander-in-chief of the army of the northern provinces to suppress the rebels. Within a few

下兵马大元帅。自离了沙陀，不数日之间，到此压关楼前，聚齐二十四处节度使，取胜长安。被吾儿存孝擒拿了邓天王，活挟了孟截海，挝打了张归霸，十八骑误入长安，大破黄巢，复夺了长安。圣人的命：犒劳某手下义儿家将，但是复夺的城池，着某手下义儿家将去各处镇守，提备盗贼。今日太平无事，四海晏然，正好与夫人众将饮酒快乐。小校安排下酒骰，可怎生不见周德威来？（周德威上，云）帅鼓铜锣一两敲，辕门里外列英豪；三军报罢平安喏，紧卷旗旛不动摇。某姓周，名德威，字镇远，山后朔州人也。今从李克用共破黄巢，太平无事，某为番汉都总管。今日元帅有请，不知有甚事，须索走一遭去。可早来到也。报复去，道有周德威来了也。（卒子云）理会的。报的元帅得知：有周德威在于门首。（李克用云）道有请。（卒子云）理会得。有请！（做见科）（周德威云）元帅，周德威来了也。（李克用）将军，今日请你来不为别的，想存孝孩儿多有功劳，我许与了他潞州天党郡与存孝孩儿镇守，把邢州与李存信康君立镇守去。怎生不见李存信康君立来了也？（李存信同康君立上）（李存信云）阿妈心内想，忽然到跟前。哥哥你放心，我这

days of leaving the steppes I reached the pass, and rallied the governors of twenty-four regions to win back the capital. My adopted son Cunxiao captured Deng Tianwang, brought back Meng Jiehai and killed Zhang Guiba. Then with eighteen horsemen he galloped to Chang'an, routed Huang Chao's army and regained the capital. By imperial decree my adopted sons and officers have been rewarded and given the towns they captured to garrison against the rebels. Now the empire is at peace. Quiet reigns within the four seas. I should drink and be merry with my wife and generals. Orderlies, prepare wine and food! Why is General Zhou Dewei not here yet?

(*Enter Zhou Dewei.*)

ZHOU:

Twice the gong at headquarters has sounded;
Brave men are arrayed at the gate.
The troops raise a shout of greeting;
And the furled banners are still.

I am Zhou Dewei of Shuozhou. I helped Li Keyong to defeat Huang Chao, and now that the empire is at peace I have been appointed general of the Han and Tartar forces. Today the commander has summoned me to his headquarters, I must see what he wants. Here we are. (*To a Soldier.*) Announce my arrival, man.

SOLDIER: Yes, sir. Commander Li, General Zhou is at the gate.

LI: Ask him in.

SOLDIER: Yes, sir. Please come in, General Zhou.

(*Li and Zhou greet each other.*)

ZHOU: Here I am, commander.

LI: I'll tell you why I asked you here today, general. My adopted son Cunxiao has won such glory that I promised him Luzhou as his garrison area, and I want Cunxin and Junli to garrison Xingzhou. Why aren't they here yet?

(*Enter Cunxin and Junli.*)

CUNXIN:

The old man thinks of us
And we arrive!

一过去，见了阿妈说了呵，便着存孝往邢州去。（康君立云）兄弟，只要你小心用意者。（李存信云）阿妈、阿者，想当初一日，阿妈的言语，将潞州天党郡与俺两个镇守来；今日阿妈与了存孝，可着俺两个邢州去！（做悲科）（李克用云）孩儿存信，你做什么哭？（李存信云）阿妈，俺两个也早起晚夕舞者唱者，扶持阿妈欢喜，怎下的着您两个孩儿往邢州去？（康君立云）阿妈，想邢州是朱温的后门，他与阿妈不和。倘若索战，俺两个不会什么武艺，倘若拿将俺两个去了，俺两个死不打紧，阿妈吃起酒来，寻俺两个舞的唱的不在眼面前，阿妈不想成病？那其间生药铺里赎也赎不将俺两个来！（李存信云）阿妈，怎生可怜见着俺两个去潞州去，把邢州与存孝两口儿镇守罢。可也好？（李存信把盏科，云）哥哥，将酒来与阿妈把一盏。（李克用云）好两个孝顺的孩儿！我着你潞州天党郡去呵便了也。（康君立云）既是这等，谢了阿妈者！（周德威云）他两个有什么功劳？把他潞州天党郡去！想飞虎将军南征北讨，东荡西除，困来马上眠，渴饮刀头血，他可以潞州去；他两个去不的！（李克用云）周将军说的是，小校，与我唤将存孝儿两口过来者！（卒子云）理会的。（正旦同李存孝上）（李存孝云）岩前打虎雄心在，敢勇当先敌兵败；上阵全凭铁飞挝，扶立乾坤唐世界。某本姓安，名敬思，雁门关飞虎峪灵丘县人氏。幼小父母双亡，

Don't worry, brother. When I get there and talk to the old man, he will send Cunxiao to Xingzhou.

JUNLI: Watch your step, brother.

CUNXIN: Father! Mother! Not long ago father promised to let us garrison Luzhou, but now you are giving it to Cunxiao and sending us to Xingzhou instead.

(*He pretends to shed tears.*)

LI: Why are you crying, son?

CUNXIN: We have danced and sung day and night to keep you happy, father. Why should you send us to Xingzhou?

JUNLI: Xingzhou is Zhu Wen's back door, father, and Zhu Wen is not on good terms with you. He may attack us, and we are no good at fighing. If he captures us we don't mind dying ourselves; but when you want us to sing and dance while you are drinking, and we aren't there, you may fall ill. Then you won't find us among all the herbs in the medicine shops.

CUNXIN: Have a heart, father! Let us go to Luzhou and send Cunxiao and his wife to Xingzhou. How about it? (*He picks up a wine cup.*) Brother, bring the wine and we'll pour a cup for father.

LI: What good sons you are! All right, you may go to Luzhou.

JUNLI: Thank you, father!

ZHOU: What have they done that they should go to Luzhou? Cunxiao the Winged-Tiger General fought up and down the country, slept in the saddle, and drank blood from his sword when thirsty. He should go to Luzhou, not they.

LI: You are right, general. (*To a Soldier.*) Call Cunxiao and his wife.

SOLDIER: Yes, commander.

(*Enter Cunxiao and his wife.*)

CUNXIAO:

I fought the tiger on the precipice,
Defeated the foe in battle
And with my iron mace
Saved the house of Tang.

My name was An Jingsi. I am a native of Lingqiu near Swan Pass. My

多亏邓大户家中抚养成人，长大我就与他家牧羊。有阿妈李克用见某有打虎之力，招安我做义儿家将，封我做十三太保飞虎将军李存孝，就着我与邓大户家为婿。自从跟着阿妈，十八骑误入长安，大破黄巢，天下太平无事。圣人的命：将俺义儿家将复夺的城池，着俺各处镇守。阿妈的言语：着俺两口儿去潞州天党郡镇守。今有阿妈呼唤，不知有甚事，须索走一遭去。可早来到此也。夫人，我和你休过去；你看阿妈、阿者：大吹大擂，敲牛宰马，烹炰美味，五百番部落胡儿胡女扶持着，是好是受用也。（正旦云）存孝，今日父亲饮宴，唤俺两口儿，俺见阿妈、阿者去。听了这乐韵悠扬，常好是受用也呵！

【仙吕点绛唇】则听的乐动声齐，他是那大唐苗裔，排亲戚。今日俺父母相随，可正是龙虎风云会。

【混江龙】则俺这沙陀雄势，便有那珠围翠绕不稀奇。置造下珍羞百味，又不比水酒三杯。每日则是炰凤烹龙真受用，那一日不宰羊杀马做筵席！把些个那义儿家将得都成立，一个个请官受赏，他每都荫子封妻。

（正旦云）存孝，我和你未过去，先望阿妈咱，可早醉了也。（李存孝云）咱不过去，见阿者、阿妈身上瀽的那酒呵，你见两边厢扶持着呵，十分的醉了也。

parents died when I was young, and Landlord Deng took me in and brought me up. I tended his sheep for him till my lord Li Keyong knew that I had killed a tiger and made me his officer and adopted son, giving me the titles of Winged Tiger and Thirteenth General. After that I married Deng's daughter. Since joining Li Keyong, I charged into Chang'an with eighteen horsemen and routed Huang Chao's army. Now that the empire is at peace, His Majesty has ordered us to garrison the towns and territory seized. My father has told me and my wife that we are to garrison Luzhou, and today he has sent for us. We must see what he wants. Here we are. Wait a moment before going in, ma'am. Look at our parents among all those flutes and drums, beef, horseflesh and abundance of delicacies, with five hundred Tartar boys and girls in attendance. Excellent!

DENG: Yes, today they must want us to join them at a feast. Listen to that beautiful tune! They are making very merry.

Listen to the music played in unison!
He is descended from the house of Tang.
We come to pay respect to our step-parents —
Dragons and tigers met in wind and clouds.
On the great steppes of Tartary
Beauties in pearls and emeralds count as nothing,
Here are rare food and dainties,
Not just three paltry cups of watered wine.
Each day we dress the flesh of dragon and phoenix,
And slaughter sheep and horses for our feasts;
His adopted sons and retainers
Receive official posts as their reward,
Their sons and wives are granted ranks and titles.

Don't go over just yet, Cunxiao. Look at father — he has drunk too much already.

CUNXIAO: Yes, he has spilt wine on his gown. See how they are holding him: he must be quite drunk.

【油葫芦】我见他执盏擎台忙跪膝，他那里撒滞殢。阿妈那锦袍上全不顾酒淋漓，可正是的他不择不减乾乾的吃，他那里刚扶刚策醺醺的醉。一壁厢动乐器是大体，将一面鼍皮画鼓冬冬擂，悠悠的慢品鹧鸪笛。

【天下乐】你觑！兀那大小的儿郎列的整齐，端的是虚也波实，享富贵。我则见傍边厢坐着周德威，一壁厢摆着品馔，番官每紧紧随，我则见军排在两下里。

（正旦云）咱过去见阿妈去来。（李存孝云）咱过去来。（做见科）（李存孝云）阿妈，您孩儿存孝两口儿来了也。（李克用云）存孝孩儿来了。别的孩儿每各处镇守去了；今日吉日良辰，你两口儿便往邢州镇守去；康君立，李存信，你两个孩儿往潞州天党郡镇守去。（李存孝云）阿妈，当日未破黄巢时，阿妈的言语："若你破了黄巢，天下太平，与你潞州天党郡镇守。"阿妈失其前言！今日阿妈着你孩儿镇守邢州，那邢州是朱温家后门，终日与他相持，可怎了也！（正旦云）存孝，我阿者行再告一告去。阿者，与存孝再说一声咱！（刘夫人云）孩儿，你去邢州镇守。阿妈醉了也，你且去咱。（李存孝云）阿者，当日与俺潞州天党郡，如今信着康君立、李存信，着俺去邢州去。阿者，怎生阿妈行再说一声，可也好也？（刘夫人云）你阿妈醉了也。（李存孝云）康君立、李存信，你有什么功劳？倒去潞州天党

DENG:

One is kneeling with cup and wine pot,
The other is making jokes.
Father does not care if his gown is stained with wine,
He helps himself absently,
Completely drunk.
Sweet music sounds beside him:
The roll of painted crocodile drums
And slow notes of cuckoo flutes.
See how smartly the troops are drawn up,
What pleasure he takes in wealth and nobility!
On one side sits General Zhou,
On the other Tartar officers serve food,
Between two ranks of soldiers.

Let us go over now.

CUNXIAO: Very well. (*He greets Li.*) We have come, father.

LI: So you have. My other sons have already gone to their posts. Today is an auspicious day. The two of you can set off to Xingzhou, while Junli and Cunxin start for Luzhou.

CUNXIAO: Before we defeated Huang Chao, father, you promised that if we crushed the revolt and restored peace you would give me Luzhou. But now you are going back on your word. Today you tell me to garrison Xingzhu, which is Zhu Wen's back door, where I shall have to be fighting all the time. What does this mean?

DENG: Let me ask mother to put in a word for us. Mother, please speak up for Cunxiao.

LIU: You had better go to Xingzhou, son. Your father is drunk. You had better go.

CUNXIAO: Father promised me Luzhou, but now he has more confidence in Junli and Cunxin and has ordered me to go to Xingzhou instead. Won't you speak to him for us, mother?

LIU: Your father is drunk.

CUNXIAO: Junli and Cunxin, what great deeds have you two done that you

郡镇守去？（李存信云）阿妈的言语，着你邢州去；都是一般好地面，谁和你论是什么功劳！（李存孝云）想当日在压关楼前，觑三层排栅，七层围子，千员猛将，八卦阵图，那其间如踏平地也。（正旦云）咱阿妈好失信也！

【节节高】今日呵便太平无事，全不想用人那用人得这之际。存孝与你安邦定国，他也曾恶征战图名图利。他觑的三层鹿角，七层围子，如登平地；端的是八卦阵图，千员骁将，施谋用计。阿者，他保护着唐朝社稷！

（李存孝云）康君立、李存信，你两个有什么功劳，倒去潞州镇守去也？

【元和令】端的是人不曾去铁衣，马不曾摘鞍辔；则是着阿者今日向父亲行提：想着他从前出力气。可怎生的无功劳，倒与他一座好城池？阿者，则俺这李存孝图个甚的！

（刘夫人云）孩儿也，你阿妈醉了也，等他酒醒时再说。（正旦云）想康君立、李存信他有什么功劳也！

【游四门】你则会饮酒食，着别人苦战敌。可不道

should go to Luzhou?

CUNXIN: Father told you to go to Xingzhou. It's just as good. Who said anything about great deeds?

CUNXIAO: When I stormed the citadel at Chang'an, there were three palisades, seven lines of defence, and a thousand of the enemy's best fighters drawn up in battle formation. But I trampled them under my feet as if they were nothing.

DENG: Our father is breaking his word.

Now the world is at peace you forget
How when you needed men
Cunxiao quelled the rebels for you,
How he battled so that you
Might win fame and riches.
Defences and palisades
Were nothing to him.
Despite their battle formations,
Fierce generals and cunning strategy,
He preserved the great Tang empire.

CUNXIAO: You, Junli and Cunxin! What great deeds have you done that you should go to Luzhou?

DENG:

He never unbuckled his armour,
His horse was never unsaddled.
Mother should remind our father
Of all Cunxiao did for them.
Why should men with no feats to their credit
Receive good cities
While Cunxiao goes unrewarded?

LIU: Your father is drunk, child. We will speak to him again when he is sober.

DENG: But what have Junli and Cunxin done?

You two fellows are nothing but gluttons
Who let others fight the fierce battles

生受了有谁知？阿妈，你则是抬举着李存信、康君立；他横枪纵马怎相持？你把他亏，人面逐高低。

（李存孝云）康君立、李存信，想当日十八骑误入长安，杀败葛从周，攻破黄巢，天下太平，是我的功劳；你有什么功劳也？（李存信云）俺两个虽无功劳，俺两个可会唱会舞也里。

【胜葫芦】他几时得鞭敲金镫笑微微，人唱着凯歌回，遥望见军中磨绣旗。则你那滴羞碟躞身体，迷留没乱心肺，唬的劈留扑碌走如飞。

（李存孝云）你两个有是么功劳？与你一匹劣马不会骑，与你一张硬弓不会射。则会吃酒肉，便是你的功劳也！

【后庭花】与你一匹劣马不会骑，我与你一张弓不会射，他比别人阵面上争功效，你则会帐房里闲坐的。咱可便委其实，你便休得要瞒天瞒地。你饿时节挝肉吃，渴时节喝酪水，闲时节打髀殖，醉时节歪唱起，醉时节歪唱起。

And never consider the hardships that they have suffered.
Father, you are favouring Cunxin and Junli.
Remember how Cunxiao fought with his horse and lance!
Now you are letting him down
And treating your sons unjustly.

CUNXIAO: Junli and Cunxin, I charged into the capital with eighteen horsemen, defeated Ge Congzhou, routed Huang Chao and restored peace. That was my work — what have you done?

CUNXIN: We have never distinguished ourselves in battle, but we can sing and dance.

DENG:

While he rode back victorious
With songs of triumph,
Smiling as he beat his golden stirrup with his whip,
And saw his embroidered standard float in the wind,
You were trembling,
Scared out of your wits,
Running away as fast as you could from the battle.

CUNXIAO: What have you two to your credit? Can you ride a spirited horse, or bend a strong bow? All you can do is gorge meat and wine. That is all you are fit for.

DENG:

Can you ride a spirited horse
Or bend a strong bow?
While he covered himself with glory in the field,
You lounged in camp.
This is the truth —
You need not try to deceive us.
Hungry, you clamour for meat;
Thirsty, you look for koumiss;
To pass the time you dice,
And once you are drunk
What ludicrous songs you sing.

【柳叶儿】你放下一十八般兵器，你轮不动那鞭简挝槌，您怎肯袒下臂膊刀厮劈？闹吵吵三军内，但听的马频嘶。早唬的悠悠荡荡，魄散魂飞。

（正旦云）存孝，则今日好日辰，收拾驮马辎重，辞别了阿者，便索长行。（李存孝云）今日好日辰，辞别了阿妈阿者，便索长行也。

【尾声】罢，罢，罢！你可便难依弟兄心，我今日不可公婆意。（刘夫人云）孩儿，你且休要性急，待你阿妈酒醒呵，再做商议。（正旦云）去则便了也。（唱）别近谤俺夫妻每甚的，止不过发尽儿掏窝不姓李，则今日暗昧神祇。（带云）惭愧也！（唱）执得一个远相离，各霸着城池；不恁的呵，这李存信、康君立断送了你。这一个个瞒心昧己，一个个献勤买力。存孝，这两个巧舌头奸狡赖功贼！（下）

（刘夫人云）康君立、李存信，你阿妈醉了也，我且扶着回后堂中去也。（下）（周德威云）想着存孝破了黄巢，复夺取大唐天下。他的好地面与了这两个，可将

You cannot handle one of the eighteen weapons,
You cannot wield mace or club,
And you will not bare your arms
To fight with a sword;
When horses neigh
In the bustle and din of the camp,
You nearly die of fright.

Cunxiao, today is an auspicious day. Let us collect our baggage and horses, say goodbye to our parents and set off on our long journey.

CUNXIAO: Yes, today is an auspicious day. Let us say goodbye to our parents and set off on our long journey.

DENG: Say no more.

Your brothers are no true brothers to you,
And now I have offended our parents.

LIU: Don't be so impatient, child. When your father wakes up, we can discuss this again.

DENG: No, we must be giong.

You need reproach us no more;
After all, we were not born in the house of Li.
May Heaven see this injustice!

It is lucky —

That we shall be far apart,
Each in our own city,
Otherwise Cunxin and Junli
Would be in for trouble —
One a downright liar,
The other a fawning flatterer,
Two glib, deceitful knaves!

(*Exeunt Cunxiao and Madam Deng.*)

LIU: Junli and Cunxin, your father is drunk. I will take him inside.

(*Exeunt Madam Liu and Li.*)

ZHOU: Cunxiao defeated Huang Chao and re-established the Tang empire, yet his good land has been given to these two, while he gets Xingzhou.

邢州与了存孝。元帅今日醉了也，待明日酒醒，我自有话说。还着存孝两口儿潞州天党郡去，方称我之愿也！元帅殢酒负存孝，明日须论是与非。（下）（李存信云）康君立，如何？我说咱必然得潞州，今日果应其心。若是到那潞州的丰富地面，不强似去邢州与朱温家每日交战？（康君立云）兄弟，想存孝这一去，必然有些见怪。等俺到的潞州，别寻取存孝一桩事调唆阿妈，杀坏了存孝，方称我平生之愿。则今日收拾行装，先往邢州，诈传着阿妈言语：着义儿家将各自认姓。他若认了本姓，咱搬唆阿妈杀了存孝，方称我平生之愿也。阿妈好吃酒，醉了似烧猪。害杀安敬思，称俺平生愿。（同下）

Today the commander is drunk. Tomorrow when he is sober I must speak to him, and persuade him to send Cunxiao and his wife to Luzhou. Nothing less will satisfy me.

The drunken commander has wronged Cunxiao.

Tomorrow we must set this injustice right. (*Exit.*)

CUNXIN: Well, Junli, what do you say now? I told you we'd get Luzhou, and you see I was right. Going to a rich place like that will be better than being in Xingzhou and fighting every day with Zhu Wen's men.

JUNLI: But now Cunxiao bears a grudge against us, brother. Once we get to Luzhou we must accuse him of some fault so that the old man has him killed. That's the only way we'll be safe. I tell you what — let's pack up today and go to Xingzhou. Then we can pretend that we have orders from the old man that all his adopted sons and retainers are to use their own names again; and once Cunxiao uses his old name, we can accuse him and have him killed. Then our greatest wish will be granted.

The old man is fond of drinking,
Once drunk he is like a swine;
We are going to kill An Jingsi
To have our own way.

(*Exeunt.*)

第二折

（李存孝领番卒子上，云）铁铠辉光紧束身，虎皮妆就锦袍新；临军决胜声名大，永镇邢州保万民。某乃十三太保李存孝是也，官封为前部先锋，破黄巢都总管，金吾上将军。自到邢州为理，操练军卒有法，抚安百姓无私；杀王彦章，不敢正眼视之；镇朱全忠，不敢侵扰其境。今日无甚事，在此州衙闲坐，看有是什么人来。（李存信同康君立上）（李存信云）自离上党郡，不觉到邢州。自家李存信，这个是康君立。可早来到也，这个衙门就是邢州。小校报复去，道有李存信康君立在于门首。（卒子云）理会的。（做报个云）报的将军得知，有李存信、康君立来了也。（李存孝云）两个哥哥来了，必有阿妈的将令，道有请。（卒子云）理会的。有请！（做见科）（康君立云）李存孝，阿妈将

ACT II

(*Enter Cunxiao with Tartar Troops.*)

CUNXIAO:

In shining helmet and close-fitting habit,
A tiger-skin above my new silk robe,
I have won great fame in battle,
And garrison Xingzhou to protect the people.

I am Li Cunxiao the Thirteenth General, formerly I was commander of the vanguard, conqueror of Huang Chao, and halberdier-general. Since coming to govern Xingzhou, I have trained my troops well and governed with justice. I have defeated Wang Yanzhang, who dared not look me in the face, and kept Zhu Wen from invading our territory. Today I have no business. I am sitting in my office to see if anyone comes.

(*Enter Cunxin and Junli.*)

CUNXIN:

From Luzhou we come to Xingzhou;
I am Cunxin, he is Junli.

Here we are. This is the Xingzhou office. Go in, fellow, and report that Li Cunxin and Kang Junli are at the gate.

SOLDIER: Yes, sir. (*Announcing them.*) General Li! Li Cunxin and Kang Junli are here.

CUNXIAO: So my brothers have come. They must have brought orders from our father. Ask them in.

SOLDIER: Yes, sir. Please come in.

(*Cunxin and Junli greet Cunxiao.*)

JUNLI: Cunxiao, this is our father's order. You have done many great deeds

令：为你多有功劳，怕失迷了你本性，着你出姓，还叫做安敬思。你若不依着阿妈言语，要杀坏了你哩！你快着的改姓，我就要回阿妈的话去也。（李存孝云）怎生着我改了名姓？阿妈将令不敢有违。小校安排酒骰，二位哥哥吃了筵席去。（康君立云）不必吃筵席，俺回阿妈话去也。诈传者阿妈将令，着存孝更名改姓；调唆的父亲生嗔，耍了头也是干净。（同下）（李存孝云）阿妈，你孩儿多亏了阿妈抬举成人，封妻荫子，今日怎生着我改了姓？阿妈，我也曾苦征恶战，眠霜卧雪，多有功勋；今日不用着我了也！逐朝每日醉醺醺，信着谗言坏好人；我本是安邦定国李存孝，今日个太平不用旧将军。（下）

（李克用同刘夫人上）（李克用云）喜遇太平无事日，正好开筵列绮罗。某乃李克用是也。奉圣人的命，着俺义儿家将各处镇守。四海安宁，八方无事，正好饮酒作乐。看有是什么人来。（李存信同康君立上，云）阿妈，祸事也！（李克用云）你为什么大惊小怪的也？（康君立云）有李存孝到邢州，他怨恨父亲不与他潞州，他改

and he fears your own family name may be forgotten, so he orders you to give up the surname Li and take the name of An Jingsi again. If you disobey him, he will have you killed. You had better make the change at once. We must leave now to report back to our father.

CUNXIAO: Why should he want me to change my name? Still, this is my father's order, and I dare not disobey. Men, prepare a feast for my brothers.

JUNLI: We won't stop to eat. We must go back to the old man.

We have given him a false order
To make him change his name;
The old man will be angry,
Then off with his head!
And all will be well for us!

(*Exeunt Junli and Cunxin.*)

CUNXIAO: Ah, father, it was you who helped me win my present rank with a wife and son to share my high position. Why do you want me to change my name now? I fought hard, endured frost and snow, and distinguished myself in battle; but today you cast me off.

He is drunk every day,
He listens to liars and injures honest men.
I am Cunxiao who pacified the land,
But now there is peace the veteran is not wanted. (*Exit.*)

(*Enter Li Keyong and Madam Liu.*)

LI:

Happy days of peace and quiet —
Time to feast with silk-clad girls.

I am Li Keyong. By imperial decree my adopted sons and retainers are garrisoning different parts of the empire. The whole world is at peace — we can drink and be merry. Let us see who is coming here.

(*Enter Cunxin and Junli.*)

JUNLI: Father, trouble has started!

LI: What is the matter now?

JUNLI: After Cunxiao went to Xingzhou, because he was angry with you

了姓——安敬思，他领着飞虎军要杀阿妈哩！怎生是好？（李存信云）杀了阿妈不打紧，我两个怎生是好？我那阿妈也！（李克用云）颇奈存孝无礼。你改了姓便罢，怎生领飞虎军来杀我？更待干休！罢，则今日就点番兵，擒拿牧羊子走一遭去。（刘夫人云）住者！元帅，你怎生不寻思？李存孝孩儿他不是这等人。元帅，你且放心，我自往邢州去。若是存孝不曾改了姓呵，我自有个主意；他若改了姓呵，发兵擒拿，未为晚矣。也不用刀斧手扬威跃武，鸦脚枪齐摆军校；用机谋说转心回，两只手交付与一个存孝。（下）（李克用云）康君立、李存信，你阿者去了也。倘若存孝变了心肠，某亲拿这牧羊子走一遭去。说与俺能争好斗的番官，舍生忘死家将：一个个顶盔擐甲，一个个押箭弯弓，齐臻臻摆列剑戟，密匝匝搠立枪刀；三千鸦兵为先锋，逢山开道，遇水叠桥；左哨三千番兵能征惯战，右哨三千番兵猛烈雄骁，合后三千番兵推粮运草；更有俺五百义儿家将，都要的奋勇当先，相持对垒，坐下马似北海的毒蛟，鞍上将如南山猛虎。某驱兵领将到邢州，亲捉忘恩牧羊子。家将英雄武艺全，番官猛烈敢

for not giving him Luzhou he changed his name to An Jingsi, and means to lead his Winged-Tiger Army against you. What shall we do?

CUNXIN: If he kills you, what will become of us, father?

LI: How dare Cunxiao do such a thing? He could change his name, but why lead an army against me? I won't let him off lightly. Today I shall mobilize my Tartar troops and arrest that shepherd myself.

LIU: Wait a bit, commander. Why not think this over? Young Cunxiao would never do a thing like that, you can be sure. Let me first go to Xingzhou. If he has not changed his name, well and good. If he has, we can still mobilize our troops to capture him.

We need no swordsmen, halberdiers,
Or lancers to show our might;
I shall make use of cunning
And deliver Cunxiao to you with my bare hands. (*Exit.*)

LI: Junli and Cunxin, your mother has already gone there. If she finds Cunxiao has really revolted, I shall go myself to catch that shepherd boy. Tell my brave officers and men to make ready.

Put on your helmets and armour,
Fit arrows to your bows,
Shoulder your lances and halberds,
Brandish your swords and sabres.
Our vanguard, three thousand strong,
Will cross the mountains and streams;
My left troops are skilled soldiers,
My right troops are fierce and brave,
My rearguard will bring up supplies,
And my five hundred retainers
Will fight like heroes in front.
Our chargers are fierce as dragons,
Our officers brave as tigers;
I shall lead my men to Xingzhou
To seize that ungrateful cub.
My men are seasoned campaigners,

当先；拿住存孝亲杀坏，血溅东南半壁天。（同下）

（李存孝同正旦、卒子上）（李存孝云）欢喜未尽，烦恼到来。夫人不知，如今阿妈的言语，着康君立、李存信传说，但是五百义儿家将，着更改姓。休教我姓李，我不免改了安敬思。我想来阿妈信着这两个的言语呵，怎了也？（正旦云）将军，你休要信这两个的贼说！则怕你中他的计策，你也要寻思咱。（李存孝云）他两个亲来传说，教我改姓，非是我敢要改姓也。（正旦云）既然父亲教你改姓，则要你治国以忠，教民以义。

【南吕一枝花】常言道“官清民自安，法正天心顺”，他那里家贫显孝子，俺可便各自立功勋。无正事尊亲，着俺把各自姓排头儿问，则俺这叫爹娘的无气忿。今日个嫌俺辱末你家门，当初你将俺真心断认！

（李存孝云）夫人，想当日破黄巢时，招安我做义儿家将；那其间不用我，可不好来！

【梁州】又不曾相趁着狂朋怪友，又不曾关节做九眷十亲；俺破黄巢血战到三千阵，经了些十生九

My Tartar officers are brave and daring;
I shall kill him with my own hands,
Splashing the blood over the eastern sky!

(*Exeunt.*)

(*Enter Cunxiao with his wife and soldiers.*)

CUNXIAO: Before we can enjoy happiness, fresh trouble has started, ma'am. My father has told Junli and Cunxin to inform me that his five hundred adopted sons and retainers are ordered to change their names. I am to give up the name of Li and call myself An Jingsi again. It seems to me our father puts too much trust in that couple. What shall we do?

DENG: You had better not believe those two scoundrels, my lord. Be careful that you don't fall into a trap.

CUNXIAO: It was they who came to order me to change my name. It is not that I want to change it.

DENG: If your father has ordered you to change, you must. But govern loyally and show the people justice,

The proverb says:
Good magistrates make happy people;
Just laws are pleasing to Heaven;
Poor families may have filial sons;
Let us do what good we can.
If our father orders us to change our name,
We need not stamp with rage;
Today he fancies we disgrace his house,
But there was a time when he wanted you for his son.

CUNXIAO: When we were fighting Huang Chao, ma'am, he made me his son and a member of his family. He would have done better not to adopt me then.

DENG:

We relied not on powerful friends,
Nor on family connections.
We fought Huang Chao
In three thousand bloody battles,

死，万苦千辛。俺出身入仕，荫子封妻，大人家达地知根。前后军捺袴摩裩，俺、俺、俺，投至得画堂中列鼎重裀，是、是、是，投至向衙院里束杖理民，呀、呀、呀，俺可经了些个杀场上恶哏哏捉将擒人。常好是不依本分！俺这里忠言不信，他则把谗言信；俺割股的倒做了生忿，杀爹娘的无徒说他孝顺：不辨清浑！

（李存孝云）夫人，我在此闷坐。小校觑者，看有是什么人来。（孛老儿同小末尼上）（孛老儿云）老汉李大户。当日个我无儿，认义了这个小的做儿来；如今治下田产物业、庄宅农具，我如今有了亲儿了也，我不要你做儿，你出去。（小末尼云）父亲，当日你无儿，我与你做儿来；你如今有了田产物业、庄宅农具，你就不要我了！明有清官在，我和你去告来。可早来到衙门首也。冤屈也！（李存孝云）是什么人在这门前大惊小怪的？小校与我拿将过来者！（卒子做拿过科，云）理会得。已拿当面。（孛老儿同小末尼跪科）（李存孝云）兀的小人，你告什么？（小末尼上，云）大人可怜见！当日我父亲无儿，要小人与他做儿；他如今有了田业物产、庄宅农具，他如今有了亲儿，不要我做儿子了，就要赶我出去，小人特来告。大人可怜见，与我做主也！（李存孝云）这小的和我则一般：当日用着他时便做儿，今日有了儿就不要他做儿。小校将那老子与我打

Braved many dangers and hardships,
And at last gained official rank,
Both wife and sons sharing the honour.
Before we reached high estate
And lived in painted halls,
Before we governed the people in this office,
We conquered and captured foes...
But now he doubts our loyalty,
Believes wicked lies about us,
Doubts a filial son
And puts trust in heartless rogues,
Unable to distinguish good from evil.

CUNXIAO: Let us wait here, ma'am. (*To a Soldier.*) Go and see who is outside.

(*Enter an Old Man with a Boy.*)

OLD MAN: I am Landlord Li. Because I had no son I adopted this boy. Now I have land, a fine house and farm tools, as well as a son of my own. I don't need you now. Get out.

BOY: Father, when you had no son of your own, I became your son. But now that you have land, a house and farm tools, you don't want me. Here is a good official. Let us ask him to decide between us. Here we are at the office. Justice!

CUNXIAO: Who is that shouting at the gate? Bring him in.

SOLDIER (*bringing them forward*): Here they are, sir.

(*The Old Man and the Boy kneel before Cunxiao.*)

CUNXIAO: Well, boy, what is your complaint?

BOY: Mercy, Your Honour! When my father had no son he adopted me. But now that he has land, a house and farm tools, as well as a son of his own, he has no further use for me and wants to drive me out. So I come to appeal to you. Have mercy, and decide between us!

CUNXIAO: This boy's fate is like mine. In time of need, my father had a use for me; but now he has other sons he casts me off. Guards, beat that old man!

着者！（正旦云）你且休打，住者！

【牧羊关】听说罢心怀着闷，他可便无事哏，更打着这入衙来不问讳的乔民。则他这爷共儿常是相争，更和这子父每常时厮论。（李存孝云）小校，与我打着者！（唱）词未尽将他来骂，口未落便拳敦。常好背晦也萧丞相，（正旦云）赤瓦不剌海！（唱）你常好是莽撞也祇候人。

（李存孝云）小校，与我打将出去！（卒子云）理会的。出去。（孛老儿云）我干着他打了我一顿，别处告诉去来。（同下）（刘夫人上，云）老身沙陀李克用之妻刘夫人是也。因为李存孝改了姓名，不数日到这邢州；问人来，果然改了姓，是安敬思。这里是李存孝宅中，左右报复去，道有阿者来了也。（卒子云）理会的。报的将军得知：有阿者来了也。（正旦云）你接阿者去，我换衣服去也。（做换服科）（刘夫人做见科）（李存孝云）早知阿者来到，只合远接；接待不着，勿令见罪！（做拜科）（刘夫人怒科，云）李存孝，阿妈怎生亏负你来？你就改了姓名，你好生无礼也！（李存孝云）阿者且息怒。小校安排酒果来者！（卒子云）理会的。（李存孝

DENG: Wait! Don't beat him.

I listen with sinking heart,
It is not right
To beat this foolish old man.
If father and son have quarrelled
That is only natural.

CUNXIAO: Guards, beat that man!

DENG:

You condemn him unheard,
You beat him before he can speak;
What a wrong-headed judge you are!

Oh, you will kill him!

And what rough guards you have!

CUNXIAO: Drive him out.

SOLDIER: Yes, sir. Get out!

OLD MAN: So I have been beaten for nothing. I shall lodge a complaint somewhere else.

(*Exeunt.*)

(*Enter Madam Liu.*)

LIU: I am Li Keyong's wife, Madam Liu. Hearing that Cunxiao has changed his family name, I have come post-haste to Xingzhou. When I made inquiries, I found it was true that he calls himself An Jingsi now. Here is Cunxiao's house. Go and announce me, fellow.

SOLDIER: Yes, ma'am. Your Excellency, Madam Liu is here.

DENG: Go and welcome mother while I change my clothes.

(*She steps aside and changes her clothes.*)

CUNXIAO (*greeting Madam Liu*): If I had known you were coming, mother, I should have gone to welcome you. Forgive me for failing in respect. (*He bows.*)

LIU (*angrily*): Cunxiao, what wrong has your father done you? Why should you change your name? How could you do such a thing?

CUNXIAO: Please don't be angry, mother. Men, prepare wine and sweetmeats.

递酒科，云）阿者满饮一杯！（刘夫人云）孩儿，我不用酒。（正旦云）我且不过去，我这里望咱；阿者有些烦恼，可是为何也？

【红芍药】见阿者一头下马入宅门，慢慢的行过阶痕；见存孝擎抬把盏两三巡，他可也并不曾沾唇。我则他迎头里嗔忿忿，全不肯息怒停嗔。我这里傍边侧立索殷勤，怎敢道怠慢因循！

【菩萨梁州】我这里便施礼数罢平身，抄着手儿前进。您这歹孩儿动问，阿者，你便远路风尘！（刘夫人云）休怪波，安敬思夫人！（唱）听言罢着我去了三魂，可知道阿者便怀愁忿。这公事何须的问，何消的再写本！到岸方知水隔村，细说原因。

（刘夫人云）孩儿，俺老两口儿怎生亏负着你来？你改了名姓！若不是康君立李存信说呵，你阿妈不得知；如今你阿妈便要领大小番兵来擒拿你。我实不信，亲自到来，你果然改了姓名。俺怎生亏负你来？（正旦云）存孝，你不说待怎么？（李存孝云）阿者，是康君立、李存信的言语，着俺五百义儿家将都着改了姓，着您孩儿姓安。想你孩儿多亏着阿妈阿者抬举的成人，封妻荫子，偌大的官职，怎敢忘了阿者阿妈的恩义！（做哭

SOLDIER: Yes, sir.

CUNXIAO (*presenting wine*): Mother, please drink this cup.

LIU: No, Cunxiao, I will not drink.

DENG: I won't go to her yet but watch from here. Mother seems rather upset. I wonder why?

I saw her alight from her horse and enter the gate,
Walking slowly up the steps.
I see Cunxiao with cup and wine pot,
But she will not touch a drop.
I see how angry she looks,
Refusing to be appeased.
Standing humbly on one side
I dare not show any lack of due respect,
But curtsey and advance with folded hands —
Did you have a good journey, mother?

LIU: Please excuse me for disturbing you, Madam An Jingsi.

DENG: This is most disquieting!

Now I know why she is angry,
And need not ask the reason.
But we can explain what happened.

LIU: Child, have we two old people done you any wrong? Why should you change your name? If Junli and Cunxin had not told us, we should not even have known. Your father wanted to bring Tartar troops to arrest you, but I could not believe it was true so I came myself. However, I find you really have changed your name. Tell me what wrong we have done you.

DENG: Cunxiao, now is the time to speak.

CUNXIAO: Mother, it was Kang Junli and Li Cunxin who told me that our father had ordered all his five hundred adopted sons and retainers to change their names and made me take the name of An again. It was you, father and mother, who helped me reach my present position, win noble titles for my wife and son, and occupy such a high official post. How could I ever forget your kindness? (*He weeps.*)

科，云）不由人嚎咷痛哭，提起来刀搅肺腑；抬举的立身扬名，阿者，怎忘你养身父母！（刘夫人云）我道孩儿无这等勾当，你阿妈好生的怪着的。

【骂玉郎】当初你腰间挂了先锋印，俺可也须当索受辛勤。他将那英雄慷慨施逞尽，他则是开绣旗，聚战马，冲军阵。

【感皇恩】阿者，他与你建立功勋，扶立乾坤；他与你破了黄巢，敌了归霸，败了朱温。那其间便招贤纳士，今日个俺可便偃武修文。到如今无了征战，绝了士马，罢了边尘。

【采茶歌】你怎生便将人不偢问？怎生来太平不用俺旧将军？半纸功名百战身，转头高家卧麒麟。

（刘夫人云）媳妇儿，你在家中；我和孩儿两个见你阿妈，白那两个丑生的谎去来！（正旦云）阿者休着存孝去；到那里有康君立、李存信，枉送了存孝的性命也！（刘夫人云）孩儿，你放心！这句话到头来要个归着，要个下落处。孩儿，你在家中，我领存孝去，则有个主意也。（李存孝云）我这一去别辩个虚实，邓夫人放心也！

【尾声】到那里着俺这刘夫人扑散了心头闷；不恁的呵，着俺这李父亲怎消磨了腹内嗔！别辩个假共真，

I cannot help shedding tears;
My heart is racked with pain.
You raised me to high estate and fame,
How could I forget my adopted father and mother?

LIU: So you did not do this yourself. In that case your father has no reason to be angry.

DENG:

As vanguard commander
He strove with all his might,
Exerting his strength and courage to the utmost,
Galloping with silken standard
To storm the enemy's camp.
He won glory for you, mother,
Restored the empire and routed Huang Chao for you,
Fought Zhang Guiba and defeated Zhu Wen.
In those days you welcomed his talents,
But now we have laid down arms —
No more battles, soldiers, horses and frontier alarms —
You have forgotten us!
In time of peace you no longer need your general.
Hundreds of battles just for a scrap of paper —
But the dead are forgotten now in their high tombs.

LIU: Stay here, daughter, while I go with Cunxiao to his father to expose those two scoundrels' lies.

DENG: Don't take him with you, mother. If Junli and Cunxin are there, he will lose his life for nothing.

LIU: Set your mind at rest, child. We must clear up this slander. Wait here while I take Cunxiao with me. I know what to do.

CUNXIAO: This time I must clear myself. Don't worry, ma'am.

DENG:

Let mother clear up the trouble,
Or father will still be angry.
We count on the god of luck

全凭着这福神，并除了那祸根。你把那康君立、李存信，用着你那打大虫的拳头着一顿！想着那厮坑人来陷人，直打的那厮心肯意肯，可与你那争潞州冤仇证了本。（下）

（刘夫人云）孩儿收拾行装，你跟着我见你父亲去来。万丈水深须见底，止有人心难忖量。（同下）

（李克用同李存信、康君立上）（李克用云）李存信、康君立，自从你阿者去之后，不知虚实。将酒来我吃。则怕存孝无有此事么？（李存信云）阿妈，他改了姓也。我怎敢说谎？（康君立云）我两个若是说谎了呵，大风里敢吹了我帽儿！（李克用云）此是实。将酒来，与我吃几杯。（康君立云）正好饮几杯。（刘夫人同李存孝上）（刘夫人云）孩儿来到也。小校报复去，道有阿者来了也。（李克用云）阿者来了，请过来饮几杯。（卒子云）理会得。有请！（李存孝云）阿者先过去，替你孩儿说一声咱。（刘夫人云）孩儿，你放心，我知道。（刘夫人见科，云）李克用，你又醉了也！不是我去呵，险些儿送了孩儿也！（李存信报科）（云）阿者，亚子哥哥打围去，围场中荡马也！（刘夫人慌科，云）似这般如之奈何？我索看我孩儿去。（存孝扯科，云）阿者，替您孩儿说一说！（刘夫人云）亚子孩儿打围去，在围场中落马，我去看了孩儿便来也。（李存孝云）阿者去了，阿妈带酒也，信着这两个的言语，送了您孩儿的性命也！（刘夫

To distinguish true from false
And root up the source of our calamity.
Use those fists that have killed tigers
To pound Junli and Cunxin
Till they confess their crime
Of seizing Luzhou from you,
And we are avenged. (*Exit.*)

LIU: Pack up your luggage, son, and come with me to your father.
We can see to the bottom of deep pools;
Only the human heart is hard to fathom.

(*Exeunt.*)

(*Enter Li Keyong, Cunxin and Junli.*)

LI: Junli and Cunxin, since your mother left we have heard nothing to confirm that rumour. Bring me wine. Weren't you mistaken about Cunxiao?

CUNXIN: He *has* changed his name, father. How dare I lie to you?

JUNLI: If we lied, may a big gust of wind blow my hat away!

LI: So it is true. Bring me wine. I'll drink a few cups.

JUNLI: A good idea. Yes, drink a few cups.

(*Enter Liu and Cunxiao.*)

LIU: Here we are, son. (*To the Guard.*) Go in, man, and announce me.

LI: So she is back. Ask her to come in to drink a few cups.

GUARD: Yes, sir. Please come in, ma'am.

CUNXIAO: Go in first and say a good word for me, mother.

LIU: Don't worry, son. I will. (*She greets Li.*) So you are drunk again, husband. If I hadn't gone, you would have done Cunxiao a serious wrong.

CUNXIN: Mother! Brother Yazi has been thrown from his horse in the hunt.

LIU (*alarmed*): What's that? I must go to my son!

CUNXIAO (*seizing her sleeve*): Put in a good word for me, mother!

LIU: My son Yazi has been thrown in the hunt. I must go and see him. I shall come back very soon.

CUNXIAO: You are leaving me, mother, and my father is drunk. He will listen to those two villains and have me killed.

人云）存孝无分晓：亲儿落马撞杀了，亲娘如何不疼？可不道"肠里出来肠里热"，我也顾不得的，我看孩儿去也。（打推科，下）（李存孝哭科，云）阿者，亚子落马痛关情，子母牵肠割肚疼；忽然二事在心上，义儿亲子假和真。亚子终是亲骨肉，我是四海与他人；"肠里出来肠里热"，阿者，亲的原来则是亲！（李存信把盏科，云）阿妈满饮一杯。（李克用醉个，云）我醉了也。（康君立云）阿妈，有存孝在于门首，他背义忘恩。（李克用云）我五裂篾迭！（下）（李存信云）哥哥，阿妈道五裂篾迭。醉了也，怎生是了？阿妈明日酒醒呵，则说道："你着我五裂了来。"（康君立云）兄弟说的是。若不杀了存孝，明日阿妈酒醒，阿者说了，咱两个也是个死。小校与我拿将存孝来者。（李存孝云）康君立、李存信，将俺哪里去？（李存信云）那阿妈的言语：为你背义忘恩，五车争了你哩！（李存孝云）阿妈，你好哏也！我有什么罪过？将我五裂了！我死不争，邓夫人在家中岂知我死也？两个兄弟来，安休休、薛阿滩，将我虎皮袍、虎磕脑、铁燕挝与邓夫人，就是见我一般也。（李存孝哭科，云）邓夫人也，今朝我命一身亡，

LIU: Can't you understand? My own son has fallen from his horse and been killed. How can a mother behave as if nothing had happened? He is my own flesh and blood. I cannot look after you now — I must go to my son. (*She pushes him aside and goes out.*)

CUNXIAO (*shedding tears*): Ah, mother!

Yazi has been thrown
And she is broken-hearted,
For they are one flesh and blood.
When the choice lies between
An adopted son and her own,
The difference is clear as noonday.
Yazi was flesh of her flesh,
While I am a stranger.
She mourns for her own:
Her own child is more dear to her.

CUNXIN (*offering wine*): Father, drink one more cup.

LI (*reeling*): I am drunk.

JUNLI: Cunxiao is at the gate, father. He is disloyal and ungrateful.

LI: I feel distempered. (*Exit.*)

CUNXIN: The old man said he felt distempered, brother. He is drunk. What shall we do? Suppose tomorrow when he wakes up, we say that he told us to have Cunxiao dismembered?

JUNLI: Right! If we don't kill him, tomorrow when the old man wakes up and listens to his wife, we shall die. Men, arrest Cunxiao!

CUNXIAO: Where are you taking me. Cunxin and Junli?

CUNXIN: These are our father's orders. For your ingratitude and disloyalty, you are to be torn to pieces by five carts.

CUNXIAO: Cruel father! What wrong have I done that I should be torn to pieces? I shall die here while my wife at home does not know I am dead. Brothers An Xiuxiu and Xue Atan, send my tiger-skin robe and turban and my iron mace to her. This is my last gift to her. (*Weeping.*) Ah, wife!

Today I shall perish here,
I am on my way to the execution ground.

眼见的去赴云阳；娇妻暗想身无主，夫妇恩情也断肠。我死后淡烟衰草相为伴，枯木荒坟作故乡；夫妻再要重相见，夫人也，除是南柯梦一场！（李存信云）兀那厮，你听者：用机谋仔细裁排，牧羊子死限催来；李存孝真实改姓，就邢州斩讫报来。（李存孝云）皇天可表，于家为国多有功劳！我也曾活拿了孟截海，怒挟了邓天王，杀败了张归霸，力取了太原，复夺了并州，立诛了五将；华严川大战，杀败了葛从周，十八骑误入长安，攻破黄巢，扶持唐社稷：此乃是我功劳也！今日不用我，就将我五裂了！（哭科）（云）罢、罢、罢！志气凌云射斗牛，苍天教我做公侯。舍死忘生扶社稷，苦征恶战统戈矛。旌旗日影龙蛇动，野草闲花满地愁。英雄屈死黄泉下，忠心孝义下场头！邓夫人也，兀的不苦痛杀我也！（下）（李存信云）今日将存孝五裂了也，明日阿妈问俺，自有话说，咱去来。金风未动蝉

My wife will lose her husband,
My heart is broken as I think of our love.
Withered grass-blades on the misty plain
Will be my companions,
Dead trees and desolate tombs
Will be my home;
Only in her dreams
Shall we ever meet again.

CUNXIN: Just listen to me!

We laid our plans with cunning
To hasten the shepherd boy's death;
You fell into our trap and changed your name,
Now we have got you from Xingzhou to have you killed!

CUNXIAO: As Heaven is my witness, I have served the Li family and the empire well. I captured Meng Jiehai alive; in my rage I seized Deng Tianwang, defeated Zhang Guiba, stormed Taiyuan and took back Bingzhou, killing five enemy commanders. In the great battle of Huayanchuan, I defeated Ge Congzhou; then with eighteen horsemen I charged into Chang'an and routed Huang Chao, restoring the Tang empire. These are my achievements. Today I am not needed, and you want to have me dismembered. (*He sheds tears.*) Enough!

My high ambitions towered to the stars,
Heaven decreed me a noble.
I risked my life to prop the tottering throne,
And fought hard at the head of the spearmen.
Flags gleamed in the sun like serpents;
Now wild flowers bloom over sad battlefields,
The hero is wrongly killed —
This is the fruit of loyalty and goodness!

Ah, wife, I am dying of bitterness! (*Exit.*)

CUNXIN: Today we will have him torn limb from limb. When the old man questions us tomorrow, we can think of some answer. Come on.

The cicada knows when autumn is at hand,

先觉，暗送无常死不知。（同下）

（周德威上）（云）事有足濯，物有故然。某乃周德威是也。此事怎了？谁想李克用带酒杀了存孝！竟信着康君立、李存信谎言，直将飞虎将军五裂身死。昨日带酒不知，今日小官直至帅府，问其详细走一遭去。二贼子用计铺谋，将存孝五裂身卒；众番官亲临帐下，我看那李克用怎的支吾！（下）

But death comes stealthily and unforeseen.

(*Exeunt.*)

(*Enter Zhou Dewei.*)

ZHOU: Events may surprise us, but there is a reason for all things. I am Zhou Dewei. This is a fearful business — Li Keyong while drunk has had Cunxiao killed. Taken in by Junli and Cunxin's lies, he had the Tiger General dismemberd. Yesterday he was in a drunken stupor. I am on my way now to his headquarters to find out exactly what happened.

Two scoundrels plotted together
And had Cunxiao dismembered.
Now Tartar officers are crowding his tent —
Let us see what Li has to say! (*Exit.*)

第三折

（刘夫人上，云）描鸾刺绣不曾习，劣马弯弓敢战敌，围场队里能射虎，临军对阵兵机识。老身刘夫人是也。昨日引将存孝孩儿来阿妈行欲待说也，不想亚子在围场中落马。我亲到围场中看孩儿，原来不曾落马，都是李存信、康君立的智量。未知存孝孩儿怎生？使一个小番探听去了，这早晚敢待来也。（正旦扮莽古歹上，云）自家莽古歹便是。奉阿者的言语，着吾打探存孝去。不想阿妈醉了，信着康君立、李存信的言语，将存孝五裂了。不敢久停久住，回阿者的话走一遭去也。

【中吕粉蝶儿】颇奈这两个奸邪，看承做当职忠烈，想俺那无正事好酒的爹爹！他两个似蚖蛇，如腹蝎，心肠乖劣。我呸呸的走似风车，不付能盼到宅舍。

ACT III

(*Enter Madam Liu.*)

LIU:

I never learned needlework or embroidery,
With bent bow on horseback I fight the enemy;
I shoot tigers with the hunters,
And know stratagems of war.

I am Madam Liu. Yesterday I brought Cunxiao to see his father, but just as I was going to explain matters I heard that my son Yazi had been thrown while hunting. When I hurried to see him, I found nothing had happened — it was a trick played by Cunxin and Junli. I wonder what has happened to Cunxiao. I have sent a messenger to find out. She should be back now.

(*Enter Manggudai.*)

MANGGUDAI: I am Manggudai. Our mistress told me to find out what happened to Cunxiao. It seems that when the master was drunk he believed Junli and Cunxin, and had Cunxiao dismembered. I dare not delay, but must report this at once.

Two treacherous villains
Were treated as loyal men
By our heartless, drunken master.
Those two are like vipers and scorpions:
Their hearts are evil.
I move as fast as a windmill
To hurry back to the house,
Running the whole way,

【醉春风】一托炁走将来，两只脚不暂歇；从头一一对阿者，我这里便说、说。世做的泼水难收，至死也无对，今日个一庄也不借。

(刘夫人云)阿的好小番也！暖帽貂裘最堪宜，小番平步走如飞；吾儿存孝分诉罢，尽在来人是与非。你见了存孝，他阿妈醉了，康君立、李存信说是么来？喘息定，慢慢的说一遍。

【上小楼】则俺那阿妈醉也心中乖劣；他两个巧语花言，鼓脑争头，损坏英杰。他两个厮间别，犯口舌，不教分说；他两个傍边相倚强作孽。

(刘夫人云)小番，他阿妈说是么来？存孝说是么来由？李阿妈醺醺酒殢，李存孝忠心仁义，子父每两意相投，犯唇舌存信君立。他阿妈与存孝谁的是？谁的不是？再说一遍咱。

【上小楼】做儿的会做儿，做爷的会做爷，子父每无一个差迟，生各札的意断恩绝！阿妈那里紧当者，紧拦者，不着疼热，他道是："你这姓安的怎做

Giving my feet no rest.
I shall tell our lady the truth from the beginning.
It is done, the water is spilt,
The dead cannot speak;
There is no remedy now.

LIU: What a fine young Tartar!
With well-fitted cap and sable coat,
She runs as if she had wings.
She will give me news of Cunxiao,
And tell me the truth of the matter.

Well, you must have seen Cunxiao. His father was drunk — what did Junli and Cunxin say to him? When you are less out of breath, tell me all that happened.

MANGGUDAI:
Our master has no sense when he is drunk,
Junli and Cunxin wagged their tongues,
Shook their heads,
And slandered the hero.
They gave him no chance to answer,
But worked hand in glove to destroy him.

LIU: What did your master say, girl? What did Cunxiao say?
My husband was drunk;
Cunxiao is good and loyal;
Son and father loved each other
Till Cunxin and Junli made trouble.

What words did your master have with Cunxiao, tell me that.

MANGGUDAI:
One was a good son,
The other a good father,
But their love was destroyed by others.
An evil influence on the father's side
Made him unkind to his son;
And slanderers said:

李家枝叶！”

（刘夫人云）小番，阿妈那里有两个逆贼么？（莽古歹云）是那两个。（刘夫人云）一个是康君立，双尾蝎侵人骨髓；一个李存信，两头蛇谗言佞语。他则要损忠良英雄虎将，他全无那安邦计赤心报国。那两个怎生支吾来？（莽古歹云）阿者，听您孩儿从头至尾说与阿者，则是休烦恼也！

【十二月】则您那康君立哏绝，则你那李存信似蝎蜇；可端凭着他劣缺，端的是今古皆绝。枉了他那眠霜卧雪，阿妈他水性随邪。

（刘夫人云）俺想存孝孩儿，华严川舍命，大破黄巢定边疆。他是那擎天白玉柱，端的是驾海紫金梁。他两个无徒，怎生害存孝来？

【尧民歌】他把一条紫金梁，生破做两三截。阿者休波，是他便那里每分说！想着十八骑长安城内逞豪杰，今日个则落的足律律的旋风踅，我可便伤也波嗟。将存孝见时节，阿者，则除是水底下捞明月！

（刘夫人云）小番，你要说来又不说，可是为什么来？（莽古歹云）李存信、康君立的言语，将存孝五车争死

"How can a son of An be an heir of Li?"

LIU: Do you know that there were two traitors with your master, girl?

MANGGUDAI: Who were they?

LIU:

Kang Junli, that two-tailed scorpion,
Li Cunxin, that double-faced snake.
With no loyalty to the state
They plotted to harm the hero.

How did those two men argue their case?

MANGGUDAI: I will tell you all, ma'am, if you can bear to hear it.

Junli is a savage wolf,
Cunxin a poisonous snake;
Their dastardly deed
Was something unheard of before.
Cunxiao's loyalty was vain;
Our master is fickle.

LIU:

My son Cunxiao risked his life at Huayanchuan
To defeat Huang Chao and pacify the state.
He was the jade pillar supporting the vault of heaven,
The golden bridge spanning the ocean.

What did those two scoundrels do to him?

MANGGUDAI:

The golden bridge was broken:
How could he defend himself, ma'am?
Once he charged with eighteen horsemen into Chang'an,
Now he is only a spirit riding the wind —
It's enough to break your heart.
You will no more see him again
Than catch the moon in a pool.

LIU: What are you keeping back, girl?

MANGGUDAI: Thanks to Cunxin and Junli, Cunxiao was torn to pieces by five carts.

了也！（刘夫人云）苦死的儿也！他临死时，将存孝棍棒临身，毁骂了千言万语，眼见的命掩黄泉。存孝儿衔冤负屈，孩儿怎有生死了来？

【耍孩儿】则听的喝一声马下如雷烈，恰便似鹘打寒鸠哏绝。那两个快走向前来，那存孝待分说怎的分说？一个指着嘴缝连骂到有三十句，一个扶着软肋里扑扑扑的装到五六靴。委实的难割舍，将存孝五车争坏，霎时间七段八节。

（刘夫人云）想必那厮取存孝有罪招状，责口词无冤文书，知赚的推在法场，暗送了七尺身躯。

【三煞】又不曾取罪名，又不曾点纸节；可是他前推后拥强牵拽，军兵铁桶周围闹，棍棒麻林前后遮，扑碌碌推到法场也。称了那两个贼汉的心愿，屈杀了一个英杰！

（刘夫人云）想当日俺那存孝孩儿多有功劳：活挟了孟截海，杀了邓天王，枪槊杀张归霸，十八骑入长安，挝打杀耿彪，火烧了永丰仓，有九牛之力，打虎之威。怎生死了我那孩儿来！（莽古歹云）存孝道：

LIU: Ah, my unhappy child!

They must have beaten him
And cursed him again and again!
His spirit has gone to the shades
With unavenged wrongs.

How did he meet his death?

MANGGUDAI:

With a shout like a thunderbolt,
Like a cruel hawk catching a dove,
The pair rushed forward.
They gave Cunxiao no chance to speak.
One abused him thirty times,
The other kicked him six times in the ribs.
It was a fearful sight!
He was torn limb from limb,
Torn to pieces by the carts!

LIU: Did they try to extract a confession from him before they took the hero to the execution ground and murdered him?

MANGGUDAI:

They did not ask him to confess,
Nor did they sign a warrant for his execution.
He was pushed away,
With soldiers around him like iron hoops,
With a forest of clubs before and behind,
He was dragged to the execution ground.
Two scoundrels had their wish,
And one gallant man was murdered.

LIU: Think of all my son Cunxiao did for the country! He captured Meng Jiehai alive, killed Deng Tianwang, pierced Zhang Guiba with his lance, and charged with eighteen steeds into Chang'an. He killed Geng Biao with his mace, and burned the Yongfeng Granary. He had the strength of nine bulls and could kill a tiger. How did he meet his death?

MANGGUDAI: Cunxiao said:

【二煞】我也曾把一个邓天王来旗下斩，我也曾把孟截海马上挟，我也曾将大虫打的流鲜血，我也曾双掀打杀千员将。今日九牛力，当不的五辆车，五下里把身躯拽。将军死的苦痛，见了的那一个不伤嗟！

（刘夫人云）五辆车，五五二十五头牛，一齐地拽，存孝怎生者？

【尾声】打你那头口门惊惊跳跳，叫道是“打打俫俫”。则见那忽剌鞭飕飕的摔动一齐拽，将您那打虎的将军命送了也！（下）

（刘夫人云）李克用，你信着这两个贼子的言语，将俺存孝孩儿屈死了。李克用，你好哏也！五辆车五下齐拽，铁石人嚎咷痛哭；将身躯骨肉分开，血染赤黄沙地土。再不能子母团圆，越思量越添凄楚；刘夫人苦痛哀哉，李存孝身归地府。（做哭科，云）哎约！存孝孩儿也，则被你痛杀我也！（下）

I killed Deng Tianwang beneath his flag,
Dragged Meng Jiehai from his horse,
Beat a tiger till it streamed with blood,
And killed a thousand men with my two maces.
But today the strength of nine bulls
Cannot withstand five carts.
The general died in agony,
All that saw it were appalled.

LIU: When the five carts with five times five bulls started pulling, what then?

MANGGUDAI:

They beat the bulls to make them jump with fright,
Shouted to urge them on;
Whips cracked and the bulls strained together,
So the Winged-Tiger General was killed. (*Exit.*)

LIU: Cruel Keyong! You believed two lying scoundrels and had Cunxiao killed so unjustly.

Five carts pulled in five directions —
Even a man of iron would utter a cry.
Bone and flesh were torn apart,
His blood stained the yellow sand.
Never again shall I see my son —
The thought of it breaks my heart.
I am bowed with sorrow,
And Cunxiao has gone to the shades.

(*Weeps.*) Ah, Cunxiao, my son, your mother will die of grief! (*Exit.*)

第四折

（李克用、李存信、康君立领番卒子上）（李克用云）塞上羌管韵，北风战马嘶；缕金画面鼓，云月皂雕旗。某乃李克用是也。昨朝与众番官饮酒，我十分带酒。说道存孝孩儿来了也，小番与我唤存孝孩儿来者。（李存信云）如之奈何？（刘夫人上，云）李克用，你做的好勾当！信着两个丑生，每日饮酒，怎生将存孝孩儿五裂了？我亲到的邢州，并不曾改了名姓；都是康君立、李存信这两个贼丑生的见识，着他改做安敬思。昨日我领着存孝孩儿来见你，你怎生教那两个贼子五车争了？存孝媳妇儿将着骨殖，背将邓家庄去了。孩儿也，兀的不痛杀我也！（李克用云）夫人，你不说我怎生知道！都是这两个送了我那孩儿也！我说道五裂篾迭，我醉了也。他怎生将孩儿五裂了！把这两个无徒拿到邓家庄上杀坏了，剖腹剜心，与俺孩儿报了冤仇也！便安排灵位祭物，便差人赶回媳妇儿来者。（做哭科，云）哎约！存孝儿也！我听言说罢泪千行，过如刀搅我心肠。义儿家

ACT IV

(*Enter Li Keyong, Cunxin, Junli and Tartar Troops.*)

LI:

Shepherd pipes flute in the wilderness,
A north wind blows, chargers neigh.
We beat painted drums inlaid with gold,
Black banners flutter against the clouds and the moon.

I am Li Keyong. Yesterday I made merry with my officers till I was drunk. They say that Cunxiao is here. Scout, bring Cunxiao to me.

CUNXIN: Now what shall we do?

(*Enter Madam Liu.*)

LIU: A fine thing you have done, Li Keyong! How could you listen to those two scoundrels who make you drunk every day, and have Cunxiao dismembered? I went to Xingzhou myself to find out the truth, and discovered that he did not change his name: it was those devils Cunxin and Junli who tricked him into calling himself An Jingsi. Yesterday I brought Cunxiao to see you. How could you let those wicked men dismember him? His wife has taken his bones to Deng Village. Ah, you have broken my heart!

LI: Madam, I knew nothing of this. It was all their doing. I said that I felt distempered because I was drunk — how dare they have him dismembered! Let those two wicked men be taken to Deng Village and killed. Let their bellies be opened and their hearts taken out, to avenge my son. Have a shrine and sacrifice prepared, and let someone fetch Cunxiao's wife. (*He sheds tears.*) Ah, Cunxiao, my son, my son!

My tears stream down,

将都悲戚，只因带酒损忠良。颇奈存信康君立，五裂存孝一身亡。大小儿郎都挂孝，家将番官痛悲伤。哎！你个有仁有义忠孝子，休怨我无恩无义的老爹娘！（同下）

（正旦拿引魂旛哭上，云）闪杀我也，存孝也！痛杀我也，存孝也！

【双调新水令】我将这引魂旛，招飐到两三遭，存孝也，则你这一灵儿休忘了大阳关大道。我扑簌簌泪似倾，急穰穰意如烧，我避不得水远山遥，须有一个日头定到。

【水仙子】我将这引魂旛，执定在手中摇，我将这骨殖匣，轻轻的自背着。则你这悠悠的魂魄儿无消耗，（带云）你这里不是飞虎峪那，（唱）你可休冥冥杳杳差去了！忍不住、忍不住痛哭嚎咷，一会儿赤留乞良气，一会家迷留没乱倒，天那！痛煞煞的心痒难挠。

（刘夫人上，云）兀的不是媳妇儿邓夫人！我是叫他一声咱：媳妇儿，邓夫人，你住者！

【庆东原】踏踏的忙那步，呸呸的不住脚，是谁人吖吖的脑背后高声叫？（刘夫人云）邓夫人，是我也。（做

My heart seems pierced with a sword,
All my adopted sons and retainers mourn,
Because in my cups I killed a loyal man.
It was Cunxin and Junli, the scoundrels,
Who had Cunxiao dismembered.
Let all my sons put on mourning,
Let my Tartar officers and men lament.
Alas, my good and loyal son,
Do not think too harshly of your faithless parents!

(*Exeunt.*)

(*Enter Madam Deng carrying the pennant to call the dead man's spirit.*)

DENG: Ah, Cunxiao, my heart is broken.

I wave the pennant from side to side —
Your spirit must not lose its way!
My tears stream unceasingly,
My heart is burning with anguish.
No matter how long the road,
I shall reach my goal in the end.
I wave the pennant,
I carry the box with your ashes on my back.
Your spirit flies on high — where is it now?

Surely this is Winged-Tiger Valley?

You must not miss the place and pass us by.
I cannot stop sobbing with anguish,
Faint with sorrow.
Oh, Heaven!
My heart is racked with pain!

(*Enter Madam Liu.*)

LIU: Isn't that my daughter-in-law? Let me call her to make sure. Madam Deng! Daughter! Wait a moment.

DENG:

I hasten on without a pause.
Who is that calling me?

见哭科，云）痛杀我也，存孝孩儿也！（唱）阿者，你把我这存孝来送也！（刘夫人云）我说是么来？（唱）你可道“不着落，保到头来须有个归着”。（刘夫人云）媳妇儿也，你不曾忘了一句儿也。（唱）这烦恼我心知，待对着阿谁道？

（刘夫人云）孩儿，你且放下骨殖匣儿，你阿妈将二贼子拿将来与存孝孩儿报仇雪恨也。（李克用同周德威领番卒子拿李存信、康君立上）（李克用云）媳妇儿也，你也辞我一辞去，怕做是么？将那祭祀的物件来，将虎磕脑、螭虎带、铁飞挝供养在存孝灵前，将康君立、李存信绳缠索绑祭祀了，慢慢地杀坏了这两个贼子。周将军与我读祭文咱。（周德威读祭文科）维大九月上旬日，忻、代、石、岚、雁门关都招讨使，破黄巢兵马大元师李克用等，致祭于故男飞虎将军李存孝之灵曰：惟灵生居朔漠，长在飞虎，累遇敌战，猿臂善射。两张弓，两代箭，左右能射之；手舞铁挝，爱将不及三合。曾打虎在山峪之中，破贼兵禁城之内。挝打死耿彪，立诛三将，杀坏五虎。击破一字长蛇阵，

LIU: Madam Deng, it is I! (*She greets her and weeps.*) Alas, Cunxiao, sorrow will carry me to my grave.

DENG:

Mother, you caused my husband's death.

LIU: What did I do?

DENG:

You promised that all would be well,
That the misunderstanding would be explained away.

LIU: Ah, daughter, not a word have you forgotten.

DENG:

My heart is bursting,
But to whom can I speak?

LIU: Child, put down the box with his remains. Your father is bringing those two scoundrels here to avenge Cunxiao.

(*Enter Li Keyong, Zhou Dewei and Tartar Troops escorting Cunxin and Junli in chains.*)

LI: I am to blame for this, daughter. You need not be afraid to reproach me. Now bring the sacrificial objects. Put the tiger-skin turban, the tiger-belt and the iron maces before the shrine. Let Kang Junli and Li Cunxin be tied up and brought here. Those wicked men shall die a lingering death. Now General Zhou will read the funeral speech.

ZHOU (*reading*): On the tenth of the ninth month of the first year of Qianning[37] of the Tang Dynasty, Li Keyong, commander-in-chief of the northern provinces and conqueror of Huang Chao, offers sacrifice with his generals before the shrine of his late adopted son, Li Cunxiao the Winged-Tiger General. Here is the dirge: "Reared in the northern steppes, you spent your youth in Winged-Tiger Valley and fought countless battles against the enemy. You were skilled in the use of the bow, and could shoot both right and left. You were invincible when you wielded your maces, and could fell an opponent with a single blow. You overcame a tiger in the mountains and routed the rebels in the capital. You struck Geng Biao dead with your mace, killed the three commanders and the five tiger generals, smashed the enemy's serpent formation and defeated

杀败葛从周。渭南三战，十八骑误入长安。箭射黄巨天，恶战傅存审，力伏李罕之，活挟邓天王，病战高思继，生擒孟截海，大败王彦章。救黎民复入长安城，享太平再临京兆府。祭奠英灵，亲藩悔罪。今克用因殢酒听信狂言，故损坏义男家将。今将贼子尽该诛戮，与公雪冤。众将缟素，俺哭的那无情草木改色，青山天地无颜。将军阳世不将金印挂，阴司却掌鬼兵权。众将番官痛嚎咷，壁上飞挝血未消，阶下枉拴龙驹马，帐前空挂虎皮袍。英雄存孝今朝丧，多曾出力建功劳，赤心报国安天下，万古清风把姓标。呜呼哀哉，伏惟尚飨！

【川拨棹】则听的父亲道，将孩儿屈送了。家将每痛哭嚎咷，想着盖世功劳，万载名标，都与他持服挂孝，众儿郎膝跪着。

【七弟兄】你兀的据着，枉了见功劳。沉默默两柄燕挝落，骨剌剌杂彩绣旗摇，扑冬冬画鼓征鼙操。

Ge Congzhou. Then you fought three battles at Weinan, and with eighteen horsemen galloped into the capital. You shot Huang Juyao, fought Fu Cunshen, vanquished Li Hanzhi, and captured Deng Tianwang. You beat Gao Siji during an illness, caught Meng Jiehai and routed Wang Yanzhang. Then you entered Chang'an a second time so that the people might live in peace again. But I, Li keyong, after drinking listened to slander and wronged my adopted son. I shall execute these murderers now to avenge you, and all my generals shall mourn for you.

We wail till the grass and trees,
Green hills, earth and sky turn pale.
No more will you wear the commander's golden seal,
But, a shade, will command ghostly troops.
The Tartar officers mourn with their men,
Your maces hanging here bear blood-stains still,
Your charger in the court misses its master;
Your tiger robe hangs limp before your tent.
Brave Cunxiao is no more.
He achieved many deeds of valour,
He served the state loyally.
And gave peace to the empire;
His name will live for all eternity.

May your spirit come to the sacrifice!"

DENG:

His father has admitted wronging him,
His comrades-in-arms are wailing bitterly;
Recalling his mighty deeds and immortal fame,
Thay have put on mourning for him
And are kneeling before the shrine.
Alas, your achievements were vain —
Quiet hang the two iron maces,
The bright embroidered flag flutters in the wind,
The painted drum sounds and the bugle.
In tiger-skin turban

【梅花酒】你戴一顶虎磕脑，马跨着黄骠，箭插着钢凿，弓控着花梢，经了些地寒毡帐冷，杀气阵云高。我这里猛觑了，则被你痛杀我也李存孝！

【收江南】呀，可怎生帐前空挂着虎皮袍？枉了你忘生舍死立唐朝！枉了你横枪纵马过溪桥！兀的是下梢，枉了你一十八骑破黄巢！

（李克用云）小番，将李存信、康君立拿在灵前，与我杀坏了者！（番卒子做拿二净科，云）理会得。（李存信云）阿妈，怎生可怜见饶了我两个罢！（康君立云）阿妈，若是饶我这一遭，下次再不敢了也！

【沽美酒】康君立你自道，李存信祸来到。把存孝赚入法场屈送了，粹碎了我浑家大小，任究禁罪难逃。

【太平令】也是你争弱，拿住你该剐该敲。聚集的人员好闹，准备车马绳索，把这厮绑了，五车裂了，可与俺李存孝一还一报！

（李克用云）小番将二贼子五裂了者！（番卒子做杀李存信、康君立科，云）理会的。（李存信云）我死也。（下）

On bay charger,
Bearing steel-tipped arrows
And bow with painted tassels,
You stayed in frosty tents in ice-bound country
Where battles raged and enemy forces swarmed.
Seeing these relics now,
My heart bleeds for you, Cunxiao.
The tiger-skin robe hangs limp before your tent,
In vain you risked death to restore the house of Tang,
Or galloped across the bridge with lance in hand —
This is the end!
In vain you routed Huang Chao with eighteen horsemen.

LI: Take Cunxin and Junli to the shrine, men, and have them killed.

SOLDIERS (*seizing them*): Yes, sir!

CUNXIN: Have pity, father! Spare us!

JUNLI: If you spare us this time, father, we won't do it again.

DENG:

Junli and Cunxin,
You brought this on yourselves,
You murdered Cunxiao,
And destroyed my family;
You shall not escape retribution,
But receive your due deserts.
You should be sliced and pounded,
The crowd clamours for your blood!
Get carts and horses ready,
And ropes to tie them up,
Then have them torn to pieces
So that Cunxiao is avenged!

LI: Have the villains dismembered, men!

(*The soldiers shout their assent, making ready to kill them.*)

CUNXIN: It's all up with us.

(*Exeunt.*)

（李克用云）既然将二贼子五裂了，与我存孝孩儿报了冤仇，将孩儿墓顶上封官，邓夫人与你一座好城池养老。您听者：李存信妒能害贤，飞虎将负屈衔冤。邓夫人哀哉苦恸，为夫主遇难遭愆。康君立存信贼子，五车裂死在街前。设一个黄箓大醮，超度俺存孝生天。

LI: Now that the murderers are being torn limb from limb, my son Cunxiao is avenged. Let posthumous honours be granted at his grave, and you, Madam Deng, shall have a good city to support your old age. Mark what I say:

Li Cunxin envied an able man,
And the Winged-Tiger General was unjustly accused.
His wife is stricken with grief,
Bowed down by her husband's death.
Now wicked Junli and Cunxin
Have been torn apart by five carts in the public square,
We shall hold a grand sacrifice
To send Cunxiao's spirit to Heaven.

(*THE END*)

NOTES

[1] Zhuo Wenjun, the daughter of a rich man, who eloped with Sima Xiangru, a famous Han Dynasty scholar. Since they were poor, they kept a small tavern in Chengdu where she served as barmaid.

[2] Wife of Liang Hong of the Later Han Dynasty.

[3] Thousands of the men conscripted by the First Emperor of Qin to build the Great Wall died. According to a legend Meng Jiangnü, the wife of one of these conscripts, wept so bitterly at the wall that part of it crumbled.

[4] During the Spring and Autumn Period (770-475 B.C.), Wu Zixu fled from the state of Chu to Wu. A woman washing by a river took pity on him and fed him. Upon leaving, he asked her not to tell his pursuers which way he had gone. To set his mind at rest she drowned herself.

[5] This legendary woman, whose husband left home, climbed a hill every day to watch for his return, till at last she was transformed into a boulder.

[6] Zou Yan of the Warring States Period (475-221 B.C.) was a loyal subject of the Prince of Yan, but because an enemy slandered him he was imprisoned. Since such great injustice had been done, frost appeared in summer.

[7] The favourite of Xiang Yu, who contended with Liu Bang for the empire at the end of the Qin dynasty but was defeated. Before Xiang Yu went into battle for the last time, Lady Yu bade him a touching farewell.

[8] Minister of the King of Yue, who fought against the Kingdom of Wu during the Warring States Period. To make the King of Wu forget affairs of state, Fan Li presented him with the celebrated beauty Xi Shi.

[9] A beautiful court lady of the Han Dynasty. Legend has it that she was given in marriage to a Hunnish Khan to win the friendship of the Huns.

[10] Headquarters of the peasant revolt during the Song Dynasty, described in the famous novel *Water Margin*.

[11] In Chinese Lu Zhailang (鲁斋郎) and Yu Qiji (鱼齐即) look very similar.

[12] A quotation from the Taoist classic, the *Dao De Jing*.

[13] A statesman and scholar of the Jin Dynasty.

[14] A famous alchemist of the Tang Dynasty.

[15] A minister of the first emperor of the Han Dynasty.

[16] When Zhuang Zi's wife died, a friend who came to offer condolences found the philosopher singing and beating a basin.

[17] A euphemism for passing the examination.

[18] Which announced the names of successful candidated in the examinations.

[19] Diligent scholars in the old days sometimes fastened their hair to a beam or pricked their legs to keep themselves awake.

[20] A Kind of water-lily.

[21] A fruit also known as Longyan.

[22] In the southern opera several characters sometimes sang together.

[23] These were signs of good luck.

[24] The *Book of History* relates that when King Wu fell ill, the Duke of Zhou prayed to die in his place, putting his prayer in a golden casket. After Cheng became king the Duke of Zhou was accused of trying to usurp the throne; but when the king opened the casket and found the prayer, he realized the duke's loyalty.

[25] A quotation from the *Book of Rites*.

[26] There is a legend that when a certain foreign envoy came to the Tang court, Li Bai, the great poet, was the only one able to understand his language and write a reply.

[27] Jiang Gan was a follower of Cao Cao. On Zhuge Liang's advice, Zhou Yu planted a letter casting suspicion on two of Cao Cao's generals where Jiang Gan was bound to find it. This made Cao Cao lose trust in these men. Then Huang Gai, one of Zhou Yu's generals, pretended to have been driven out by him and went over to Cao Cao, later betraying him.

[28] Cao Cao was persuaded by false friends to rope his boats together at Red Cliff. As soon as the wind was in the right direction, the enemy started a fire which destroyed his entire fleet.

[29] Generals who helped the first emperor of the Han Dynasty to win his kingdom.

[30] Lü Shang, who helped King Wen of Zhou to overthrow the Shangs.

[31] A hermit of the time of King Yao.

[32] Duke Mu of the State of Qin met the King of Chu at Lintong, meaning to capture him.

[33] Xiang Yu invited Liu Bang to a banquet at Hongmen, meaning to kill him; but Liu Bang escaped.

[34] 770-475 B.C.

[35] Famous orators.

[36] Leader of a peasants' uprising towards the end of the Tang Dynasty (618-907 A.D.).

[37] A.D. 894.

ABOUT THE TRANSLATORS

Yang Xianyi was born in Tianjin in 1915. His wife Gladys Yang was born in England in 1919. They both graduated from Oxford University in England in the 1930s. They were married in 1940 in China.

After teaching at several universities, they went to work for the National Compilation and Translation Bureau in 1943, in charge of translation of literary works. In 1952, they joined the Foreign Languages Press (now the China International Publishing Group) in Beijing, where Yang Xianyi worked as the chief editor of the magazine *Chinese Literature*. At the same time, he was a foreign literature research fellow of the Chinese Academy of Social Sciences, a council member of the Chinese Writers Association and a council member of the Chinese Translators Association.

For many decades, Yang Xianyi and Gladys Yang have devoted themselves to translating and research into Chinese and foreign literary legacies. Their translations of classical Chinese works of literature especially have brought them global fame, making a great contribution to the cultural exchanges between China and the rest of the world. Apart from their monumental translation of *A Dream of Red Mansions*, they have translated the *Verses of Chu, Selected Records of the Historian, The Dragon King Daughter, The Courtesan's Jewel-box, The Man Who Sold a Ghost, Palace of Eternal Youth, The Scholars* and a number of works by the famous modern Chinese writer Lu Xun.

图书在版编目(CIP)数据

关汉卿杂剧选 / （元）关汉卿 著；杨宪益，戴乃迭 译.
－北京：外文出版社，2004.1
（大中华文库）
ISBN 978-7-119-03395-2
Ⅰ. 关… Ⅱ. ①关… ②杨… ③戴… Ⅲ. 英语－对照读物，戏剧－汉、英
Ⅳ. H319.4: I
中国版本图书馆CIP数据核字（2003）第073296号

出版策划：徐明强 胡开敏
责任编辑：蔡莉莉
重印修订：刘奎娟
重印编辑：杨 璐
重印监制：冯 浩

大中华文库
关汉卿杂剧选
〔元〕关汉卿 著
吴晓铃 单耀海 李国炎 刘坚 编校
杨宪益 戴乃迭 译

出 版 人：徐 步
出版发行：
外文出版社
（中国北京百万庄大街 24 号）
邮政编码 100037
http://www.flp.com.cn
电话：008610-68320579（总编室）
008610-68995852（发行部）
008610-68327750（版权部）
制 版：北京维诺传媒文化有限公司
印 刷：深圳市碧兰星印务有限公司
开 本：960mm × 640mm 1/16 **印 张：**31.5
2004 年第 1 版第 1 次印刷
2020 年第 1 版第 3 次印刷
（汉英）
ISBN 978-7-119-03395-2
（精装）
定价：80.00 元